UNDERSTANDING THE GIFT OF
SALVATION

UNDERSTANDING THE GIFT OF
SALVATION

And a concise history of how the church through
ignorance and unbelief lost the power of the Holy Spirit

IRPEEL EBENEZER

AuthorHouse™
1663 Liberty Drive
Bloomington, IN 47403
www.authorhouse.com
Phone: 1-800-839-8640

© 2012 by Irpeel Ebenezer. All rights reserved.

No part of this book may be reproduced, stored in a retrieval system, or transmitted by any means without the written permission of the author.

First published by AuthorHouse   01/31/2012

ISBN: 978-1-4685-4166-3 (sc)
ISBN: 978-1-4685-4165-6 (hc)
ISBN: 978-1-4685-4164-9 (ebk)

Library of Congress Control Number: 2012900734

Printed in the United States of America

Any people depicted in stock imagery provided by Thinkstock are models, and such images are being used for illustrative purposes only.
Certain stock imagery © Thinkstock.

This book is printed on acid-free paper.

Because of the dynamic nature of the Internet, any web addresses or links contained in this book may have changed since publication and may no longer be valid. The views expressed in this work are solely those of the author and do not necessarily reflect the views of the publisher, and the publisher hereby disclaims any responsibility for them.

Contents

Dedication
Acknowledgement
Introduction xi
Chapter 1 1
    What is Salvation?
Chapter 2 10
    Receiving the Gift of Salvation
Chapter 3 27
    Salvation—A Covenant Relationship
Chapter 4 52
    The Early Church and the Ante-Nicene Church Fathers
Chapter 5 85
    The Imperial Church and the Post Nicene Church Fathers
Chapter 6 105
    'Heresies' and Schisms of the Early Church
Chapter 7 115
    The Church During the Dark Ages—(c500-1100 AD)
Chapter 8 131
    The Byzantine Empire and the Greek Orthodox
    Church—(450-1055 AD)
Chapter 9 144
    The Church in the Middle Ages (c1000-1500)
Chapter 10 168
    Theologians, Philosophers and Reformers of the Middle Ages
Chapter 11 193
    Controversies, 'Heresies' and Schisms of the Middle Ages
Chapter 12 205
    Monastic Movements of the Middle Ages
Chapter 13 210
    Renaissance and Renaissance Humanism

Chapter 14 223
    The Reformation and the Reformers—1450-1750 AD
Chapter 15 252
    European Wars of Religion
Chapter 16 261
    The Roman Catholic Counter-Reformation
Chapter 17 267
    The Enlightenment and Enlightenment Philosophers—17th & 18th Centuries
Chapter 18 278
    Global Evangelization and Re-Evangelization
Chapter 19 294
    Three Revolutions and the Impact on Christianity—1760-1850
Chapter 20 302
    The Great Awakenings and Protestant Missions and Missionaries
Chapter 21 318
    Theologians and Philosophers of the 19th and 20th Centuries
Chapter 22 332
    Global Trends in Christianity in the 19th and 20th Centuries
Chapter 23 381
    The Christian and Christianity Today
Chapter 24 391
    Evolutionary Trends from the Early Church to the 21st Century
References 419

DEDICATION

This book is dedicated to every true seeker of God.
To all who take God at His Word when He said:
"You will seek Me and find Me
When you seek Me with all your heart"—Jeremiah 29:13

To all who believe Jesus Christ when He said:
". . . I have come that they may have life,
And that they may have it more abundantly"—John 10:10

To both of my parents of blessed memory
For the godly heritage they gave me.
To my family, nuclear and extended
And to God Almighty for revealing His Truth
And the privilege to share it

ACKNOWLEDGEMENT

To my love and "God's Special Gift"; I say a big thank you.

And to Emmanuel, "God's blessing and my Joy"

Thanks to both of you for your encouragement and unflappable patience during the writing of this book; when months became years with multitudes of missed deadlines. Thanks for your faith in me; you are indeed God's blessing.

To 'Wumi', a friend indeed, thanks.

And to Ope for the Cover Design, thanks and God bless.

To all the facilitators and the children of the Friday Evening Ministry and the members of my Sunday school class who were used of God to clarify His Word during the preparation of the book; thanks and may God bless you all.

To AuthorHouse, what can I say but Thanks, for your patience? The next ones will not be as exasperating by God's grace.

Introduction

*"Beloved . . . I found it necessary to write to you
Exhorting you to contend earnestly for the faith
Which was once for all delivered to the saints;
For certain men have crept in unnoticed . . .
Men who turn the grace of our God into lewdness
And deny the only Lord God and our Lord Jesus
Christ"—Jude 3.*

A Christian friend going through a rather rough patch health wise asked: **"What exactly did Jesus Christ save us from, other than from hell?"**

Most professing Christians can identify with our friend's apparent frustration and or resignation in regard to the Christian life.

The notion that the Christian life is one of drudgery and pain is very pervasive that it approaches the status of doctrine in many circles. This fact is illustrated by this statement in an instruction manual for children's ministry of one of the mainstream denominations about Salvation—***"Jesus came to save people from sin, which separates us from God, not to change our circumstances."***

This kind of sentiment, considering what the bible likened being saved to, reveals a lack of understanding of the fullness of the Gift of Salvation.

What change of the human condition or circumstance can surpass that which occurs when a man is redeemed from Sin and Satan by the Blood of Jesus Christ?

The change is so **fundamental** and so **monumental** that Jesus Christ called it being **"Born Again"**—**(John 3:3-8),** and the Apostle Paul called it becoming a **"New Creature"**—*(2Corinthians 5:17)*.

If being born again or becoming a new creature is not a change of circumstance then what is?

While Christians are warned to expect persecutions and tribulations on account of their faith, and while they are not exempt from the vicissitudes of life, some of the kinds of suffering and afflictions that Christians embrace are not in accordance with the Will of God.

Ignorance of the scope of the gift of Salvation as revealed in the Bible is also the reason the walk of the majority of Christians is characterized by inconsistencies and does not match the talk.

For instance, the Scriptures affirm that believers have victory over Sin and Satan through the blood of Jesus, but many who identify themselves as Christians live continually defeated by Sin and oppressed by Satan. Jesus came to set the captives free but many remain in bondage to various addictions; and while Christians speak of the joy of Salvation they top the list of the depressed and anxious.

The contemporary Church, compared to the Church of the Apostolic Age is largely devoid of **power**. While Paul and Silas, just two believers, were accused of turning the world upside down in the apostolic era—*(Acts 17:1-8),* the hordes of professed Christians today have little or no impact on the society, and most of the time actually take their cues from the world.

The dichotomy between what professing Christians are in actuality and what they profess and ought to be has made Christianity unattractive for centuries and continues to cause unbelievers to blaspheme the Name of God.

While Jesus Christ prayed for the unity of His Church, the divisions among those who call themselves by His Name number in the thousands—thirty-eight thousand denominations globally as of the year 2001 [1].

Contemporary Christians are divided over a wide range of issues ranging from the serious to the mundane in areas of beliefs, practices and ethics. They differ in their Christology, quibbling over whether Jesus Christ is only divine, only human or both divine and human and they do not agree on the process, the substance or the essence of the Salvation that He brings. There is disagreement based on whether Salvation is by election or predestination by God or whether free will of man is involved. There is also controversy as to whether salvation is instantaneous and permanent no matter what, or whether the possibility of apostasy is real. Then there is the controversy over whether ordinances like Baptism and the Lord's Supper are Sacraments, that is, ordinances necessary for salvation, or mere symbols.

Believers cannot contend meaningfully for the faith if they are ignorant of who Jesus Christ is, what he accomplished for mankind and who believers are in Christ or what their inheritance are in Him.

In researching this book, I found a lot, to disagree about doctrinally with the denomination I have espoused since childhood and some things with which to agree with denominations with which I had thought I had nothing in common.

The quest was never to promote or put down any denomination, it was a honest desire to understand the Christian faith, using as the primary resource, the Holy Bible and combing through the history of the Church to find out how the Church has evolved.

It is obvious that The Church Universal is not what she was during the "Apostolic Age"; so how did the Church get to this point? How and why has she veered so sharply from Scriptural standards?

This book explored the Scriptures for the full meaning of Salvation as purchased by the Blood of Jesus Christ and the evolution of the Church through the ages as she lost the true faith and power and filled in by setting up structures that hold a form of godliness but deny the power of God.

Chapter 1

What is Salvation?

"For God so loved the world, that He gave His only begotten Son, that whoever believes in Him, should not perish but have everlasting Life."—John 3:16

Salvation means: *"the act of rescuing, keeping or preserving the soul from sin or the punishment for sin.*

It also means: *"the act of being rescued, kept or preserved from destruction, ruin, calamity or loss."*

Why does Man need Salvation?
To address this question fully, it is necessary to go to the very beginning, to creation and the Garden of Eden.

In the beginning, God created the heavens and the earth; He made Man the crown of His creation, made Him the keeper of it and gave him dominion over it, God even made Adam a partner in His creative work by giving him the honor of christening every living creature—*Genesis 1:27-28; Genesis 2:15-23.*

God made man for fellowship with Himself; Adam and Eve frolicked in Eden and communed with God "in the coolness of the day" until the fellowship was broken by Satan. By deception, Satan convinced Eve to desire "to be like God." She disbelieved God and disobeyed by eating the forbidding fruit and so did her companion, Adam. Rather than becoming like God, they died spiritually, the glory of God departed and they became naked.

The idyllic life which Adam and Eve enjoyed in Eden was destroyed and the fellowship they had with God was broken. The disintegration of their bodies set in and physical death was just a matter of time—Genesis 3. By choosing to believe and obey Satan rather than God, Adam and Eve unwittingly, but voluntarily, changed the power equation. Man lost the authority and dominion that God gave them over His creation to Satan because, as the Scriptures say: **"you are the slave of the one you choose to obey"—*John 8:34; Romans 6:16*.**

Man fell to the same Sin that got Satan kicked out of heaven—**"the desire to be like God"—*Genesis 3:1-6; Isaiah 14:12-14*.**

Therefore, at the heart of every Sin is the rebellion springing from the desire to be like God. Adam and Eve were kicked out of Eden with the natural consequences of their actions—curses instead of blessings.

Children born to slaves in the house of their masters are also slaves, therefore all the descendants of Adam and Eve remain slaves to Satan and Sin unless they are **"Redeemed",** that is, **"bought back"**. That is why the entire human race needs Redemption or Salvation.

What is Sin?

As stated earlier, at the core of every Sin is rebellion arising from the desire to be like God. However according to the Scriptures, it manifests in many ways:

  a) **Sin is breaking the Law—(also characterized as lawlessness)—1John 3:4.**
  b) **Sin is wrongdoing; or unrighteousness—1John 5:17**
  c) **Sin is Failing to do what is known to be right—James 4:17**
  d) **Sin is doing anything, the rightness of which is doubtful—Romans 14:23.**

Sin is not only wrongdoing or breaking the law; it is also failing to do what is right. In other words, sin can be by **commission** or **omission.**

Sin can also be **intentional** or **unintentional**.

According to the Bible, guilt is imputed even for unintentional sins and these also require propitiation—*Leviticus 4:13, 27; Leviticus 5:17.*

The Bible talked about **Trespass, Transgression, and iniquity**—*Leviticus 5:15; Leviticus 6:2;* Psalm 51:2-3; Isaiah 59:12. **Trespass** and **Transgression** imply violating a lawful boundary, in essence, breaking a law or command, by commission or omission and whether intentional or unintentional. **Iniquity** is acts of wickedness or injustice, more likely intentionally by commission or omission.

The Consequences of Sin
The main consequence of Sin is separation from God—Isaiah 59:1-2.

Because God is Holy, He cannot tolerate Sin nor can sinful man behold a holy God without disintegrating—(Exodus 33:20; Isaiah 6:1-5); therefore, man in sin cannot fellowship with God.

The separation from God resulted in **devastating derivatives** for mankind, namely—**Disasters, Diseases, Defeat, Despair, Desperation, Desolation, Destitution, Diminution, Destruction, Disillusionment and finally Death—Leviticus 26:14-39; Deuteronomy 28:15-68.** These derivatives operate at individual, family, community, national and global levels.

Without Salvation, the inexorable end result of Sin is Death—Romans 6:23.

The Sin Problem
The Scriptures say—*"For all have sinned and come short of the glory of God"—Romans 3:23.*

As the human race inherited slavery to Satan, Sin was also inherited because, with the departure of the glory of God as covering from Adam and Eve, their nature changed to that which is corruptible. Therefore, every human being is conceived and born in Sin—Psalm 51:5.

In other words, the entire human race was under a death sentence because, *"the wages of Sin is death . . ."—Romans 6:23a.*

The Solution
According to Scriptures, the forgiveness or remission of Sin can only be accomplished through the **'Shedding of blood'**:

> *"For the life of the flesh is in the blood, and I have given it to you upon the altar to make atonement for your souls; for it is the blood that makes atonement for the soul."—Leviticus 17:11.*

And, *"Without the shedding of blood, there is no remission for sin"—Hebrews 9:22.*

Therefore, for Sin to be forgiven, the shedding of blood is vital.

In the Old Testament, there were specific stringent guidelines for the animals used for sacrifices but even then those were not effective as the sacrifice had to be repeated time and time again. ***The blood of calves, bulls and goats could not take away sins—Hebrews 10:3-4.***

In addition, not just anyone can offer sacrifices for sin, but only the High Priest who alone can enter the Holy of Hollies once a year. In making atonement for the people, the High Priest, under the Levitical order, first had to offer sacrifices for his own sins before he could offer the same for the people.—***Hebrews 9:1-9.***

Under this arrangement, neither the priests nor the blood of the animals used in the sacrifices were perfect and therefore the process did not provide the perfect solution for the Sin problem. Man could only approach but not really reach God. There was still a veil.

No man can atone for his own sins by shedding his own blood or shed his blood for the redemption of another because, as already stated, there is the heredity of Sin from Adam in every human being. **Even the blood of the holiest martyrs cry out for justice and vengeance, as the blood of Abel, and not for mercy—*Genesis 4:10; Psalm 49:7-8; Revelations 6:9-10.***

What then is the Remedy for the situation? How can man return to fellowship with his Creator?

The Remedy:
Jesus Christ, the perfect Sacrifice and High Priest.

The solution, as already stated, is **"the shedding of blood"**; but the snag is that the blood of animals are inadequate and ineffective and the blood of Man is unacceptable.

Thankfully, God never gave up on human beings, the crown of His creation. The omniscient God knew that Man may fall even before the world began and He had made plans for man's restoration and reconciliation with Himself.

The Scriptures say that, before the world began, God ordained Jesus Christ as the **"Lamb without blemish and without spot"**—1peter 1:18-21—the perfect sacrificial Lamb.

What made Jesus Christ suitable as the Sacrificial Lamb?

- He was conceived of the Holy Spirit and therefore was untainted by the "Adamic 'gene' of Sin"—***Luke 1:26-35***.
- He lived as man and was tempted in every way but did not sin—***Hebrew 2:14-18; Hebrews 4:14-15***.

Therefore, the Blood of Jesus is <u>UNIQUE</u>.
It is the only Blood that speaks better things than that of Abel. His blood speaks MERCY and GRACE before the throne of God—Hebrews 12:24.

It is *only the Blood of Jesus Christ* that has the power to wash away sins and propitiate or make atonement for sins.

He was also foreordained to be the Perfect High Priest.

What Made Him the Perfect High Priest?
- As the Son of Man, He knows the nature of Man, sympathizes with human weaknesses but he was able to transcend and live a sinless life—***Hebrews 2:14-18; Hebrews 4:14-15***.
- He never sinned and therefore he does not need to atone for His own sins before He can make atonement for others as the Levitical priests had to do—***Hebrews 7:26-28***
- His priesthood is Eternal, in the order of Melchizedek, King of Salem. Therefore, the need for yearly sacrifices for Sin is obviated—***Hebrews 7:23-25; Hebrews 10:11-14***.
- He did not offer the blood of animals but offered His own Blood—***Hebrews 9:24-26, 28***.
- His perfect Sacrifice is once and for all, not repeated as under the Levitical order—***Hebrews 7:26-27; Hebrews 10:11-12***.

Comment

Theologians often talk of the substitutionary or vicarious death of Jesus Christ for sinners on the Cross.

However, the use of such terms can be misleading as it suggests that we could have gone on the Cross or die to atone for our own sins. This is not the case at all. No human being as already explained can die for his sins or the sins of others. Without Jesus Christ Man is doomed and without any hope in regard to the atonement for sin and salvation.

Jesus Christ is God's remedy for Man's sins and the means to reconcile Man to God; a plan God had made even before the foundations of the world—*1 Peter 1:18-21*

What did the Blood of Jesus Christ Accomplish for Sinners?

According to Scriptures, the Blood of Jesus accomplished the following for sinners: **Forgiveness, Redemption, Justification, Sanctification, Reconciliation, Healing, Victory and Eternal Life.**

1) Forgiveness

   To forgive means to remit, to release from punishment, to pardon

   Because God is Just, The Sin of the human race cannot be simply overlooked. The penalty had to be paid, the requirement of the law fulfilled and atonement made for sin.

   The problem, as earlier noted is that no human being can pay the price or atone for his own sin or that of anyone else.

   God Himself made forgiveness possible by giving His **only begotten** Son, Jesus Christ who carried the sins of the whole world on the Cross and shed His Blood for the propitiation of the Sin of all mankind—*2Corinthians 5:21; Mathew 26:28; Ephesians 1:7.*

   ❖ *"This is my blood of the New Covenant, which is shed for many for the forgiveness of sins".*

2) Redemption

   Redemption means to buy back, to free from bondage by paying a price.

   - **Believers are redeemed from Satan.**

   Adam and Eve sold out to Satan and became, with the whole of Mankind, **slaves of Satan.** But God in His mercy, at the appointed time, stepped in and re-purchased Man. The bible says, not with silver or gold, **"but with the Precious Blood of Jesus Christ . . ."—1Peter 1:18-19; Revelations 5:9.**

   - **Believers are redeemed from Sins and Iniquity.**

   Jesus said: **". . . Everyone who sins is a slave of sin"**—John 8:34. Thankfully, He went on to say: **"If the Son sets you free, you will be free indeed"**—John 8:35.

   Jesus redeemed Mankind **"from every kind of sin"**—Titus 2:14 (NLT)

- **Believers are redeemed from the curse of the law.**

Apart from becoming slaves of Sin and Satan, Man came under a curse because, breaking faith with God by breaking His Covenant and Law automatically places Man under a curse. Jesus Christ, by His death on the Cross, **"redeemed Man from the curse of the Law"—Galatians 3:13**; and **"wiped out the records that were against us"—Colossians 2:14**.

- **Believers are also redeemed from Self or the Flesh.**

Paul, in Romans 7:24 **(NIV),** detailed man's struggle with sin and his anguished cry was: **"What a wretched man I am! Who will rescue me from this body of death"?** He answered: "Thank God, the answer is in Jesus Christ our Lord . . ."—***Romans 7:25 (NLT).***

> ❖ *"For you know that you were not <u>redeemed</u> with corruptible things like silver and gold . . . but with the <u>precious blood</u> of Christ as a Lamb without blemish"—1Peter 1:18-19*

3) **Justification**

To be justified means to be acquitted, declared not guilty and free from blame.

Again, because God is Just, He acquits anyone who trusts in Jesus Christ because Jesus had fulfilled the requirements of the Law by His death on the Cross and paid the penalty for Sin—***Romans 3: 24—26; Romans 5:1,9; Romans 8:1-4***—things that Man was simply unable to do.

> ❖ *"Since we have now been <u>justified</u> by <u>His blood</u>, how much more shall we be saved from God's wrath through Him!"—Romans 5:9*

4) **Sanctification**

Sanctification means to be made holy, consecrated and free from sin.

God, who is Holy, demands that man be holy—***1Peter 1:15-16; Leviticus 11:44 & 45; Leviticus 19:2*** and without holiness, Man cannot see God—***Hebrews 12:14.***

Jesus Christ frees from Sin by washing/cleansing with His Blood—***1John 1:7; Hebrews 13:12; Revelations 1:5.***

> ❖ *"Therefore, Jesus also, that He might <u>sanctify</u> the people with <u>His own blood</u>, suffered outside the gate"—Hebrews 13:12.*

5) **Reconciliation**

Reconciliation means to make peace, settle differences or quarrel, become friends again and bring into harmony.

Fellowship between God and Man was broken after Adam and Eve sinned in Eden. The bible says the unrepentant Man is God's enemy—***Colossians 1:21-23.***

Through the shedding of His Blood, Jesus Christ made peace and reconciled Man with God. He mediated a New Covenant between God and Man with His Blood and restored Man's fellowship with God—***2Corinthians 5:18-19; 1Peter 3:18; Colossians 1:19-23;***

- ❖ *"For God was pleased to have all His fullness dwell in Him and through Him to <u>reconcile</u> to Himself all things, whether things on earth or things in heaven, by making peace through <u>His blood</u> shed on the Cross"—Colossians 1:19-20*

6) Healing

To heal means to make whole, to cure or return to health.

Sin damaged everything and diseases/sicknesses are part of the consequences of Man's Sin.

The Scriptures say that we are healed by the stripes of Jesus Christ—*1Peter 2:24; Isaiah 53:4-5*. Jesus Christ fulfilled God's promise in *Exodus 15:26* for all who believe and obey.

Psalm 107:20 says: *"He sent <u>His Word</u> and healed them and saved them from their destructions . . ."* Jesus is the Word of God—***John1:1-3***.

Again, Malachi prophesied: *"But for you who fear My Name, the Sun of Righteousness will arise with healing in His wings"—**Malachi 4:2.***

Jesus is the 'Sun of Righteousness' and he has come with healing in His wings for all who fear the Name of God.

- ❖ *"But He was wounded for our transgressions, He was bruised for our iniquities; the chastisement for our peace was upon Him, and by His stripes we are healed"—Isaiah **53:5***

7) Victory

Through Jesus Christ, and His shed Blood, we have victory over:

- The Accuser, Satan—***Revelations 12:10-11***
- Principalities and Powers—***Colossians 2:13-15***
- The World—***1John 4:4; 1John 5:4-5***.

Believers are overcomers in Jesus Christ.

> ❖ *"And they <u>overcame</u> him by <u>the blood of the Lamb</u> and by the Word of their testimony, and they did not love their lives to the death"—Revelations 12:11.*

8) Eternal Life

Eternal Life means life without end, everlasting life.

According to Scriptures, there are two eternal destinations, life and death or heaven and hell.

All who put their faith in Jesus Christ will have eternal life while all who reject Him will have eternal death in hell, forever separated from God—(John 3:16)

- Eternal Life is for only those who are victorious, the overcomers—Revelations 21:7-8
  - ❖ *"Whoever eats My flesh and drinks <u>My Blood</u> has <u>Eternal Life</u>, and I will raise him up at the last day"—John 6:54*

All that the Blood of Jesus accomplished when it was shed for sinners on the Cross—**Forgiveness, Redemption, Justification, Sanctification, Reconciliation, Healing, Victory and Eternal Life—are contained in God's "Gift of Salvation".**

Everything is accomplished by Jesus Christ through the Blood He shed on the Cross and is **FINISHED.**

Jesus did everything and there is nothing any man can contribute.

Chapter 2

Receiving the Gift of Salvation

"Sirs, what must I do to be saved?"—Acts 16:30

Salvation is a gift of God's love and is free, but as noted earlier, it is not at all cheap. It costs God Almighty His one and only Son—***John 3:16.***

How is the Gift of Salvation received?
Salvation is obtained only by **Grace** through **Faith**.
Therefore, it is man's part to believe; God extends the grace and gives the Gift, but man has to believe in order to receive—Ephesian 2:8-9.
It is often said that because "Salvation is a gift and is given freely; man has no part to play." However, while the 'Gift' is free, it is only accessible to **"whoever believes"**.

What does it mean to Believe or have Faith?
Faith is often considered as something abstract and many who claim to believe in Jesus Christ do not know who He is and so do not really know what to believe about Him.
A.W. Tozer said: **". . . it is not enough that we believe; we must believe the *right things* about the *right One*. True faith requires that we believe everything God has said about Himself and also that we believe everything He has said about us."** [1]
True faith means that the believer holds to be true, even when he does not fully understand, and agree with God about:

- All that God said about Himself
- Who the Scriptures say Jesus Christ is and what His birth and life mean, and also what His death and resurrection accomplished for sinners.
- Who the Holy Spirit is and what He does

- Who a believer was before Christ and who, according to Scriptures he becomes after Christ.

Therefore, to believe means to hold to be true that:
God the Father is:
- The Creator of Heaven and Earth—***Genesis 1***
- Almighty God—***Genesis 17:1***
- The "I AM"—***Exodus 3:14***
- The God-Head of the Trinity

To believe means to hold to be true:
- That Jesus Christ was conceived by the Holy Spirit in the Virgin Mary—Luke 1:26-28
- That Jesus Christ is both Divine and Human—Luke 1:35; Luke 3:21-22; John 8:58.
- The teachings of Jesus Christ—in Mathew, Mark, Luke and John Gospels
- The Redemptive Death on the Cross—Mathew 20:18-19, 28; Revelations 5:9-10
- All that the death of Jesus, and the shedding of His Blood accomplished for sinners
- The Resurrection of Jesus from the Dead—Mathew 28:1-10; Luke 24:1-7
- The Ascension of Jesus to Heaven—Mark 16:19; Luke 24:50-51; Acts 1:1-9
- The Return of Jesus at the end of Time—Mathew 16: 27; Mathew 24:29-31; Mark 13:24-27; Luke 21:25-28; Acts 1:10-11.

To believe means to hold to be true that The Holy Spirit is:
- The third Person of the Trinity
- The Believers' Helper—John 14:16-17
- The Believers' Guide—John 16:13
- The Believers' Teacher—John 14:26
- The Revealer of God and Jesus Christ to Believers—John 16:13-14; 1Corinthians 2:10-11
- The One who empowers and enables every Believer to be who God intends for them to be—true witnesses to Christ—Acts 1:8

To believe means to hold to be true that:
Anyone who does not know Jesus Christ:
- Has sinned and come short of God's glory—Romans 3:23
- Is a slave of Sin and Satan—Roman 6:16-17
- Is under God's wrath—Ephesians 2:1-3
- Is God's enemy—Colossians 1:21
- Is lost, without hope and heading for hell—Ephesians 2:12-
- Is under a death sentence—Romans 6:23
- Needs a Savior—Luke 19:10
- Must be Born Again—John 3:1-7

To believe means to hold to be true and agree with God that:
Sinners need to repent—Mathew 3:1-2; Mathew 4:17; that is:
i) Confess all known sins specifically and express genuine sorrow for them *2Corinthians 7:10*
ii) Ask God for forgiveness on the basis of only the Blood of Jesus Christ that was shed on the Cross and believe that it is granted—*1John 1:8-10*
iii) Commit to forsaking all previous sinful ways and trust Jesus and the Holy Spirit for help to live the new life—*2Corinthians 5:17*
iv) Ask Jesus to take over and become the Lord and commit to a life of obedience to Him and the Holy Spirit—J*ohn 14:15, 21, 23; John 15:14; John 1:12*
   - **This is true Repentance that leads to Salvation—2Corinthians 7:10.**

To believe means to hold to be true and agree with God that:
i) A sinner who has confessed his or her sins, repented and believed in Jesus Christ is saved—**Acts 10:43; Acts 16:31**
ii) All that the Blood of Jesus Christ accomplished are available to the believer—Ephesians *1:13-14*

When a man *acknowledges his sinfulness, confesses his sins, repents, trusts Jesus Christ's atoning sacrifice, asks for forgiveness based on the Blood of Jesus Christ, asks Him to become Lord in his life and believes all that His blood accomplished*, he is **Saved, Born Again!—Acts 4:12; 1Peter 1:22-23; John 3:3.**

Next: He submits himself to a course of instruction in the faith, receives the ***Believers' Baptism*** and joins fellow believers in a community of fellowship and in observing the ***Lord's Supper or Holy Communion.***

Then he commits to living a life of obedience to the teachings of Jesus Christ within the family of fellow believers—Mathew 28:19—20.

- ❖ *This is how the 'Gift of Salvation" is received.*

What is in the "Salvation Gift Package"?

The **"Gift of Salvation"** consists of **EVERYTHING** that the Blood of Jesus accomplished, that is—***Forgiveness, Redemption, Justification, Sanctification, Reconciliation, Healing, Victory and Eternal Life.***

- ➢ **To believe means to hold to be true and agree with God that once the Gift of Salvation is accepted, all that the Blood of Jesus accomplished is available and accruable to the believer.**

Therefore:

As the Redeemed, the believer:
- Can resist and overcome Satan, the old master—***James 4:7; 1Peter 5:8-9***
- Is free from the bondage of sin to live in righteousness—***John 8:34; Romans 6:18,22***
- Has the power of Sin over his life broken—***1John 3:8-10***
- Is assured of help in time of temptation so that he will not sin—***Hebrews 2:18; Hebrews 4:15; 1John 5:18; 1Corinthians 10:13.***

As the Forgiven and Justified the believer:
- Has peace with God—***Romans 5:1***
- Has the peace of God—***Philippians 4:7***
- Is no more under condemnation and can approach God with confidence because of the Blood of Jesus—***Romans 8:1; 1John 3:21-23; Hebrews 4:16.***
    - ❖ Believers are <u>Justified</u> by <u>Grace</u> through the <u>Redemption</u> that is in <u>Christ Jesus</u>—Romans 3:24-25.

As the Sanctified, the believer:
Can live in holiness through the power of the Holy Spirit by:
- Living in obedience to the Word of God—***Psalm 119:9, 11, 105***
- Being taught, guided and helped by the Holy Spirit—***John 14:15-17, 26;***
- ***John 16:13-14.***
- Guarding his heartv—***Proverbs 4:23; Mark 7:21-23.***
- Having zero-tolerance for Sin—***Mathew 18:8-9***
- Keeping the right company—***1Corinthians 15:33; 2Corinthians 6:14-18.***
- Relying on the faithfulness of God.—***1Thessalonians 5:23-24; Jude 24.***
  - ❖ **Redeemed** from Sin, Satan and Self, believers can live a **Sanctified** life.

As the Reconciled, the believer:
- Lives in Covenant relationship with God—***Hebrews 12:24; Mark 14:24.***
- Has intimacy with God, becomes God's confidant—***Psalm 25:14; Amos 3:7***
- Is reconciled to God and all who have the same faith whatever their race or color—***2Corinthians 5:18-19; Ephesians 2:14-19.***
- Has unhindered access to the Presence of God—***Ephesians 3:11-12, Hebrews 4:16.***
- Can see God—***Hebrews 12:14.***
  - ❖ **Sanctification is the condition for Reconciliation with God—Hebrews 12:14**

As the Healed the believer:
- Enjoys divine health and healing: *(1Peter 2:24; Isaiah 53:5; James 5:14-15)*
- Is healed spiritually—***Hosea 14:4.***
- Is healed emotionally—***Psalm 147:3; Isaiah 61:1***
- Is healed physically—***Exodus 15:26; Psalm 103:3; Psalm 107:20***
  - ❖ **Healing is a consequence of Forgiveness**

As the Overcomer, the believer:
- Lives in triumph through Christ over Satan, the accuser—***Revelations 12:11; 2Corinthians 2:14***
- Lives in victory over the world—***John 16:33; 1John 4:4; 1John 5:4-5; Revelations 12:11.***
- Lives in victory over Sin and the flesh—***Romans 6:6, 13-14;***
  - ❖ **Victory derives from Christ's Redemption and only the overcomers attain to Eternal Life**

Assurance of Eternal Life:

Redeemed, forgiven and justified; sanctified, reconciled and victorious through the blood of Jesus Christ, the believer is assured of Eternal Life—***John 10:28; Romans 6:22; Revelations 21:7.***

- ❖ Therefore, it is clear that "Faith has content"; and to believe is not an abstraction. The body of the teachings to believe constitutes the *"Doctrines"*. Anyone who doubts the tenets or doctrines of the faith cannot in all honesty be considered an adherent of the faith.

  Unfortunately, the Church has deviated from the catechumenate system of the early Church. In the Apostolic era, when most of the converts were Jews, the apostles emphasized the importance of instructing converts on doctrine—***Acts 2:42; Acts 5:42.*** The importance of doctrinal instruction was underscored when the apostles encouraged the people to select seven deacons to oversee the distribution of food rather than be distracted from teaching—***Acts 6:1-7.*** The apostle Paul also emphasized the importance of sound doctrinal instructions repeatedly—***1Timothy 4:13, 16; Titus 1:9; Titus 2:1.***

  In the early Church, the catechumenate period could last as long as three years for adult converts before they are admitted into full communion after baptism.

  Converts start out as *"**Enquirers / Hearers**"* during which period they learn the rudiments of ***doctrine, morals and liturgy***. At this stage they participate in the worship service only up to a point after which they are dismissed. From this stage they graduate to *"**catechumens**",* the stage in which deeper doctrinal, moral and liturgical instructions are given. In addition, at this stage, the behavior of the catechumens are watched and assessed to know if their lives are been impacted by the instructions. This will determine the catechumens' readiness for baptism and subsequent participation in the Holy Communion. Catechumens stay longer and participate in the worship service longer than the Hearers but they are also dismissed before the administration of the Holy Communion. After the required period of catechumenate, the catechumens are prepared for baptism with fasting, prayers and vigils together with the whole congregation according to the early Church fathers. After baptism, catechumens become part of the *"Faithful"* and they are accepted into full membership and communion. Tertullian was scandalized about the practice of some sects considered heretics who were "initiating" catechumens before they were instructed and also allowing them to participate in every aspect of worship as the faithful. Catechetical schools were common between the second and fourth centuries and it is not surprising that Christians of that era were more consistent and hold up under persecution even unto death.

In many evangelical circles today, there are but only vestiges if at all, of the early catechumenate system. Those who "accept" or "decide for" Christ undergo instructions that span aggregately less than one day and are then baptized. The teaching nowadays is that simply walking down the aisle in response to a pastor's invitation to "accept" Christ or confession of "faith" in Christ by anyone constitute eternal salvation irrespective of what the person does or fails to do subsequently because some Scripture passages say "anyone who believes shall be saved".

The problem is that for many, there is ignorance of what it really means to believe.

The clichés of contemporary evangelism has obscured what it means to be truly saved. In awareness of this, A.W. Tozer said: "**Salvation comes not by 'accepting the finished work' or 'deciding for Christ'. It comes by believing on the Lord Jesus Christ, the whole, living, victorious Lord Who, as God and man, fought our fight and won it, accepted our debt as His own and paid it, took our sins and died under them and rose again to set us free**". [1]

It cannot be considered as true Salvation for anyone to give mere verbal accent to a preacher's prepared "sinners' prayer" while entertaining doubts about or even rejecting what the Scriptures affirm concerning Jesus Christ such as the Virgin birth or His resurrection.

Among those identified as Christians today, there is a whole plethora of doctrines, beliefs and teachings that reject Scriptural truths.

Everything in the Salvation gift package is available to every believer and true faith requires that believers trust God for the forgiveness as well as the justification; the redemption as well as the sanctification; reconciliation as well as the healing and the victory as well as the Eternal Life. Reconciliation would have been impossible without sanctification or justification without forgiveness and Eternal Life is for only those who overcome.

True faith means embracing the ***"Salvation Gift Package"*** wholesale.

Ignorance of the scope of what the Blood of Jesus accomplished as revealed in the Scriptures has emasculated Christians for centuries and is the reason the contemporary Church is a mere shadow of the early Apostolic Church.

Concepts of Salvation in Christianity [2, 3, 4]

The concepts of salvation among those identified as Christians today in the various church traditions range from the 'Limited and Exclusive' to 'General and Universal'.

Broadly, the concepts can be categorized as follows:

a) Moral Transformation

According to this concept, man experiences moral transformation by imitating Christ's example and living according to His teachings. The concept is rejected by many church traditions because it is felt that it underestimates sin's seriousness and undermines Christ's atonement and suggests salvation by works. This concept prevail in contemporary time among some 'liberal Christians who consider the idea of Christ's death on the Cross or His vicarious suffering repugnant

b) Christus Victor

This is a concept of a victorious Jesus Christ who triumphed over Satan and destroyed Satan's power over death.

He disarmed principalities and powers and destroyed the power of sin over those who believe in Him.

c) Ransom from Satan

According to this concept, Jesus Christ redeemed (bought back) man from slavery to Satan consequent to man's fall in the Garden of Eden.

d) Satisfaction

The Satisfaction concept of salvation states that Jesus Christ provided satisfaction for divine justice by His death on the Cross. His death on the Cross is considered both "a gift from God to man" as well as "a sacrifice of man to God" which restores man to the state of 'original justice'.

e) Penal Substitution

The Penal Substitution concept states that humanity committed crimes or sins against God and God in His love for man put the punishment on Christ. Jesus Christ therefore suffered punishment for the sins of mankind to fulfill divine justice. Some also find this concept repugnant.

f) Theosis

This is the concept of salvation commonly found in the Eastern, Oriental and Russian orthodox traditions. In these traditions, salvation is considered in terms of drawing closer to God through the merits procured by the suffering and death of Jesus Christ on the Cross and following His teachings. Through faith, it is believed that as Christ became man, man becomes the son of God and therefore a *'god'*. This concept is enunciated in the writings of some early church fathers and others later. For example:

> St. Iranaeus said*: "The Word became flesh and the Son of God became the Son of Man, so that man, by entering into communion with the Word and thus receiving divine sonship, might become a son of God"*
>
> St. Aquinas said: *"The Only-begotten Son of God, wanting us to be partakers of His divinity, assumed our human nature so that, having become man, He might make men gods".*

The Process

There are also deferring concepts about the process of salvation. While some are of the view that God's grace and man's will are involved, others think man's will is not involved and salvation is purely by God's grace as well as His predestination and election which nothing can change.

The importance of 'works' in the process of salvation is also contentious. Some Christian traditions insist that works are essential in the process of salvation while others strongly believe that works play no part; only grace and faith.

The Nature

There are also differing opinions about the nature of salvation.

Is salvation instantaneous and permanent no matter what? Or is salvation instantaneous and reversible?

Is salvation progressive and reversible?

Or is it only aspirational and futuristic?

At the core of this issue is what is believed about how Jesus Christ's atonement dealt with believers' sins. In other words:

What sins are atoned for by Christ's sacrifice at conversion?

The Roman Catholic Church believes that Christ's sacrifice on the Cross did not blot out individual sins but only provided the means (available to all men) for blotting out individual sins. Baptism is regarded as the washing of regeneration which removes the guilt of original sin and past sins. Subsequent sins are dealt with according to the *"Penitential Discipline"* developed by the Church. Therefore, in the Catholic dogma, baptism provides the means of salvation for children and those permanently deprived of reason while the Eucharist provide the means of continuing sanctifying grace for adults with reason. For adults with reason, faith can be lost and grace broken by unrepented mortal sins, ultimate salvation requires final perseverance.

A few Protestant sects also believe that past sins are atoned for, that there is grace for subsequent sins and that believers should eschew sinning deliberately and espouse holy living after baptism. These believe that salvation is both instantaneous and progressive and also reversible.

Some Protestants believe that past, present and future sins are forgiven; these are those who subscribe to the idea of instantaneous and permanent salvation no matter what the believer does or fail to do—the so called *"Eternal Security"* or *"once saved, always saved"* doctrine.

Most of these themes will be further discussed in relevant portions later in the book.

The Result / Effect

There is consensus across different Christian traditions that the ultimate result of salvation is eternal life. However, there is a wide range of opinions about the effect of salvation for living Christians. While some believe that Christ gives believers victory over sin and therefore they can live righteously, others believe that righteousness is only imputed and that man cannot but commit sin even after conversion. For the latter group, the grace of God through Christ is a cover for sins of believers much like a carpet under which their sins are swept rather than empowering them not to sin. The only difference between a believer and an unbeliever according to this school of thought therefore is that one group has "professed faith in Jesus Christ".

The majority of Christian traditions believe in two destinations for mankind in the after life; namely heaven for believers and hell for unbelievers. Some liberal Christians today deny the reality of hell.

The Ordinances and Salvation

In some Church traditions, the ordinances of Baptism and the Holy Communion (called the Eucharist) are sacraments that are necessary for salvation; while in others they are viewed merely as ordinances of remembrance with no salvific property.

In the early Church, Baptism was essentially for adult believers and is considered the washing of regeneration after which Christians feared to sin so as not to lose their salvation. Therefore many put off baptism till much later in life or even just before death. However, in the Roman Catholic Church, with the development of the doctrine of 'original sin', the doctrines of *infant baptism* and sacramental penance followed.

The tendency to put off baptism until the point of death and infant baptism also changed the method. Baptism, which used to be by immersion, usually in a flowing stream or river, was being administered by affusion (pouring) or aspersion (sprinkling) because the candidate's condition precluded immersion.

Many Protestant traditions also practice infant baptism while a few subscribe only to the *'Believer's Baptism'* and consider it an ordinance performed in obedience to Christ's instruction but made available to those old enough to profess faith in Christ.

In the Roman Catholic Church, the Holy Communion is a sacrament and participation in its celebration is considered necessary for salvation. However, in some Protestant churches, the Holy Communion is observed merely as a remembrance.

Another bone of contention with the Holy Communion is the properties or nature of the Bread and Wine once they have been blessed. While some believed that there is ***transubstantiation***—literal presence of Christ in the elements), others believe in the real presence but no transformation of the elements and some believe that the bread and wine remain just that; that the meal is just a memorial with no spiritual significance.

Comment:
Concepts of Salvation

It would appear that the various traditions hold some aspects of the concept of salvation and as explained before, salvation involve aspects of all the concepts—the sacrificial, satisfaction, Christus Victor, Redemptory and up to a point substitutionary concepts. And of course moral transformation, not by imitation but by fundamental transformation of the human nature which Jesus summed up as being "Born Again".

Jesus Christ, as the 'Lamb of God', foreordained before the foundations of the world, provided the perfect sacrifice for the atonement of the sins of mankind by the blood He shed through His death on the Cross—1Peter 1:19; Hebrews 9:22.

The blood of animals and human beings cannot propitiate the sins of mankind, only the unique Blood of Jesus Christ which speaks better things than that of Abel provided propitiation for sins and procured satisfaction for divine justice—Isaiah 53; Hebrews 9:22; Hebrews 10:12, 14.

By His death on the Cross, Jesus Christ destroyed the works of the devil, destroyed death and the devil who held the power of death, He triumphed over powers and principalities and ransomed man from Sin and Satan—1John 3:8; Colossians 2:14-15; Hebrews 2:14-15, 18; John 8:34; Romans 6:15-18, 20-22; Titus 2:11-14.

Jesus Christ bore the sins of mankind on the Cross and was in fact made Sin so that believers can be the righteousness of God—(2Corinthians 5:21). "He was pierced for our transgressions, crushed for our iniquities; His punishment brought us peace and by His wounds we are healed"—Isaiah 53:1-12. These all happened by the design of God Almighty, a plan He had even before the foundation of the world.

However, it would be misleading to use the words 'substitutionary' or 'vicarious' as these suggest that He suffered what we would have suffered. The fact of the matter is that the death of every man that has ever lived on the Cross cannot propitiate the sins of mankind and were Man to be subjected to God's just wrath, it could not have earned man eternal life. Therefore, the words should be used with caution as they can distort the truth about the process of salvation. There is no way man could ever have done what Christ did for the redemption of mankind.

True salvation does result in moral transformation. A believer is described as "a new creation, a new man" etc. A believer did not just get a makeover or reformed, he is fundamentally transformed—2Corinthians 5:17; Titus 2:11-12; Romans 6:1-4; Mathew 7:15-23.

The idea of man becoming a god through Jesus Christ may sound sacrilegious to some people; however, the concept is actually scriptural. In Genesis 1:26, God said: "Let us make man in our image, according to our likeness . . ." and Man became a living being by the breath of God. Therefore, inherently, man shares some nature of God. After that nature was corrupted by the fall, fellowship with God was lost. However, in John 1:12, the Bible says that those who receive Christ are given the power to become children of God. Through Christ, there is restoration to God's original purpose and through Him, the Apostle Peter said we once again become partakers of the divine nature—2Peter 1:3-4. Carried to its logical end, children of God are "gods"—Psalm 82:6.

Although certain passages in the New Testament talked about predestination and election, this concept of 'limited atonement' and 'unconditional election' cannot stand in the light of other preponderant Scriptures that support 'universal atonement' but 'conditional election '. God loved the world and has no pleasure in the death of the wicked—John 3:16; Ezekiel 18:21-23, 32.

However, there is no Scriptural basis for the position of 'liberal Christians' who deny the existence of hell.

Process

As regards 'works' in relation to salvation, it is absolutely true that no one can work for his salvation; however, good works is a natural result of salvation——Mathew 5:16; Ephesians 2:10 (8-10); 2Timothy 3:16-17; Titus 2:11-14.

It is obvious that, while 'good works' cannot procure salvation, it is a vital indicator of true salvation in all true believers and the absence of good works puts the claim of salvation in question—Mathew 7:15-23; James 2:18-26.

Nature

The permanence or otherwise of salvation is also a contentious issue among differing Christian traditions. While many believe apostasy is possible, some subscribe to "Eternal Security" of believers no matter what they do or fail to do after professing faith in Jesus Christ. This school of thought believes that a life of sin after salvation results only in the loss of fellowship and eternal rewards but not the loss of eternal life. However, Jesus made it clear that simply professing faith in Him is useless if not attended by real change—Mathew 7:15-23. He also stressed that only those who endure to the end will be saved—Mark 13:13. In His letter to the Seven Churches, Jesus made it clear that only those who overcome will reign with Him—Revelations 1-3.

In His charge to the church in Sardis, Jesus observed that the church's appearance of life was phony; it was dying though it had the appearance of being alive. He urged the church to repent and be watchful. He further went on to say that He would not **'blot out'** from the Book of Life the names of those who overcome. The logical inference from this passage is that the names of those who fail to repent and therefore fail to overcome would be blotted out from the Book—Revelations 3:1-5.

Other warnings of the Apostles in their epistles support the fact that apostasy is a possibility.

According to the scriptures, when Jesus Christ is believed and confessed, salvation is received at that moment. However, this is the beginning of a journey; Jesus said he who endures to the end will be saved. Therefore, salvation is instantaneous as well as progressive and futuristic.

As for which sins are atoned for at conversion, some Scripture passages shed some light.

Romans 3:24-25 says:
> *"Being justified freely by His grace through the redemption that is in Christ Jesus, whom God has set forth to be propitiation through faith in His blood, to declare His righteousness for the **remission of sins that are past**, through the forbearance of God".*

Hebrews 9:14-15 says:
> *"How much more shall the blood of Christ, who through the eternal Spirit offered himself without spot to God, cleanse your conscience from dead works to serve the living God? And for this reason He is the Mediator of the New Covenant by means of death, **for the redemption of the transgressions under the first***

covenant, that those who are called may receive the promise of eternal inheritance".

These passages suggest that at conversion, past or previous sins are forgiven. This is the understanding of many early Church fathers before the development of St. Augustine's doctrine of original sin.

The question which then arises is what happens if a believer sins after conversion and baptism?

The Scripture says that a true believer does not make a habit of sinning, that is, a true believer should not sin willfully—***1John 3:1-9; 1John 5:17-18***.

In fact the Bible says there is no more sacrifice for sin for those who sin willfully after receiving the knowledge of truth as such actions insult the Holy Spirit and treat the blood of Jesus Christ with contempt—***Hebrews 10:26-31***.

However, should a Christian sin inadvertently, such sins should be repented of and forgiveness sought through Jesus Christ also—***1John 2:1-2***.

Effect

As to the impact of salvation on the life of obedient individual believer, the Bible made it clear that it is transformative. Jesus called it being "Born Again"—***John 3: 3-8;*** the Apostle Paul called believers "new creatures"—***2Corinthians 5:17*** and the Apostle Peter said believers are partakers of the divine nature—***2Peter 1:3-4***. Believers are no longer slaves of sin but slaves of righteousness and of God for holiness and the end, eternal life—***Romans 6:16-22***. The grace of God, rather than being a passive thing and covering over sin is active and transforming.

Titus 2:11-12 say:

> *"The grace of God that brings salvation has appeared to all man, teaching us that denying ungodliness and worldly lusts, we should live soberly, righteously and godly in the present age".*

Baptism and Holy Communion

The question of whether or not Baptism and the Holy Communion are observances crucial to the Christian life or mere memorials is important.

From the references in the Bible, they do have intrinsic value and are not mere symbols or observances with no spiritual meaning.

In ***Luke 7:30***, the Bible referred to the Baptism of John the Baptist as *"the Will of God" (NKJV)* or *"the Purpose of God"* (NIV) which the Pharisees and the

Lawyers rejected. Something that is the Will of God cannot be inconsequential or just mere symbolism. Jesus said only those who do the Will of the Father will enter the Kingdom of Heaven—*Mathew 7:21.*

In *Mark 16:16,* Jesus said: **"He who believes and is baptized will be saved; but he who does not believe will be condemned"**.

This presupposes that true believers should be baptized.

The Apostle Paul in **Roman 6:1-4** explained what the crucifixion, burial and resurrection of Jesus Christ mean for the believer. The believer's old nature of sin, he said was crucified with Christ, he is 'buried' with Christ in baptism, and just as Jesus Christ resurrected, the believer rises from the water of baptism into newness of life.

In *Colossians 2:12,* it is written that believers are *"buried with Him (Christ) in baptism and raised with Him through your faith in the power of God, who raised Him from the dead".* (NIV)

In *Acts 2:38,* baptism in the name of Jesus Christ is tied to the remission of the sins of believers and the reception of the gift of the Holy Spirit. In *Acts 22:16,* baptism is equated with the washing away of sins and in *1Peter 3:21-22,* the Apostle Peter linked baptism with salvation through the resurrection of Jesus Christ. Also in *Titus 3:5,* salvation and the "washing of regeneration" (baptism) are linked as well with the renewal by the Holy Spirit.

In *Colossians 3:1,* the Apostle Paul continued: "Since you have been raised with Christ, set your hearts on things above where Christ is seated at the right hand of God".

Therefore believers are to trust in the power of God for baptism to produce in their lives what it signifies—burial with Christ and resurrection into newness of life.

In *1Peter 3:21*, the Apostle Peter also concurred with Paul saying: **"There is also an antitype which now saves us—baptism (not the removal of the filth of the flesh, but the answer of a good conscience toward God), through the resurrection of Jesus Christ".**

As for the method, since the root of the word baptism imply immersion and since Jesus Christ was baptized by immersion, if there are no genuine reasons to preclude immersion, baptism ought to be by immersion rather than aspersion or affusion.

Baptism is viewed as the 'rite of initiation' into the Christian faith by many of the early Church fathers.

When the Holy Communion was instituted by Jesus Christ; regarding the Bread He told the disciples: **"Take, eat, this is <u>My Body</u>"** and regarding the

Wine, He said: *"This is <u>My Blood</u> of the New Covenant which is shed for many..."—Mathew 26:26-27.*

It is instructive that He did not say: this represents or this is a symbol of my body or blood.

In *John 6:32-66*, Jesus told His disciples and the people that He is the "***Bread of Life***", the *"Living Bread"* and the *"Bread from Heaven"*.

He said further: *"I am the Living Bread... If anyone eats of this bread, he will live forever; and the bread that I shall give is <u>My Flesh</u>, which I shall give for the life of the world"—John 6:51*

Again He said: *"Most assuredly, I say to you, <u>unless you eat the flesh of the Son of Man and drink His Blood,</u> you have no life in you. <u>WHOEVER EATS MY FLESH and DRINKS MY BLOOD has ETERNAL LIFE</u> and I will raise him up at the last day"—John 6:53-54. "... He who feeds on Me will Live because of Me"—John 6:57*

When Jesus said the above, many of his disciples were offended and they actually stopped following Him!

In *1Corinthians 11:23-30*, the Apostle Paul said those who ate bread and drank the wine of the Holy Communion unworthily were guilty of the body and blood of the Lord. He went on to say that in so doing, they were eating and drinking judgment to themselves and that for that reason many were ***weak, fell sick and some even died.***

It is unlikely that such dire consequences would attend an observance which is merely a memorial with no spiritual import or consequence.

The Scriptural evidence is that the Bread and the Wine of the Holy Communion are not ordinary and that the observance of the ordinance is spiritual and not just a mere symbolic memorial.

*The Holy Communion is a covenant meal which only worthy believers, (the initiated in good standing) can partake of for spiritual renewal.

Chapter 3

Salvation—A Covenant Relationship

Receiving the "Gift of Salvation" means:
- Entering into a **New Covenant** with God in the **Blood of Jesus Christ'**
- The beginning of "the journey of a **New Life**" by a **"New Creature"** in an entirely **'New Direction'** under the **'New Management'** of the **Holy Spirit.—Mathew 7:13-14; Romans 6:4; 2Corinthians 5:17.**

Covenants in the religious context are spiritual contracts between two or more people which have terms and conditions, the breaching of which have attendant consequences.

Right from the beginning, God has always related to Man in covenants. Hence there was the Adamic, Noahic, Abrahamic and the Mosaic covenants in the Old Testament.

Likewise, salvation brings a Christian into **a Covenant relationship** with God. The Covenant is written and sealed with the Blood of Jesus Christ, who is *the Mediator of the New Covenant—Mark 14:24; 1Timothy 2:5-6; Hebrews 12:24.*

The relationship is maintained and sustained by the power of the Holy Spirit.

By reason of the redemption which Jesus Christ procured for Christians with His own Blood, believers come under a new management, and, freed from Sin and Satan, believers are subject to the Lordship of Jesus Christ—Romans 6:15-19.

The relationships forged by the Blood of Jesus include:
- ❖ **Father—Child—(John 1:12; Romans 8:14) with God the Father**
- ❖ **Master—Servant—(Mathew 23:8; John 13:13) with Jesus Christ**

- ❖ **Teacher—Student—(Mathew 23:10; John 14:26) with Jesus Christ and The Holy Spirit**

It is often alleged by some that because Salvation is a Gift of God's Love given by God's Grace, God has no expectations of and expects nothing from believers.

However, as stated above, believers who accept the gift of Salvation enter into a relationship with the **Trinity** and it is obvious that none of these relationships is devoid of expectations and all have fundamental reciprocal expectations.

So, after being saved and becoming children of God:

- ❖ **What can believers expect from God, Jesus Christ and the Holy Spirit?**
- ❖ **What do God and Jesus Christ expect of believers?**
- ❖ **What can believers expect from the world?**

A) What Can Believers Expect From God and Jesus Christ?

1) First, believers can expect the fulfillment of all that Jesus Christ accomplished on the Cross, that is—**Forgiveness, Redemption, Justification, Sanctification, Reconciliation, Healing, victory and Eternal Life** with all the benefits accruing there from as already discussed.

2) Secondly, believers can expect the **Holy Spirit.**

When Jesus Christ was leaving the earth, He commanded the disciples to wait for **"The Promise of the Father"**—which is the Holy Spirit *(Luke 24:49; Acts 1:4-5 & 8)* who is responsible for actualizing in the lives of believers all that Jesus Christ accomplished for them by His death, resurrection and ascension.

At His valedictory address to the disciples, Jesus Christ took pains to explain to the disciples who the Holy Spirit is and what He will do in the lives of true believers. Jesus promised to pray to the Father to send the Holy Spirit who will:

- **Be the abiding / indwelling Counselor and Helper—John 14:15-17**
- **Teach and remind believers of all things taught by Jesus Christ—John 14:26**
- **Testify about Jesus Christ to believers—John 15:26**

- **Convict the world of Sin, Righteousness and Judgment—John 16:7-8.**
- **Guide believers into all Truth—John 16:13**
- **Tell believers things to come—John16:13**
- **Tell believers what He hears from Jesus—John 16:13-14**
- **Glorify God by sharing with believers things that belong to Jesus Christ—John 16:14.**
- **Empower believers to be true witnesses of Jesus Christ—Acts 1:8**.

Who is the Holy Spirit?
- The Holy Spirit is the third Person of the Trinity. Present at Creation, His operations are recorded throughout the Old and New Testaments—**Genesis 1:1-2;**
- He empowered people for special duties and spoke through the Prophets—**Exodus 31:1-6; Exodus 35:30-35; Numbers 11:24-27; Judges 15:14-15; 1Samuel 16:13-14; Daniel 4:18 etc.**
- Jesus Christ was conceived in the Virgin Mary by the Power of the Holy Spirit—**Luke 1:35—38.**
- The Holy Spirit descended on Jesus Christ at His Baptism and the beginning of His Ministry and He was affirmed by the Voice of the Father. On this occasion, as at Creation, the three Persons of the Trinity—the Father, the Son and the Holy Spirit were present—**Mathew 3:16-17.**
- The Holy Spirit seals the accomplishments of Jesus into the obedient believer—**Ephesians 1:13-14**; and then He enables and empowers him to live the redemptive life by counseling, teaching, guiding and helping.
- Through the indwelling of the Holy Spirit, the obedient Believer is in constant / perpetual communion with Jesus Christ and the Father—**John 14:21, 23**. Jesus Christ promised that the Holy Spirit will dwell in the believer; put in another way, Jesus Himself will abide in the believer because believers have His Spirit—**1John 3:24.** In fact, according to **Romans 8:9**, anyone who does not have the Holy Spirit does not belong to Jesus Christ.
  - ❖ **Therefore, the principal thing that believers need to expect is the Holy Spirit—"The Promise of the Father".**

All other things derive from the imparted **Characteristics, Gifts and Fruit of the Holy Spirit.**

The Characteristics of the Holy Spirit
The characteristics of the Holy Spirit are enunciated in **Isaiah 11:2.**
- "And the **"Spirit of the Lord"** shall rest upon Him,
- The Spirit of **Wisdom**
- and **Understanding**
- The Spirit of **Counsel**
- and **Might**
- The Spirit of **Knowledge**
- And of the **Fear of the Lord."**

The Spirit of the Lord
The Holy Spirit is "*the Spirit of the Lord*". He **proceeds from the Father—John 15:26.** This is important because there are other types of spirits which are dangerous and are to be avoided by believers. Believers are warned not to believe every spirit but to test the spirits and be sure they are of God—**1John 4:1-3.**

"The Spirit of the Lord" is **the Spirit of Authority;** He anoints to make all other things possible. Jesus said:

"The <u>Spirit of the Lord</u> is upon me,
Because He has anointed me
To preach the gospel to the poor;
He has sent me to heal the brokenhearted,
To proclaim liberty to the captives
And recovery of sight to the blind,
To set at liberty those who are oppressed;
To proclaim the acceptable year of the Lord"—Luke 4:18-19 (NKJV)

Jesus Christ said that He sends the disciples and by extension, all believers, out to the world just as the Father had sent Him—John 20:21 and then breathed the Spirit on them—John 20:22. He therefore sends believers out with same Spirit and the same authority.

While sending the disciples on a mission, Jesus Christ said: **"Behold, I give you the authority to trample on serpents and scorpions, and** over all the power of the enemy, and nothing shall by any means hurt you."—**Luke 10:19**.

Again, in His valedictory charge to the disciples, Jesus Christ said: **". . . All Authority has been given to me in heaven and on earth. Go therefore and make disciples of all the nations . . ."**—**Mathew 28:18-20**.

Therefore, the Spirit of the Lord is the Authority behind the Great Commission given to believers to preach, teach, deliver and heal just as Jesus Christ did.

- ❖ **The <u>Authority</u> of "the Spirit of the Lord" is essential for effective service.**

The Spirit of Wisdom

Jesus Christ is the personification of Wisdom. He is both the **"Wisdom of God"** and **the "Wisdom from God"—1Corinthians 1:24, 30**. Therefore, the Holy Spirit is the Spirit of Jesus Christ.

- **The Wisdom from God is: ". . . first pure, then peaceable, gentle, willing to yield, full of mercy and good fruits, without partiality and without hypocrisy."—James 3:17.**
- The Bible says the man who finds this Wisdom is blessed because **'Wisdom is more profitable than silver and gold and more precious than rubies'—Proverbs 3:13-15.**
- The dividends of possessing this kind of Wisdom are—**long life, riches, honor and peace—Proverbs 3:16-18.**
- This godly Wisdom:
- **"Is better than strength"—Ecclesiastes 9:16 (NKJV).**
- **"Is better than weapons of war"—Ecclesiastes 9:18 (NKJV).**
- **"Brings success"—Ecclesiastes 10:10 (NKJV).**
- Jesus promised: **". . . I will give you a mouth and wisdom which all your adversaries will not be able to contradict or resist . . ."—Luke 21:15.**

There is another kind of wisdom that Believers are warned to avoid. This kind of wisdom is: **'earthly and sensual; and is characterized by envy, bitterness and selfishness'**.

The dividends of this kind of wisdom are confusion and all kinds of evil—**James 3:14-16**. God calls this kind of wisdom foolishness—**1Corinthians 3:19**.

The Preacher said:
- ❖ **"The fear of the Lord is the beginning of Wisdom…"—Proverbs 9:10a.**

The Spirit of Understanding

The Holy Spirit gives true understanding.

To understand is to comprehend, that is, to grasp the meaning or significance of something.

The Bible says: **". . . the knowledge of the Holy one is understanding"—Proverbs 9:10b.**

- Real Understanding is from God—**Job 32:8.**
- Understanding can be acquired through meditation on the Word of God and the keeping of His precepts—**Psalm 119: 99,100, 104 & 130.**
- It is the understanding of the Word of God that makes the believer grow, prosper and bear fruit—**Mathew 13:23.**
- Daniel and his colleagues, Shadrach, Meshach and Abednego were endowed with **"understanding in all visions and dreams"** because they dedicated themselves to God and refused to be defiled—**Daniel 1:8-18.**
- God wants believers to glory or boast in only one thing, their knowledge and understanding of Him—**Jeremiah 9:23.**
- The dividends of true understanding include: **uprightness in conduct, calmness of spirit and prosperity—Proverbs 15:21 (NKJV); Proverbs 17:27 (NKJV); Proverbs 19:8 (NIV).**

The Spirit of Might

Might mean great power:

Power belongs to God—Psalm 62:11.

One of the prophetic Names of Jesus Christ is **"The Mighty God"—Isaiah 9:6.**

- The Spirit of God and of His Christ therefore is the Spirit of Might.

When Jesus sent out the disciples, He 'gave them *power* over unclean spirits—**Mark 6:7.**

- After His resurrection and before His ascension, Jesus Christ asked the disciples to remain in Jerusalem until they were **endued with 'Power'** from on high. The Great Commission is

not to be undertaken until the Holy Spirit empowered them for service—**Acts 1: 4-5, 8.**
- Paul the Apostle testified in many instances that his preaching of the Gospel was not in **'mere words'** only but in demonstration of the Spirit and of **power—1Corinthians 2:4-5; 1Corinthians 4:20; 1Thessalonians 1:5.**

The Holy Spirit gives believers power for service and for living the godly life—2Peter 1:3-4

> ❖ **The Spirit that Believers receive from God is the <u>Spirit of Power</u>, of Love and of a sound mind—2Timothy 1:7.**

The Spirit of Counsel

Another prophetic Name of Jesus Christ is **"Counselor"** or **"Wonderful Counselor"—Isaiah 9:6.**
- Jesus Christ promised to pray the Father to send another **"Counselor"** to believers who will indwell, teach and guide the believer. He will bring to the believers' remembrance what has been learnt and even tell about the future—**John 14:16-17, 26; John 16:13.**
- Because the Spirit knows the mind of God, He is able to counsel and intercede for believers according to the Will of God—**Romans 8:26-27.**

The Holy Spirit is the believer's Counselor and Guide through the labyrinth of life.

> ❖ **"You will guide me with Your counsel and afterward receive me into glory"—Psalm 73:24.**

The Spirit of Knowledge

Knowledge means to have the facts, have information about, have experience with or be aware of and be familiar with.
- Knowledge is the building block of Wisdom and Understanding—**Proverbs 9:10; Ecclesiastes 7:12**.
- Knowledge, like Wisdom and Understanding is from God—**Proverbs 2:6;** and true Knowledge begins with the fear of God—**Proverbs 1:7**
- Godly knowledge is more than mere accumulation of facts and figures; it embodies thorough comprehension of the subject.

- Both the pursuit and the acquisition of knowledge should be within the ambience of the fear of the Lord. The pursuit of Knowledge without the fear of God will usually ultimately prove to be destructive.
- To walk worthy of the Lord and to please Him requires that Believers seek deeper knowledge of God: "in all wisdom and spiritual understanding"—**Colossians 1:9-10.**
- God wants believers to make their boast only on their Knowledge and understanding of Him—Jeremiah 9:23-24

True knowledge can be acquired only through the guidance of the Holy Spirit

❖ The Bible says: "**My people are destroyed for lack of knowledge**"—Hosea 4:6

The Spirit of the Fear of the Lord

Fear in this context is not terror but **"Reverence", "honor" or "great respect."**

- **The fear of the Lord is the key to God's treasure of true Wisdom, Knowledge and Salvation—Isaiah 33:6 (NIV); Proverbs 1:7; Proverbs 9:10; Proverbs 15:33 (NIV).**

The Spirit of the fear of the Lord confers on the believer many benefits, namely:
- **Intimacy with God—Psalm 25:14; Amos 3:7**
- **Security—Psalm 34:7; Proverbs 19:23**
- **Blessings—Psalm 128:1-2 (NIV)**
- **Fulfillment of desire by God—Psalm 145:19**
- **It is the fountain of life—Proverbs 14:27**
- **Divine Guidance into God's ordained path—Psalm 25:12.**
- **Prosperity—Psalm 25:12-13**
  ❖ Prayer:—*"Teach me Your Way O Lord; I will walk in your Truth; unite my heart to fear Your Name"—Psalm 86:11*
❖ **Believers can expect the Baptism of the Holy Spirit from God with the impartation of the characteristics.**

The Gifts of the Holy Spirit:

The Holy Spirit gives gifts to believers—**Romans 12:5-8; 1 Corinthians 12; Ephesians 4:11-13.**
- Diversely as He wills

- For the profit of all
- To build up the Body of Christ, the Church
- To equip Believers for Service/Ministry
- To promote unity in the faith and in the knowledge of Christ
- To help Believers mature and resemble Jesus Christ in true holiness and righteousness—***Romans 12:6; 1Corinthians 12:4-7; Ephesians 4:12-13.***
  - The gifts of the Holy Spirit, as recorded in the Scriptures include:
- Prophecy—**Romans 12:6; 1Corinthians 12:10 & 28; Ephesians 4:11**
- Teaching—**Romans 12:7; 1Corinthians 12:28; Ephesians 4:11**
- Exhortation/Encouragement—**Romans 12:8**
- Giving—**Romans 12:8**
- Leadership/Administration—**Romans 12:8; 1Corinthians 12:28**
- Mercy/Helps—**Romans 12:8; 1Corinthians 12:28**
- Wisdom—**1Corinthians 12:8**
- Word of Knowledge—**1Corinthians 12:8**
- Faith—**1Corinthians 12:9**
- Healing—**1Corinthians 12:9**
- Miracles—**1Corinthians 12:10, 28**
- Discernment of spirits—**1Corinthians 12:10**
- Tongues—**1Corinthians 12:10,28**
- Interpretation of Tongues—**1Corinthians 12:10**
- Apostles—**Ephesians 4:11; 1Corinthians 12:28**
- Evangelists—**Ephesians 4:11**
- Pastors—**Ephesians 4:11**
  - ➢ "But the <u>manifestation</u> of the Spirit is given to <u>each</u> one for the profit of <u>all</u>;"—1Corinthians 12:7. (NKJV)
- ❖ Believers can expect the Gifts of the Spirit from God.

The Fruit of the Spirit—Galatians 5:22-23.

The Holy Spirit, who is the Counselor, Teacher, Guide and Enabler, lives in the obedient believer.

As the believer learns to yield to the counsel and guidance of the Holy Spirit, he grows and matures and the 'Fruit of the Spirit' is produced—**Galatians 5:22-23. (NIV)**

The 'Fruit of the Spirit' include:

- **Love, joy, peace, Patience, Kindness, Goodness, Faithfulness, Gentleness, Self-control.**
  - Jesus Christ said: "You will know them by their fruits . . ."—**Mathew 7:16;**

And again: ". . . A tree is known by its fruit."—**Mathew 12:33.**
  - If indeed a believer has the Holy Spirit, he will bear fruits in keeping with His presence.
- ❖ **Believers can expect the Fruit of the Spirit.**

➢ **"And we are witnesses to these things and so also is the Holy Spirit whom God has given to <u>those who obey."</u>—Acts 5:32. (NIV)**

B) What do God and Jesus Christ expect of / from Believers?

According to Scriptures, based on what Jesus Christ accomplished and made available to believers who trust in Him and the empowerment by the Holy Spirit promised to them, God and Jesus Christ expect:

1) **Real Change**

Real Salvation results from true repentance and true repentance is always accompanied by real change. Jesus made it clear that believers cannot patch up the old nature with the new cloth of the of the Good News or pour the New Wine of the Holy Spirit in the old wine skin of the old sinful nature—**Mathew 9:16-17**.
  - According to the Bible, a person who is Born Again is a **"New Creature"—2Corinthians 5:17; old things for such a one have passed away, all things become new.**
  - If there has been genuine repentance and Salvation is real, the conduct will be in keeping with the new nature. John the Baptist urged those responding to his message of repentance to **"bear fruits worthy of repentance"—Mathew 3:8.**
  - Paul's message was that his audience—" . . . **repent, turn to God and do works befitting repentance"—Acts 26:19-20.**
  - Paul repeatedly called on believers to **"put off the old man"**, the **"old sinful nature"** and put on **"the new man"** created according to God in true righteousness and holiness—**Ephesians 4:21-31; Colossians 3: 1-14; Ephesians 5:1-7.**
    - ❖ **God expects real change in true Believers**

> **The One who changed water to vintage wine can be trusted to make real changes in the lives of believers.**

2) Reverence for God, Jesus Christ and the Holy Spirit
   To revere means to love and respect deeply and to honor greatly.

All the relationship types of man with God, Jesus Christ and the Holy Spirit in the Bible, namely—Father-Child, Master-Servant and Teacher-Student require / demand respect.

- The Bible made it clear that, as God's children, believers must revere the Father.

In Malachi 1:6 God says**: "A Son honors his father and a servant his master. If I am the Father, where is my honor? And if I am a Master, where is my reverence?**

- The first three of the Ten Commandments are about honoring and respecting God—**Exodus 20:1-7.**
- The Model Prayer (The Lord's Prayer), opened with a call to honor the Name of God—**Luke 11:2**
- Believers are also called to honor the Son just as they honor the Father—**John 5:22-23**
- Believers are expected to revere the Holy Spirit too—Mathew 12:31-32
- Believers are called to honor God in:
- Thoughts—**Philippians 4:8**
- Words—**Exodus 20:7; Colossians 3:17**
- Actions—**Colossians 3:23-24**
- Bodies—**1Corinthians 6:19-20; 1Thessalonians 4:3-5**
- And with their possessions—**Proverbs 3:9-10**

That is, with the totality of their beings.

❖ **God expects Believers to honor Him, Jesus Christ and the Holy Spirit**

3) Open Identification

Jesus expects anyone who comes to Him to openly and unashamedly identify with Him and His message.

- He said: **"For whoever is ashamed of me and My Words in this adulterous and sinful generation, of him the Son of Man also will be ashamed when He comes in the glory of His Father** with the holy angels."—**Mark 8:38; Mathew 10:32-33; Luke 12:8-9**.

Jesus made it clear He too will be ashamed of anyone who is ashamed of Him or His Word before the Father.

> ❖ **Jesus expects Believers to identify openly with Him**

4) Loyalty & Total Commitment

Jesus expects absolute loyalty and total commitment from anyone who comes to Him in the New Covenant and is very succinct in this regard.

- Loyalty to Jesus Christ transcends filial affections, affinities and affiliations. Jesus said: **"He who loves father or mother more than me is not worthy of Me. And he who loves son or daughter more than me is not worthy of me . . ."—Mathew 10:37-39; Mark 3:31-35; Luke 14:25-27.**
- Entering into a Covenant relationship with God through the Blood of Jesus Christ leaves no room for half measures. Jesus said: **"Therefore whoever does not forsake all that he has cannot be my disciple."—Luke 14:33.**

What is Jesus saying here? Is He implying that believers abandon family and possessions?

No, what He is saying is that obedience to Him transcends everything and should be paramount. Nothing must conflict with the believer's devotion to Him; not relationships, possessions or circumstances—**Mathew 6:24.**

> ❖ **Jesus Christ expects Believers to be loyal and be totally committed to Him**

5) Faithfulness & Accountability

In the parable of the talents, Jesus revealed that everyone will give account to God—**Mathew 25:14-30.**

- Jesus stated clearly that everyone will give account of everything—thoughts, speeches, actions, bodies, talents, possessions etc.

He said: **"But I say to you that <u>for every idle word</u> men may speak, <u>they will give account</u> of it in the Day of Judgment."—Mathew 12:36.** (NKJV)

In regards to actions He said: **". . . Behold I come quickly and my reward is with me, to give every one according to his works."—Revelations 22:12.**

- Paul said: **"So then, each of us shall give account of himself to God"—Romans 14:12. (NKJV)**
- Paul again said: **"For we must all appear before the judgment seat of Christ, that each one may receive the things done in the body, according to what he has done, whether good or bad."—2Corinthians 5:10 (NKJV)**
  - ❖ Jesus Christ expects believers to be faithful and accountable

6) Growth & Fruitfulness

Growth and fruitfulness, from creation have always been integral parts of God's Covenant with Man.

- God told Adam and Eve to: **". . . Be fruitful and multiply . . ."—Genesis 1:28.**
- After the destruction of the first world by floods which only Noah and his family survived; God again pronounced the blessing of fruitfulness on him saying—**"Be fruitful and multiply . . ."—Genesis 9:1.**
- After Abraham honored God by offering his Son Isaac, God renewed His Covenant with him saying: **". . . Because you have done this . . . . in blessing I will bless you, and in multiplying, I will multiply your descendants . . . ."—Genesis 22:16-18.**

The New Covenant that believers have in the Blood of Jesus Christ is not different; it is the will of God that believers be fruitful.

- Jesus said: "**By this, My Father is glorified, that you bear much fruit; so you will be my disciples**"—**John 15:8.**
- To bear fruit, a tree first has to grow and mature. In the same way, believers have to grow and mature by remaining connected to Jesus Christ as the branches of a tree are connected to the stem. This is very important because **"without Him we can do nothing"—John 15:5-6**
- *Fruitlessness is a violation of the divine principle.* The branch that does not abide in the vine cannot grow or mature and therefore cannot bear fruit and it is therefore cut off, thrown into the fire and burnt.—**John 15:6**.
- It is not only important to bear fruit, it is essential to bear **"good fruit"**. The fate of the tree that bears bad fruit is the same as that of the fruitless tree—**Mathew 3:10; Mathew 7:19.**

Fruitfulness, apart from serving the purpose of propagation also serves as means of identification.
- Jesus said: "**You will know them by their fruits.**"—Mathew 7:16

   ❖ **God expects Believers to Grow and be Fruitful**

7) **Forgiveness**

Forgiveness is an essential part of salvation gift package; God *demands* that believers forgive others too.

In the Model Prayer,
- Jesus taught believers to pray: "**And forgive us our debts, as we forgive our debtors.**"—Mathew 6:12.

Several theologians have looked into what this may mean, is it saying God should forgive in the manner or in the measure that believers forgive others?
- Either way, Jesus Christ left no one in doubt about what He meant, He said: "**For if you forgive men their trespasses, your heavenly Father will also forgive you. But if you do not forgive men their trespasses, neither will your Father forgive you your trespasses.**"—Mathew 6:14-15.

Many have argued that refusing to forgive does not mean that a believer would lose God's forgiveness.

However, for anyone who might still be in doubt about what is required in regard to forgiving others, Jesus gave the parable of the *"Unforgiving Servant"* in **Mathew 18:23-35.**
- The King forgave a servant a large amount of debt, however, the forgiven servant failed to forgive a fellow servant who owed him a very small debt. When the King heard what happened, he was angry with the unforgiving servant. **He reversed the forgiveness and clamped him in jail with hard labor**.
- Jesus Christ ended the story by saying: "**So My heavenly Father will do to you if each of you, from his heart, does not forgive his brother his trespasses**"—**Mathew 18:35.**
- Jesus Christ also underscored the importance of forgiveness to effective worship and prayer. He said: "**Therefore, when you bring your gift to the altar, and remember that your brother has something against you, leave your gift there before the**

altar, and go your way. First be reconciled to your brother, and then come, and offer your gift."—Mathew 5:23-24.
- Again He said: "**And whenever you stand praying, if you have <u>anything</u> against <u>anyone</u>, <u>forgive</u> him, so that your Father in heaven may also forgive you your trespasses. <u>But if you do not forgive, neither will your Father in heaven forgive your trespasses.</u>"—Mark 11: 25-26**. (NKJV)
  - ➢ **It is clear that for Believers to retain the forgiveness from God, they also have to forgive others from the heart.**
- ❖ **God expects Believers to sincerely forgive all who offend them.**

7) Faith

"**. . . Faith is the substance of things hoped for, the evidence of things not seen."—Hebrews 11:1. (NKJV)**
Faith is very central to a believer's life.
- *"Salvation is by Grace through Faith"*—**Ephesians 2:8** and
- Believers live by faith—**Hebrews 10:38**
- "Believers walk by faith, not by sight."—**2Corinthians 5:7.**
- **Faith is the currency with which believers can do business with God**.

The Bible says: **"But without <u>faith</u>, it is impossible to <u>please</u> Him (God), for he who comes to God <u>must believe</u> that He is, and that He is a <u>Rewarder</u> of those who diligently seek Him."—Hebrews 11:6. (NKJV)**
- Jesus said that by faith believers can move mountains and do the humanly impossible—**"For assuredly, I say to you, whoever says to this mountain, 'Be removed and be cast into the sea, and does not doubt in his heart, but believes that those things he says will be done, he will have whatever he says."—Mark 11:22-24; Mathew 17:20; Mark 9:23**
- Jesus promised believers that if they believe, they will see the glory of God—John 11:40.

Jesus emphasized the importance of faith on numerous occasions. He wondered at the disciples' lack of faith in the storm—**Luke 8:22-25** and He rebuked Peter for entertaining fear and doubt instead of faith while walking on water—**Mathew 14:22-32.**

❖ **Jesus expects Believers to have faith in Him and in God**

9) Prayer & Watchfulness

Prayer is communication with God. A child has a lot to say to and ask a loving Father, so it should be natural, as God's children, for believers to want to pray.

- Jesus prayed often and fasted too—**Luke 5:15-16; Mathew 4:1-2.**
- Sometimes He prayed all night—**Luke 6:12.**
- Sometimes, He prayed corporately with the disciples—**Luke 9:28-29**

Many times privately and solitarily—**Mathew 14:23; Mark 1:35; Mark 6:46; Luke 9:18.**

- And He prayed publicly too—**John 11:41.**
- Jesus taught believers **how** to pray, **where** to pray, **when** to pray and **what** to pray for and He did this by His life of prayer as the example—**Mathew 6:5-15**.
- He encouraged believers to pray—**Luke 11:9-13;** and pray with importunity—**Luke 18:1-8.**
- He gave assurance that prayer will be answered—**Mark 11:24; Luke 11:9-10; John 14:13; John 16:23.**
- He emphasized the need for watchfulness and alertness and warned against carelessness—**Mathew 24:42-51; Mathew 25:1-13; Mark 13:32-36.**
- He expects believers to be watchful for end time signs such as societal lawlessness, proliferation of false prophets and tribulations—**Mathew 24; Mark 13 and Luke 21**.
- ❖ **Jesus Christ expects Believers to pray, and to be alert and watchful.**

10) Holiness—(Zero Tolerance for Sin)

To be holy means to be set apart, and free from sin. The process of being made holy is sanctification which means to make holy, to purify or to be consecrated and free from sin. Sanctification is a component of the 'Salvation Package'.

- God expects those who have truly accepted the Gift of Salvation to be sanctified, that is holy. Sanctification made Reconciliation

- possible because the Bible says: **"without holiness, no one will see God—Hebrews 12:14.**
- God's intention is that through the redemption obtained in Christ Jesus, believers will serve Him in holiness and righteousness—**Luke 1:74-75.**
- Jesus made it clear He expects believers to have zero tolerance for Sin. He said: **"If your right eye causes you to sin, pluck it out and cast it from you And if your right hand causes you to sin, cut it off and cast it from you; for it is more profitable for you that one of your members perish than for your whole body to be cast into hell."—Mathew 5:27-30.**

This should not be construed as a call to self mutilation; however, it is certainly a call to zero tolerance for Sin. It means nothing is off limit for believers to do away with in the effort to maintain the right relationship with God. It is a call to the highest standard possible.

Why would Jesus expect that believers be holy or perfect?
- He prayed for the Sanctification of believers—**John 17:17.**
- He committed Himself to doing it—**John 17:19,** and
- He followed through by His death on the Cross. The Bible says: **"For He (God) made Him (Jesus Christ) who knew no sin to be sin for us, that we might become the righteousness of God in Him"—2Corinthians 5:21.**

On the Cross, Jesus Christ did not just have the sins of the world placed on Him, **He was made SIN!**

No wonder, the Father had to forsake Him; for a holy God cannot look at Sin.
- Believers need not be intimidated by the holiness issue, though it is impossible by human effort, God has said—**"I am the Lord who sanctifies you."—Leviticus 20:8; Leviticus 22:32.**

As believers trust God for forgiveness through faith in Jesus Christ and His atoning death following repentance, so also they ought to trust Him for sanctification as He promised He will do. To hold otherwise would be to deny God, Jesus and the Holy Spirit and tantamount to trusting God for some part of the Salvation package while disbelieving some others, **"For with God, nothing shall be impossible"—Luke 1:37.**

❖ **God expects Believers to be Holy**

11) Endurance & Perseverance

Jesus Christ left no one under any illusion about what life would be like for believers. He warned: **". . . . In the world you will have tribulations; but be of good cheer, I have overcome the world."—John 16:33.**

- He warned that believers will experience persecutions, betrayals and hatred just as He did.—**Mathew 10:21-22; Mathew 24:9-13; John 15:20.**
- However, in spite of all these, Jesus Christ expects believers to endure and not turn back. **He said: "But he who endures to the end shall be saved."—Mathew 24:9-13; Mark 13:12-13**
- And again, He said: **"No one, having put his hand to the plow, and looking back, is fit for the kingdom of God—Luke 9:62.**
- Paul called for **"enduring hardship as a good soldier of Christ"—2Timothy 2:3.**
    - ❖ **Jesus Christ expects Believers to endure and persevere in spite of persecutions and tribulations.**

12) Good (Charitable) Works:

Jesus said: **"Let your light so shine before men, that they may see your good works and glorify your Father in heaven."—Mathew 5:16.**

- Jesus made it clear; God expects "Good works" from believers. In fact, the very verse after the often quoted verses that characterized Salvation as a gift by Grace through Faith says: **"For we are His workmanship, created in Christ Jesus for 'good works' which God prepared beforehand that we should walk in them."—Ephesians 2:10.**

Believers are **"created in Christ Jesus for good works as ordained by God"**!

While no one can do anything to earn Salvation, Salvation in Christ Jesus commits believers to good works and is a natural product of the New Creature.

- Paul said that Jesus **"redeemed us from every lawless deed and purified for Himself His own special people, zealous for good works."—Titus 2:14.**
    - ❖ **Jesus not only expects good works from Believers, He wants their good works to be seen (not advertised) so that God will be glorified.**

13) Love (of God & Neighbor) and Obedience

It is incontrovertible that God loves Mankind, the crown of His creation. It was love that made Him give His one and only Son to die on the Cross so that Man can be forgiven, sanctified and reconciled to Him.

How can man love the One to whom he owes everything?

- Jesus Christ showed believers the acceptable way. He said: "**If you love me, keep My Commandments."—John 14:15.**
- Again He said: "**He who has My Commandments and keeps them is he who loves me. And he who loves me will be loved by My Father, and I will love him and manifest myself to him."—John 14:21.**
- He went further to say: **"If anyone loves me, he will keep My Word; and My Father will love him, and we will come to him and make our home with him."—John 14:23**.
- <u>**OBEDIENCE,**</u> therefore is the Way to love God; not sentiments, proclamations or activities.
- **1John 5:3** says: **"For this is the love of God, that we keep His Commandments. And His Commandments are not burdensome."**

It is through obedience that believers:

- Get to know Jesus Christ—**John 14:21; 1John 2:3-6**
- Abide in the Love of Jesus Christ and of the Father—**John 14:23; John 15:10.**
- Become and remain the friend of Jesus Christ—**John 15:14.**
- Receive the Holy Spirit—**Acts 5:32**
- ▪ Believers' love for others is also measured by obedience to God's Commandments. 1John 5:2 says: **"By this we know that we love the children of God, when we love God and keep His Commandments."**

It is impossible to truly love others outside of obedience to the Word of God, because Jesus expects believers to not only love the lovable, but also the humanly unlovable.

In **Mathew 5:43-48;** Jesus Christ asked that believers love their enemies, bless those who curse them, do good to those who hate them and pray for those who persecute them.

- ▪ **Obedience is the acid test of true Conversion and Salvation.** Jesus Christ made it clear that it is futile to call Him Lord without living in obedience to His Word—**Mathew 7:21-29.**

- The Apostle John said: **"Now, by this we know that we know Him, if we keep His Commandments. <u>He who says 'I know Him' and does not keep His Commandments is a liar and the truth is not in him.</u>"**—1John 2:3-4
  - ❖ **Jesus expects Believers to LOVE and OBEY Him**

14) Evangelism

The last charge Jesus gave to the disciples and all who would come to believe in Him was—**"Go therefore and make disciples of all the nations, baptizing them in the Name of the Father and of the Son and of the Holy Spirit, teaching them to observe all things I have commanded you; and lo I am with you always, even to the end of the age." Amen**—Mathew 28:19-20.

How will this to be done?

- Believers are to: "**preach the gospel** to every creature; and In His Name, **cast out demons**, **heal the sick** and do what Jesus did while on the earth; in other words, *be his true witnesses*—**Mark 16:15-20.**
- However, believers cannot be true witnesses until they receive the Promise of the Father, the Holy Spirit—**Acts 1:4-5, 8.**
- Paul said: "Preach the Word, be instant in season and out of season; reprove, rebuke, exhort with all long suffering and doctrine"—*2Timothy 4:2.*
  - ❖ **Jesus expects Believers to preach, teach and heal; in short, be His true witnesses.**

C) What can Believers expect from the World?

Jesus Christ said: **'If you belong to the world, it would love you as its own. As it is, you do not belong to the world, but I have chosen you out of the world. That is why the world hates you"**—John 15:19 (NIV).

James said: **".... Do you not know that friendship with the world is enmity with God? Whoever wants to be a friend of the world makes himself an enemy of God"**—James 4:4

- Those who are not Christians are under the influence of what the Apostle Paul called—**"the prince of the power of the air, the spirit that works in the sons of disobedience."—Ephesians 2:2.**

- However, Christians are controlled by the Holy Spirit—**Romans 8:14.**

Therefore, it is not surprising that the people of the world are constantly in hostility towards those who profess and live the faith in the Lord Jesus Christ.

What then can Believers expect from the World?

1.) Hatred & Persecutions
- Jesus Christ said: **"And you will be hated by all for My Name's sake . . ."—Mark 13:13** and
- **"If the world hates you, keep in mind that it hated me first . . . If they persecute me, they will persecute you also"—John 15:18 & 20.** (NIV)
- The Apostle Paul said: **". . . all who desire to live godly in Christ Jesus will suffer persecution"—2Timothy 3:12. (NKJV)**

What should be the attitude of Christians to hatred and persecution by the world?

- Jesus Christ said: **"Blessed are those who are persecuted for righteousness' sake, for theirs is the kingdom of heaven. Blessed are you when they revile and persecute you, and say all kinds of evil against you falsely for my sake. Rejoice and be exceedingly glad, for great is your reward in heaven, for so they persecuted the prophets who were before you"—Mathew 5:10-12.**
- Peter said Christians should not be surprised when persecution arises on account of their faith in Jesus Christ; he said: **"Beloved, do not think it strange concerning the fiery trial which is to try you, as though some strange thing happened to you; but rejoice to the extent that you partake of Christ's sufferings, that when His glory is revealed, you may also be glad with exceeding joy . . ."—1Peter 4:12-14 (NKJV).**
- He went on to say: **". . . If anyone suffers as a Christian, let him not be ashamed, but let him glorify God in this matter"—1Peter 4:16.**
- James said: **"My brethren, count it all joy when you fall into various trials, knowing that the testing of your faith produces patience"—James 1:2-3.**

The Apostles and the early Church were threatened, beaten, imprisoned and many were killed; but as instructed by Jesus, they rejoiced that they were counted worthy to suffer for the Name of Jesus—**Acts 5:41; Acts 7:54-60; Acts 12:1-4; Acts 14:19-20; Acts 16:19-24**

The believers' attitude should be no less than theirs; counting it all joy and being exceedingly glad, knowing that, as Jesus said, they are blessed.

The assurance of blessedness should enable believers to **"love enemies, bless those who curse, do good to those who hate and pray for those who are spiteful and persecute them"—Mathew 5:44.**

2.) Tribulations

Tribulation means great trouble, severe trials, oppression, distress or misery; that is Persecution on a higher scale.

- Jesus said: **". . . In the world you will have tribulation; but be of good cheer, I have overcome the world"—John 16:33.**
- The hatred of Christians and what they stand for brings them into conflict with the world. All over the world, it is becoming increasingly more difficult for Christians to operate freely and it is more likely they will get into conflict with the secular laws in many nations.
- The trend in many "developed nations" is that the Christian views and values are not only being degraded, they are being criminalized. A Christian who merely states the facts of his or her faith is in danger of being accused of hate speech or worse and by all indications it can only get worse.
- Jesus warned that: **". . . there will be great tribulation such as has never been since the beginning of the world . . ."** and He warned that only those who endure to the end will be saved—**Mathew 24:21; Mathew 24:13.**

The early disciples, quite unlike many prosperity preachers today, prepared new Christians for tribulations and told them plainly that their lives would not be easy.

- Paul and Barnabas told the disciples at Derbe, Lystra, Iconium and Antioch that: **"We must through many tribulations enter the kingdom of God"—Acts 14:22.**

However, Christians have the assurance of God's comfort;

- Paul said: **"Blessed be the God and Father of our Lord Jesus Christ, the Father of mercies and the God of all comforts, who**

comforts us in all our tribulations, that we may be able to comfort those who are in any trouble, with the comfort with which we ourselves are comforted by God"—2Corinthians 1:3-4.

The Apostles practiced what they preached; Paul wrote to the Corinthians: **". . . I am filled with comfort. I am exceedingly joyful in all our tribulation"—2Corinthians 7:4.**

The consolation for Christians is that they have been warned and therefore can be at peace within.

❖ **Christians can expect tribulation from the world**

6.) Betrayal

Profession of faith in Jesus Christ can split families and friends when values are at variance. To live uncompromisingly in such situations may eventually bring frictions into relationships to the point where Jesus described as: **"bringing a sword on the earth"—Mathew 10:34.**

- Jesus said: **"brother will betray brother to death, and a father his child; and children will rise up against parents and cause them to be put to death"—Mark 13:12.**

As the world grows more rebellious, these scenarios, already playing out in many places around the world, will become more commonplace.

❖ **Christians can expect betrayal from the world**

The Christian Identity in Christ

The relationship established with God the Father, Jesus Christ the Son and the Holy Spirit through the New Covenant in the blood of Jesus creates for the believer a new identity. The Bible says: "If any man is in Christ, he is a New Creature . . ."

It is important for a believer to know what his new identity is in Christ Jesus because if Satan was so audacious as to challenge Jesus Christ on His identity, he will surely challenge Christians too.

The experience of Jesus Christ's temptation in the wilderness at the beginning of His ministry illustrated the importance of knowing one's true identity. The Devil challenged Him for forty days and nights on His identity saying: *"If you are the Son of God . . ."—Mathew 4:3, 6,* quoting scriptures to tempt Him.

The implication was clear, to get Jesus Christ to doubt himself or goaded into acting in ways that tempt God. Jesus defeated the Devil because He was confident about who he was and by His knowledge and understanding of the scriptures; therefore He avoided being lured to eat stone, tempt God or worship the Devil.

To drive home the importance of knowing one's true identity, Jesus Christ asked the disciples, first who the people thought He was—***Matthew 16:13-14.*** They told Him he was thought to be a re-incarnation of one of the old prophets like Elijah, Jeremiah or some others.

Jesus then asked the disciples who they thought He was and Simon Peter by revelation correctly identified Him as "the Messiah, the Son of the Living God"—***Matthew 16:16.***

To His neighbors, Jesus Christ was defined by His family background and remained ***"the Carpenter, son of Mary, the brother of James, Joseph, Judas and Simon.*** And of course they knew the sisters!—***Mathew 13:54-56; Mark 6:3***.

For another group, Christ's town of domicile defined Him so they didn't expect much of him so they said: ***"Can anything good come out of Nazareth?—John 1:46.***

For the religious leaders, Christ was defined by his geographical district and history and their learned opinion was: ***"Shall Christ come from Galilee? . . . Search and see, for out of Galilee arises no prophet"—John 7:41, 52.***

In the same way, people will try to define believers by family background, zip code, race, color, life history, profession, socio-economic status etc. While these to some extent can serve the purpose of physical identification, a believer is much more than these.

What is the Christian's identity in Christ?
- First, the Bible says that a believer is empowered to become a ***child of God—John 1:12*** As such he has unhindered access to the throne of Grace and Mercy by the blood of Jesus to obtain help in time of need—***Hebrews 4:16.***
- As a child of God, he becomes a ***"Joint Heir"*** with the one and only begotten Son of God, Jesus Christ—***Romans 8:16-18; Galatians 4:7.***
- As an obedient child and joint heir, he has the Father and Jesus Christ living in him through the Holy Spirit and he becomes the ***Temple of God—John 14:16, 21, 23; 1Corinthians 3:16; 6:19.***
- He has the Holy Spirit as his teacher, guide and helper—***John 14:16, 26; John 16:13***

- He becomes a member of a ***holy nation of peculiar people and royal priesthood**—1Peter 2:9*
- He changes his citizenship to that of heaven and becomes an alien in the world—***Philippians 3:20.***
- His role in the world becomes that of an ***Ambassador of Christ*** and His *soldier*—***2Corinthians 5:20; 2Timothy 2:3-4.***
- He is also expected to be ***light and salt*** in the world—***Matthew 5: 13-16.***

These are just a sample of who a Christian is in Christ.

Although the composite picture of a Christian according to scriptures is that of an exceptional and extraordinary being, only very few agree with God on their true identity. Although the Bible says Christians are overcomers, many only see themselves as Satan's punch bags; although the Bible affirm that believers are set free from sin and are saints, many think it is humility to harp on their sinfulness—***John 8:34-36***. And while the Bible says the one inside the believer is greater than the one that is in the world—*(1John 4:4),* many speak of the power of the devil than of the power of the resurrected Christ "who has through death destroyed him who had the power of death, that is the devil"—***Hebrews 2:14-15.***

Ignorance and lack of understanding of the Christian's true identity is responsible for the state of the Church today. Many believers are being deceived by the devil to eat stone, tempt God and some even unwittingly worship him. In addition, believers are being defined and limited by the world's stereotypes.

The situation is reminiscent of the story of an eaglet, rescued by a farmer and raised among chickens on the farm. It grew up behaving like a chicken, scratching and pecking around in the dirt, a grotesque site and object of derision; totally oblivious of its true identity and potential; it did not realize that it was born, not only to fly but to soar.

In spite of the wonderful heritage that Christians have in Christ, and the divine power made available to them to be partakers of the divine nature—(2Peter 1:3-4)—most Christians limp through life instead of soaring like eagles.

How did the Church get to be this way? How has her gold become dross?

To answer these questions, it is important to trace her history from the beginning to the present time.

Chapter 4

The Early Church and the Ante-Nicene Church Fathers

"See to it that no one takes you captive
Through hollow and deceptive philosophy,
Which depends on human tradition and the basic
principles—
Of this world rather than on Christ"—Colossians 2:8
(NIV)

The Apostolic Church—(35AD-120AD)
The Apostolic Church comprised eye witnesses; many walked and worked with Jesus and others had first hand information about Jesus Christ or contact with those who did. The Apostolic fathers, represented by Peter, James, John, Paul and others, energized by the Holy Spirit that Jesus promised them and all believers, literally turned the world up side down. Of them it was said: ***"And through the hands of the Apostles, many signs and wonders were done among the people . . ."—Acts 5:12.***

Their exploits were recorded in the "**Acts of the Apostles**"; a permanent testament to the potency of their faith and the faithfulness of the one in whom they trusted. Powered by the Holy Spirit, the Apostolic Church lived up to the expectation of the Master; their witness was not in "**words only but also in power**" and those who disagreed with them could neither ignore their boldness nor deny their exploits. Needless to say, they won many to the fold, sometimes in their thousands as happened on the day of Pentecost—**Acts 2:37-41.**

The church comprised baptized believers whose activities were directed by the Holy Spirit who gave members spiritual gifts for the perfecting of believers, for effective witnessing and the edification of the church collectively as well as individually—**Ephesians 4:11.**

The Apostle Paul compared the Church to the human body with different parts, each serving different but crucial role with Jesus Christ as the Head—**1Corinthians 12:12-27**.

However, even during the time of the Apostles, doctrinal differences reared its head. Peter and Paul contended with the Judaizers who insisted that the Gentiles who converted to Christianity must observe Jewish ceremonial laws and customs to be truly Christian. The issue was resolved at the '***Council of Jerusalem***' where Peter shared his vision in the house of Simon the Tanner and later, his experience in Cornelius' household, with the other elders of the nascent Church—**Acts 10:1-48**. It was resolved that Gentile Converts need not observe the Jewish ceremonial laws including circumcision ̄**Acts 11:1-18; Acts 15:1-20**. However, some of the early Jewish Christians continued to hold on to the view that Gentiles must become Jews before they can be truly Christians. This was a particular problem in Galatia that Paul had to address but also one he had to contend with throughout his ministry in other places.

Initially, the early church, being essentially Jewish, worshiped in the Temple and the synagogues but also met from house to house—**Acts 2:46; Acts 3:1**. However, as more Gentiles believed and persecution intensified, the disciples had to find alternative places for meeting and worship and often, these were houses of individuals within the church—**Acts 2:46; Acts 13:49-52; Acts 16:8-9; Acts 18:4-11; Acts 19:8-10; Romans 16:3-5; Colossians 4:15.**

The Apostles superintended the churches, instructed and encouraged them through visits and epistles. They also ordained elders and overseers over the Churches as well as gave guidelines on how and who to chose for leadership positions in the church—**Acts 8:14-25; Acts 14:23; 1Timothy 3:1-13; Titus 1:5-9.** They emphasized the fact that the leaders should serve the people and not lord it over them and for the people to respect and obey the leaders—**1Peter 5:1-5**. Both Peter and Paul warned Believers to be wary of false teachers who would bring in 'destructive heresies'; they also warned the churches about agents of Satan masquerading as 'angels of light'—**2Corinthians 11:12-15; 2Peter 2:1-3.**

Paul also had reasons to warn the Christians of his time about what he called ***"hollow and deceptive philosophy"* based on 'human tradition' and the 'basic principles of the world' rather than on Jesus Christ—Colossians 2:8 (NIV).**

By the second century AD, this problem was already insidiously creeping into the Church.

The Apostolic and Ante-Nicene Fathers
Clement of Rome[1] (c.30—100 AD)

Clement of Rome is thought to be the associate of St. Paul mentioned in his epistle to the Philippians in **Philippians 4:3.** He is therefore regarded as one of the Apostolic fathers by his direct contact with them.

He wrote a letter to the Corinthian Church to address the problem of emulation, envy, strife and sedition. He contrasted their state then with what they were before—obedient to God's commandments, forgiving, not deliberately sinning, hospitable, and full of good works, uncorrupted, sympathetic and empathetic and living in the fear of God. He attributed their moral decline to the abandonment of the fear of God and enjoined them to:

- Live in love, purity and holiness,
- Live in peace and concord with others and
- Avoid seditions, envy and schisms which he said, discourages people and cause grief to all.
- He asked the guilty to confess their sins and repent and
- For all to make sacrifices for the sake of peace.

Ignatius of Antioch[2] (c.30-107 AD)

Legend has it that he was the little child set among the disciples in Mathew 18:2, and that he was a disciple, together with Polycarp, of St. John the Apostle.

He wrote many letters to both individuals and to churches, many of which aroused controversy. So much controversy attended his writings that eight of the fifteen letters were set aside as spurious. Of the remaining seven considered authentic, there were two versions, the short and the longer. Many scholars consider the short version as the authentic and the longer a corrupted version.

His letters were exhortations for congregations and individuals to:
- Live in unity according to the will of God,
- Pray without ceasing,
- Live in the fear of God,
- Avoid deception by false teachers and defilement,
- Forgive one another and fellowship together and
- Obey their spiritual leaders.

It was on the last point that he seemed to be very controversial as his exhortation regarding obedience to bishops has a disturbing ring to it.

- For example, in his letter to the Magnesians he said: ***"I exhort you to study to do all things with a divine harmony while your bishop presides in the place of God and your presbyters in the place of the assembly of the apostles along with your deacons . . ."***
- In the epistle to the Tarsians or Trallian he said: ***"In like manner, let all reverence the deacon as an appointment of Jesus Christ, and the bishop as Jesus Christ who is the son of the father, and the presbyter as the Sanhedrin of God, and assembly of the apostles;*** <u>***apart from these, there is no Church."***</u>.
- In the letter to the Romans he said: ***"For what is the bishop but one who beyond all others possesses*** <u>***all power and authority***</u>***, so far as it is possible for a man to possess it, who, according to his ability has been made an imitator of the Christ of God."***
- To the Smynaeans he wrote: ***"He who honors the bishop has been honored by God; he who does anything without the knowledge of the bishop does in reality serve the devil."***

Again he said: ***"And I say, honor thou God indeed, as the Author and the Lord of all things but the bishop as the high priest, who, been the image of God inasmuch as he is a ruler, and of Christ, in his capacity as a priest. After him we must honor the king, for there is no one superior to God or ever like Him among all beings that exist. Nor is there anyone in the church greater than the bishop who ministers as priest to God for the salvation of the whole world."***

His flowery words regarding the office of the bishop and other clergy disturbingly sounded like deification of the office and the person.

He was martyred in Rome by being thrown to the wild beasts.

Polycarp of Smyrna[3] (c.65-c.155)

Polycarp, according to Irenaeus was a disciple of John the Apostle.

He was said to have visited Rome c. 150 AD and met with the bishop of Rome (Pope), to discuss the date for the celebration of Easter. Easter was being celebrated in Asia Minor on the fourteenth day of Nisan, the same time as the Jewish Passover, whatever day of the week it fell, a tradition he said derived from St. John the Apostle. In the rest of Christendom it was celebrated on Sunday, a tradition supposedly from St. Peter. Neither won the other to his point of view but fellowship was not broken. The issue

however resurfaced during the time of another bishop of Rome, (Pope) Victor I (189-199), in what is called the ***Easter Controversy.***
- In his letter to the Philippians he called on them to:
- Walk worthy of God's Commandments,
- Live righteously, to be temperate and to avoid the love of money,
- Live in purity and avoid fornication, homosexuality and other lusts,
- Be obedient to the overseers and to have faith.

He enjoined the leaders to:
- Take care of the weak and the poor,
- Avoid showing partiality and to maintain justice,
- Forgive and show mercy,
- Live in the fear of God, avoid hypocrisy and false brethren
- And persevere in hope and patience.

The church in Smyrna wrote to other churches to give account of Polycarp's martyrdom. They spoke of how he did not seek martyrdom but was betrayed by a youth who was tortured to give information about his whereabouts.

How a man named Quintus volunteered himself for martyrdom but recanted and was persuaded to swear and sacrifice to idols. They therefore admonished other Christians not to seek suffering or commend those who do as it was contrary to the gospel to do so.

They revealed that Polycarp was urged, to reproach Jesus Christ, swear by Caesar and to offer incense to save himself but refused saying: ***"Eighty and six years I have served Him and He never did me any injury; how then can I blaspheme my king and my Savior?***

Threatened with being thrown to wild beasts unless he denied Christ, he answered, ***". . . we are not accustomed to repent of what is good in order to adopt that which is evil".***

Then threatened with fire he said: ***"Thou threatenest me with fire which burneth for an hour and after a little is extinguished, but art ignorant of the fire of the coming judgment and of eternal punishment reserved for the ungodly."***

He was said to have been burnt at the stake, but according to legend had to be pierced with a dagger by the executioner when the flame failed to burn him.

Justin Martyr [4, 5]—(c.100-c.165)

Justin Martyr was born in Neapolis (modern day Nablus) in Samaria to Gentile parents. He was well educated in the philosophies of his day before his conversion to Christianity. In his search for the truth, he attached himself to a succession of prevailing philosophical schools such as Stoicism, Aristotelianism, Pythagorianism and Platonism until he came in contact with and embraced Christianity. For him, Christianity was the true Philosophy and he dedicated his life to defending orthodox Christianity against other philosophies of his time.

As a notable figure among the first Christian Apologists, his writings are the earliest still extant. The persecution of Christians was very rampant during his time and Justin Martyr in his Apology used his knowledge of prevailing philosophies to:
- Appeal to the Roman authorities to desist from persecuting Christians solely on the basis of their name even when no definite wrongdoing could be proven against them.
- Call for justice and due process in prosecuting, convicting and acquitting Christians charged with wrongdoing simply on account of the name they bore. (It was the practice to convict those who refuse to deny they are Christians and acquit all who deny).
- Highlight the folly of worshipping idols made by men and that the deities, based on what people believed about them were wicked spirits
- Show that the poets and philosophers taught the same thing as the Christians about the deities though less clearly and with less understanding. That it was unfair that the Christians were persecuted while the philosophers and poets were celebrated.
- Show that the philosophers garnered some truth from the ancient biblical prophets but did not have full understanding and that demons perverted the little they knew.

He cited as examples of demonic perversion of biblical events
- The practice of removing shoes before entering some pagan temples (Moses and the burning bush)
- The sprinkling of water on or even entire body washings of devotees of some deities (baptism).
- The sharing of bread and water during the initiation rites of devotees of Mithras—(the Eucharist)

On Jesus Christ
- He chronicled the prophesies relating to the birth of Jesus Christ to show that He was not a magician but the Son of God.
- He believed Jesus Christ was in the world as the Word before He became flesh and was born and that those who lived by the Word of God like Abraham, Daniel etc, were in essence Christians.
- He warned the people to avoid deception by demons working in heretics like Marcion, who was teaching that Jesus Christ was not the Son of the Old Testament God.

On Baptism

Justin Martyr considered baptism a rite; the washing of regeneration for the remission of *former* sins. He believed it transforms Christians to children of choice and knowledge, leading to illumination and understanding in the Name of Jesus Christ. He described the preparation for baptism as including repentance with prayer and fasting by the candidates, (joined by the church), for the remission of *past sins*.

He gave the qualification for baptism as:
- Those persuaded and who believe the Christian teachings about God, Jesus Christ, the Holy Spirit and Man
- Those who have been made new through Jesus Christ
- And are committed to living a changed life

The baptism was then administered after these have been ascertained; he thus affirmed *"Believers' Baptism"*.

He wrote: *"And for this rite (baptism), we have learned from the Apostles this reason, . . . in order that we may not remain the children of necessity and of ignorance, but may become the children of choice and knowledge; and may obtain in the water the remission of sins formerly committed, there is pronounced over him who chooses to be born again, and has repented of his sins, the Name of God the Father and Lord of the universe; he who leads to the laver the person that is to be washed calling him by this name alone and in the Name of Jesus Christ who was crucified . . . and in the Name of the Holy Ghost . . ."*

On the Eucharist

Justin Martyr believed that the consecrated Bread and Wine for the Eucharist are not common (ordinary) but are as the Flesh and the Blood of Jesus Christ transmuted by the Word.

It was shared with baptized believers at the weekly service and with newly baptized believers. The qualifications for partaking of the Eucharist include:
- Those who have consented to and are convinced of Christian teachings
- Those who have been baptized.

He wrote: *"**And this food is called among us the Eucharist, of which no one is allowed to partake but the man who believes that the things we teach are true, and who has been washed with the washing that is for the remission of sins, and who is living as Christ has enjoined. For not as common bread and common drink do we receive these; but in like manner as Jesus Christ our Savior, having been made flesh and blood for our salvation, so likewise have we been taught that the food which is blessed by the prayer of His Word and from which our blood and flesh by transmutation are nourished is the flesh and blood of that Jesus who was made flesh**".*

On Weekly Worship Service

Justin described the typical weekly service as:
- Being held on the first day of the week, Sunday
- Readings from the Prophets and the Gospel
- Exhortation by the presiding officer
- Prayers and Thanksgiving
- The sharing of the Eucharist among those present and deacons taking portions to those absent.
- Collection made for the poor and needy—(widows, orphans, the sick and the stranger)—with people giving according to their ability.

On Freewill

Justin Martyr believed that Man has freewill and that the predestination of Jesus Christ's birth, passion and death do not mean that Man is governed by unalterable fate over which he has no choice. That if Man had no power to choose good or evil, there could be no grounds for rewards or punishment based on choice. He said that the Bible supports the fact that man has free will from the experiences of Adam—Genesis 3; Moses—Deuteronomy 30:15-20; and Isaiah 1:16-19.

He was martyred during the persecution of Christians by Marcus Aurelius around 165 AD.

Irenaeus of Lyons [6,7] (c.115-c.202)

Irenaeus was born in Smyrna and he studied under Polycarp who was said to have been a disciple of John the Apostle. He later joined the school of Justin Martyr in Rome. ***However, he rejected the philosophical approach to Christianity espoused by Justin Martyr and believed that Christianity rested on revelation, tradition and the power of the Holy Spirit.*** Much of what is known of his writings came from the writings of other early Christian historians who cited him.

He was said to have cautioned the Bishop of Rome (Pope) Victor I (189-199) against his decision to excommunicate the Church in Asia Minor because they insisted on celebrating Easter on the fourteenth day of Nisan, whatever day of the week it fell and not on Sundays as was the custom in Rome, Gaul and Africa—*(The Easter Controversy).* He reminded Bishop Victor I that his predecessors were aware of the issue and yet did not allow it to cause a break in fellowship.

His main ministry was in writing apologetics against heresies. He identified the methods of heretics as:
- Falsification of the oracles of God
- Misinterpretation of the Word and revelations of God and
- Pretence of superior knowledge.

The heresies that he refuted included:
a) **The Valentinians**—a Gnostic heretical movement with 'endless genealogies' that mixed a lot of fables with biblical truth.
b) **The Marcosians**—who used a mixture of magic and familiar spirits to prophesy and deceive people, especially women who were possessed. The heresy was also filled with biblical misinterpretations.
c) **The Carpocrates**—the advocates of this heresy claimed that good and evil are a matter of human opinion. They practiced plurality of wives, promiscuity, magic, love potions, incantations, familiar spirits and dream-sending through demons and philters.

The Carpocrates also believe in transmigration of souls through repeated incarnations and preached the need to experience every kind of life and actions. They honored the image of Jesus Christ and philosophers like Pythagoras, Aristotle and Plato.
a) **The Encratites**—led by Tatian, who preached against marriage and called marriage corruption and fornication.

b) **The Cerinthuans**—led by Cerinthus, were versed in the wisdom of the Egyptians. They denied that the world was created by God, denied the virgin birth of Jesus Christ and taught that he was delivered normally by the union of Mary and Joseph; but being more righteous than others, Christ descended on Him at His Baptism. That up to the point of Baptism, Christ was an ordinary man and that at His crucifixion, Christ departed from Him and only Jesus the man suffered and rose again while Christ remained "impassible" being a spiritual being.

c) **The Ebionites**—Held the same opinion about Jesus Christ as the Cerinthuans though they agreed that God created the world. They obeyed Mosaic laws and practiced circumcision. They accepted only the Gospel of Mathew and rejected all Pauline epistles, considering Paul an apostate.

d) **The Nicholaitanes**—these were the followers of Nicholas whom some thought was one of the seven deacons appointed in Acts 6 but others have refuted this claim. The members practice licentiousness and unrestrained indulgence; they were promiscuous and ate food offered to idols. The heresy was mentioned in Revelations 2 as present and thriving in the church at Pergamos but hated in the church at Ephesus

Irenaeus was said to have been martyred during the reign of the Emperor Severus, c202.

Clement of Alexandria[8, 9]—(c 153-c 215)

Titus Flavius Clemens was born in Athens or Alexandria. A pagan philosopher before embracing Christianity, he became the head of the catechetical school in Alexandria. He wrote copiously on paganism, philosophies and virtually every facet of the Christian life and quoted copiously from philosophers and poets as much as he did form the Scriptures in his writings.

On the Heathen gods

- He denounced the heathen gods as pervert demons and human haters who demand cruel oblations and human sacrifices; said that though they were called divinities, they were worse than the human beings who worship them.

- Denounced the celebration of the heathen gods as profane rites filled with indulgences, lasciviousness and licentiousness. He derided as absurd the worship of creatures or their images.

On Philosophies and Philosophers
- Clement defined Philosophy as *"the cultivation of right reason"*.
- He believed that philosophy was Knowledge given by God and that all sects of philosophy contained some germs of the truth but that they convey the knowledge of God imperfectly.
- He believed philosophy was given to the Greeks as preliminary training before the advent of Christianity just as the Jews were given the Commandments.
- Although he believed that true doctrine can only be found in the prophets, he held that philosophy helped in the comprehension of the Divine Truth and that it is *"the handmaid of theology, the schoolmaster to bring the Hellenistic mind to Christ"*.
- He dismissed the objection of those who cautioned against mixing philosophy and Christianity and considered philosophy 'a work of Divine Providence'.

On Sin and Repentance
- Believed that sinlessness is the prerogative of God alone.
- He defined **sin** as *"Everything that is contrary to right reason"*; that disobedience in reference to reason is the generating cause of sin and "whatever is done through error of reason is transgression".
- He believed that man falls into sins through ignorance and that acquisition of knowledge disperses the darkness.
- He counseled against sinning after repentance but made allowance for the second repentance which he said should not be repented of. He believed that voluntary sin and involuntary transgression can be avoided or minimized by learning and training.
- He also believed that sin originated from free choice and inclination

On Faith and Salvation
- He defined **faith** as *"a comprehensive knowledge of the essentials"*; and that the first step of faith is to know God.
- He believed that the knowledge of God can only be attained through faith.

- He held that faith is not a product of nature and that the foundation of salvation is voluntary faith
- He believed that faith is the foundation of all knowledge.
- He held that: *"God called all equally and that Jesus is Lord of all but the Savior of only those who believe"*.
- He held that human knowledge is necessary for understanding the scriptures and dismissed the arguments of those who held that faith alone is required.

On Christian Living
- Clement of Alexandria wrote compendiously on various aspects of life including marriage, eating, drinking, clothing, etiquette, etc.
- Marriage, Celibacy, Continence and Chastity:
- He recommended that those who meet the conditions and could should marry as ordained by God for procreation. He considered it also a duty to society. He held that marriage should be indissoluble except on account of fornication and adultery.
- He believed sexual intercourse in marriage is pure but should be with self control for the purpose of procreation.
- He supported the idea of a second marriage following the death of a spouse for those who find it hard to be continent.
- He denounced forced celibacy but viewed favorably celibacy for those who are so gifted by God who supplies the divine power and grace.
- He rejected as blasphemy the notion that what the Serpent tempted Adam and Eve with and to which they fell in the Garden of Eden was the use of sexual intercourse.
- He held that continence is more than sexual abstinence and apply also to temperance in other areas of human desire like possessions, eating and drinking etc.
- He denounced the perversion of the scriptures that some heresies like the Carpocrates used to justify promiscuity on the one hand and the strict asceticism and celibacy of sects like the Encratites who regarded human sexuality as evil on the other.

Eating:
- He denounced gluttony and recommended eating only for growth, health and strength. He advocated the eating of simple, light and

digestible foods rather than delicacies and pastries which he said caused diseases. He believed that overeating is injurious to man, deteriorates his spirit and renders his body prone to diseases.
- Denounced the eating of such things as sweet meats, honey cakes and sugar plums
- Denounced the use of refined flour for bread as he believed the nourishing part had been strained off and recommended whole grain bread. (Amazingly ahead of his time!).

Drinking:
- Recommended that young people keep away from wine entirely as it tends to inflame the passions
- Recommended that adults who can handle wine drink moderately and only in the evenings when it cannot interfere with sober judgment.
- Recommended that the elderly, 'moored by reason and time' could drink liberally to 'warm the chill of age' but also reasonably.

Furniture and other possessions
- Recommended that furniture and all possessions reflect necessity rather than luxury
- Denounced the inordinate acquisition of gold and other precious stones and articles made from expensive and rare materials

Clothing and Grooming
- Recommended that clothing materials be simple and plain, preferably white and not dyed. Heavily embroidered and variegated materials to be avoided.
- Denounced the use of silky and diaphanous materials that showed the contours of the body and recommended that women should be well covered from head to toe.
- Denounced the use of cosmetics or hair dyes on the ground that ultimately these destroy the skin and that old age need not be concealed.
- Recommended that men shave their heads, trim the moustache but keep the beard; in fact he considered it reprehensible to be clean shaven.
- Recommended simple shoes for women, for modesty; shoes he believed were not essential for men except when on military service.

- Denounced the use of jewelry by both men and women except for finger rings worn for legal transactions. Considered necklaces and anklets as fetters.
- Denounced all forms of extravagance in clothing and living

On Etiquette
- He counseled against sneezing loudly among people
- He denounced the habit of speaking loudly and counseled that speech be in even, measured tones.
- He advised that Christians eat and drink decently at banquets, not pick their teeth in public and to leave early.
- Counseled against sitting near a woman in a banquet and considered it scandalous for unmarried women to be in attendance at banquets

Other Issues
- Denounced the practice of keeping exotic pets while neglecting the widow, the orphans, the old and the poor.
- Recommended baths for both men and women, men for health and women for both cleanness and health. He said none should use the baths for pleasure, and denounced the public nudity that was common in the baths. He therefore recommended the use of baths at night and without using the assistance of slaves or domestic help.
- Condemned the games, the shows and the theaters as the *"seats of plagues, full of confusion and iniquity"*. He denounced the games as "cruel contests for glory" and not sport.
- Recommended exercises for both men and women, gymnasium for men and household chores like spinning for women.
- He recommended honesty in trading.

Clement of Alexandria was regarded by many as the ***Christian ethical philosopher*** but others found his work difficult to organize into doctrine while some even accuse him and the Alexandrian school of encouraging the development of heresies.

Clement left Alexandria during the persecution of the Emperor Severus and is believed to have gone to reside with one of his students, bishop Alexander of Jerusalem. He is believed to have died around 215-217 AD.

Comment—Clement was a philosopher who sought to graft philosophies to Christianity and vice versa. Though he regarded Christianity as the true philosophy, nevertheless, he did not totally renounce the other philosophies but believed they were from God and contained imperfect revelations of Him. He felt that a true 'Gnostic' would avail himself of all human knowledge. His copious referencing of philosophers and poets sometimes made him seem more like an apologist for philosophies rather than Christianity and this tends to create a sense of uneasiness about his orthodoxy.

The question is, if, indeed he had found Christianity to be the 'true philosophy' which perfectly reveals God, why cling to those philosophies which he admitted were imperfect? Why hang on to pieces if Christ is the embodiment? Why keep looking at the flickers of light when Christ is the "Sun of Righteousness"? And why continue to scrape at broken cisterns of philosophies when Christ is the fountain?

He addressed sin, faith and salvation from the standpoint of reason and knowledge; however while the right kind of knowledge is necessary for salvation and Christian growth, the scriptures made it clear God cannot be known through human reasoning or philosophical deductions but by revelation. His position about philosophy is diametrically opposed to that of other fathers like Tertullian and the Apostle Paul.

Tertullian of Carthage[10, 11, 12]—(c.160-c.225)

Tertullian was born of pagan parents in Carthage. The son of a centurion, he was educated as a lawyer in Rome and later became a Christian and a presbyter in Carthage.

On Philosophies and Philosophers

- Tertullian, like Irenaeus but unlike Clement of Alexandria, was a Christian Apologist who rejected vigorously the philosophical approach to Christianity.
- He considered philosophy the material of the world's wisdom; ***that philosophies bred heresies and that Philosophers were the "patriarchs of heretics"***.
- He rejected 'the idea of a Stoic, a Platonic or dialectic Christianity.' He said the various schools of philosophy reflected the characters of their masters, thus the school of Plato reflected dignity, Zeno, vigor, Aristotle, equanimity, Epicurus, stupidity, Heraclitus, sadness and Empedocles, madness.

- He decried the perversion of Christian doctrines by philosophers to serve their own purposes. He said because they were devoid of real faith and understanding of God's revelations, they had no qualms about changing Christian doctrines and creating complexities out of simple issues by disputations.
- He accused philosophers of disputing about the nature, properties and the abode of God instead of believing the simple revelations of God. He averred that the speculations of philosophers only lead to uncertainties and confusions.
- He derided the fact that philosophers never seem to agree on any point about God or anything at all. While the Platonists thought God was incorporeal, the Stoics said He had a body; on the other hand, the Epicureans said He was composed of atoms while the Pythagoreans said numbers. Platonists believed that God is involved in the affairs of the world but the Epicureans thought He was indifferent and inactive. The philosophers also disagreed on the creation of the world and its eventual fate and disagreed on the Soul whether it is divine and eternal or whether it is dissoluble.
- He rejected the corruption and adulteration of Christian revelations into systems of philosophic doctrines by the introduction of fables and speculations.
- Tertullian called Aristotle's dialectics ***"the art of building up and pulling down, evasive in its propositions, far fetched in its conjectures, harsh in its arguments, productive of contentions, embarrassing to itself, retracting everything and resolving nothing".***

On the Games and the Theatre Shows
- Tertullian traced the origins of the games to the dedication of pagan gods.
- He contended that *"that which sprung from sin, shamelessness, violence, hatred or fratricidal founder cannot be good"* He pointed out that the arenas were usually adorned with altars on which sacrifices were made to the gods on special days and that some of the games were instituted in honor of specific gods.
- He considered the theatres and the amphitheatres as the temples of demons and traced their origins to human sacrifices to the dead veiled as sport. He did not believe Christians should participate in the games or seek earthly laurels and crowns as they had been

dedicated to gods like Bacchus and Apollo. Similarly, he did not believe that Christians should join the military.
- He identified elements of idolatry in the origins, titles, equipment, places of celebration and the arts of the shows and therefore considered them unsuitable for Christians. He contended that the circus elicit baseless passionate excitement that may give rise to sinful emotions of hatred.
- He denounced the violence, profanities and licentiousness that tend to accompany the tragic and comic plays and contended that they could engender crimes and lusts. He also considered that the things that happen in the shows were an antithesis of Christian virtues and constitutes cruel enjoyment.
- He gave the example of a woman who became demon possessed in a theatre and during exorcism; the demon justified its actions on the grounds that the woman was in its domain when it possessed her.
- He called on Christians not to accept in the theatre and the shows what they would otherwise reject in the home or the street. He said: *". . . never and nowhere is it right to do what you may not do at all times and in all places."*
- He held that it is the heathen, devoid of God's full revelation that practice situation ethics, holding a thing to be good in one place and evil in another to suit self-will and passion. He said: *"It is the freedom of the truth from change of opinions and varying judgments which constitutes its perfection and gives it its claim to full mastery, unchanging reverence and faithful obedience . . . in all things, the truth of God is immutable"*

On Heathenism and Idolatry
Tertullian in his apologetics
- Showed that the worshippers of idols and State gods believed a lie and that the so called gods were demons.
- He highlighted the immorality, perversion and depravity of the Greco-Roman gods.
- He held that God equally prohibited the making and the worshipping of idols—Exodus 20:4; Exodus 32:6; Leviticus 26:1; Deuteronomy 5:8; 1Corinthians 10:7.

Tertullian believed that idolatry had permeated many areas of life in his time and warned Christians to beware of inadvertently participating in idol worship.

- He warned Christians not to participate in the observance of special days like heathen midsummer and New Year celebrations as those days were dedicated to idols. He condemned Christians who participate in heathen celebrations by decorating their doors with laurels and lighted lamps explaining that the decorations were actually in honor of "gods of entrances" like doors, hinges, thresholds, gates etc. That Christians who had renounced temples of idols should not make their gates temples for idols.
- He was scandalized by the fact that some in the church, even in ministries, were in vocations that supported the making of idols; he believed that making idols was tantamount to worshiping them and that Christians should not engage in such vocations. While he agreed that Christians can work with secular authorities, he believed that obedience to them should be within the limits of Christian discipline and idolatry avoided like Daniel and his colleagues did.
- He warned against Christians being bound by oaths and contracts or accepting blessings made in the name of heathen gods.

On the Persecution of Christians
- Tertullian challenged the Roman authorities about the persecution of Christians; he wondered why poets and philosophers who mock the gods were not persecuted or forced to make sacrifices to the gods as the State required Christians to do.
- He debunked the idea that Christians were responsible for the woes of the empire; that the imperial power was never attributable to the gods and that the true God of the Christians is the One that rules in the kingdoms of men and dispenses it as He wishes.
- He said Christians were known for their chastity, virtue, justice, patience and sobriety; and that though Christians would not sacrifice to idols for the Emperor, they prayed for him because the Scripture required that they do so.
- He condemned casuistry and dissembling in order to avoid being discovered to be a Christian and said this is actually denying Jesus Christ.

- He made it clear that Christians were not afraid of death and said: ***"The oftener we are mown down by you, the more in number we grow; the blood of Christians is seed".***

On Human Sexuality

Tertullian addressed human sexuality directly and defended marriage, he said:
- ***"Now, let no one take offence or feel ashamed at the interpretation of nature which is rendered necessary (by the defense of truth). Nature should be to us an object of reverence, not blushes; it is lust, not natural usage which has brought shame on the intercourse of the sexes. It is the excess, not the normal state which is immodest and unchaste. The normal condition has received a blessing from God and is blest by Him: 'be fruitful and multiply and replenish the earth'"***

He considered that both the body and the soul are involved in the sexual act and said:
- ***"Well now, in this usual function of the sexes which brings together the male and the female in their common intercourse, we know that both the soul and the flesh discharge a duty together; the soul supplies the desire, the flesh contributes the gratification of it. The soul furnishes the instigation and the flesh affords the realization".***

On the Soul, the Body and Sin
- Tertullian believed that the human soul has its origin in the breath of God at creation and is superior to the body because it is the soul that Jesus Christ came to save and it is the soul that will suffer the consequences of sin in hell—Ezekiel 18:4, 20; *
- Tertullian believed that the soul and body were simultaneously conceived and that the idea of some philosophers that the soul joins the body at birth was erroneous. He believed that the co-existence of both body and soul from conception was the reason Moses legislated against causing abortion in a pregnant woman.
- He believed that the body is ancillary to the soul in the commission of sin, that the body of itself, being a mere vessel for the soul, is incapable of committing sin on its own. He backed up this position with what Jesus taught in Mathew 5:27-28 and Mark 7:20-23

- He believed that sin can be corporeal, that is by deeds; and spiritual, that is by thought or the will only and that both species of sin require confession and repentance.
- He believed that every soul, by reason of birth has its nature in Adam until it is born again in Christ; and remains unclean all the while that it remains without regeneration; and because it is unclean, it is actively sinful.
- Tertullian believed that even though the Adamic nature of sin is present in everyone and obscure the good as an opaque object obscures the rays of light, still, as the light remains so does the good in human beings too. He believed that there are elements of good and bad in varying proportions in all men.

On Repentance, Salvation and Second Repentance
- Tertullian believed that the second birth is about the soul coming under the power of the Holy Spirit and being freed from the influence of the inherited sin tendency. The body, he said, is also freed from the evil influence which was aiding and abetting the soul to sin.
- He believed that there is no redemption without repentance.
- He advocated true repentance and real change; and counseled that Christians should not return to sin after repentance—1John 3:9.
- He said sinning after repentance is akin to renouncing Jesus Christ and pronouncing Satan the better master; for in repenting, such a one with volition chose Jesus Christ as Lord. Backsliding, he said, is worse than the previous state because the sinner is saying, in essence, having tried both, he prefers Satan.
- Rejected the notion that sinning may do no damage to a man's faith and said this is as true as saying that adultery does no damage to chastity.
- He believed that there is a second chance for anyone who sins after baptism. He advocated full public confession and penitential discipline—*exomologesis*—for anyone requiring a second repentance.
- He considered the second repentance the last one and encouraged people to avail themselves of it not minding the shame; that compared to hell, the open confession and repentance is really trivial and like bitter medicine for the cure of a serious illness. He

encouraged the church to join the penitent in supplication to God for forgiveness.

On Baptism

- Tertullian regarded baptism as the washing away of *previous sins* and necessary for salvation based on John 3:5 and Mark 16:15-16.
- He described how baptism was given during his time: The candidate prepared with prayers, fasts and vigils; then after the washing, he was anointed with oil and then had hands laid on him and the benediction pronounced with the invocation of the Holy Spirit. Afterwards, he was encouraged to pray for the gifts of the Holy Spirit.
- He believed that baptism should neither be hastily given nor presumptuously received; that those to be baptized should show true repentance evidenced by real change in lifestyle.
- Warned those awaiting baptism not to act on the presumption of anticipated remission of sins to continue sinning, rather they should spend the time learning not to sin. He said: *"We are not washed that we may cease sinning, but because we have ceased, since in heart we have been bathed already; for the first baptism of a learner is this, a perfect fear".*
- He believed baptism should be administered only to believers saying: *"Those who believe in His blood might be bathed with water; those who had been bathed in the water might likewise drink the blood."*
- Believed that every believer can administer baptism but out of respect for the church hierarchy, he believed the bishop should or delegate the function to the priest, the deacon or any other in that order.
- *He did not recognize the baptism administered by heretics since according to him these have another God and Christ.*

On the Trinity

- Tertullian vigorously defended the doctrine of the Trinity with several Scripture passages and analogies against what he called the heresy of **Praxeas** who taught, (in order to preserve the doctrine of "One God") that God the Father and the Son are one and the same; that it was the father who became incarnate as the son.

- *He argued that the persons of Trinity though separate in personality were unified in substance and though distinct are not divided.*

For Tertullian, the very substance of the Church was the **Holy Spirit** and not the **Episcopacy** whose right to wield the *'power of the key'* he rejected.

He aligned himself with a group of Believers called **Montanists** who believed in prophecy and the holiness of the Church as the holiness of its members but considered heretics by the Roman Catholic Church. Eventually the Montanists separated from the Roman Catholic Church and formed an independent schismatic Church.

Tertullian was branded as anti-intellectual and has received opprobrium in the Roman Catholic Church history for his stand on Church holiness and discipline. Today, the majority of scholars believe that the Montanists were doctrinally orthodox and Tertullian's contribution to theology need not be rejected. In fact he is considered by some as the founder of the Latin Church.

Origen of Alexandria[13, 14, 15] (c.185-c.254)

Origen is considered one of the most prolific, brilliant and greatest of the Christian theologians and apologists. He was born into a devoutly Christian family circa 185AD.

Throughout his life time, spanning the reign of Emperors Severus, Maximin and Decius, the persecution of Christians was rife and his father died a martyr. He was well educated in Biblical and Hellenistic studies becoming the headmaster of the Catechetical school at Alexandria at about the age of seventeen or eighteen when persecution forced the incumbent head, Clement to withdraw.

During the time of Origen, there was little or no doctrinal consensus among the various regional churches and Christianity had no system of theology as basis of orthodoxy. There were therefore many opinions as well as sects all claiming to possess the truth of the faith. Origen is considered the first systematic theologian and philosopher of the Christian Church.

Origen's philosophy and doctrines were influenced by Platonic, Stoic and Pythagorean philosophies.

Origen's Philosophy and Doctrines

(a) The Trinity [13, 14].

Origen propounded the doctrine of a hierarchical Trinity comprising the Father, the Son and the Holy Spirit. This was said to have been influenced by the Platonic divine triad of Monad, Dyad and World Souls. According to Origen, The Father is a perfect Unity, complete, without body, purely spiritual, personal and active. Existing always with Him is the Son, the Logos or the Wisdom through whom He exercises His intellectual activities. The Holy Spirit proceeds from the Son. The Father holds the universe together, is superior to and is the creator of every being in existence. The Son is less than the Father in power and is superior to only rational beings while the Holy Spirit is less than the Son and resides only in those who have achieved salvation, that is, the Saints.

However, he also stated the simultaneous concurrence of the Father, the Son and the Holy Spirit; that whoever the Holy Spirit indwells also possess the Father and the Son. To some, Origen subordinated the persons of the Trinity while others defend him on the grounds that the apparent subordination arose only from his attribution of different and unequal spheres of action to each of them, that is, the Father—Creator, the Son—Redeemer and the Holy Spirit,—the Sanctifier.

This concept of the subordination of the persons of the Trinity was to be a source of major controversies later on in Christendom.

(b) The Origin and the Fall of Rational Beings (Souls) [14, 15]

According to Origen, God created rational beings to be in proximity to Him and to contemplate divine mysteries eternally. In time, they became weary from intense contemplation and fell away from God, not because of imperfection, but from the misuse of God's greatest gift to His creation: freedom. As rational beings, through boredom and distraction, they moved away from God and divine warmth and became cold. As they became cold, they got clothed in various bodies of varying thickness ranging from the invisible ethereal to the more visible and solid bodies depending on the distance from God. This, he said, explained the hierarchies of angels, stars, men and demons.

(c) Universal Redemption and Final Restoration for All [14, 15].

Origen believed in the eventual restoration of all beings even though it may take several life times to achieve salvation. He believed that the falling away of souls from God was not a conscious choice of evil but only out of ignorance and that no rational being would choose evil; he recognized freedom only in reason and rationality.

To Origen, evil is not the polar opposite of the good but only the absence of it and therefore evil does not really exist and what is considered as "choosing evil" is merely acting in ignorance of rational decision. Because irrationality is ignorance and the absence of the conception of good, the ignorant person cannot be held responsible for his ignorance or sin, and therefore is not to be punished. Punishment, according to Origen would only lead to deeper ignorance and sin since the punished would grow resentful for lack of understanding as to why he is being punished. Ignorance, according to Origen, can only be remedied by education.

Origen did not believe in hell or the eternal suffering of unrepentant sinners in it. He believed that God can soften any heart, no matter how hard though it may take indefinite trials.

Taking Origen's doctrine to its logical conclusion would mean that even the devil would be saved; Origen was said to have become angry when this was pointed out to him.

(d) The Scripture and the Church [14, 15].

Origen believed that if the Bible is inspired by God, it cannot be irrelevant or unworthy of God and where it seems to be in error, the deeper meaning is being missed. He therefore believed in Scriptural allegorism and accepted the literal meaning of Scriptures only if they 'made sense'.

He proposed three levels of Scriptural meaning, the body, the soul and the spirit corresponding to Pauline (and Platonic) trichotomy divisions of a person. The bodily level is the mere letter, the psychic (soul) level is for making progress in perfection and the spirit level allows humanity to partake of the doctrines of the Spirit's counsel. He believed the Scriptures must be interpreted in a manner worthy of God and the literal meaning must be rejected if it is absurd or unworthy of God.

Origen believed that the two lights that guide Christians on earth are Christ and the Church; the Church, he said, reflected faithfully the light received from Christ as the moon reflects the rays of the sun.

Origen refuted the heresies of the Valentinian Gnostics and pagan Celsus' attack on Christianity.

He was imprisoned by the Emperor Decius and tortured. He outlived the Emperor and was released from prison. He is believed to have died in Tyre around 254 AD.

Origen drew upon pagan philosophy in his attempt to elucidate the Christian faith and in a manner acceptable to the intellectuals of his time.

During his lifetime and for quite a while after his death, Origen influenced many and drew many followers, giving rise to a movement called ***Origenism***. However, the voices of dissent, present during his lifetime became more strident after his death and degenerated into **"Origenist crises"** until during the reign of Emperor Justinian, part of his writings and doctrines were reportedly anathematized.

Origen's legacy was however not lost, as the Renaissance Humanists and modern day Existentialist Christians found inspiration from his doctrine of universal restoration.

Comment:—Origen's concept of salvation, the process and end point, his concept of sin and evil and his disbelieve in hell are all unscriptural and exposed the dangers inherent in attempting to philosophize the gospel. The Catechetical school in Alexandria, with its tradition of teaching philosophies and the gospel had a reputation of producing heretics.

Cyprian of Carthage [16, 17, 18, 19, 20]—(c.200-c.258)

Cyprian was born of pagan parents in North Africa. He was a wealthy lawyer and teacher of rhetoric. He became a Christian around 246 AD and was elected the Bishop of Carthage in 248 AD. In 250 AD, Emperor Decius ordered the persecution of Christians and Cyprian and some other bishops went into hiding, an action for which he was censured.

Cyprian wrote treatises on the '*Unity of the Church*', '*The lapsed*', *Baptism* and *the Lord's Prayer* among others

On the Church and the Papacy
- Cyprian held the belief that the unity of the Church is essential and that to separate from the Church is also to separate from Christ's promises and rewards for the Church.
- He believed that the ***'universal episcopate'*** is the ***'chair of Peter'***. In his own words—***"Assuredly, the rest of the apostles were also the same as was Peter, endowed with a like partnership both of***

honor and of power; but the beginning proceeds from unity". "And this unity we ought firmly to hold and assert, especially those of us that are bishops who preside in the Church, that we may also prove the episcopate itself to be one and undivided. Let no one deceive the brotherhood by falsehood: let no one corrupt the truth by perfidious prevarication. The episcopate is one, each part of which is held by each for the whole."

- Cyprian did not relate to the bishop of Rome as a superior but only as first among equals. He believed in the independence and responsibility of individual bishops but always consulted with other bishops to find a consensus on matters of faith. He wrote; *"For neither does any of us set himself up as a 'bishop of bishops', nor by tyrannical terror does any compel his colleague to the necessity of obedience; since every bishop, according to the allowance of his liberty and power, has his own proper right of judgment and can no more be judged by another than he himself can judge another".*

On the Bishops and Priests and the people

"Each one was desirous of increasing his estate; and forgetful of what believers had either done before in the times of the apostles, or ought always to do, they, with insatiable ardour of covetousness, devoted themselves to the increase of their property themselves to the increase of their property".

"Among the priests there was no devotedness of religion; among the ministers, there was no sound faith, in their works, there was no mercy; in their manners, no discipline".

"Not a few bishops who ought to furnish both exhortation and example to others, despising their divine charge, became agents in secular business, forsook their throne, deserted their people, wandered about over foreign provinces, hunted the markets for gainful merchandise while brethren were starving in the Church. They sought to possess money in hoards, they seize estates by crafty deceits and they increase their gains by multiplying usuries".

"But how can they follow Christ, who are held back by the chains of their wealth? . . . They think that they possess, when they are rather possessed".

"In the men, their beards were defaced; in women, their complexion was dyed: the eyes were falsified from what God had made them; their hair was stained with falsehood . . . They would swear, not only rashly, but even more, would swear falsely; . . . would speak evil of one another with envenomed tongue, would quarrel with one another with obstinate hatred".

On the Lapsed
- On the question of what to do with *"the lapsed",* that is, those who denied the faith during persecution, Cyprian believed and practiced readmission after those concerned have shown evidence of repentance.
- Cyprian was in agreement with **Stephen I (254-257),** the bishop of Rome on the issue of the lapsed. However, he disagreed with other bishops like **Novatus** who decided to readmit the lapsed on the presentation of "letters of peace" written by martyrs or confessors; while **Novatian** was against their readmission into communion.
- He warned the Church against the abuse of the letters of peace given by martyrs and confessors. He wrote: *"Let no one cheat himself, let no one deceive himself, the Lord alone can have mercy, He alone can bestow pardon for sins which have been committed against Himself who bore our sins, who sorrowed for us, whom God delivered up for our sins. Man cannot be greater than God, nor can a servant remit or forego by his indulgence what has been committed by a greater crime against the Lord . . . We believe, indeed that the merits of martyrs and the works of the righteous are of great avail with the Judge; but that will be when the day of judgment shall come . . . when His people shall stand before Christ. But if anyone, by over hurried haste, rashly thinks that he can give remission of sins to all or dares to rescind the Lord's precepts, not only does it, in no respect advantage the lapsed, but it does them harm."*

On Baptism and Re-baptism
- Cyprian believed that baptism removes all sins and that the Holy Spirit is received during baptism.
- Believed that infants can be baptized as soon as they are born and not wait till the eighth day as recommended by others to conform to the tradition of circumcision.

- Rejected the validity of the baptism given by heretics or schismatics, and disagreed with Stephen I (254-257), the Bishop of Rome who believed that baptisms by heretics are valid and such people should not be re-baptized. For Cyprian, there was no valid baptism outside the Orthodox Church.

The bishop of Rome, Stephen I, had contended that the baptism administered by heretics was valid on the ground that it was performed in the Name of the Trinity—The Father, Jesus Christ and the Holy Spirit—and therefore the "right formula". He said all that was required by heretics returning to the Church was for the bishop to lay hands on them and claimed that his position was based on apostolic tradition. (St. Augustine of Hippo later expanded on this dogma). He wrote to the African bishops and others to stop re-baptizing heretics or face excommunication.

On the Eucharist
- Cyprian considered the Eucharist a sacrifice to be received only by the baptized.
- He believed that the Cup should be wine mixed with water.
- He said being baptized and receiving the Eucharist are unprofitable unless matched by a godly life.

On Games and Shows

Cyprian condemned the games and the shows in very strong terms. He said: *"The gladiatorial games are prepared that blood may gladden the lust of cruel eyes . . . Man is slaughtered that man may be gratified and the skill that is best able to kill is considered an exercise and an art . . . Crime is not only committed, but is taught . . . and the achievement of murder is its glory"*.

About the theatre he said: *"In the mimes, moreover, by the teaching of infamies, the spectator is attracted . . . Adultery is learnt while it is seen and while the mischief, having public authority, panders to vices, the matron who perchance had gone to the spectacle a modest woman returns from it immodest . . . What a degradation of morals, what a stimulus to abominable deeds, what food for vice, to be polluted by histrionic gestures . . . Can he who looks upon such things be healthy minded or modest? Men imitate the gods they adore and to such miserable beings, their crimes become their religion"*.

He warned about the lure of riches and called riches "gilded torments" that enslave the owners. He said the wealthy only have the appearance of security but are in actual fact insecure. He said those truly at peace are those **anchored at the harbor of salvation** through Jesus Christ.

Cyprian believed that obedience is the mark of the true Christian and that anyone who does not do what Christ commanded cannot claim to be a believer in Christ. He believed that a baptized person can lose the grace attained and that believers should live a steadfast life. He said: ***"It is a slight thing to have been able to attain anything, it is more to be able to keep what you have attained; even as faith itself and saving birth makes alive, not by being received, but by being preserved"***.

He therefore enjoined new Christians to learn to study God's Word without distractions, speak to God and learn to listen to God speak, and to live a life of uncorrupted discipline.

Cyprian's treatises constituted the beginnings of the systematization of Church dogmas.

During the reign of the ***Emperor Valerian (253-260)***, another persecution arose and Cyprian was arrested, tried, exiled and was later beheaded.

COMMENT:

Cyprian is respected by both the Roman Catholic and Protestant traditions. His writing on the unity of the Church is often quoted for and against the institution of the Papacy by the Roman Catholics and Protestants respectively. Protestants allege that his work had been corrupted by interpolations to slant it in favor of the papacy; an institution they believed is unscriptural.

The Roman Catholics deplored his position on re-baptizing of heretics and suggested that his opposition to Stephen I, the contemporaneous bishop of Rome, was in error and due to his relative inexperience as a Christian and his ignorance of Christian literature other than the Holy Scripture.

However, this is an unwarranted condescending position because Cyprian was not alone in insisting that heretics be re-baptized. All of the eighty-seven African bishops at the **Seventh Council of Carthage, 258 A.D** and all in Cappadocia believed the same thing. Many of these were bishops in places with older Christian traditions than Rome.

In fact, **Firmilian (d. 269)**, the bishop of Caesarea, responding to the situation was scandalized by ***Bishop Stephen I's (254-257 A.D.)*** position and wrote that the practice of re-baptizing heretics was not new in the east and that he would answer Stephen by "opposing tradition to tradition". *He pointed out the hollowness of*

Bishop Stephen's appeal to tradition on the grounds that Rome had deviated from the Apostolic tradition in the observance of Easter and other mysteries.

Firmilian was also indignant about Bishop Stephen's claim to primacy and considered it preposterous that he would think that he had power to excommunicate anyone who differed from his position based on his being a 'successor to the chair of Peter'. Almost derisively he said: **"I am justly indignant with Stephen's obvious and manifest silliness, that he so boasts of his position and claims that he is the successor of St. Peter on whom were laid the foundations of the Church; yet he brings in many other rocks and erects new buildings of many churches when he defends with his authority the baptism conferred by heretics; for those who are baptized are without doubt numbered in the Church and he who approves their baptism affirms that there is among them a church of the baptized".**

He actually believed that Bishop Stephen's position was heretical.

Other African bishops expressed their views and made comments that revealed how scripturally illogical (tradition or not) Bishop Stephen's position was.

Victorious of Thabraca asked: *"If heretics are allowed to baptize and give remission of sins, wherefore do we brand them with infamy and call them heretics?*

Successus of Abbir Germaniciana said: *"Heretics can either do nothing or they can do all. If they can baptize, they can also bestow the Holy Spirit. But if they cannot give the Holy Spirit, because they have not the Holy Spirit, neither can they spiritually baptize".*

Libosus of Vaga said: *"In the Gospel, the Lord said, 'I am the Truth', He said not 'I am the custom'. Therefore, the truth being manifest, let custom yield to truth; so that although for the past, anyone was not in the habit of baptizing heretics in the Church, let him now begin to baptize them".*

Caecilius of Bilta said: *"I know only one baptism in the Church . . . For thus it is written, one faith, one hope, one baptism; not among heretics where there is no hope and the faith is false; where all things are carried on by lying, where a demoniac exorcises . . . the faithless give faith and the wicked bestows pardon of sins. The antichrist baptizes in the Name of Christ, he who is cursed of God blesses, he who is dead promises life, he who is unpeaceful gives peace, the blasphemer calls upon God, the profane person administers the office of the priesthood, the sacrilegious person establishes an altar . . . and the priest of the devil dare to celebrate the Eucharist; or else let those who stand by them say that all things concerning heretics are false".*

The Lapsed & the Penitential Discipline[21, 22]

The lapsed was the term used in the third century AD for those who, after baptism, denied the faith during the Decian and Diocletian persecutions. There were various categories:

i) Those who actually sacrificed or burned incense—*the sacrificati and the thuruficati.*

In this category were sub categories:
   a) Those who voluntarily sacrificed or burned incense to idols
   b) Those who sacrificed or burned incense to idols under torture

ii) Those who bought certificates indicating that they had sacrificed or burned incense to idols without actually doing so, through bribery of officials—*the libellatici.*

iii) Those who sent slaves who assumed their names to actually sacrifice or burn incense to idols.

iv) Those who bribed pagans to assume their names to actually sacrifice and burn incense to idols.

v) *Traditores*—these were members of the clergy who cooperated with the authorities by surrendering sacred texts.

The question of what to do with the lapsed who wanted to return to the church, created controversies and even schisms in the church.

The established principle from the apostolic period was the obligation of true believers to confess the Christian faith under all circumstances. Jesus Christ and the Apostles taught that Christians would be persecuted and that it is important to persevere, endure and remain faithful even unto death—**Mathew 10:16-23, 32-33; Luke 12:4-9; Luke 21:12-19; 1Timothy 3;12; 1Peter 4:12-19.**

Jesus said He would deny before the Father, anyone who denies Him—**Mark 8:38.** Therefore, the well established penitential discipline up to that point in the history of the church was that an apostate even after penance, was permanently excluded from communion if not completely from fellowship.

However, following the ***Decian (249-251) and Diocletian (284-305)*** persecutions, the penitential rules were relaxed. The reasons advanced for the relaxation include:

- The large numbers and categories of the lapsed

- It was felt that many did not really want to return to idolatry out of conviction but that they only lacked the courage to confess the faith out of fear of torture, banishment, forced labor or death.
- The letters of recommendation from dead martyrs and sometimes imprisoned confessors to bishops and other clergy in favor of the lapsed.

Many craved immediate re-admittance into the church solely on the merit of such letters and were obliged by some clergy.

However, Cyprian, the bishop of Carthage insisted that cases should be treated on their individual merit and due penance had to be performed before anyone could be re-admitted into communion with the church. ***Novatus*** admitted them unconditionally on the recommendations of martyrs or confessors; while ***Novatian*** insisted on the pre-existing penitential discipline and refused to readmit the lapsed into communion. Eventually Novatianism became a separate sect with Novatian as the bishop of his followers in Rome. (Novatian is now usually referred to as an anti-pope though at the time the position of the pope was non-existent).

It was decided that all who lapsed would do penance, the length of which would be determined by the severity of their sin. Those who sacrificed voluntarily would be readmitted only at the point of death. Later, with another impending persecution, a general amnesty was declared and all the lapsed who had done penance were absolved and readmitted into full communion of the church, ostensibly to 'strengthen' them for the impending persecution.

During the Diocletian persecution, another category, ***the traditores*** was added to the lapsed. These were clergymen who cooperated with authorities by surrendering sacred texts, though some claimed they submitted only secular books. The controversy over the fitness of such clergymen to retain their leadership positions in the church led to the ***Donatist schism***. Again, the Roman Catholic Church relaxed the rules and left the clergymen in their positions. The Donatists maintained that ***the holiness of the church is the holiness of its members*** and insisted that lapsed clergy no longer merited their positions.

COMMENT: A subtle but dangerous idea crept in during the persecutions and the subsequent attempts to resolve the cases of the lapsed. This was the idea that martyrs and confessors, by their martyrdom and sufferings respectively could somehow propitiate the sins of the Lapsi. As already observed, ***the remission of***

sins is possible only through the shedding of the unique Blood of Jesus Christ which alone 'speaks better things than that of Abel'—**Hebrews 12:24.**

On the basis of their "letters of peace or recommendation", some clergy re-admitted the lapsed unconditionally. Cyprian protested this and said: *"And does anyone think that, in opposition to the Judge, a man can become of avail for the general remission and pardon of sins, or that he can shield others before he himself is vindicated? The martyrs order something, to be done; but only if this thing be just and lawful, if it can be done without opposing the Lord Himself by God's priest . . ." "Let no one, beloved brethren, let no one decry the dignity of martyrs, let no one degrade their glories and their crowns. The strength of their uncorrupted faith abides sound; nor can he either say or do anything against Christ, whose hope, and faith, and virtue, and glory, are all in Christ: those cannot be the authority for the bishops doing anything against God's command who themselves have done God's command. Is any one greater than God or more merciful than God's goodness, that he should either wish that undone which God has suffered to be done or, as if God had too little power to protect His Church should think that we could be preserved by his help?*

From the perceived 'merits' of the martyrs and saints later grew the **dogma of indulgences**; but as Cyprian observed, the merits of the saints accrue only to them personally and that, only on the Day of Judgment according to the Scriptures—*2Corinthians 5:10*. The souls of martyrs are resting under the altar, crying for vengeance for the evils of the world—**Revelations 6:9-11.**

Cyprian warned that the lapsed should not be misled to put their trust in man but rather be reminded of the need for repentance. He emphasized the danger of giving assurance of peace to the unrepentant apostate or sinner under a misguided notion of mercy; that rather than being kind to them, they were actually being injured. He considered that the prerogative of mercy belong to God and cannot be guaranteed on the promise of the martyrs, saying: *"The martyrs order something to be done; but if what they order be not written in the law of the Lord, we must first know that they have obtained what they ask from God and then do what they command. For that may not always appear to be immediately conceded by the divine majesty, which has been promised by man's undertaking.*

Chapter 5

The Imperial Church and the Post Nicene Church Fathers

Emperor Constantine [1,2,3]—**(c.274—c.337) and The Imperial Church**
Constantine was born about 274 AD to Constantius Chlorus and Helena. He became the Emperor of the Roman Empire in 306 AD at the death of his father.

While involved in battle over the control of Italy with **Maxentius (c278-312)** in 312**,** he was said to have seen a vision of a shinning Cross with the inscription—*"By this thou shall conquer".* Constantine won the battle, became the sole ruler of the Western Roman Empire and ascribed his victory to the "spiritual experience" he had, and therefore converted to Christianity.

Prior to Emperor Constantine's conversion to Christianity, persecution of Christians in the empire was common for two reasons. First, Christians refused to participate in state worship of idols and secondly, they often refused to enlist in the army so they were seen as insubordinate and dangerous.

From 312 through 323 AD, Constantine promulgated several edicts that gave equal recognition to Christianity as a state recognized religion, allowed free worship by Christians, gave reparations for previous loses, restoring confiscated properties to Christians and recalling those on exile. In addition, the Christian clergy were given exemption from all municipal burdens and Christian slaves were somewhat emancipated.

In 321 AD, the edict making Sunday a work free day and the day for Christian worship was promulgated.

When Constantine defeated **Licinius (c263-325)**, the Emperor of the Eastern Roman Empire in 324, he became the Emperor of the whole Empire and moved the capital to Constantinople. The edicts then applied to the whole realm. As a result of the Emperor's embrace of Christianity, many in the realm also converted, albeit nominally to Christianity.

The Emperor Constantine noticed, and was puzzled by, the various controversies that plagued the Church. In 314 AD, he called the *'Council of Arles'* to resolve mainly the **Donatist Controversy** and some other issues. The assembled bishops decided against the Donatists who rejected the decision of the Council. The Donatists, unlike the mainstream orthodoxy of the day, were wary and unwelcoming of the Emperor's involvement in the Church.

Eventually, the Donatists separated from the Roman Catholic Church and in many places, especially in North Africa; congregations were divided between Donatists and non-Donatists. In 317 AD, Constantine sent troops to Carthage to deal with the sect, a precedent in Christian persecuting other Christians. This effort failed and Constantine called off the operation in 321 AD.

In 325 AD, Constantine convened the *'Council of Niceae'*, mainly to address the **Arian controversy**; this gave birth to the **Nicene Creed**, a summary of Christian doctrinal beliefs about the relationship of the Persons of the Trinity to one another. The Council decided against Arius who was banished. Thus, effectively, the Emperor Constantine succeeded in making the Roman Catholic Church the only lawful church in the empire while the other sects were suppressed and members sometimes actually persecuted.

Although Constantine is still venerated in some Church traditions, many remain skeptical about the veracity of his conversion to Christianity which is considered a change of policy rather than of moral character. This cynicism is not without basis as Constantine's conducts, after his alleged conversion, were not in keeping with Christian ethics. He was said to have killed his own son and wife in 326 AD, killed other relatives and some intimate friends, retained the title of Pontifex Maximus—(that is the highest priest of the Roman polytheism)—and was not baptized until shortly before his death. He was said to have been baptized by the Arian bishop with whom he mended fences before his death.

The conversion and involvement of the Emperor Constantine in Christian affairs marked the beginning of the concept of **Christendom** (that is Christ Kingdom on earth) and the intertwining of the Church and State for many centuries with the idea that Christianity can or should be enforced and defended by the power of the State.

Emperor Constantine died in 337 AD.

Flavius Gratian—(375-383)[4, 5]

Gratian became emperor in 375. With continued onslaught on the empire by barbarians, he appointed Theodosius 1 as co-emperor in 379.

Influenced by Ambrose, the bishop of Milan, Gratian promoted religious intolerance by outlawing pagan worship, persecuting pagan priests and confiscating their shrines and temples. He also renounced the title of Pontifex Maximus.

Instigated by some Catholic bishops in the region of Spain, he decreed ***Priscillianism*** illegal, sentenced the sect's leaders to exile and dispossessed them of their churches. However, the sect's leaders, failing to get help from Bishop ***Ambrose of Milan (374-397)*** and ***Pope Damasus (366-383)*** sought redress from the imperial court and successfully had the decree against them rescinded. They returned home and recovered their properties and status in the society.

However, when the emperor Gratian was killed by Magnus Maximus in 383, the calumny against the Priscillians was rekindled. Priscillian and the other leaders were tried and convicted for heresy and magic and were executed.

No writings on the teachings of the sect are extant, and all that is known about them is what their accusers said about them so it is difficult to ascertain independently the veracity of the charges of heresy and others. Unfortunately, this is a common situation throughout the history of the Church as the writings of dissenting sects were usually destroyed by burning.

Theodosius I (346—395)[6, 7]

While Emperor Constantine made Christianity one of the recognized religions of the empire, Emperor Theodosius made Roman Catholicism the only acceptable religion. In 380 AD, he and his co-emperor, Gratian (375-383 AD) published the edict that mandated every citizen to subscribe to Roman Catholicism.

They expelled the Arian bishop of Constantinople and closed down Arian places of worship. During his reign, he also persecuted the Jews, the Manicheans and pagans whose temples he destroyed in Egypt, Syria and Asia Minor and paganism became a capital offense. Hence, religious toleration gave way to intolerance, only this time, a Christian Emperor and Christians were the persecutors.

Bishop Ambrose of Milan had a great influence on the Emperor. He had, courageously refused communion to the emperor for his massacre of seven thousand men, women and children in Thessalonica on account of a public disturbance. The Emperor however humbly accepted the eight months of penance imposed by the bishop for the offence. The emperor's intolerance of other religions and any view opposed to Roman Catholicism is thought by some to be an attempt to further please the bishop and demonstrate his fervency in the Catholic faith.

He died in 395 AD.

COMMENT:—
The apparent conversion of the Emperor Constantine I greatly impacted the course and development of Christianity, many would argue, negatively. Although Emperor Constantine is venerated in some Church traditions, many are of the opinion the Church actually apostatized during his time.

Jesus Christ made it clear that His Kingdom is not of this world and never instructed His disciples to use force in presenting the Gospel or in making more disciples but rather to depend on the power of the Holy Spirit. According to the Bible, the *'sword of the Spirit'* is the ***Word*** of God—***Ephesians 6:17***; it is therefore unlikely that Christ would instruct anyone to conquer by the use of the physical sword.

If the Emperor's vision were truly divine, it was definitely wrongly interpreted. In retrospect, many would make bold to say that the vision was demonic.

The immediate effect of the Emperor's conversion was the cessation of the persecution of Christians throughout the empire. Although initially Christianity was just one of the religions recognized by the State, many, for expediency embraced Christianity because the Emperor identified with it and not out of genuine conversion. The population of Christians was therefore increased by nominal Christians and in time morality, virtues and discipline suffered even as the catechumenate system gradually fell into disuse.

A new and ominous dimension was introduced into Church Procedures as the Emperor became the convener of Councils and synods for the purpose of resolving doctrinal controversies. For instance, even though the Emperor was technically not yet a full member of the Church—(as he was not baptized until shortly before his death)—he convened and attended both the Council of Arles (314) and the Council of Niceae (325) and took sides in the controversy by using the instruments of the State to enforce the views of the majority even though he personally had no deep knowledge of the issues in dispute.

The practice of referring cases of Christian doctrinal disputes to the Emperor reached a dangerous point in the case of the ***Priscillian 'heresy'*** when the orthodox Catholics accused him and his colleagues of heresy before the civil court. The Donatists and Arians were also severely persecuted. The persecution of Christians by other Christians therefore became the accepted norm.

St. Hilary (300-368), the erudite bishop of Poitiers decried the use of State instruments to persecute other Christians with differing doctrinal views and said:

"I ask you bishops to tell me, whose favor did the Apostles seek in preaching the Gospel and on whose power did they rely in preaching Jesus Christ? Today, alas, while the power of the State enforces divine faith, men say that Christ is powerless. The Church threatens exile and imprisonment; she in whom men formally believed while in exile and prison, now wishes men to believe her by force . . . exiling the very priests who once spread her Gospel. What a striking difference between the Church of the past and the Church of today". [8]

However, from public order standpoint, the position of the Emperors was understandable; doctrinal acrimony did not bode well for peace in the empire.

St. Gregory of Nazianzus (325—389 AD) [9]

Gregory Nazianzus was from a Christian family and his father was the bishop of Nazianzus. He was well educated in Caesarea, the capital of Cappadocia where he met and befriended St. Basil and the two again studied together in Athens.

He lived a monastic life with his friend Basil and together they edited some of Origen's exegetical works. Basil was elected the Bishop of Caesarea and Metropolitan of Cappadocia and he made Gregory the bishop of Sasima and his brother Gregory the bishop of Nyssa. Gregory of Nazianzus hated the place and abandoned it, returning to Nazianzus to help his father run his see; thereby causing a strain in his relationship with Basil.

After his father's death, he turned down the bishopric and urged the appointment of someone else then withdrew to a monastery in Seleucia. He was summoned from there to Constantinople by the Emperor Theodosius and there, at the Council of Constantinople eloquently defended the Nicene Creed and the concept of the Trinity while preserving the Unity of the Godhead. He was made the bishop of Constantinople but had to resign soon after and retired to his native Nazianzus for the rest of his life.

St. Basil the Great (c.329-379 AD) [10, 11]

Basil was born into a devoutly Christian family and many members of the family were canonized.

He lived a monastic life for some time but succeeded Eusebius as the bishop of Caesarea. He defended the Nicene Creed against the Arians and founded a coenobitical monastery which became the model in the east and later the Byzantine Empire. He was a friend of St. Gregory Nazianzus and together with his brother, St. Gregory of Nyssa, constituted "**the Cappadocian Fathers**".

St. Gregory of Nyssa (340-390 AD) [12]

Gregory of Nyssa was the younger brother of St. Basil of Caesarea.

He was more reluctant in his embrace of the ecclesiastical life and was believed to have married at some point before. He was made the bishop of Nyssa by his brother.

He suffered persecutions under the Emperor Valens (364-378) who was an Arian Christian. He was credited with being the first to clearly put into words the idea of the transformation of the Communion Bread. He said: *"Rightly do we believe that now also the bread which is consecrated by the Word of God is changed into the Body of the Word;"* . . . *"As the Word Himself has said: 'This is My Body'. "The consecrated Bread is changed into the Body of the Word and it is needful for humanity to partake of that".*

Gregory of Nyssa, like Basil and Gregory Nazianzus was an ardent Origenist though he differed from Origen in some detail. In his attempt to employ philosophy to explain Christianity, he also stumbled into inconsistencies and contradictions like most of the early Church fathers.

Gregory of Nyssa disapproved of pilgrimages, especially by women because, while on pilgrimage to Jerusalem, he observed the behavior of pilgrims who, veiled by anonymity, were committing indecent acts, immorality, lewd behavior, adultery, theft and murder. He said:

". . . . If the divine grace was more abundant at Jerusalem than elsewhere, sin would not be so much the fashion amongst those that live there; but as it is, there is no form of uncleanness that is not perpetuated amongst them—rascality, adultery, theft, idolatry, poisoning, quarreling and murder are rife . . . Nowhere in the world are people ready to kill each other as there; where kinsmen attack each other like wild beasts and spill each other's blood, merely for the sake of lifeless plunder".

He wrote on a number of theological issues and defended the Catholic faith against many 'heresies' of the day. Like the other Gregory, he was also in Constantinople to defend the doctrine of the Trinity.

The Cappadocian fathers and the cult of Martyrs [13]

The cult of martyrs and veneration of icons and relics was prevalent in Cappadocia during the time of the Cappadocian fathers. Many scholars are of the opinion that these fathers, though not the originators, promoted, encouraged and were instrumental in institutionalizing the practice.

It was the vogue, considered a display of piety, for the aristocracy to build shrines or Churches where the relics or bodies of martyrs were kept. Such places became centers of attraction to the people while the aristocrats consolidated their power. The mother and sister of St. Basil and St. Gregory of Nyssa built a shrine to *"the twelve martyrs"* on their property.

The feasts of the saints were developed into elaborate ceremonies including vigils, fasts, candle-light prayers, chanting of psalms and homilies. It also included the celebration of the Eucharist followed by the delivery of long panegyrics to the martyrs and the procession of the martyrs' relics on a decorated bier. The festival often lasted for many days and tended to become unruly.

At the festival, the faithful venerated the relics or body of the martyr through touching, kissing or embracing. Such actions were believed to:

(i) Facilitate an exchange of spiritual or physical gifts
(ii) Afford the faithful participation in the martyr's sanctity and miracles.
(iii) Initiate the process of sanctification and blessing

Basil said: *"greeting the relics expressed a bond of blood relation or kinship with the saint and those who touched the relics or bowed, participated in the sanctity of the martyr."*

Gregory Nazianzus claimed that *"the martyrs' bodies touched or worshiped possessed equal power with their holy souls."*

The martyrs were regarded as *'intercessors most worthy to intercede with Jesus the Lord and master'*.

Incubation, (sleeping at the shrine), was believed to enhance the likelihood of experiencing a miracle.

Such practices probably developed in an effort to wean the people from 'hero-worship' and other pagan practices as illustrated by the issue of **"child registration"**.

It was the practice for parents to 'register' their children with apotropaic jewelries and incantations placed on the children as amulets. Many professing Christians were still involved in the practice, so Gregory of Nyssa admonished them to stop the practice as it was diabolical and instead have the children baptized. He told them that baptism was a more potent form of exorcism because the Trinity is more powerful than demons and that the sacrament is a greater phylactery than amulets. (This was probably the origin of or at least a major contributor to infant baptism before the Augustinian doctrine of original sin and infant baptism, as the earlier fathers were emphatic about the Believers' baptism).

St. Jerome (345—420 AD) [14]

St. Jerome was born to Christian parents in 345 AD in Stridon and had a good secular education.

Later he turned his passion towards spiritual matters and spent five years with monks in the desert of Chalcis where he embraced the ascetic mode of life. He then left for Rome and formed a community of ascetics with like minded people sponsored by a wealthy widow who also had decided to embrace asceticism.

They left Rome for Bethlehem when the Pope and the Romans became antagonistic to their mode of life. In Bethlehem, they built a monastery and a hospice, catering to the need of pilgrims to the Holy Land.

Jerome was a prolific writer; he wrote many letters, commentaries and apologia and was responsible for the translation of the bible from original Hebrew to the Latin Vulgate. The Latin Vulgate was the main bible text for over a millennium. He is also credited with introducing monasticism to the west.

St. Jerome lived at the time the Roman Empire was in decline politically and he witnessed the reign of several Emperors—*Julian (361-363 AD), Valens (364-378AD), Valentinian I (364-375 AD), Gratian (375-383 AD), Theodosius (379-395AD)* and through to the fall of Rome in 410 AD.

St. Jerome on Women

"The women ... paint their cheeks with rouge and eyelids with antimony; whose plastered faces, too white for human beings, look like idols; and if

in a moment of forgetfulness they shed a tear, it makes a furrow where it rolls down the painted cheeks of women to whom years do not bring the gravity of age; who load their head with other people's hair and enamel a lost youth upon the wrinkles of age . . ."

And the Clergy
"All their anxiety is about their clothes . . . you would take them for bridegroom rather than for clerics; all they think about is knowing the names and houses and doings of rich ladies".

St. Jerome studied under Origenists like Gregory Nazianzus and he also admired Origen's Scholarship and this caused ecclesiastical controversies for which he had to defend himself against detractors. He refuted the writings of the Pelagians whose adherents burnt down his monastery in Bethlehem.

During his time among the monks of Chalcis, he was also embroiled in the Arian controversy. He also interacted with other Church Fathers like Ambrose of Milan, Basil of Caesarea, Gregory of Nazianzus, Gregory of Nyssa, Augustine of Hippo and Chrysostom.

St. John Chrysostom (347-407 AD) [15]

John Chrysostom was born in Antioch in 347 AD to a Christian mother and a military officer father. The father died in Chrysostom's childhood and he and his sister were raised by their young mother who refused to remarry.

Like many of his time such as Basil of Caesarea, Gregory of Nyssa, Gregory of Nazianzus, Jerome and Augustine of Hippo, John Chrysostom was not baptized in infancy. (*Tertullian had argued against infant baptism because it was viewed as the sacrament of regeneration and that committing sins after baptism could lead to the forfeiture of the baptismal grace*).

He had an excellent secular education and became a successful lawyer in Antioch. However, he was dissatisfied with the corruption of the society and considered as *'the wages of Satan' the reward from a profession which 'made the worse cause appear as the better cause'*.

Influenced by his mother, an ascetic friend and bishop Meletius, he joined the Catechumen class and was baptized after the required three years catechumenate. To escape temptations and pursue holiness, he wanted to embrace monasticism but had to defer this aspiration because of the entreaties of his widowed mother. Nonetheless, he practiced asceticism and committed himself to bible study with some of his friends.

After the death of his mother, he entered the monastery and was an advocate of *"useful monasticism"* as opposed to *"idle contemplations"*.

He was ordained a deacon and then a presbyter becoming a preacher of renown and earning the sobriquet of "***chrysostom***" or golden mouth.

The Antioch of John's days was very worldly; he had this to say about the Christians of his city: **"*So great . . . is the depravity of the times that if a stranger were to compare the precepts of the gospel and the actual practice of the society, he would infer that men were not the disciples but the enemies of Christ"*.**

John Chrysostom observed in the society he lived in, a dichotomy in their profession and the actual realities of their daily lives. He enjoined them not to be Christians only on Sundays or at festival times; that it was important for the difference between them and the gentiles to be visible at all times. He admonished them to form Christian habits in thoughts and actions through rehearsal of Scriptures and singing psalms rather than bawdy or meaningless folk songs. He also encouraged them to keep a short account of their sins with God by daily thinking about sins committed and asking for forgiveness from God. He noticed that many took a bath before attending Church out of respect for the holy place, and encouraged them to be even more concerned about spiritual purity, though it was alright to be physically clean.

He alerted them to the danger that lurked in every facet of life—business, theatre, songs, fashions, cosmetics, conversations, eating and so on.

He noticed some practices which derived from paganism or Judaism which the people still practiced such as in:

- **Child Care**: Wearing of amulets made from selected Scripture verses and making mud signs on the forehead of children to keep away the evil eye, witchcraft and envy. Instead, he encouraged women to use the sign of the Cross on their children. (St. Gregory of Nyssa had encouraged infant baptism as alternative to similar practices).
- **Naming of Children**: The practice of choosing a child's name by lighting several lamps with names and choosing the name on the longest burning lamp. He countered this by encouraging them to choose the names of saints.

- **New Year Celebration**: The practice of decorating market stalls and shops, doors of homes, lighting lamps in the market, drinking mixed wine during the New Year celebrations and watching for omens which was believed would influence the whole year. John urged Christians not to participate in such rituals and that if Christians would please God daily, each day of the year would bring good omens and not just one day in which they got drunk. When he failed to sway them from observing the day, he tried to modify their activities by admonishing them that rather than getting drunk, they should use the day to give thanks to God, meditate on the passage of time, their faith and God's judgment rather than omens.
- **The Marriage Custom:** John Chrysostom deplored the custom in which the bride was garishly dressed and paraded through the market accompanied by obscene songs and insults from the crowd. Many acts that would normally not be tolerated were allowed on such occasions and 'Chrysostom could not understand the logic of breaking everyday rules for a special event. He contended that if it was wrong, then it should not be done even once in the name of custom and that if it was good, it should be done always'.
- **Funerals**: The funeral custom was another that Chrysostom tried to modify. He deplored the excessive emotional displays that accompanied funerals and the hiring of pagan women to sing dirges. He tried to make them understand that the fact of resurrection radically modified the Christian attitude towards death and mourning.

St. Chrysostom's extravagant praise of saints and martyrs, like the Cappadocian fathers, encouraged and promoted the 'cult of martyrs' akin to a refined form of idolatry and a substitute for the pagan 'hero worship'.

St. John Chrysostom was a ***Synergist***, who believed in the cooperation of the human free will with the divine grace in the work of salvation. He believed that ***"Christ died for all, is able to save all, but not against their will or their free consent"***. He preached that faith and good works were necessary for salvation, though Christ's merits alone are the efficient cause.

He disapproved of second marriages following spousal death; though legal, he felt remarrying was less pious. In his writings he exalted the virginal state above marriage.

He regarded the other patriarchs also, for example the bishop of Antioch, as the successor of Peter just like the bishop of Rome. In this regard, it would seem that like Cyprian, he believed that the universal episcopacy is the chair of Peter and not only Rome.

St. Chrysostom wrote a number of homilies against the Jews expressing opinions that were to be used, unfortunately for unsalutary political purposes by anti-Semites through the ages.

St. John Chrysostom was elected the bishop of Constantinople in 398 AD. However, his uncompromising stand against vices and sin set him on a collision course with the Empress and some licentious clergy. An ascetic to the core, he gave no parties and refused invitations to banquets; he sold the expensive furnishing in the Episcopal palace and used the proceeds for the poor. He disciplined immoral priests and forbade the practice in which the clergy lived with *"spiritual sisters"*.

He was tried, deposed and sent on exile on trumped up charges. He died in 407AD en route another more remote exile location on the order of the Empress and was buried in a monastery in a remote part of the empire.

Thirty-one years later, his remains were brought to Constantinople and buried with other patriarchs and emperors in the church of the Holy Apostles.

He is regarded as a preacher of morals rather than dogma.

Augustine of Hippo [16, 17] (354-430 AD)

Augustine was born in Thagaste, in present day Algeria, North Africa in 354 AD to a Christian mother and a pagan father.

Though well educated, he led a riotous and licentious lifestyle as a youth and had a long relationship with a woman who bore him a son, Adeodatus.

In his quest for knowledge, he studied Platonism and at the age of nineteen years joined the Manichaeans, a sect which was an amalgam of Zoroastrianism, Buddhism and Christianity founded by a Persian named Mani.

Manichaeism had strange teachings and Augustine commented on one such teaching thus: *"I was foolish enough to believe that we should show more kindness to the fruits of the earth than we should to mankind for whose use they were intended. If a starving man, not a Manichaean were to beg for a mouthful, they thought it a crime worthy of mortal punishment to give him one."*

Disillusioned with Manichaeism, he turned to neo-Platonism until he met *St. Ambrose (c.340-397), the bishop of Milan.* At the age of thirty-three years, in Milan, Augustine embraced Christianity which for him became the 'true philosophy' and he sought harmony between Christianity and Platonism.

He returned to Thagaste and later became the bishop of Hippo, also in present day Algeria.

The fractiousness that characterized the Church in the ante-Nicene era continued during the time of Augustine who spent a lot of time writing refutations against sects considered as heretic or heterodox. He refuted the teachings of the Manichaeans, the Pelagians, the Arians and the Donatists.

The systematization of Church dogma which started with Cyprian of Carthage was fully developed by Augustine of Hippo. Through his writings, Augustine effected a paradigm shift in the attitude of the early Church to issues of holiness, sin and sinners. While the Apostolic Church viewed itself as the congregation of saints that strove to remain holy, Augustine defined the Church essentially as the congregation of sinners striving to become saints; an aspiration he said was more or less unattainable.

The theological system that Augustine developed was dominant in the Church till the medieval period and even to the present time.

St. Augustine on Doctrines: [17, 18, 19, 20,]
  ❖ *On Grace and Nature* [17]
St. Augustine said:
- *Man's nature was created faultless and without any sin, but this nature was corrupted by the **'original sin'** committed by the free will of Adam and Eve.*
- *The resulting flawed nature is passed on to all humanity and requires healing and illumination by God.*
- *This healing is received through God's grace. God's grace is given **gratis** through Jesus Christ, that is, without any merit on man's part.*
- *Both adults and infants require this grace for salvation.*
- *The works of the flesh, which proceeds from carnal concupiscence, not the substance of the flesh, oppose the spirit.*

- ❖ ***On Sin, Concupiscence, Forgiveness and Infant Baptism*** [18, 19]
- *Pride is the commencement of every sin because that was what caused the expulsion of Satan from heaven and was also the underlying factor in the fall of Man when Satan enticed them to disobey God to 'become as gods'.*
- *'Original sin passed from Adam to all of humanity through natural birth but every rational man also commits, from his own willfulness, actual or personal sins.*
- *Infants are born with the original sin and although they have no attributable personal sins, they require baptism for the remission of the original sin to escape damnation.*
- *Unbaptized infants will be condemned, albeit, mildly.*
- *"God heals us, not only that He may blot out the sins which we have committed, but that He may enable us even to avoid sinning."*
- *Arguing four propositions, Augustine concluded that it is possible to guard against sin after being freed by Jesus, but only by the grace of God and man's free will. However,* ***he believed that in actual fact, "there is not, nor has been, nor ever will be, a human being who is free from all sin except the one mediator, Christ"****
- ***"It is really necessary to man, in order to take from him all occasion for pride and boasting, that he should be unable to exist without sin."***
- *Sin with knowledge is graver than sin in ignorance.*
- *Bodily death is the result of Adam's sin.*
- ***Works of mercy remedies against guilt and bonds of sins committed after baptism.****
- *Baptism removes the guilt of concupiscence but the old nature still remains though the spirit is renewed.* ***"The remnant of the law of sin is mitigated by good works done by the baptized as they do not mold their understanding according to its principles and because they make good use of even death, the penalty of the first sin when they encounter it with fortitude and patience."***
- *Augustine considered this as the* ***"sin which dwells in our bodies"*** *and that it is* ***"a sin that is a punishment for sin"*** *and the law of sin or concupiscence operating in the human body.*
- *Those who are born again are not considered guilty though concupiscence remains, and the children propagated through concupiscence inherit the sinful nature.*

- *Since the propagation of the human race is through concupiscence, everyone is born with the original sin.*
- *Infants are born with concupiscence and need baptism for regeneration.*
- *In baptized adults, endowed with reason, those who yield consent to concupiscence for the commission of unlawful deeds are guilty; only repentance, works of mercy and intercession by Jesus Christ can prevent the second death.*
- *Conjugal chastity, which prevents adultery, is God's gift just as perfect continence which foregoes all cohabitation.*
- **"In marriage, man makes a good use of an evil thing when he restrains his concupiscence by matrimony".**
- *"The good of marriage lie not in passion of desire, but in a certain legitimate and honorable measure in using that passion, appropriate to the propagation of children, not the gratification of lust"*

❖ **Grace, Free Will, Faith, Salvation and Baptism** [19, 20]
- *Grace is not given according to merit, but given gratis*
- *Grace effects the fulfillment of the law, the liberation of nature and the suppression of sin's dominion.*
- *There is in man, a free choice of will.*
- *Free will is involved in heart's conversion but is of use only by the ability provided by the grace of God.*
- *The wills of men are in the power of God and He can turn them in any way He pleases whether to good deeds according to His mercy or to evil according to their own deserts.*
- *He who falls, falls by his own will and he who stands, stands by God's will for God is able to make him stand.*
- *Faith, from the initiation to the end is a gift of God.*
- *Faith without good works is not sufficient for salvation.*
- *Good works are also from and ordained by God.*
- *Justification is entirely by grace, but eternal life is grace and reward.*
- *Eternal life is both a reward for service and a free gift of grace.*
- *Salvation is through baptism which is the washing of regeneration and the way for believers to come to Jesus Christ.*

- In baptism, full and perfect remission of sin takes place. However, the character of the individual does not undergo total change all at once but by a process of daily renewal
- .Augustine believed that salvation is 'accomplished in hope' and not in actuality for as long as we are on earth—". . . . **We are children of God; but inasmuch as we are <u>not yet actually saved</u>, we are also not yet fully renewed, nor yet fully sons of God but children of the world."**
- ❖ **On Predestination and Perseverance** [21]
- The perseverance by which believers persevere to the end is a gift of God as is obedience.
- No one can claim to have received the gift of perseverance as long as he is still alive, because the possibility of falling remains until the final moments in the flesh.
- God has fore-knowledge of those who would believe, in other words, those who would be saved are predestined.
- Predestination is the preparation for grace; and grace is the effect of predestination.
- The purpose of election or predestination is holiness.

COMMENT:

Augustine's use of philosophical arguments in his exegetical writings sometimes created the same problems that earlier philosophers encountered; as his conclusions often seem to confute the very point he set out to prove. For example, On Free Will and Predestination:

Augustine's position on free will evolved over time from a firm believe that God gave man free will which is involved in conversion and salvation to the point where he defended predestination, a situation where man's will becomes virtually irrelevant.

On the one hand he said *"To the grace of God must be added the exertion of our own will . . . For God does not work our salvation in us as if he were working in insensate stones or in creatures in whom nature has placed neither reason nor will."*

On the other hand, he posited that *"the wills of men are so much in the power of God that He can turn them wherever He wants and whenever He wills . . ."*;—even in the hearts of the wicked. In addition he said that *"God can turn wills from evil to good and convert those inclined to fall and direct them into a way pleasing to Him."*

However, he recoiled from attributing to God bad or evil wills, the logical conclusion of his position, by contending that somehow in spite of his claim that God has absolute control over man's will, good wills are from God and bad or evil wills are entirely from man and can never be from God. Hence he said *"he who falls, falls by his own will and he who stands, stands by God's will.*

Although he decried *"the tendency to so defend God's grace as to deny man's free will or to suppose that free will is denied when grace is defended"*; that was actually what he did by his doctrine of Predestination.

Augustine recognized the problems and the questions posed by the doctrine of predestination. For example, if God already predestinated some to be saved no matter what, while others have also been predestined for reprobation, why preach repentance, obedience or perseverance or anything?

He stated to be a fact that *"anyone who lives in obedience but predestined to be rejected will have the power to obey and persevere withdrawn and will not obey to the end; whereas, anyone living in damnable sins but predestined for election will receive grace for election"*.

Augustine held that the obvious conclusions from the doctrine of predestination were true; that is, that God had predetermined some for salvation while he had also predetermined others for perdition and that man has no power to change this predetermined fate.

However, he admitted that, *"to preach predestination <u>unvarnished</u> was abominable, excessively harsh, hateful, monstrous and inconsiderate"*.

He therefore instructed that it should be "*applied with 'discrimination' and preached so as not to 'engender despair or give offence' to 'people of slower understanding'"*.

By Augustine's own admission therefore, God is ultimately responsible for the unrepentant and the damned because in His sovereignty (which the adherents of this doctrine seek to protect) He could turn their wills as He wishes but doesn't.

This doctrine sacrificed God's love, grace, mercy and justice on the altar of His sovereignty and made man no more than a mere robot—(no better than an insensate stone after all)—in the hands of a capricious 'God'.

Although Augustine admitted that the implications of the doctrine were obnoxious; amazingly, it gained credence in some Christian circles and is held as a dogma even to this day by many Calvinist denominations in one form or the other.

The Roman Catholic Church does not subscribe to this doctrine.

On Original Sin:

By Augustine's exegesis, Sin is inextricably tied to human concupiscence, principally, sexual desire. He believed concupiscence arose from man's rebellion against God in the Garden of Eden and that as punishment, God made man's genitalia—(pudenda)—to also become rebellious to man's soul such that penile erections are largely involuntary and not subject to man's will.

He said*: "It is with a natural instinct of shame that the rational soul is now indeed affected, because in that flesh, over whose service it received the right of power, it can no longer, owing to some indescribable infirmity, prevent the motion of the members thereof, notwithstanding its own unwillingness; nor excite them to motion even when it wishes. Now these members are on this account, in every man of chastity, rightly called pudenda, because they excite themselves just as they like, in opposition to the mind which is their master, as if they were their own masters . . ."*

Sexual desire therefore is essentially the "Original Sin" (or as he also put it, punishment for man's sin of disobedience) and since every human being is born as a result of sexual relations, all are born with the Original Sin.

Based on this concept, Augustine validated the practice of **infant baptism** and stated that infants need the washing of baptism to remove the inherited sin otherwise if they die, they'll be damned.

However, the concept of sexual desire being the 'Original Sin' raised more doctrinal questions than it answered; for instance, why does sexual desire remain after baptism which is supposed to wash away sin and renew man?

St. Augustine tried to resolve the issue by stating that, at baptism, though there is complete remission of sin, only the 'guilt' of concupiscence is removed while the sin itself is left for man to struggle with to end that he may remain humble.

As a result of the persistence of concupiscence, notwithstanding the washing of regeneration at baptism, he concluded that in theory, with the help of God, man can be sinless, but in practice he averred *"that no man has ever been, no man ever was and no man could ever be sinless while still in the world".*

While he admitted that God commanded perfection in righteousness and for man to live without sin; he concluded that, given man's nature, in effect, *God prescribed what He knows cannot be observed and which no man living could ever perform or fulfill in order that we may know what to ask Him in prayer.*

In fact, he reasoned that *"it was necessary that man should be unable to exist without sin so that all occasion for pride and boasting might be taken from him."*

When critics challenged him that he was in essence suggesting the '*use of sin to prevent sin*', he more or less affirmed this by his analogy that, to treat pain, sometimes, painful measures are employed.

St. Augustine's concept of Original Sin is speculative at best and unsubstantiated by Scripture, science or tradition. To accept the idea that the involuntary nature of penile erections is as a result of Original Sin would mean that by extension, going by Augustine's logic and doctrine, other bodily functions not subject to voluntary control but controlled by the autonomic (involuntary) nervous system like breathing, intestinal motility and heart beats are the result of sin and also sinful.

Contrary to St. Augustine's view that sexual desire is evil and sinful, Jesus Christ affirmed marriage and said that "**in the beginning, God made them male and female . . .**"—and advised celibacy only for those so endowed by God—*Mathew 19:1-12*.

The Apostle Paul advised continence within marriage **only** by mutual agreement and for a **limited** period of time for the purpose of prayer and fasting; and he encouraged prompt resumption of sexual relations by married couples after such abstinence to avoid temptation and sin—*1Corinthians 7:1-7.*

Further in the same chapter and in the general belief of the time that Christ's second coming was imminent, Paul gave his opinion that those who could, should be celibate and those who couldn't should marry. He stressed the need for each person to act within his or her God given gift and ability.

Many of the earlier Church Fathers (Tradition), except the heretics, considered sexuality, used according to God's design within marriage as pure and not sinful.

Augustine's view of sex and sexuality, as essentially evil and something to be grudgingly allowed for procreation, and to be endured rather than enjoyed even in marriage, though unscriptural, prevailed for centuries in Christendom and resulted in a culture of sexual ambivalence. The backlash is still being felt till today.

Augustine's view of the flesh and concupiscence as being essentially evil and his doctrine of "original sin" are thought by some to have been influenced by the Manichean philosophy with which he dabbled before he embraced Christianity.

St. Augustine's notion that sin is necessary to prevent sin is not only illogical scripturally, it is supremely scandalous because it suggests that Christ blood is inadequate for sanctification. Nowhere in the Scriptures can this idea be found. Believers are sanctified by the Blood of Jesus Christ—Hebrew 10:29 and by the Word of God—John 17:17; it is highly preposterous that God would use sin, which defiles and separates to prevent man from sinning.

Jesus Christ, by His blood shed on the Cross is the propitiation of believers' sins; by the same blood he removed the power of sin and they are kept sanctified by the Word of truth—1John 2:2; Hebrews 9:13-15, 26; John 17:17-19.

Also preposterous is the idea that, in asking that man live in righteousness, God commanded what He knew was impossible because it suggests that God was just being facetious. God and Jesus Christ promised to sanctify man; God said He is the sanctifier—Leviticus 20:8; Leviticus 21:8; Leviticus 22:32; and Jesus Christ said He is committed to the believer's sanctification—John 17:19. To suggest therefore, that God was not serious or unreasonable by requiring that man through Jesus Christ be righteous bordered on blasphemy.

This mind set, unfortunately, has also governed the attitude of the Church towards holiness for centuries.

Chapter 6

'Heresies' and Schisms of the Early Church

> "... There will be false teachers among you.
> They will secretly introduce destructive heresies,
> Even denying the sovereign Lord ...
> Many will follow their shameful ways and will bring the
> Way of Truth into disrepute"—2Peter 2:1-2

- ❖ **Marcionism** [1]

This was a heretical sect founded in 144 AD by Marcion, reportedly the son of a bishop in Rome.

He rejected the Old Testament and the God of the Old Testament; taught that Jesus Christ was not the Son of the God of the Old Testament, the God of the Jews but of the "good God". He denied the resurrection of the body and the second coming of Jesus Christ to judge the living and the dead because the 'good God' is all Love and would never punish those who reject Him. Punishment would be administered by the 'bad God' who will send those deserving to hell. He rejected marriage and baptized only celibates, virgins, widows and eunuchs; all others remained catechumen. Marcion was thought to have evolved his doctrine in an effort to have Christianity 'undefiled' by Judaism.

- ❖ **Montanism** [2,3]

Montanism was started by Montanus of Phrygia in Asia Minor. Although Montanists were well rooted in Christianity and essentially doctrinally agreed with the Catholic Church of the time, they also believed in the operations of the Holy Spirit through prophesies, visions and miracles; as well as the imminent return of Jesus Christ.

They practiced strict asceticism and a very rigorous penitential discipline. Montanists preached avoidance of sin and maintained a stricter church discipline than the Roman Catholic Church such that those who committed 'mortal sins' were excommunicated. ***They held that the holiness of the Church was the holiness of its members.***

Chastity was encouraged, second marriage was forbidden and the first was not encouraged. Martyrdom was highly extolled as the crown of human life and members were taught not to hide or flee but to sometimes offer themselves.

Another area of conflict with the Catholic Church was the Montanists' belief in the universal priesthood of believers and allowing female prophetesses; contrary to the clerical aristocracy which was becoming established in the Catholic Church.

In fact, the prophesies of the Montanists were regarded by many in the Catholic Church as demon inspired because they were mainly through women considered fanatical rather than the clergy; and some attempted to have them exorcised.

The opposition to Montanism by some was so great that a group called the *Alogi* or *Alogoi* rejected the authenticity of the Gospel and the epistles of John and the book of Revelations because John's Gospel, more than any other spoke about the Holy Spirit on whom the Montanists heavily relied.

Tertullian was a prominent adherent of the movement and was for this reason considered a heretic by the Roman Catholic Church. The Montanists' doctrines were pronounced heretic and they were excommunicated from the Roman Catholic Church. They formed an independent schismatic church which survived for centuries.

Many now consider Montanism as the reaction of the primitive Church to the moral laxity that was creeping into the Church during the time of **Bishops Zephyrinus (199-217)** and **Callistus I (217-222)** of Rome when the penitential discipline was relaxed even for grievous sins to the point where the line between the Church and the world was being blurred.

Today, some hold that the Montanists were not heretics; that they were orthodox in both belief and practice and only different in aspects of faith in which they placed emphasis. Aspects of Montanism can be found today in groups like the **Anabaptists, Puritans, Quakers, Pietists and Pentecostals.**

- ❖ **Monarchianism** [4, 5]

Monarchianism is a **Christological heresy** which arose in the second century AD from an attempt to maintain monotheism in the doctrine of the Trinity. There were two groups, the **Dynamic** and the **Modal Monarchians**.

The Dynamic group held that there is only one God, the Father; Jesus Christ was just a human being on whom the Father entered and empowered at baptism.

The Modal group trying to achieve the same end held that there is only one God, the Father and the Son and the Spirit are just *'modes'* or different expressions of the same Person. In other words they are not simultaneous and separate but consecutive modes of one Person.

Modern day groups with similar beliefs as the Dynamic Monarchians include the **Jehovah Witnesses, Unitarians** and **Christadelphians** while the **United Apostolic Church** and the **United Pentecostals** have similar Christological doctrine to the Modal Monarchians.

Hippolytus of Rome (170-235), a prolific writer, theologian and presbyter in Rome, accused the Bishop of Rome, **Calixtus I**, of tolerating the Christological heresy of Monarchianism as well as subverting Church discipline by re-admitting gross sinners. Therefore he formed a schismatic group and was elected as an antipope by his followers.

Hippolytus' Christology stated that there is a real difference between the Father and the Son (Logos). The Son is almost completely separate from and altogether subordinate to the Father.

He apparently later reconciled with the Roman Church and is regarded as a respected theologian and venerated as a Saint and martyr.

- ❖ Manichaeism [6]

Manichaeism, an amalgamation of Zoroastrianism, Buddhism, Gnosticism and Christianity was founded by ***Mani (c.216-276),*** a Persian in the third Century AD.

It is a dualistic religious philosophy of a world in perpetual struggle between good and evil derived from Zoroastrianism; the strict asceticism by the higher order of the sect derived from Buddhism and the doctrine of salvation through knowledge derived from Gnosticism.

The founder claimed to have had a divine revelation to perfect all the other religions before him. In Mani's theology, there are two opposing kingdoms of good (light) and evil (darkness) and the world and individuals, as it were, are the battleground. Therefore, each individual is simultaneously a son of light with a good soul and son of darkness with substantially evil body and corresponding evil soul. Christ is the sun spirit who effects the redemption of light from the bonds of darkness and moral regeneration is by a process of physical refinement.

Followers were divided mainly into two groups, **'the elect'** and **'the hearers'**. The elects were those committed to three seals, namely:
1.) The seal of the mouth by which they maintained purity in words and diet. Strictly vegetarian, they abstained from eating any form of animal flesh and drinking of strong drinks.
2.) The seal of the hand in which they are forbidding to engage in any kind of labor or trade. They were forbidding from uprooting plants, cutting down trees or killing any animal.
3.) The seal of the heart in which they committed to a life of absolute celibacy.

They were to renounce all earthly possessions and properties and they spent their time in preaching and prayers.

The greater percentage of the sect were 'hearers'; they could do all that were forbidden to the 'elects' and were the growers and the suppliers of the food that the elects ate. The elect would succeed in releasing the entrapped light at death while hearers hoped to be reincarnated as elects in another life.

St Augustine was a Manichean for about nine years but became a critic when he embraced Christianity refuting many of the teachings of the Manicheans in many of his apologetics. Augustine considered the Manicheans teaching that fruits weep when plucked, that the trees shed tears and that it was a crime to give a starving non-Manichean man a fruit absurd and foolish as it presupposes that more kindness should be shown to fruits than to mankind for whom the fruits were intended.

Manichaeism persisted for many centuries and elements of the religion may still persist in some contemporary New Age religious systems sometimes under the guise of Environmental or Animal rights groups.

❖ **Novatianism** [7, 8]

Novatianism, founded by *Novatian (c200-c258),* an ordained presbyter in Rome in the mid third century, arose from the controversy of whether or not to re-admit into the Church those who fell into apostasy—(lapsed)—during the Decian persecution of 250 AD.

The Catholic Church, up to about 220 AD, practiced the excommunication of those who committed 'mortal sins' like idolatry, murder, adultery and fornication until Calixtus 1.

As the Bishop of Rome, Calixtus 1 reversed the practice and through an edict established the opposite practice of re-admitting such sinners who were considered to have truly repented.

This step by Calixtus 1 was criticized by Tertullian and was in part responsible for the **Hippolytus Schism**.

Following the Decian persecution, the controversy reared its head again. The Bishop of Rome, Cornelius, decided to re-admit the lapsed after due penance without re-baptism, Cyprian in Carthage was for re-admission after penance but with re-baptism, Novatus in North Africa was for unconditional re-admission but Novatian, also in Rome was for restored fellowship but not full communion.

The position of the Catholic Church was said to have hinged on two reasons: The first was the huge numbers of the lapsed which threatened the survival of many congregations. The other was the Church's developing dogma of the 'authority of the Church and the episcopacy' which says that ***"a man can enter into relationship with God only through the Church and the priest.*** In other words, a man's salvation is absolutely dependent on his connection with the clergy and the Church; as such, a man that is refused absolution would have no hope here and in the hereafter.

Novatian, on the other hand saw the Church as a communion of Saints and that those who committed mortal sins post baptism had committed 'sins unto death' and could only be absolved by God and not bishops. Therefore, although he would encourage repentance and even admit the lapsed into fellowship, he would not give them the Eucharist. Novatian and his followers were declared heretics and excommunicated from the Catholic Church by a Roman synod in 251AD.

They formed an independent schismatic group and had adherents among Christians everywhere with separate clergy.

However, when Roman Catholicism found favor with the secular Roman establishment, they were persecuted by both the state and the Catholic Church.

The Novatians' positions on Church holiness and discipline are regarded by many today as unquestionably closer to those of the apostolic era and their idea of the Church as a communion of saints corresponding to that of the early days of Christianity.

❖ Donatism [9, 10, 11]

Donatism was a schismatic movement that started after the persecution of the Church by the Emperor Diocletian in 303 to 305 AD. Like the Novatian Schism, the controversy was on how to deal with professed Christians, in particular, priests and other leaders who in one way or another denied or betrayed the faith during the period of persecution.

The Donatists held that priests who fell into apostasy during persecution could not validly administer Church Sacraments. Like the Montanists and the Novatians, the Donatists held that: *"the holiness of the Church is the holiness of its members and that the Church must be a communion of saints not of sinners".*

The Roman Catholic Church on the other hand maintained that: *"the validity of Sacraments does not derive from the worthiness or holiness of the priests but on the holiness of God.*

The priests are believed to be merely instruments in the observance of the Sacraments.

In fact the Roman Catholic Church position is that: *"even an unrepentant priest committing mortal sins can administer Sacraments once the 'formula' is properly spoken; that it is the office, not the personal character of the incumbent that gives validity to the celebration of Sacraments".*

At stake was the developing Roman Catholic Church's *'Sacrament of Penance'*; refusing to re-admit the apostates would call into question the very basis of that Sacrament.

The controversy came to a head in 311 AD when Bishop Felix of Aptunga joined other Bishops to consecrate Caecilian, the Bishop of Carthage. Felix was a known *'traditor'* (that is he had surrendered sacred books and relics to the Roman authorities during persecution) and therefore the Donatists considered that his participation in the consecration rendered the exercise invalid. The Bishop was therefore not recognized by them and a schism ensued.

The Donatists also rejected the union of Church and State that Constantine had forged and which the Roman Catholics had embraced. At a point, there were more Donatists in North Africa than there were Catholics. In 314 AD, the Emperor Constantine, who had embraced Christianity sought to resolve the schism and convened the **Council of Arles.** The issues were debated and a ruling given in favor of the Roman Catholic Church. The verdict was rejected by the Donatists and they were persecuted by Constantine who sent troops to Carthage against them in 317 AD. This use of force however failed and Constantine stopped the persecution in 321 AD. However, it set an unfortunate precedent in Christians persecuting other Christians.

Successive Roman Emperors persecuted the Donatists and in 409 AD, Marcellinus of Carthage, secretary of State to Emperor Honorius, issued an edict proclaiming the group heretical and demanded that they give up their churches. This was made possible by the legal documents provided by St. Augustine of Hippo that proved that Emperor Constantine had chosen the Catholic Church over the Donatists as the official church of the empire.

The Catholics requested that the Emperor convene a conference in Carthage to resolve the division in 410 AD. In 411 AD, hundreds of Bishops from both sides met to debate the issue. The outcome, with the imperial power behind one group was a foregone conclusion. Marcellinus declared the Roman Catholic Church the winner. With this clear authority, Augustine and other Catholic leaders moved to enforce compliance of the imperial decree.

The Donatists were denied civil rights in 414 and in 415 were prohibited from assembling together to worship.

However, in spite of intense persecution, Donatism persisted in North Africa till the seventh century AD.

- ❖ **Arius (c260-c336) and Arianism** [12]

Arianism is considered a Christological heresy popularized and propagated by Arius, a Libyan and presbyter in Alexandria. Arius contended that Jesus Christ is not of the same essence with the Father and that although he is divine, he was one of God's greatest creations before the creation of the world. This view was not new and had been held by some in the Church for years before Arius in Alexandrian circles.

Subordination of the divine Persons was a part of Origenism, the theology propounded by Origen more than a century earlier in Alexandria.

However, views that subordinated the Persons of the Trinity conflicted with the popular doctrine of Trinity which held that the Persons, though distinct are of the same essence. The ensuing controversy was so great and involved every level and region of Christendom that the Emperor Constantine had to wade in and sought reconciliation through the ***Council of Nicaea*** which he convened in ***325 AD.*** The majority of the bishops at the Council of Nicaea signed the creed which evolved—*The Nicene Creed*—except three including Arius. Arius and his co-dissidents were therefore anathematized and banished to Illyria. As time went on, he had sympathizers in the court of the Emperor and was later recalled from exile through the influence of the Emperor's sister.

The Arian controversy raged for centuries in Christendom and elements of it persist in some religious systems today.

❖ **Nestorianism** [13, 14]

Nestorianism is a Christological doctrine considered to be heretical and propagated by *Nestorius,* a monk who became the patriarch of Constantinople from 428-431. The doctrine held that Jesus Christ had two distinct and separate natures, namely divine and human which were in contact but not united.

Therefore, Mary gave birth to the human, not the divine Jesus; as such he preached against calling Mary the *'Mother of God'*. He also said that the human Christ suffered and died on the Cross as God cannot suffer or die. Taken to its logical conclusion, Jesus Christ had to be two separate persons and if that were so, it had implications for many other theological doctrines on Salvation.

The controversy led to the **Council of Ephesus in 431 AD** where it was affirmed that "Christ is one Person and that Mary was the 'Mother of God' and Nestorius' doctrine was anathematized. Nestorius and his followers rejected the verdict and this led to the formation of a Schismatic Church, *the Assyrian Church of the East*.

This Church evangelized China, Korea, Persia and India and there are still adherents of the doctrine in Iraq, Iran and India. There are also some elements of Nestorianism in some protestant Reformed Churches. Mohammed was thought to have had contact with Nestorian Christians.

❖ **Pelagius (c354-425) and Pelagianism** [17, 18]

Pelagianism was a theological doctrine propounded by Pelagius, a British monk, which denied the doctrines of 'original sin', sanctifying grace and predestination being propagated by his contemporary, St. Augustine of Hippo.

Pelagius taught that Adam's sin did not hurt anyone but Adam, that man, by the exercise of his will can live a righteous life without the grace of God because God has given man the free will to choose between good and evil.

He affirmed the naturalness of concupiscence and the death of the body; that Adam might have died even without the fall. His position on original sin conflicted with and invalidated the practice of infant baptism.

Pelagius also believed that man sins by imitation of Adam and not heredity, in the same way, man's salvation is through instruction and the imitation of Jesus Christ.

St. Augustine wrote extensively to refute Pelagianism and was instrumental in securing an imperial condemnation of the doctrine in 418 AD.

The doctrine was condemned at the Council of Ephesus in 431 AD. Although Pelagianism and semi-Pelagianism faded off after the sixth century, the questions raised about man's responsibility versus God's sovereignty in salvation continued to cause controversy till today.

- ❖ **Eutychianism & Appollinarianism** [15, 16]

The **Council of Ephesus** did not completely resolve the Nestorian Christological controversy.

In an effort to develop a coherent doctrine in opposition to Nestorianism, Eutyches, a monk in charge of a large monastery in Constantinople propagated the idea that Christ's *'divine nature absorbed the human so much so that the human nature was like a drop of honey in the sea'*.

Taken to its logical conclusion, Christ has only one nature, the divine; this was called '*Monophysitism*'. However, this was vehemently rejected by the Roman Catholic Church.

Appollinarianism was propounded by Appolinaris, the bishop of Loadicea; it held that Christ had a human body and soul, but that His Spirit was taken over entirely by the Divine Logo. This was also considered a form of *Monophysitism.*

To address these Christological doctrines that were also considered heresies, another Council was convened at *Chalcedon* in **451 AD**. At the **Council of Chalcedon**, the *'Dyophysite'* Christological position was adopted. *This position holds that* ***'Jesus Christ is One Person in two natures (divine and human) which are inseparably united (hypostasis)'.***

However, this position was also rejected by a faction that formed ***the Schismatic Church, the Oriental Orthodox Church***. The Oriental

Orthodox Church adopted the '***Miaphysite***' position and held that **"*In one Person, Jesus Christ, Divinity and Humanity are united in one nature (physis); united without separation, without confusion and without alteration*."**

The Oriental Orthodox Church today include: ***the Syriac Orthodox, Coptic Orthodox, Ethiopian Orthodox, Eritrean Orthodox, Malankara Orthodox Syrian Church (India) and the Armenian Apostolic Churches***.

These churches, though in communion, have independent clerical hierarchy.

Chapter 7

The Church during the Dark Ages—(c500-1100 AD)

The fall of Rome and the Western Roman Empire [1, 2, 3]

In 410 AD, *Alaric*, the Visigoth sacked the city of Rome. The Capital of the western Roman Empire was moved to *Ravenna* and the western empire remained, though bombarded on many fronts, until *Odoacer*, another Visigoth deposed the last western Roman Emperor, *Romulus Augustulus* in 476 AD.

Many reasons have been adduced for the fall of Rome including the size of the empire, moral decadence and the adoption of Christianity by the empire.

While pagans blamed the neglect of the Roman gods with the adoption of Christianity for the fall, others who blamed Christianity said that, as Christian values became the norm, the empire depended more on mercenaries to fight wars and that some of these very mercenaries later attacked and destroyed the empire.

However, Christianity could not be blamed for the fall of the western half of the empire because the equally Christian eastern half survived for about a thousand years after the fall of the west.

The western empire fragmented into smaller kingdoms engaged in constant wars for supremacy. The political instability with its attendant infrastructural decay resulted in economic, social, cultural and spiritual decline. This ushered in what some historians have dubbed the *'Dark Ages'*.

Other effects of the fall of Rome include:
a) The bishop of Rome became more prominent politically and spiritually in the absence of an emperor and the exodus of the prominent political elites to the eastern half of the empire. The bishop stayed and earned the respect of the barbarian invaders who were predominantly Arian Christians.

b) Some of the barbarians were converted to Roman Catholicism from Arianism. ***Clovis***, the king of the Frankish tribes was the first, together with his whole regimen followed by the whole tribe. The authenticity of such mass conversions has been questioned and thought to be more political than spiritual.
c) The growth of monasticism. Increased worldliness in the church led those willing to lead a holy life to embrace monasticism.

Monasticism [4]

Monasticism is a mode of living characterized by withdrawing from the society by religious people. It is practiced by many religions including Buddhism, Judaism and Christianity.

In the Bible, the Nazirites were examples of people who took vows to dedicate themselves to God for a period of time or for life. They do not shave their heads and refrained from drinking wine or any strong drink; a biblical example was Samson. Biblical characters like Elijah and John the Baptists were ascetic in lifestyle but were not eccentric like the hermits of the early Church nor did they reject society, on the contrary, they were fully engaged in what was going on in the society; they confronted evil head on and tried to make the leaders accountable

Monastics—(monks and nuns)—renounce the pursuit of anything considered worldly with the goal of serving and loving God without distractions. Therefore Christian monastics take the oaths of poverty, chastity and obedience.

St. Anthony (251—356 AD) [5, 6]

Although Christian hermits existed before **St. Anthony,** organized Christian Monasticism was said to have begun with him. Born into a wealthy family in Egypt, he felt led to give his fortune to the poor and embrace the monastic life circa 270 AD.

He withdrew from society to live in a tomb where he lived in strict asceticism, tormented by demons with memories of his wealth, filial affections, impure thoughts and with lust. His struggles with demons was said to have been so intense and vivid that he was once severely beaten by the demons but eventually allegedly received help from Jesus Christ.

He left the tomb and went into the desert of Egypt where he lived in solitude as a hermit for twenty years. At the end of his years of solitude, he was said to have been "initiated into the mysteries and filled with the Holy Spirit" such that he was able to heal illnesses and exorcise demons.

Soon, others joined him, each in his own cave and he taught them from his own experience how to resist demons. He encouraged his followers to use the sign of the Cross to ward off demons and prevent demonic attacks.

St. Anthony deplored the practice of not burying martyrs and the veneration of their bones; he considered such practices unholy and unlawful and admonished the bishops to stop such among the people. To prevent his own grave from being made a shrine and his bones from being made objects of veneration, he instructed two trusted aides to bury him without disclosing the location.

He died at about the age of 105 years circa 356 AD. He is regarded as the "Father of Christian Monasticism"; especially the *eremitical* or hermit type of monasticism.

St. Pachomius (290-346 AD) [7]

St. Pachomius was a younger contemporary of St. Anthony and is regarded as the founder of the **coenobitical** type of monasticism.

He started out as a hermit but allegedly received the vision to build a monastery where the monks and nuns lived communally. He organized the members of each commune into groups according to their vocations such that they were involved in labors for the benefit of all and he wrote rules regulating life within the monasteries. However, each individual was free to choose his or her level of austerity. By the time he died in 346 AD, he had built nine monasteries for men and two for women.

St. Basil the Great (c330-379) [8] and St. Benedict (c480-543) [9]

St. Basil the Great and St. Benedict modified the Pachomian monastic system by expanding and refining the rules of association. For instance, dinner time was made common as well as work and prayer time. The degree of asceticism was also determined by the superior and not left to the individual as was the case in Pachomius monasteries.

Through St. Basil and St. Benedict, monasticism then spread to the east and west respectively.

Prior to the time of the Emperor Constantine, many embraced monasticism to escape the heathenism around them that had permeated the whole fabric of the society. After Christianity became the popular religion and nominalism became the order of the day, morality among Christians declined and many more were also driven to embrace the monastic life.

Simeon Stylites (c. 390-459) [10, 11]

St. Simeon Stylite was a hermit who lived atop a pillar for thirty-seven years come rain or shine, refused to take a bath or take care of his body. He joined a monastery as a young teenager but was asked to withdraw because of his extreme asceticism. He reportedly lived in a dry well for some time before adopting the pillar in order to escape from the throng of people seeking his advice. It is said that he eats only once in seven days and would fast through the lent. He also practiced other forms of flagellations like standing for hours or other body contortions.

He became famous and attracted pilgrims and disciples to whom he delivered sermons and teachings from atop his pillar. It was said that Emperor Theodosius II and his empress consulted him and that he wrote to Emperor Leo of the Eastern Empire in support of the Council of Chalcedon.

He developed an ulcer on his thigh which he felt was inflicted by Satan for briefly indulging in self-righteousness and died in 459. He is venerated as a saint in many Church traditions including the Eastern Orthodox, the Coptic Orthodox, the Eastern Catholic and the Roman Catholic. He inspired generations of Stylites monks many of whom were also venerated as saints.

Extreme asceticism in form of prolonged fasts and other practices designed to subjugate the body were common among the earlier hermits. Some like **St. Macarius of Alexandria and St. Eusebius** lived in caves and dry wells and carried loads around while others lived in tombs chained themselves in fetters, neglected body hygiene, and engaged in various forms of flagellations. These hermits were under the misguided notion that their souls were better served the worse their bodies were treated.

However, these practices among the early monks are questionable and tended more towards eccentricity than holiness. Nevertheless, many of them attracted pilgrims and disciples as they were held in high regard as "holy men".

COMMENT:
The idea of holiness through the infliction of bodily pain or neglect of bodily hygiene is unscriptural. Holiness is part of the package of the gift of Salvation.

When believers trust Christ as Lord and Savior, their sins are forgiven and they become new. Believers avoid future sins as they live in obedience to the Word of Truth by the power of the Holy Spirit and are thereby sanctified—***John 17:17-19***. ***No amount of pain inflicted on the body can wash away sin;*** only the Blood of Jesus Christ can wash away sins and purify the hearts of sinners. Sanctification is also received by faith and manifest as believers live in obedience. Neither is the Holy Spirit obtained by years of isolation or asceticism but by faith in Jesus Christ and obedience—***Acts 2:38-39; Acts 5:32.***

Believers are renewed day by day as they submit to the transformation by the Holy Spirit. True, Jesus said believers are not of the world, but he prayed that the father would keep them from the evil one and not that they be taken out of the world—***John 17: 14—16.***

It is also true that the Bible enjoins believers to "come out and be separate"—***2Corinthians 6:17***, but the separation called for is more of spiritual rather than physical because for Christians to make disciples of all nations as commanded by Jesus Christ they must of necessity live in the world but at the same time not be of it. Jesus said though believers are not of the world, they remain in the world of necessity; He therefore prayed the Father to protect them from the evil one—***John 17:14-15.***

In any case, the lives of many now regarded as saints, who lived both as hermits or coenobitical monks revealed that though they retreated physically from the world, they could not retreat from sin, the demon(s) within or from Satan as many were tormented by evil and lustful thoughts. There were also many stories of envies, jealousies, strife etc within the monasteries. For example, some disgruntled monks in one monastery tried unsuccessfully to poison St. Benedict. In addition, many of the Monastic Orders founded relapsed into the worldliness and the decay which informed their formation sooner or later; in fact the very things they hoped to escape tend to become obsessions for them.

Christians are called to be transformed by the renewal of the mind—***Romans 12:2;*** this transformation is from the inside out as they submit to the teaching and guidance of the Holy Spirit and live in obedience.

The Apostle Paul addressed the futility of extreme asceticism in restraining concupiscence when he said: ***"Such regulations (don't touch, don't handle, don't taste) indeed have an appearance of wisdom, with their self-imposed worship, their false humility and their harsh treatment of the body, but they lack any value in restraining sensual indulgence"—Colossians 2:23 (20-23) NIV.***

How can a hermit grow in love or patience? How can someone living in isolation and silence learn how to truly control his tongue? Can virtues be mastered by the avoidance of real choices between good and evil? Such mastery can only be apparent rather than real. Therefore the very basis of withdrawing from the world for the purpose of loving God or living a holy life is questionable.

The Church—State Alliances

With the fall of the Western Roman Empire, the people of the fragmented old empire were ravaged by cycles of wars and plagued by epidemics of diseases.

The people were therefore impoverished and ignorance and superstitions were pervasive.

Christianity retreated to the monasteries which became the centers of learning and religious activities. The Church hierarchy turned to the strongest warlords for protection but these alliances were to be sources of controversies and problems later on.

Clovis (466-511 AD.) [12, 13]

In 496, Clovis, king of the Frankish tribes, influenced by his Roman Catholic wife, converted to Roman Catholicism together with about three thousands of his army and he became the founder of the **Merovingian dynasty**.

He was an ally of the Catholic bishops of Gaul and convoked the first ***Council of Orleans*** in 511 AD which came up with canons that were applicable to both Franks (the conquerors) and the Romans (the conquered) thus establishing equality; an uncommon phenomenon during the time.

Some of the decrees revealed the cooperation between the Church and the State; for instance, no free man could be ordained into the priesthood without the consent of the king and the authorization of a judge. Subsequent Councils of Orleans also included the approval of the king in the election of bishops. Other decrees placed the care of the sick and the poor under the jurisdiction of the bishop and the practice of divination was forbidden.

Charles the Hammer (688-741 AD.) [14]

While Christianity largely retreated into the monasteries, Islam, which started around 600 AD, was advancing rapidly. Within a century, it had swept through Arabia, North Africa and crossed into Portugal and Spain through the Strait of Gibraltar.

By 732 AD, the Moslems, led by Abdul-Rahman invaded France but they were effectively repelled by Charles Martel (Charles the Hammer), a brilliant Frankish General and adroit political leader, at the "Battle of Poitiers".

The decisive victory of Charles Martel over the Moslem Jihadists was considered an historical landmark in stopping the march of Islam into Europe.

By the time of Charles Martel's death in 741 AD, the Merovingian dynasty had become weak and ineffective, therefore effective rule of the State was being carried out by the sons of Charles Martel, Pepin the Short and his older brother.

Pepin the Short [15] **(714—768 AD).**
After some time, the older brother gave the whole realm to Pepin and embraced the monastic life. Pepin then deposed the last king of the Merovingian dynasty **Childeric III** and, with the blessing of the pope and the local Bishop was declared the king, thus beginning the **Carolingian dynasty**.

The pope's territory was being threatened by the Lombards and therefore the papacy needed the protection which at the time, the Merovingian crown could not give; therefore the Church turned to the military and accepted Pepin as the king. It was therefore expediency that instructed the shift of allegiance of the papacy from the legitimate, albeit ineffective king to a very powerful military strategist. The new alliance was mutually beneficial as the blessing of the Church on what otherwise would have been treason, legitimized the usurper.

Pepin attacked the Lombards and conquered them in 755 AD; he strengthened the Church-State alliance by donating the Lombard lands that he conquered to the papacy. This *"**Pepin Donation**"* became the Papal States which, for the first time extended the papal temporal rule beyond the traditional diocese of Rome.

Charlemagne (742-814 AD) and the Holy Roman Empire [16, 17, 18, 19]
Pepin died in 768 AD and his kingdom passed on to his two sons Charlemagne and Carloman II. The younger brother, Carloman II died in 771 AD and Charlemagne became the sole ruler of the realm. He fought the Lombards who were trying to retake the Papal States donated to the Church by his father and re-confirmed the 'Donation of Pepin'. He became the "protector of the Church" and he waged wars *"**by the sword and the Cross**"* and forced those conquered to convert to Christianity or be killed.

In 799 AD, the *Pope, Leo III* **(795-816 AD)**, was harassed by the Roman nobility who accused him of corruption and he sought out Charlemagne for help to put down the rebellion.

In 800 AD, on Christmas day, while kneeling to pray, Charlemagne was crowned the "**Emperor of the Holy Roman Empire**" by Pope Leo III. This was considered a deft political move by the Pope because it:

(1) Secured a strong ally for the papacy against its enemies
(2) Freed the papacy from the Byzantine Empire which hitherto could not be relied on to protect the papacy and
(3) Ensured increased political power for the papacy as the king maker.

By this action, the amalgamation of politics and the Roman Catholic Church, the main bastion of Christianity in the West, became complete.

Charlemagne combated illiteracy in his realm by building schools for the children of all classes of people. He himself committed to learning as an adult and had a school in the palace for his family.

He made laws that incorporated Christian values and waged war on paganism, banning divinations and soothsaying.

He was not always in lock-step with the papacy over ecclesiastical issues and at the Council of Frankfort in 794 AD, took a different position from that of the papacy on the Iconoclastic Controversy. The *Council of Frankfort (794 AD)* [20] condemned the canon of the *Second Council of Niceae (787 AD)* [21] that sanctioned the veneration of images though the Pope supported it but concurred with the Pope in condemning the Adoptionist heresy.

Charlemagne divided the empire between his three sons but two of them died before him and he crowned his son, Louis the Pious as the next Emperor before his death in 814.

Louis the pious (778-840 AD) [22]

Louis the pious was very religious and tried to reform the Frankish church.

He had priests among his chief advisers and strove to improve morality and spirituality among the clergy by making adherence to the Benedictine Rules mandatory in the monasteries.

Initially, he divided the kingdom between his three sons; but after a fourth child was born to him by his second wife, an attempt to give an inheritance to the youngest by taking from the others resulted in civil wars with the older children and even grandchildren. The civil wars continued after his death in 840.

As the Carolingian empire fragmented between the descendants of Charlemagne, it became weaker and suffered invasions from the Vikings, the Magyars and the Moslems.

In 881, **"Charles the Fat"** [23] was crowned the emperor by Pope John VIII. In 884, he inherited the whole empire but he was deposed in 887 and died in 888, bringing to an end the Carolingian dynasty.

Papal Decline and Recovery 900-1122 AD

The union of church and state, which ostensibly increased the power of the papacy over the monarchy instead created frictions between the imperial and the ecclesiastical powers. While the monarchy frequently interfered in ecclesiastical issues, the papacy also frequently got embroiled in intrigues of imperial succession.

However, both sides largely got the expected benefits, the monarchy got the aura of divine legitimacy and therefore due regard among the people and the papacy enjoyed the protection from many marauding forces.

The period following the demise of the Carolingian dynasty was one of the darkest in the history of the papacy. Sometimes the hapless popes were compelled by the emperors to take part in downright atrocious acts. Such was the case of **Pope Stephen VI (VII)** [24] **(896-897AD),** who was reportedly compelled by Emperor Lambert and his mother to convoke a synod which conducted a post-mortem trial of **Pope Formosus**[25] **(891-896 AD)**. The dead Pope's body was exhumed and seated on a throne with papal vestments and had charges read against him with a deacon designated to answer for him. All his orders were invalidated and his measures and acts nullified. Furthermore, the three fingers used by the dead pope in consecrations were amputated from his right hand; the papal vestments were torn off him and his body thrown into the river Tiber. Pope Stephen forced many of the clergy consecrated by Formosus to resign. He was himself killed by strangulation.

The decisions of Pope Stephen VI were reversed by **Pope John IX (898-900 AD)** [26] and in an effort to stem the tide of partisan violence in Rome decreed that no Pope be consecrated in the absence of the imperial envoys.

Sometimes, the spiritual and temporal authorities were concentrated in a single individual. Such was the case of **Pope John XII** [27] (955-964 AD). His Father, the absolute ruler of Rome, obtained the consent of the Roman nobles by oath to have his only son elected as pope. Pope cum Roman ruler John was said to be spiritually and morally bankrupt. When the Papal States were captured, he appealed to the German King, Otto I.

Otto 1 (962—973 AD) [28]

The German king, Otto 1 was a Saxon and had subdued all oppositions in Germany, including that of the Franks, Saxon's rivals, and of his half brother and son.

He married Adelaide, the widow of the Italian king who bore him his successor, Otto II.

Pope John XII crowned Otto I the Holy Roman Emperor in 962 AD and became officially **'the protector'** of the papacy. In addition, the Emperor signed a treaty—the ***'Privilegium Ottonianum'*** on the Romans which gave the Emperor and his successors, power to ratify papal elections. As soon as the emperor marched out of Rome, Pope John XII started colluding with the emperor's enemies and was subsequently deposed, accused of simony, adultery, perjury and murder.

A layman was elected as the next pope without due process and took the title **Leo VIII (963-964)**[29]. When Pope John XII died, the Roman nobility elected **Benedict V (964 AD)** but this was overturned by the emperor who re-instated Leo VIII and upon the death of the latter, appointed Pope John XIII (965-972AD).

Otto I reached across political and ecclesiastical divide to secure the marriage of the Byzantine princess Theophanos, the daughter of ***Emperor Nicephorus II Phocus***, to his son Otto II. However, the ecclesiastical reunification of the east and the west hoped for by the alliance did not materialize.

Otto II (973-983 AD) [30]

Otto II was crowned as co-emperor with his father by Pope John XIII in 967 AD and as substantive emperor in 973 AD. He fought the Moslems in southern Italy and appointed Pope John XIV (983-984 AD). He died in 984 AD of Malaria and was buried at St. Peter's in Rome.

Otto III (996-1002 AD) [31]

Otto III was born in 980 AD and was crowned the successor to his father at the age of three years by Pope John XIV.

When his father died in 983 AD, his mother served as the regent until he reached majority and was crowned the substantive emperor in 996 AD by Pope **Gregory V (996-999 AD),** his cousin, whom he personally appointed. A Roman patrician revolted against the appointment of Gregory V and appointed an antipope **John XVI in 997 AD**.

However, the Emperor re-instated his choice and quelled the revolt in 998 AD. When Pope Gregory V died in 999 AD, he appointed **Sylvester II (999-1003 AD),** his former tutor, as the next Pope. He was very religious and ascetic; and dreamt of an ecclesiastic empire. He stayed in Rome after quelling the revolt of 998 AD hoping to make Rome the seat of his government.

However, the Romans revolted in 1001 AD and he was forced out. He was planning an attack on Rome when he died in 1002 AD.

This was the state of the Church in relation to the State at the end of the Dark Ages in the west. The Church and the State had become so intertwined that the former was becoming an appendage of the State.

The spiritual decline, which was becoming noticeable from the nominalism that followed the conversion of the Emperor Constantine, progressively got worse as evidenced by the commentaries of the people of the period and historians:

Pope Gregory 1 (The Great 590-604) [32] **on the Priests and the People**

> *"For the most part, the priest who ought to give of their own, seize the property of others . . . Consider then what will become of the flock, when the shepherds become wolves".*

> *". . . Both priests and people run riot in wickedness, and when they were in any way prevailed with to come to themselves so far as to confess their fault, yet would they not submit to be censured for them nor appear in a posture becoming penitents".*

St. Eligius Bishop of Noyon (c. 590-660) [33] —Concept of a Good Christian

Eligius was a honest goldsmith whose honesty at handling works commissioned by Clotaire II, king of the Franks earned him a place as counselor in the court of the king's successor, King Dagobert. He used his position to help the poor and so when a bishopric opened up, he was appointed bishop by consensus of both the clergy and the laity.

This is, unfortunately a 7th century concept of a good Christian according to Bishop Eligius:

> *"He is a good Christian who goes frequently to church, and makes his oblations at God's altar; who never tastes of his own fruits till he has presented some to God; who for many days before the festival observes strict chastity though married, that he may approach the altar with a safe conscience. Lastly, who can recite the creed and the Lord's prayer".*

St. Boniface, the Archbishop of Mainz (c.680-c.755) on Women Pilgrims [34]

St. Boniface was the first archbishop of Mainz, and an apostle to the German people in the 8th century and is credited with forging the alliance between the papacy and the Carolingian dynasty.

In a letter to **Cuthbert, the Archbishop of Canterbury** around 747, St. Boniface wrote:

> *"Finally, I will not conceal from your Grace that all the servants of God here who are especially versed in Scripture and strong in the fear of God agree that it would be well and favorable for the honor and purity of your church, and provide a certain shield against vice, if your synod and your princes would forbid matrons and veiled women to make these frequent journeys back and forth to Rome. A great part of them perish and few keep their virtue. There are very few towns in Lombardy and Frankland or Gaul where there is not a courtesan or harlot of English stock. It is a scandal and a disgrace to your whole church".*

"It said also that the vice of drunkenness is far too common in your parishes and that some bishops not only do not prohibit it but themselves drink to the point of intoxication, and by offering large drinks to others force them into drunkenness . . ."

St. Boniface (c.680-c.755) [35] to King Aethelbald of Mercia

"But with these good tidings, one grave accusation against your otherwise good conduct, and one which we would prefer to think was false, has reached our hearing and caused us sorrow. We have learnt from several sources that you have never taken a lawful wife . . . . But have been driven by lust unto the sins of fornication and adultery and have lost your good name before God and men . . . And what is worse, those who told us add that you have committed these sins, to your greater shame, in various monasteries with holy nuns and virgins vowed to God . . . It should be noted that in this crime, another much greater crime is involved because when these harlots, whether nuns or not bring forth their children conceived in sin, they generally kill them . . ."

Emperor Charlemagne's Capitulary of 802 on Monks [36]

*"They shall in every way avoid earthly pursuit of gain, or desire for worldly things. For avarice and concupiscence are to be avoided by all Christians in this world, but chiefly by those who have renounced the world and its desires . . . Let them altogether avoid drunkenness and feasting; for it is known to all that chiefly through them, one comes to be polluted by lust. For the very pernicious rumor has come to our ears that many in the monasteries have been taken **in** fornication, in abomination and uncleanness. And most of all it saddens and disturbs us that . . . . the evil has arisen that some of the monks are found to be sodomites".*

Emperor Charlemagne's Capitulary of 811 on Clerical Avarice [37]

"We see some of them day by day, by all sorts of means, to augment their possessions; now making use for this purpose, of menaces of eternal flames, now of promises of eternal beatitude; despoiling simple minded people of their property in the Name of God or some saint, to the prejudice of their lawful heirs".

Laerius a Carthusian priest—cited by Archbishop Usher (9th Century) [38, 39]

"O worst of times! In which holy men failed and truth was rendered scarce by the sons of men . . . About this time, charity waxed very cold in every class of men, and iniquity began unusually to abound . . . Ambition and avarice and other vices, loosening the reins, persecuted the Christian faith".

Hervey [38, 39] —the Archbishop of Rheims on the People and the Bishops in the 10th Century

Archbishop Hervey lived at a time turbulent time in the history of the Church when barbarians were devastating monasteries and rendering priests, monks and nuns vagabonds. In addition rogue nobles were also encroaching on ecclesiastical properties. The whole society was degenerating into near anarchy; so he wrote in 909:

"As the first men lived without law and without fear, giving up to their passions; so every one now does as he pleases, despising all laws human and divine, and the direction of the bishops. The powerful oppress the weak; wreak violence against the poor and the plunder of ecclesiastical possessions are universal. And it may not be imagined that we spare ourselves, we who ought to correct others, we indeed have the name, but we do not fulfill the duties of bishops. We neglect preaching; we see those who are committed to our care abandon God and fall into sin, without addressing them and stretching forth our hands

and if we wish to reprove them, they say as in the gospel, that we bind on them heavy burdens and we will not ourselves touch them with the end of our fingers".

"It has happened through our negligence, our ignorance . . . that there are found in the Church, an innumerable multitude of people of every sex and condition, who arrive at old age without ever being instructed in the faith, so that they are ignorant even of the words of the creed and the Lord's Prayer".

Cardinal Baronius (1538-1607) about the 10th Century Church [38, 39]

Cardinal Caesar Baronius was an Italian priest and ecclesiastical historian. He had this to say about the Church in the 10th century:

"What was then the face of the Holy Roman Church? How exceedingly foul was it? When powerful and abandoned women ruled at Rome; at whose will the Sees were changed, bishops presented and what is horrid to speak of, false pontiffs, their lovers, intruded into Peter's chair! Thus lust, relying on the secular power and mad with rage of dominion claimed everything for itself. Then as it seems, 'Christ evidently was indeed asleep in the ship' . . ."

Ludovico Antonio Muratori (1672-1750) [38, 39] on Bishops, Abbots and Popes in the 10th Century:

Muratori, a renowned Italian Roman Catholic priest, scholar and historian said:

"What unheard of monsters filled not only the chairs of bishops and abbots, but that of St. Peter also. Everywhere might be seen the profligate morals of the clergy and monks and not a few of the rulers of the Church were more worthy of the appellation of wolves than pastors".

St. Bruno, Bishop of Segni (1048-1123) [39] **—About Priests and Bishops**
St. Bruno was priest, historian and reformer of the Church of his time who said:

> *"The whole world was placed in wickedness, sanctity had failed, justice had perished and truth lay buried. Iniquity was king, avarice was Lord, Simon Magnus held the Church, bishops and priests were given over to pleasure and fornication. Priests . . . contract nefarious marriages and endowed with laws those with whom according to the laws, they should not live in the same house . . . but what is even worse than all this, hardly anyone was found who either was not a simoniac himself or had not been ordained by simoniacs . . ."*

Chapter 8

The Byzantine Empire and the Greek Orthodox Church—(450-1055 AD)

The Byzantine Empire [1,2]
The eastern half of the Roman Empire survived the onslaught of invaders of the fifth and sixth centuries that ravaged the western half and continued as what is commonly called the ***Byzantine Empire***.

Initially, the eastern emperors tried to regain the west and re-unify the empire.

Emperor Justinian (483-565) [3]
Notable among these was the ***Emperor Justinian*** who succeeded in regaining North Africa and Italy but had to abandon the campaign when an epidemic devastated his empire and precipitated economic constraints.

The eastern half of the empire was rife in what the Roman Catholic Church considered heresies and internal tensions often arose in the empire when the emperor tried to enforce his point of view. Justinian and his predecessor, his uncle, ***Justin*** were ***Monophysites,*** but in order to secure the help of the papacy in recovering Italy, he renounced Monophysitism and in fact persecuted those who subscribed to the doctrine as well as pagans and Jews. This had an unfavorable long term effect because when Moslems invaded North Africa, the persecuted Christians cooperated with the conquerors who promised to tolerate them.

Justinian's other achievements include the compilation and codification of the Roman laws with incorporation of Christian values into the civil laws—***The Codex Justinianus.***

He was also credited with the founding of the Byzantine architecture with the construction of the ***Haggia Sophia*** in Constantinople and the ***San Vitale*** in Ravenna, Italy.

Justinian's dream of restoring the old Roman Empire through re-conquest did not materialize as it was difficult to hold the regained territories and parts of Italy were lost to invading Lombards within three years after Justinian's demise.

The empire was constantly assaulted from the west by the Slavs, Huns and Mongolians, from the east by the Persians and later from the south by the Moslems.

The Emperor Heraclius I (610-641 AD) [4]

Emperor Heraclius signed a peace treaty with the Slavs and allowed them to settle in the Balkans while he focused his effort on defeating the Persians, a goal that he achieved in 627 AD.

However, as this was being accomplished, a new enemy, Islam, was emerging from the south and the defeat of the Persians was somewhat a pyrrhic victory as the weakening of the Persians removed a formidable buffer between Byzantium and the emerging Arab forces of Islam.

Within the empire, there was a resurgence of the Monophysite controversy when the largely Monophysite North Africa and Syria were recovered from the Persians. His effort to unify the empire by subscribing to the compromise of ***"Monothelitism" (the Christological doctrine that held that Jesus had two natures but one will which is divine)*** proposed by the Patriarch of Constantinople was opposed by both the Chalcedonians and Monophysites. This internal strain was considered a factor in the conquest of Syria and Jerusalem by Moslems in 637 AD.

Heraclius Hellenized the empire by making Greek rather than Latin the official language so that with time, the empire diverged from its Latin roots and evolved into a distinct culture. He died in 641 AD.

Leo III (717-741) and **the Iconoclastic Controversy** [1, 2, 5, 6, 7]

The Moslems continued the effort to crush the Byzantine Empire and besieged Constantinople many times but were successfully repelled.

In 718 AD, *Leo III (717-741)* defeated a combined land and sea assault by Moslems on the empire. However, Leo III had to contend with Moslem offensives throughout his reign and the empire was losing territory on all fronts and shrinking.

The emperor felt that the declining fortunes of the empire was a warning from God for them to return to the recognition of the real protector of the realm, Jesus Christ and use only the sign that served Constantine and Heraclius well, the Cross.

Therefore, in 726 AD, Emperor Leo III promulgated an edict banning the *veneration* of religious icons and he had the image of Christ on the gate of the Imperial palace replaced by a cross. The emperor considered the veneration and worship of images as idolatry and fundamentally pagan. It had become the norm for people to kiss, and show reverence/devotion to icons of Jesus Christ, the Virgin Mary, angels and saints or relics supposedly associated with them. In 730 AD, he ordered all images removed from churches and monasteries and destroyed, and he also forbade the use of icons in the military.

The uproar and opposition to the emperor's edict was very great and it precipitated what became known as the *"Iconoclastic Controversy"* which raged on and off till 853 AD. Many of the clergy, the monks and the laity in Byzantine Empire opposed the edict. In the west Popes *Gregory II (715-731 AD)* and his successor *Gregory III (731-741 AD)* both vehemently opposed the edict.

The controversy worsened the relationship between the papacy and the Byzantine emperor which was already strained because of increased taxes on the papacy's area of jurisdiction and the edict was seen as an undue interference in ecclesiastical matters. Gregory III held two synods in 731 AD condemning the emperor's edict. In response, the emperor removed the imperial lands in Italy from the jurisdiction of the papacy and placed them under the Patriarch of Constantinople. This caused a fresh rift between the west and the east.

After the death of Leo III in 741 AD, his son **Constantine V (741-775)** became the emperor and continued the iconoclastic policy. He convened the **Council of Hieria**[8] in 754 AD where icon veneration and worship were condemned as idolatry. The controversy waned somewhat thereafter. When **Empress Irene** ascended the throne in 780 AD as regent for her son **Constantine VI (780-797)**[9], the first wave of iconoclasm subsided. Eventually, she called the **Second Council of Niceae in 787 AD**, which condemned the Council of Hieria as uncanonical and reversed the decrees. The Council, which used as a major resource the Apologia of **John of Damascus (c.676-754)**[10] on icons was attended by papal legates and was ratified by the Pope.

Perhaps, motivated also by military failures, iconoclasm resurged during the reign of Emperor *Leo V (814-820)*[11] and his next two successors, *Michael II (820-829)*[12] and *Theophilus I (829-842)*[13].

Theodore the Studite (759-826), an Abbot of a monastery in Constantinople and an ardent iconophile, carried out a literary campaign against Emperor Leo V's iconoclasm by writing letters to ***Pope Paschal 1 (817-824),*** the patriarchs of Alexandria and Jerusalem as well as other Abbots. In response, the emperor moved against the monasteries, removed and destroyed relics and icons from them and converted some monasteries to secular use.

Theophilus' heir *Michael III (842-867)*[14] was a minor; therefore his mother ***Theodora,*** was regent from 842 and co-empress till 855 when he reached majority. Theodora, unlike her husband was an iconophile, and she reversed her husband's iconoclast policies, replaced the iconoclast patriarch with an iconophile, restored the monasteries and convoked a Council in 843 AD which restored the 'veneration' but not the 'worship' of icons.

The Issues in the Iconoclast Controversy [15, 16]

(i) Christology

Iconoclasts were of the view that it was impossible to truly depict Jesus Christ as He has both divine and human natures and the divine nature which is incomprehensible cannot be depicted. Depicting his human nature would mean subscribing to Nestorianism while any claim to depict his divine nature would be sacrilegious. On the other hand, iconophiles, championed by ***John of Damascus,*** a monk and chief Administrator to the Moslem Caliph of Damascus, held that the incarnation of Jesus Christ, with God condescending to take on human flesh justified the making of images or icons. He argued that the incarnation meant that God had 'deified matter', affirmed the goodness of material creation and made it a vehicle for obtaining salvation rather than an obstacle.

(ii) Idolatry

Iconoclasts regarded the practice of veneration of icons and relics as the revival of paganism and idolatry inspired by Satan. In support of this position, they cited the second Commandment which forbade the making and worshipping of idols—Exodus 20:4-5.

However, iconophiles insisted that pagan idols were made to represent demons but since their own images or icons were made to represent Jesus

Christ, the Virgin Mary, angels and saints, it was acceptable. John of Damascus said God gave the commandment to the Jews because they were prone to idolatry and infants so to speak, in spiritual matters, but Christians were no longer under the law and were more mature spiritually since God had revealed Himself to them in Christ. In fact he said anyone who opposed the veneration of icons based on the Mosaic Law had fallen from grace and that whoever did not worship images did not worship the Son of God and the living image of the invisible God.

John of Damascus also tried to differentiate icons from idols on the basis of intention. He believed that the 'pious intent' of glorifying God and his saints, the promotion of goodness, avoidance of evil and salvation of souls justified the making and veneration of icons.

(iii) Tradition

Both the iconoclasts and the iconophiles appealed to both biblical and non-biblical traditions to support their positions.

The iconoclasts cited the writings of ***Eusebius of Caesarea (263-340 AD)*** and ***Epiphanius of Cyprus (315-403 AD)***.

John of Damascus and other iconophiles also cited copiously other patristic writings, particularly those of the Cappadocian fathers that supported the use and veneration of icons.

The *second Council of Nicaea—787AD* which reinstated the use of icons and repealed the decisions of the *753 AD Council of Hiereia* actually based its inspiration on itself and tradition and not on any sound theology or Scripture.

(iv) Imperial versus Ecclesiastical Power tussle.

An important undercurrent in the controversy was the perennial power struggle between the secular and the spiritual leaders.

The emperors have been involved in Church affairs since the time of Emperor Constantine I who convened the first Council of Niceae, although he did not obviously determine the outcome. Emperor Constantine V on the other hand convened the Council of Hiereia to put his stamp on a preconceived position.

Another objection from most of the ecclesiacs was that the initiative arose from the secular arm rather than the spiritual and this was vigorously resented as encroachment on ecclesiastical territory. However, it should be noted that the ecclesiacs, who resented imperial imposition of iconoclasm never resented imperial power when needed to enforce doctrines they agreed with. They welcomed the restoration of iconophilism by empresses Irene and Theodora.

(v) Economics

Many monasteries had become affluent from the commerce of icons.

Monasteries produce and display icons which attracted throngs of pilgrims especially to those with stories of miracles attributed to them. It was therefore not surprising that the monks were in the center of the controversy as iconophiles.

(vi) Salvation and Sanctification

John of Damascus said: *"Every image is a revelation and representation of something hidden . . . The image was devised for greater knowledge and for the manifestation and popularizing of secret things, as a pure benefit and help to salvation, so that by showing things and making them known, we may arrive at the hidden ones, desire and emulate what is good, shun and hate what is evil"*. He also said: *"The Holy Spirit, which indwells the saints while alive, continued to abide in their bodies in their tombs and in their likenesses in holy images by grace and divine power and that he worshipped matter, not as God, but as the instrument of salvation"*.

He believed that images allowed the contemplation of the miracles of Jesus and His power and that contemplating the image of Christ produced sanctification.

St. Basil said: *"matter is endued with a divine power through prayer made to those who are depicted in the image". And again ". . . devils have feared the saints and have fled from their shadow (Acts 5:12-16); the shadow is image, and I make an image that I may scare demons"*.

(vii) Judaism, Manichaeism and Islam

Iconophiles charged that iconoclasts were influenced by the Manichaeans' view that matter is evil or the Jewish and Islamic view that forbade image veneration as idolatrous.

(viii) Illiteracy of the Masses

John of Damascus considered the various kinds of images as the books of the illiterate and therefore instruments for education of the unlettered

COMMENT:

In his voluminous and eloquent Apologia, John of Damascus cited many biblical references that he claimed supported the 'worship' of images. For example, the Ark of the Covenant with the two Cherubim, the tabernacle with the decorations and motifs, the bronze serpent that Moses made in the wilderness to heal those bitten by snakes, Joshua's memorial at the crossing of River Jordan and even Solomon's temple. However, his claims that the Israelites 'worshipped' these things were inaccurate. There was nowhere the people were commanded to worship these things and in the case of the bronze serpent, those affected were to look at, but not worship it—*(Numbers 21:4-9)*. Moses kept it as a memorial but it was destroyed by King Hezekiah because some people had given it the name *Nehushtan* and made it an object of worship—*(2Kings 18:3—4)*.

As for the Ark of Covenant with the Cherubim, it was in the Holy of Holies, out of sight of all except the high priest who entered the inner sanctuary only once a year. And no one except the designated Levites could touch the Ark, therefore the question of worshiping it did not arise—***Exodus 25:10-22; 2Samuel 6:1-11; Hebrews 9:6-7)***.

The Cappadocian fathers that John of Damascus quoted copiously, heavily promoted and institutionalized the 'cult of martyrs'. Their teachings regarding the spiritual and physical benefits from the veneration of icons and relics of martyrs were frankly unscriptural. For example, in his homily on the Forty Martyrs, St. Basil said: ***"O sainted band, O sacred fraternity, O invincible army! Protectors of the human race, solace of the troubled, hope of your petitioners, most powerful intercessors, light of the world, bloom both intellectual and material of the churches..."***

This kind of eloquent, exaggerated and frankly erroneous panegyrics arrogated to the martyrs and their relics virtues and powers that border on idolatrous.

The martyrs were called protectors of the human race; but no human being, dead or alive can be the protector of the human race. God alone is the refuge—***Deuteronomy 33:27; Proverbs 18:10; John 17:11, 15; 2Thessalonians 3:3*** and the Scriptures warned against depending on the arm of flesh—***Psalm 146:3-5.***

He called the martyrs the 'hope' of those petitioning them. According to the Scriptures, Jesus Christ is the only sure, steadfast and living hope for mankind that does not disappoint—***Romans 5:5; 1Peter 1:3-5; Hebrews 6:17-20.***

He called them the most powerful intercessors, again this is inaccurate and unscriptural; while human beings can intercede for others when still alive, this function ceases once the person is dead; the Scriptures say: ".... It is appointed for men to die once and after this, the judgment"—***Hebrews 9:27***. And again: "Whatever your hand finds to do, do it with your might; for there is no work, or devise or knowledge or wisdom in the grave where you are going"—***Ecclesiastes 9:10.*** The dead martyrs are not interceding for anyone; according to ***Revelations***

6:9-10, the souls of martyrs are under the altar before the Lord God crying, like the blood of Abel, for vengeance on the dwellers of the earth. It is only the Blood of Jesus Christ that speaks better things than that of Abel, which is forgiveness and reconciliation with God by grace—***Genesis 4:10; Hebrews 12:24***.

The most powerful intercessors for mankind are Jesus Christ and the Holy Spirit—***Romans 8:26-27; Hebrews 7:25***. Besides, Jesus Christ is the *ONLY* mediator between God and man—*1Timothy 2:5-6*.

The whole idea of martyrs, saints, the Virgin Mary and angels as some sort of auxiliary mediators or intermediate deities between God and man or between Jesus Christ and man is contrary to the message of salvation which gave the assurance that through the Blood of Jesus Christ all true believers have access to God the Father and the Throne of Grace.

Significantly, at the crucifixion of Jesus Christ, the veil over the Holy of Hollies was torn and believers are called to approach the Throne of Grace boldly through the Blood of Jesus Christ to obtain help in the time of need—***Hebrews 4:14-16***.

Jesus Himself gave the assurance that whoever believes in Him can ask anything in *HIS NAME* and that the Father and He Himself will do it—***John 14: 12-14; John 16:23-24***. In fact Jesus promised to manifest Himself to all who obey His Commandments and make His home together with the Father with such a person!—***John 14: 21 & 23; Revelations 3:20***.

Venerating icons cannot save or sanctify anyone; salvation is only by the grace of God through faith in Jesus Christ—***Acts 4:12; Ephesians 2:8-10.*** **

The idea of using inanimate objects as 'points of encounter' with dead people; crediting them with revealing 'hidden or secret things' and seeking 'corporeal association' with dead saints through such objects all fit into the definition of idols. Jesus promised that the Holy Spirit will be the revealer of secrets and the teacher for believers—***John 14: 16-17, 26; John 16:13***.

John of Damascus averred that the intent to glorify God, promote goodness and save souls somehow justifies icon and image veneration. This is like saying it is justified to do evil so long as some good may result. The point is that God expressly forbids the making and the worshiping of idols and images and he has made it clear in His Word how He is to be glorified—***Psalm 50:23; Mathew 5:16; John 15:8 and 1Peter 2:12***—giving thanks and praising Him, living right and bearing good fruit.

While he might have had a valid point in the use of images as mediums of instruction in a culture with widespread illiteracy; some have contended that icons as books can be easily misread and it is obvious that he credited icons with much more. John of Damascus himself considered images as replacements for statues of demons and 'instruments of salvation' and made bold to say that anyone who did not worship images could not worship Jesus Christ! This casts serious doubts on the great Apologist's understanding of the Gospel message.

It was reported that the patriarch of Constantinople at the time of Emperor Leo III's edict was more concerned about the implications of the church being wrong for so long rather than with theology, in his communications with iconoclast bishops. He was said to have feared that Christians would _'play into the hands of Jews and Moslems'_ were they to accept that they had been wrong in the veneration of icons.

Furthermore, considering the clarity of the injunction against the making and worshipping of images in the second Commandment, the charge of iconoclasts being influenced by Moslems, Jews or Manicheans was baffling.

In regard to tradition, Canon 36 of the **Council of Elvira (c.306 AD)** was not in support of iconophilism and stated that: ***"Pictures are not to be placed in churches so that they do not become objects of worship and adoration"*** [17].

The Photian Schism [18, 19, 20, 21]

Influenced by Bardas, his uncle, *Michael III* overthrew his mother's regency in 856 AD and made his uncle a Caesar. A disagreement between Patriarch Ignatius and Bardas over the latter's immoral liaison with his daughter-in-law led to the deposition of the Patriarch.

He was replaced by **Photius (c.820—c.893 AD)**, an educated and accomplished bureaucrat who was the chief Secretary of State. A lay man, his ordination and elevation was hurried through the ecclesiastical orders to the Patriarchate within 6 days.

Those loyal to Ignatius protested and appealed to **Pope Nicholas 1 (858—867).** The Emperor requested the Pope to send legates to Constantinople to investigate before ruling in the case. In 861 AD, in the presence of the papal legates, a synod was held which confirmed Photius as canonically appointed and ratified Ignatius' removal.

Pope Nicholas I rejected the decision of the synod and was very angry with his legates so much so that he convened a synod in 863 AD that charged the legates with accepting bribes; they were tried, convicted and were excommunicated. He regarded the appointment of Photius as uncanonical and excommunicated him; insisting that Bishop Ignatius be re-instated.

It has been suggested that there was more to Pope Nicholas I's reaction than purely ecclesiastical because the investiture of lay persons had precedents both in the west and the east. To complicate issues, Ignatius for whom he was rooting was not elected by a synod of bishops as required by the canons either, but he was appointed by the regent Empress Theodora. It is thought that the Pope was piqued more by the refusal of Constantinople to grant his request for the return of the territories of Sicily and Calabria to papal control.

Emperor Michael III demanded that the Pope withdraw the decision against Photius but his request was denied. Therefore, with the blessing of the Emperor, Photius convoked a Council in 867 AD which also excommunicated Pope Nicholas 1, condemned his claim of primacy, his interference in Bulgaria and the addition of the *filioque clause* to the Nicene Creed.

Unfortunately, Emperor Michael III and his Caesar, Bardas were murdered by an army General, Basil who became the Emperor **Basil I (867-886 AD)**. He deposed Photius, exiled him and re-instated Ignatius.

However, Photius regained imperial favor such that he was recalled from exile to teach the Emperor's son, *Leo VI*.

At the death of Ignatius in 877 AD, Photius was once again made the Patriarch of Constantinople. In 879 AD, he convoked a Council, attended again by legates of **Pope John VIII,** which ratified his appointment and voided the canons of the previous council that had ratified his previous deposition and excommunication.

However, the Emperor rejected papal requests, namely—an apology from Photius for previously excommunicating Pope Nicholas 1 and the acceptance of the Latin addition to the Nicene Creed called the *filioque clause.* Photius refused to apologize and not only rejected the *filioque clause,* but anathematized all who subscribed to it, in effect, including the Pope.

The disagreement caused what is called the ***Photian Schism*** which is considered the beginning of the final rift between the Roman Catholic Church and the Greek Orthodox Church.

Leo VI (886-912 AD)

In 886 AD, **Leo VI** succeeded his father, Basil I and forced Patriarch Photius to resign, sent him on exile and replaced him with his brother. Photius died in exile c.893 AD.

Leo VI was regarded as a wise king who was in the habit of moving incognito among his subjects to detect injustice and corruption. He married four times before he got an heir and had four Patriarchs.

A synod was held during the tenure of his second Patriarch, Anthony (893-895 AD), during which the Photian schism was healed.

Although the Roman Catholic Church tends to attribute the beginning of the Eastern Schism to Photius, many now believe that the East-West Schism did not begin nor end with Photius. In fact previous schisms prior to Photius could be identified. There **was the Arian schism (343-398 AD), the schism following the deposition of St. John Chrysostom (404-415 AD), the Acacian schism (484-519 AD), the Monothelite schism (640-681 AD) and the iconoclastic schism (726-843 AD).**

The Great Eastern Schism [21, 22, 23, 24, 25]

The Photian schism healed and the Byzantine Empire regained some of its old glory under Emperors such as *Romanos II (959-963 AD),* the grandson of Leo VI who recaptured the Island of Crete from the Moslems and his older son *Basil II (976-1025 AD).*

Basil II was a ruthless warrior who devoted his life to expanding and securing the empire both by conquest and by diplomatic means. He regained much of Palestine short of Jerusalem from Moslems as well as most of southern Italy and he subdued the Bulgarians and Armenians. He married his sister to Prince Vladimir of Kiev Rus (present day Ukraine) resulting in the whole clan embracing Christianity and getting baptized. He reformed the tax codes to favor the masses to the detriment of the nobility and treated the army well. An ascetic in lifestyle, he left the Empire prosperous and secured but his brother *Constantine VIII (1025-1028 AD)* who succeeded him was old and not a warrior like his older brother.

During the reign of *Constantine IX Monamachus (1042-1055 AD),* the Normans invaded Southern Italy which had been under the jurisdiction of the Patriarch of Constantinople since the period of the Iconoclastic Controversy. *Emperor Henry III (1039-1056),* an ally of the papacy, confirmed *Drogo of Hauteville (1010-1051)* [26], a leader of the Normans as the Duke of Apulia and Calabria. As the Normans settled, they started replacing the Byzantine bishops with Latin bishops and thereby changing the liturgical rites. This development displeased the Byzantine *Patriarch, Michael Caerularius (1043-1058 AD)* who reacted by ordering all the Latin churches in the empire to adopt the Byzantine rites or close down.

In 1054 AD, **Pope Leo IX (1049-1054 AD)** sent a letter to Patriarch Caerularius citing the infamous ***"Donation of Constantine"*** and claimed that the Lateran Palace, the city of Rome and all the cities, provinces and districts of Italy and other parts of the western part of the empire rightly belonged to the papacy. *[The "Donation of Constantine" was a document purporting that Emperor Constantine the Great ceded to Pope Sylvester I (Bishop and Patriarch of Rome) and his successors both the temporal and spiritual authorities of the western half of the empire when he moved the capital to Constantinople].*

Patriarch Caerularius responded by rejecting not only both the claim of Primacy and the 'Donation' but also raised various doctrinal issues on which the east believed the west was in error. These doctrinal issues included—

    (i) The filioque clause,
    (ii) The use of azymic bread for the Eucharist,
    (iii) Celibacy and
    (iv) Fasting on Saturdays.

The Pope sent his legates back to Constantinople but there was no breakthrough in the ensuing negotiations. Eventually, the legates left for Rome but left a letter of excommunication of the Patriarch Caerularius. The Patriarch retaliated by excommunicating the papal delegates and removing the name of the Pope from his diptychs.

Some accounts of the event claimed that he also informed the other eastern Patriarchs and that these sided with Constantinople against Rome by removing the name of the Pope from their diptychs.

This event of 1054 AD is generally agreed to be the cause of the so far irreparable complete split of the Western (Latin) and the Eastern (Greek) Churches. From that time, the Eastern Orthodox and the Roman Catholic Churches have gone their separate ways and attempts to mend fences have generally been unsuccessful.

The Decline of the Byzantine Empire [27, 28]

The Emperor Constantine IX Monomachus took political and military decisions that adversely affected the Byzantine Empire. In purging the government of his predecessor's loyalists, he removed the General in charge of southern Italy and facilitated the region's conquest by the Normans. He annexed Armenia to the empire and then disbanded the Armenian army in 1053 AD. These steps removed Armenia as a buffer between the empire and the Turks and are believed to have set the stage for the Turk's victory over Emperor Romanus IV (1068-1071) at the battle of ***Manzikert in 1071 AD***. This event is regarded by many historians as the beginning of the end of the Byzantine Empire.

Chapter 9

The Church in the Middle Ages (c1000-1500)

By the end of the first millennium, the Church in both the east and the west of the old Roman Empire was intricately involved with the temporal powers. In the west, the warring kings, emperors and Roman nobility installed, deposed, imprisoned and even killed popes at will, sometimes electing laymen of questionable characters as bishops or even popes.

The bishops and even the popes were involved in leading troops to wage wars. While in the east, the Church from the time of Constantine had been viewed more or less as a department of the civil administration with emperors and empresses deposing and appointing Patriarchs with impunity. Sons, relations, friends and cronies were elevated to the Church's highest offices in both the West and the East without regard to ecclesiastical qualifications.

The popes of the Middle Ages tried to break free of imperial dominance with varying degrees of success. The power struggle persisted between successive popes on the one hand and emperors, kings and nobles on the other.

The Roman Catholic Church in the Middle Ages
Emperor **Henry II (1002-1024 AD)** [1,2], the cousin of *Emperor Otto III (983-1002 AD)* succeeded him as he died childless. Henry II became the king of Germany in 1002, king of Italy in 1004 and was crowned the Holy Roman Emperor in 1014 by **Pope Benedict VIII (1012—24 AD)**[3].

Pope Benedict VIII, a layman, was imposed as pope by his powerful father of the Tusculum family. He was opposed by Anti-pope Gregory VI who went into exile when Henry II recognized Benedict VIII. Henry II fostered harmony between the Church and the State and resolutely exercised his right to appoint bishops whom he made secular rulers and endowed with wealth and property. In return the bishops repaid him with their loyalty and support against rivals and rebellious nobles. In cooperation with the Pope, he attempted to effect ecclesiastical reforms. He enforced clerical celibacy to ensure that the public lands he granted the Church did not become the inheritance of the children of the clergy. He died in 1024 AD. Henry II also died childless; hence his death marked the end of the ***Ottonian dynasty***. He was canonized in 1146 by Pope ***Clement II (1046-1047 AD)***. His wife was also canonized in 1200 by Pope ***Innocent III (1198-1216 AD)***.

He was succeeded by his cousin **Conrad II (990-1039 AD)**[4, 5] who became the German king in 1024, king of Italy in 1026 and was crowned the Holy Roman Emperor in 1027 by ***Pope John XIX (1024-1032 AD)*** the brother of Pope Benedict VIII. Conrad's approach to governance differed from that of the Ottonian dynasty; he suppressed the nobility and the ecclesiastics in civil service and promoted the lesser nobles to replace them. He made the lesser nobles hereditary in 1037 by the **"Constitution of Pavia"** and reduced government reliance on the Church. In 1028, he made his eldest son, Henry the co-ruler of Germany. He died in 1039 and was succeeded by his son, **Emperor Henry III (1039-1056 AD)**[6]

Emperor Henry III was crowned the Holy Roman Emperor by Pope Clement II whom he personally appointed in 1046. There were three rival popes in 1046; namely **Benedict IX (1032-1045 AD)** [7, 8] **Sylvester III (1045-1046 AD) and Gregory VI (1045-1046 AD)**.

Benedict IX was a teenager when he became the pope, the position procured for him by his father. He was extremely immoral and irreverent and was characterized as 'feasting on immorality' and charged with turning the Lateran Palace into a brothel.

He was forced out of Rome in 1036 but was reinstated with the help of Emperor Conrad II. In 1044, he was again forced out of Rome and Pope Sylvester III elected pope in 1045 but Benedict fought his way back and ran his rival out of town.

In 1045, Benedict IX sold his office to his godfather who took the title of Gregory VI so that he could marry; however, Benedict changed his mind and returned to reclaim the papal throne. But both Sylvester III and Gregory VI continued to also stake their claim to the papacy resulting in the confusing situation of simultaneous reign of three popes. Therefore, in 1046, Henry III intervened at the **Council of Sutri**; deposed both Benedict IX and Sylvester III and encouraged Gregory VI to resign. The Emperor then appointed Pope Clement II (1046-1047 AD). While Sylvester and

Gregory complied, Benedict rejected the verdict and seized the Lateran palace in 1047 after the death of Clement II but was dislodged in 1048. The Emperor then appointed **Pope Damasus II** whose time in office was less than a month.

After him, Emperor Henry III nominated **Pope Leo IX (1049-1054 AD)** [9] who also sought and obtained canonical election. Pope Leo IX worked hard, traveling widely and holding synods where he pushed for reforms among the clergy especially in regard to simony and clerical incontinence.

In an effort to unify Italy and regain what he believed to be the papacy's patrimony, Pope Leo IX led an army to attack the Normans in the south of Italy; however, his troops were defeated and he was captured and held in *"honorable captivity"*. He negotiated his release and returned to Rome but died soon after in 1054 before the arrival of his delegates from Constantinople.

Another significant event during the time of Pope Leo IX was the formal split of the Byzantine and the Roman Churches known as East-West schism or—The Great Eastern Schism.

He was succeeded by **Pope Victor II (1055-1057 AD).**

By his exercise of temporal power over the Church, Henry III tried to rid it of corruption and materialism so that it can focus on spiritual and humanitarian services. However, judging by the events after his death in 1056, the very opposite of what he wanted happened.

Pope Victor II and his successors became the guardian of Henry's son and heir, **Henry IV.** Pope Stephen X who succeeded Victor II in 1057 died in 1058 and was succeeded by **Pope Nicholas II (1058-1061 AD)** [10, 11] and anti-pope Benedict X, the latter being the candidate of the powerful Roman Count of Tusculum who had been responsible for the election of many popes before. Nicholas II prevailed in the ensuing power struggle between the two factions and forced Benedict X to renounce his claim to the papal throne, thus ending the Tusculan papacy.

Pope Nicholas II convoked a synod in 1059 aimed at reforming the process of papal elections with a view to ending papal subservience to the emperors and the nobles. At the synod, it was decreed that:

a) The election of popes should be by a conclave of Cardinals
b) Selection of candidates should be from the Roman clergy except when a qualified candidate could not be found.

c) The privilege of confirmation of the elected pope was conceded to Emperor Henry IV and his successors.
d) The synod also prohibited:
- Simoniacal ordinations
- Lay investitures
- Assistance at mass of a priest living in notorious concubinage.

Pope Nicholas II, acting on the spurious *'Donation of Constantine'* document entered into an alliance with the Normans in southern Italy and gave the duchies of Apulia, Calabria and Sicily normally under the Byzantine Empire to the Norman leader **Robert Guiscard (1016-1085)** who was sworn under oath to protect the papacy. Pope Nicholas II died in 1061 and was succeeded by **Pope Alexander II (1061-1073 AD)** [12] and antipope Honorius II who was the candidate of the Roman nobility and the German bishops.

Pope Alexander, the candidate of the reformers within the Church prevailed in the power struggle that ensued and he deposed and excommunicated his rival.

As a consequence of the intrigues, the Empress Regent of Germany was sent to a Convent and the regency of the child king, Henry IV given to another person sympathetic with the papacy.

By this time, the German king was still a child and politically of no use to the papacy. Pope Alexander carried on with the reforms of Pope Nicholas II. He died in 1073 and was succeeded by **Pope Gregory VII (1073-1085 AD)** [13] who had been an insider with the reformist movement in the papacy since the time of Stephen X.

In 1065, **Henry IV (1056-1106 AD)** [14] reached majority and he assumed his civil duties as the German king, but a lot of grounds had been lost to papal reforms while he was growing up and he was politically weakened. The sweeping reform of Pope Gregory VII further threatened the young King's authority and eventually led to a clash of the temporal with the ecclesiastical powers.

The Investiture Controversy [15, 16, 17, 18, 19]

Elected under Pope Nicholas' guidelines, Pope Gregory VII continued with the effort to purify the Church beginning with the clergy. At the Lenten synod in 1074, the following decrees were enacted:
- Simoniacal clerics were to cease to minister in the Church

- Simony should cease forthwith
- Incontinent clerics should cease to minister
- People should reject the ministration of clerics who disobey the injunctions.

These measures were violently opposed in Germany, Italy and France because the majority of the clerics were guilty. They rejected celibacy, citing Scriptures that said celibacy was only for those who chose to be or were so gifted by God and that the Apostle Paul advised that it was "better to marry than to burn"—*Mathew 19:10-12; 1Corinthians 7:2, 7-9.*

At the **Council of Paris in 1074**, Gregory's decrees were condemned and he was accused of implying that *"the validity of the sacraments depended on the sanctity of the minister"* contrary to the Roman Catholic dogma. *(Augustine had established the Church's position that "The validity of sacraments were independent of the holiness of the clergy" and that "a clergy in mortal sin could convect valid sacraments").*

Therefore, Gregory's measures were declared intolerable and irrational. The papal legates sent to enforce the canon were physically assaulted and some nearly lost their lives.

In addition, at the Lenten synod in 1075, Pope Gregory prohibited all lay persons from selecting a successor after the death a bishop. This canon, which in effect prohibited the emperor from investiture of bishops in the realm, stripped him of military and economic powers because, for more than a century, bishops had been princes of the empire and they were influential officials in the districts who control lands and troops.

Considering the implications, it was inconceivable that the emperor would abide by the papal prohibition so he ignored it and continued to appoint bishops. Pope Gregory excommunicated members of the imperial court and threatened to also excommunicate the King.

At the **'Diet of Worms'** in January 1076, Henry IV had Pope Gregory VII deposed by his faction of bishops. Pope Gregory responded by deposing and excommunicating the emperor at the Lenten Synod in 1076 and also released all Christians in the realm from their oath of allegiance to the emperor. The emperor's domestic enemies allied with the pope and the people deserted him. This marked an apogee in the power tussle between the spiritual and secular authorities and precipitated what has been dubbed **'The Investiture Controversy'**. The emperor was obliged to apologize to the pope and observe penance and consequently, his excommunication was lifted.

For the moment, it appeared that the papacy had won and cast off the yoke of imperialism but the controversy continued to rage on for centuries.

The papal faction among the Germans ignored the reconciliation and elected a new king in 1077 and a civil war broke out.

As Henry IV gained the upper hand, he demanded that Pope Gregory excommunicate his challenger but instead the pope re-excommunicated and deposed Henry IV in 1080. By this time, most of the bishops were on the king's side and at the ***Synod of Brixen,*** deposed the pope and elected an ***antipope,*** **Clement III** (1080-1100).

Henry IV was crowned the King of Italy and Emperor by antipope Clement III in 1084. Gregory VII was declared deposed and exiled to Salerno where he died in 1085.

On both sides of the controversy were people with apparently irreconcilable convictions. *The papal supporters held" that unconditional obedience to the pope was imperative and even when <u>unjust</u>, his excommunication was valid"!* On the other hand, the imperial advocates contended that *"the emperor was above responsibility for his actions as he was God's representative on earth, not answerable to the pope but only to God".*

The power struggle continued with the successors of Gregory VII, ***Victor III (1086-1087), Urban II (1088-1099)*** **and** ***Paschal II (1099-1118)***.

Pope Urban II encouraged Conrad, Henry IV's heir to rebel against his father and was crowned the king of the Romans in 1093; and he also turned his wife against him. Later, Pope Paschal II also succeeded in instigating the emperor's younger son ***Henry V (1106-1125)*** against him. He was forced to abdicate in 1104. In 1106, loyalists of Henry IV put together an alliance which defeated that of Henry V but the Emperor died soon after at the age of fifty-six years.

Nevertheless, the investiture controversy remained a bone of contention between Henry V and Pope Paschal II because Henry V continued to invest bishops. The two reached a compromise at **Sutri** in **1111** AD in which Henry V agreed to give up the right of investiture if the bishops would return all their estates and temporal privileges and maintain themselves purely on tithes and donations.

This renunciation of temporal powers of the Church by Pope Paschal was the clearest statement on the separation of Church and State since the time of Constantine the Great. Based on his agreement with the King,

Pope Paschal promulgated an edict in 1112, for all temporalities to be returned to the Crown.

This stirred up a great opposition among the bishops who were also princes and Paschal realized that his compromise would not solve the problem.

Therefore, the King demanded that the Pope restore his right of investiture and be crowned as the Emperor. The Pope refused and was abducted by the king, with his cardinals. The Pope was released only after he granted the King's demands, that is, unconditional privilege of investiture, to be crowned as the Emperor and a promise not to excommunicate him for what had transpired.

However, the Pope was forced to rescind the privilege he granted the King by the "reformist" forces in the Church hierarchy who renewed the decrees of Gregory VII against Lay investiture at the **Lateran Synod of 1112** and declared the *'Imperial Privilegium'* null and void.

The controversy persisted until the death of Pope Paschal in 1118, and with no resolution by his successor, **Gelasius II (1118-1119 AD),** Henry V appointed an **antipope, Gregory VIII (1118 AD).** Pope **Callistus II (1119-1124 AD)** who succeeded Gelasius II, signed the *Concordat of Worms* with the Emperor in 1122.

By the agreement in the Concordat, the investiture was shared. The emperor would confer the temporal *'regalia and scepter'*, while the pope would confer the ecclesiastic *'ring and staff'* on the elected bishops. The Emperor reserved the right of arbitration in contested cases. The Concordat was a compromise that failed to attain the liberty envisaged by Pope Gregory VII but at the same time dealt a crushing blow to the divine rights of kings. It however achieved some modicum of peace between the regal and the Episcopal authorities.

The terms of the Concordat of Worms was ratified at the **First Lateran Council** in 1123 presided over by Pope Callistus II. The Council also passed canons protecting the properties of crusaders, forbade clerical marriage, appropriation of Church property and harassment of pilgrims.

In **England**, the same controversy raged. The king had officials of the church in subjection, appointing bishops and abbots and ratifying decisions of synods. This came to a head when **Anselm (1033-1109 AD)** [20] **the archbishop of Canterbury** refused to receive the bishopric from the new king of England, **Henry I (1100-1135 AD)** [21] or take the oath of fealty to him. Appeals by the king to the Pope to make Anselm comply were refused. Therefore, the king banned Anselm who was then visiting Rome from returning to England. The pope responded by excommunicating all clerics that had been appointed by the king.

Eventually, an agreement, *the Concordat of London,* was reached in 1107, whereby the king renounced the claim on investiture but retained the oath of fealty. Moreover, the king's consent was still required in the appointment of the higher dignitaries of the church.

However, neither the Concordat of London nor the Concordat of Worms permanently solved the power tussle between the popes and the European ecclesiastical potentates; the problem recurring virtually in every generation.

For example, a century later, King John of England was still at odds with the papacy over the election of the archbishop of Canterbury and his grandson, Edward 1 contested the suzerainty of Scotland with Pope Boniface VIII late in the thirteenth century. In Germany, Pope Innocent's hegemony did not leave a lasting solution as Fredrick II, a protégée of the papacy during his minority, turned out to be a maverick and was involved in a long dispute with the papacy over the Papal States.

So bad was the relationship between the papacy and Fredrick II that Popes Innocent IV, Alexander IV, Urban IV and Clement IV were all committed, not only to eliminating Fredrick II, but to the extermination of his linage.

Also in France, the Power tussle between Pope Boniface VIII and Phillip the Fair of France led to the deposition and eventual death of the former in 1303.

The Crusades [22, 23, 24]

Historical Background:
The Crusades were a series of military campaigns approved and promoted by the Church with a view to freeing the Byzantine Empire and the Holy Land from Moslem harassment and occupation respectively.

Although Jerusalem had been under Moslem occupation since 638 AD, Christians and Moslems had been living in relative peace. Though no new churches could be built and crosses could not be openly displayed, Christian pilgrims were allowed to visit holy sites unhindered provided the imposed tolls were paid.

However, the situation changed when the Fatimid Caliph of Egypt, **Al-Hakim bi-Amr-Allah (996-1021 AD)** [25] took control of Jerusalem and ordered the destruction of the Church of the Holy Sepulchre in 1009. The rebuilding of the Church was however authorized during the Caliphate of Al-Hakim's successor, **Ali-az—Zahir (1021-1036 AD)** [26]. He had a better relationship with the Byzantine Empire and signed a treaty with Emperor **Romanus III (1028-1034 AD)** for the rebuilding of the church which happened in 1042 under Emperor Constantine IX Monomachus.

In 1076, Jerusalem fell to the Seljuk Turks and Christian pilgrims were subjected to harassments, kidnappings, rapes, theft and murders. Christian Byzantium had requested the help of the West in confronting the threat of advancing Islam following the empire's defeat at the Battle of Manzikert in 1071 by the Seljuk Turks, but Pope Gregory VII was unable to help as he was distracted by the Conflict of Investitures.

Pope Urban II used the developments in Byzantium and the Holy Land to rally the people and the nobles to confront the advance of Moslems, thus gaining the advantage over the Emperor in the Conflict of Investitures.

First Crusade[16, 27]

Pope Urban II (1088-1099 AD) became the pope at a time when the Conflict of Investitures was still raging between the German Emperors and the papacy.

As a reformist in the mold of Gregory VII, he remained estranged from Emperor Henry IV and was opposed by the antipope Clement III. Therefore Urban II could not stay in Rome early in his papacy but he used his enforced exile to rally pro reformist royals and nobles in Western Europe in response to the request of the Byzantine Emperor, **Alexios 1 Komnenos (1081-1118)** for help against the Seljuk Turk Moslems in 1095. Alexios I Komnenos had inherited a collapsing empire with the eastern part overrun by the Turks.

At the *Council of Clermont* in **1095**, Pope Urban II made a passionate appeal for volunteers to fight Moslems who had taken control of Jerusalem and were harassing the pilgrims and Christians in the east. He appealed to the bishops to publish everywhere what was going on and urged the people to turn their swords from their brothers and instead join together to fight and liberate Jerusalem. He granted a **plenary indulgence** to all who decided to participate.

The response to his rallying call was phenomenal with many of the antipope bishops closing ranks with him for the crusading movement. Thus, the very first crusade was launched. When the Crusaders arrived in Byzantium in 1096 AD, Emperor Alexios I Komnenos promised to provide them with supplies but extracted by oath from every contingent that re-conquered lands would be returned to him.

The crusaders liberated Jerusalem in 1099, fifteen days before Pope Urban II died, but he did not receive the good News before he died. The first crusade thus ended on a victorious note.

However, under the pretext that the Emperor Alexios 1 Komnenos did not give adequate support to them in the siege of Antioch, the Crusaders did not return the liberated lands to the Byzantine Emperor but carved for themselves **Crusaders States** in the Holy land. The four Crusader States were the ***Principality of Antioch***, the ***Countship of Edessa,*** the ***Kingdom of Jerusalem*** and the ***Countship of Tripoli***; all administered indirectly by the papacy. The establishment of these Latin kingdoms in traditionally Byzantine territory did not please Constantinople and further strained the relationship between the east and the west.

The Second Crusade—(1147—1149)

The second Crusade was launched to liberate the countship of Edessa which was recaptured by Moslems between 1144 and 1146. The Crusade was preached by ***Bernard, the Abbot of Clairveaux*** and ***Pope Eugenius III (1145-1153)***; it was led on the eastern flank by ***Kings Louis VII of France and Conrad III of Germany*** and on the west flank by the Flemings, the Friesians, Normans and the English.

The two kings reached the Holy land but their forces were decimated by attacks from the Turks in Asia Minor such that their efforts to capture Damascus failed. They returned home without accomplishing their goal of regaining Edessa.

The western flank contingent teamed up with ***King Alfonso of Portugal*** and liberated Lisbon from Moslems in 1147. A detachment of the group also helped the ***Count of Barcelona*** to free the city of Tortosa.

Although this was not the primary purpose of the crusade, most of this contingent returned home after the victory or simply settled in the conquered areas. The second crusade therefore was essentially a failure.

The Third Crusade—(1189-1192)

The third crusade was called to recapture the city of Jerusalem which had once again fallen into Moslem hands. The city had been re-captured in 1187 by *Salah-Al-Din, the Sultan of Egypt*.

The crusade was called by Pope **Gregory VIII (1187)** and led by ***Kings Phillip II of France, Richard the Lionheart of England and Emperor Fredrick I (Barbarossa) of Germany***. Fredrick I drowned in Cilicia in 1190 before reaching the Holy Land. Richard of England detoured and conquered Cyprus from the Byzantines in 1191 before proceeding to Palestine.

Richard and Phillip II recaptured *Acre* from Moslems and the latter returned home. Richard then negotiated a treaty with Salah-Al-Din for safe passage of unarmed pilgrims to Jerusalem and the city remained under Moslem control. Richard too, departed for home in 1192.

From the standpoint of the real purpose of the third crusade, that is, the liberation of Jerusalem, it was a failure too.

Pope Innocent III (1198-1216 AD) [28, 29, 30]

Pope innocent III was born into an Italian noble family and was the nephew of Pope Clement III who made him a Cardinal-deacon during his papacy.

When Pope Celestine III died in 1198, Innocent III was elected as his successor. Although he was not a priest, he was well versed in Canon laws. He was hurried through the orders and made the pope the same year.

When he became the pope in 1198, Henry VI (1190-1197), the Holy Roman Emperor had died while preparing for a crusade to the Holy land and his heir, Fredrick II, a child, was also heir to the crown of Sicily through his mother.

Pope Innocent III took advantage of the power vacuum in Germany to consolidate the power of the papacy. First, he sacked the imperial prefect of Rome, then; he brought under papal control the areas of Italy controlled by the Emperor; Ancona and Spoleto.

When the wife of Henry VI was dying later in 1198, she made the pope the guardian of their son, Fredrick II, and hence the ruler of Sicily until Fredrick II reached majority.

Pope Innocent III backed one of the two contenders to the throne of Germany, Otto IV and explained his decision in a decretal to the princes explaining the relationship between the empire and the papacy. In summary, the decretal made the following points:

- The German princes have the right to elect the king who would later become the Holy Roman Emperor (HRE).
- The right was given to them by the "Apostolic See" when it was transferred to the Germans through Charlemagne from the Greeks.
- The Pope, who consecrates and crowns the Emperor, has the right to determine the worthiness of the candidate chosen by the princes, otherwise the pope might inadvertently crown a pagan or a heretic.
- If the pope finds the choice of the princes unworthy to be the emperor, they must elect another, and if they refuse, the pope reserved the right to confer the honor on another king as the Church always needs a defender.
- When there is more than one contender and no agreement is reached within a reasonable time, the pope must be asked to arbitrate or he will of his own accord decide in favor of one of the contenders. His decision need not be predicated on legality or otherwise of the election but only on the qualifications of the claimants.

With the decretals, Pope Innocent III overhauled centuries old process of selection of German kings and practically concentrated the power in the hands of popes.

Pope Innocent III obtained by oath the promise not to reclaim the regions of Italy the papacy had annexed before crowning Otto IV as the HRE.

However, as soon as he was crowned, he reclaimed the regions and gave them in vassalage to his friends. He also tried to take Sicily from the boy king and effectively, the Pope who was his guardian.

The Pope then excommunicated Otto IV; courted the German princes who deserted the Emperor and joined the Pope in electing Fredrick II the new King of Germany in 1211. The Pope extracted the same promise from the young king and crowned him the HRE in 1215. The dethroned emperor Otto IV died in 1218.

Pope Innocent III was involved in the politics of all Europe and beyond wielding both temporal and spiritual powers. He ended the war between England and France using the threat of interdict and the kings signed a five year truce.

Also, using the power of interdict, he forced King Phillip Augustus of France to reconcile with his wife and annulled the marriages of other kings that he deemed violated the canon laws.

In England, the appointment of the archbishop of Canterbury resulted in a conflict between the Pope and King John (Lackland). To fill the vacancy, two candidates emerged, one chosen by the monks and the other by the bishops. King John favored the bishops' candidate but the Pope invalidated both candidates and had the monks of Canterbury who were in Rome choose Stephen Langton whom he personally consecrated in 1207. King John refused to allow Langton to return to England to resume duties as the archbishop, so the Pope placed England under interdict in 1208.

When the interdict was not effective, the Pope excommunicated King John in 1209 and in 1212 deposed him, asking the King of France to effect his sentence. At this point, the feudal lords began to desert King John and he had no choice but to surrender to the Pope. The papacy drove a hard bargain and the terms of the surrender in 1213 included:
- Allowing the Pope's choice of archbishop to assume office,
- Allowing the exiled clergy to return and
- Reimbursing them for losses incurred.
- To cap it all, England was surrendered to the papacy as a vassal State and would be required to pay annual tributes.

The king's excommunication was lifted in 1213 while the interdict was lifted a year later after the reimbursement of the losses of the clergy.

The king's steps did not please the barons and a revolt ensued; they drew up a document, the *'Magna Carta'* which curtailed royal powers in areas of taxation, justice, religion and foreign policy and is acclaimed as a landmark document for governance devoid of oppression and tyranny.

The king was forced to sign the document in 1215 but the Pope invalidated it because it was supposedly signed under duress.

Pope Innocent's political tentacles reached as far as Norway, Sweden, Poland, Hungary and even the Byzantine Empire, following the fourth crusade.

Pope Innocent III called the fourth crusade, the Albigensian crusade and the fifth crusade though he did not live to see through the last mentioned. He supported crusades to Spain against the Moslem Moors as well as the missions of the Teutonic knights in the Baltic region.

He used diplomacy, mostly backed by threats (of excommunication or interdict) or blatant force to achieve his goals. He is regarded as probably the most influential Pope in the history of the papacy; wielding both spiritual and temporal powers, he made many nations in Christendom vassals of the papacy.

His ecclesiastical achievement include the approbation of the Franciscan and the Dominican Orders and the convening of the ***Fourth Lateran Council in 1215***, reported to be one of the best attended ecumenical councils in history. He died in 1216.

The Fourth Crusade—(1202—1204 AD) [31, 32]

The fourth crusade was called by Pope Innocent III with the intention of recapturing Jerusalem by a different strategy. It was considered necessary to first weaken Egypt before recapturing Jerusalem as Jerusalem could not be secured for long without dealing with Egypt.

As the group set out, it ran into the problem of inadequate funding and got embroiled in the succession dispute to the throne of the Byzantine Empire. One of the contenders in exile promised to fund the crusade in exchange for the crusaders' help to secure his claim to the throne; so the crusaders headed for Constantinople and installed their prospective sponsor.

However, he was unable to fulfill his promise and the restive crusaders, urged on by accompanying bishops and abbots then sacked the city of Constantinople, looting the Hagia Sophia and the rich monasteries.

The Abbots, in particular Abbot Martin was reputed to have made away with relics said to include:
- A trace of the blood of Jesus
- A piece of the true Cross
- A piece of John the Baptist
- The arm of the Apostle James.

Furthermore, they established a Latin Empire, replacing Orthodox bishops with Latin ones and putting Latin Abbots in the monasteries. The Byzantine seat of government moved to Niceae and did not regain Constantinople until 1261.

Pope Innocent III allegedly did not support the invasion of Constantinople, he reportedly first excommunicated the invaders for attacking fellow Christians then lifted the excommunication and ***"bowed to Providence"***.

He seized the opportunity to finally try to bring the east under the influence of the papacy and unite the Greek and Latin Churches. This is considered the final breaking point between the Roman Catholic Church and the Eastern Orthodox Church.

The Fifth Crusade—(1217-1221 AD) [33]
The fifth crusade was called by **Pope Honorius III** and led by the papal legate, **Pelagius.** The initial success of the capture of Damietta, an Egyptian strategic town was followed by a failed attack on Cairo and eventual defeat.

Prisoner exchange and an eight year truce between Egypt and Europe was all that was achieved. In essence, this too, was a failure.

The fifth Crusade was the last Church inspired multi-national Crusade undertaken.

The Sixth Crusade—(1228-1229 AD) [34, 35]
The sixth crusade was embarked on by **Frederick II (1212-1250)** of Germany in 1228.

His relationship with the Pope had soured on account of his failing to help with the fifth crusade. His earlier attempt was truncated by the outbreak of fever among his troops which caused him to turn back, but the Pope was not amused. He was excommunicated by **Pope Gregory IX (1227-1241)** in 1228.

Nevertheless, he set out for the Holy Land without the blessings of the Pope who in fact released the crusaders from their oath of allegiance to the Emperor. His excommunication by the Pope weakened his hand as crusaders already in Palestine refused to obey him. Nonetheless, through diplomacy he won back the control of Jerusalem (except the Temple Mount and the Al Aqsa Mosque), Nazareth and Bethlehem to the Christians for a period of ten years by signing a treaty with *Malik Al Kamil (1180-1238)*, the ruler of Egypt.

The sixth Crusade, without the support of the papacy was more successful than all the other Crusades except the first Crusade. Many therefore conceded that he had divine inspiration and help and the Pope's stature was somewhat diminished.

Pope Gregory IX condemned the treaty; therefore, Frederick crowned himself the king of Jerusalem in 1229. However, unable to ignore the obvious success of the Emperor, the Pope lifted the excommunication earlier imposed but he was excommunicated again in 1239 as a result of disagreement over the political control of Northern Italy.

The treaty expired in 1239 and Jerusalem was recaptured by Moslems in 1244 following a siege by the Turks; it remained under Moslem control until 1917 AD when it surrendered to the British.

The Seventh Crusade—(1248-1254) [36]

The seventh crusade was led by Louis IX of France in response to the 1244 recapture of Jerusalem by the Moslems. The strategy again was to conquer and weaken Egypt. However, his troops got into the same quagmire as the fifth crusade and the king was captured in battle; he was released only after agreeing to pay a heavy ransom in 1250. He returned home after four years of fruitless diplomacy. The seventh crusade was also a failure.

The Eighth Crusade—(1270-1272 AD) [37]

The eighth crusade was organized by Louis IX in 1270, probably to redeem his earlier failure during the seventh crusade.

He got diverted to Tunis where although he had some success, he lost his son, John Tristan who was born during the ill-fated seventh crusade. He also took ill thereafter and died without reaching his destination.

His brother, Charles of Anjou, king of Sicily, was joined by Prince Edward of England who, finding that the operation in Tunis was over, went on to Palestine and carried on the campaign until 1272, when the death of his father forced him to return home. Some historians dubbed Prince Edward's campaign the **ninth crusade**.

Eventually, the last of the Crusader states, Acre, fell back into Moslem hands in 1291; the date that is generally considered the end of the major crusades although many minor crusades continued till the fifteenth century AD.

The Impact of the Crusades [38, 39]

(i) On European Socio-political Structure

The crusades changed the socio-political structure of Europe by destroying the feudal system.

Many of the barons were bankrupted from raising money for the crusades and many died fighting in the crusades without heirs; the result in both situations was that the land reverted back to the king. The crusades also drastically reduced the internecine wars and the violence between feudal lords and knights which the "**Truce of God**" and "**The Peace of God**" instituted by the papacy did not adequately stem. The restive energies of all were diverted to fighting the common enemy—the Moslems. The elimination of the feudal lords and reduction of private warfare enhanced the authority of the King among the people.

(ii) On Intellectual Development of Europe

Those who survived the crusades had their minds and intellect broadened by their travels and contact with other cultures, art and science. Europe was enriched in arts, architecture, astronomy and medicine and the use of the compass was said to have been introduced into Europe about this time. This set the stage for the Renaissance and opened new frontiers in travel and voyages of exploration by the likes of ***Marco Polo, Vasco Da Gamma, Magellan and Christopher Columbus***.

(iii) On European Economy and Commerce

The crusades in general boosted the economy and expanded commerce in many ways. The demand for supplies and transportation for the wars soared and led to increased shipbuilding. Trade routes to the Middle East and the Orient were opened up and new articles of trade such as silk, spices, sugar and so on were introduced. The society moved from a largely barter economy to money economy.

(iv) On the Byzantine Empire

The crusaders' attack on the Byzantine Empire in 1204 has been argued by some to have contributed to its weakening and eventual fall in 1453 AD. However, many are also of the opinion that the crusades in fact prolonged the life of the Empire for more than two centuries by dissipating the energies of the Moslem powers in other theatres of war.

(v) On the Catholic Church

The crusades increased the wealth of the Church and the power of the papacy. The popes for the most part were the rallying point for the crusades. The kings, the lords, the knights and the laymen who participated in the crusades all needed the blessings and the indulgences of the Popes for the enterprise. Many returning crusaders who were broken in spirit and in health bestowed their properties on the Church and embraced the monastic life.

(vi) Formation of Military Orders

Another important development following the first crusade was the formation of Military orders, namely, the ***Knights Templar, the Knights Hospitallers and the Teutonic knights***.

The most famous of these were the Knights Templar formed in 1118 when nine knights bound themselves with an oath in the presence of the Patriarch of Jerusalem to defend the newly liberated Jerusalem.

They sought approbation from the Pope and enlisted recruits. In 1128, they also adopted the 'Rule of St. Benedict and took monastic vows in addition to the crusader's vow. As such, they were well disciplined and were respected by all. Initially called the poor knights of the Temple, they soon became wealthy from the gifts of money and land donations from the nobility. (The vow of poverty apparently thought to apply only to individual members and not the group; therefore, while individuals were sworn to poverty, it was alright for the group to be wealthy).

In 1139, Pope Innocent II by a special Bull exempted them from all local laws and taxes and they were not answerable to any authority except the Pope.

Thus appropriated by the Church hierarchy, they became very popular and powerful with chapters everywhere. They were the bankers of Europe and had thousands of estates that could not be taxed and churches that could not be put under interdict.

As the object of so much favor, friction and rivalry soon arose between them and the Knights Hospitallers. By the end of the thirteenth century, calls were being made for the merger of the military orders to secure peace and coherence of operations.

Sentiments turned against the knights with the loss of the Holy Land in 1291 AD.

vii) On the Jews and Anti-Semitism

The simmering anti-Jew sentiments among medieval Christians boiled over during the crusades into overt violent persecutions of the Jews.

The first contingent of crusaders comprising ordinary laymen and led by a priest called '**Peter the Hermit**' that marched through land for the first crusade attacked Jews along the way and robbed them of their money and property. So many Jews were killed that many dubbed it the '*First Holocaust*'. Apart from this, legal restrictions against Jews were intensified and sanctioned by some canons of the *Fourth Lateran Council* under Pope Innocent III.

The atrocities by Christians against the Jews have lingered and created a distrust of Christians by Jews.

viii) On the Islamic World and Advancement of Islam

Although the crusades failed militarily, the crusades contained the advance of Islam into Europe and arguably delayed the fall of Constantinople to Moslems by a couple of centuries by 'diverting the energies of the forces of Islam from conquest to defense'.

In spite of the failure of the crusades, they left lasting negative effects on the world of Islam. The Islamic world was ahead in astronomy, medicine and science (many believed this was inherited from the Byzantine Empire and other older civilizations) during the time of the crusades. However, as Europe opened up intellectually, culturally and commercially, Islam dug in, in an attempt to preserve its culture at all costs and as a result, its development was retarded.

Another untoward lasting effect is the Islamic world's disdain for many things western.

Pope Boniface VIII (1294-1303 AD) [40, 41, 42]

Pope Boniface was the scion of Roman nobility of Spanish ancestry. An accomplished jurist and canonist, he served the papacy in various capacities before he was elected pope in 1294 following the abdication of Pope Celestine V.

Like Gregory VII and Innocent III, Boniface VIII believed in the supremacy of the papacy in spiritual and temporal matters.

Pope Boniface VIII made it his business to interfere actively in many disputes among the Roman nobles, the Italian states and other nations across Europe, sometimes in a partisan manner and with the use of ***pontifical troops;*** but most of these attempts at mediation failed.

The most celebrated conflict he had with kings was the conflict he had with **Philip IV (the Fair), king of France (1285-1314)** over the taxation of Church properties. Pope Boniface VIII published a Bull excommunicating any laity that levied, and any cleric that paid such taxes without approval of the papacy. Philip IV retaliated with a royal ordinance forbidding exports of money, gold or other commodities from his realm. Eventually, the pope had to back down and appease the king by canonizing his grandfather, King Louis IX. The royal ordinance was retracted and there was peace for a while.

However, the same controversy flared up again and the Pope published a Bull reiterating the authority of the papacy in temporal matters and intimated the king with his plan to summon the French clergy to Rome to address the issue. The king was also invited to attend and defend himself. The king responded by prohibiting any clergy from his realm from attending the Pope's Council and confiscated the properties of those who did.

At the Council, the Pope published two Bulls; the first excommunicated anyone who impeded the movement of people to and from Rome and the second, the famous **"Unam Sanctam"**. The latter essentially stated that based on the doctrine of the *'Apostolic Succession'*, the papal authority was divine and superior to the regal temporal power. It said: ***"There are two swords (powers), the spiritual and the temporal; the first is borne by the Church, the second for the Church; the first by the hand of the priest, the second by the king, but under the direction of the priest"***.

The spiritual power, he averred had the right to instruct and correct the temporal; and, as there is no salvation outside the Catholic Church, it is in the interest of all to be subject to the representative of Christ, the Pope.

King Philip IV responded by holding a Council in France where some people brought grievous charges like simony, heresy, idolatry and sexual immorality against the Pope as well as irregularity about his ascension to the papacy. Pre-empting papal excommunication, the king sent a band of armed men to seize the Pope and imprisoned him. He was rescued after three days by his townsmen but died a few weeks after.

Some historians have postulated that Philip was collecting taxes from the clergy because he was hoping to reclaim the Holy Land and establish a Christian hegemony in Europe. However, the only person, apparently with such a dream was Pope Boniface VIII who interfered in every temporal dispute and came up with the 'Unam Sanctam' which stated in essence that he was above all temporal rulers.

Although the association is rarely made by historians, the eventual fall of the Knights Templar must have its root in the papacy of **Boniface VIII.** With powerful and wealthy knights like the Knights Templar solely under papal control, it was not surprising that King Philip IV, after his prolonged conflict with Pope Boniface VIII, plotted and succeeded in neutralizing the Knights Templar.

In 1307, King Philip IV arrested the leaders of the Knights Templar and accused them of sacrilege and idolatry especially in their secret initiation rites. Letters were sent to other nations to also investigate them. The arrested leaders were tortured and some confessed to the charges. After a lengthy trial, those of the leadership that recanted their earlier confession of guilt were burnt at the stakes, those who pleaded guilty were allowed to join other orders or revert to the secular order after the Pope had formally dissolved the order of the Knights Templar.

The Avignon Papacy (1305-1378 AD) [43, 44, 45]

After the death of Pope Boniface VIII, Rome once again descended into anarchy on account of the perennial wars between the nobility. Pope Benedict XI, who succeeded him died after just eight months, suspected to have been poisoned. Pope Clement V (1305-1314), Benedict XI's successor therefore took residence in Avignon, a French territory.

Pope Clement V was asked by King Philip IV to try Boniface VIII post-mortem but sanity eventually prevailed and the trial wound down without condemnation of the dead pope. He also had the unfortunate task of disbanding the Knights Templar in France after King Philip IV arrested and tried the leadership of the military order.

Pope John XXII (1316—1334), a Dominican monk, theologian and Canon law expert succeeded Clement V and continued in Avignon.

During his papacy, a doctrinal dispute over ecclesiastical poverty arose between the ***Religious*** and ***Conventual*** factions of the ***Franciscan Order***. While the religious faction maintained that Jesus Christ and the Apostles had no possessions either individually or collectively; the conventuals disagreed. The pope sided with the conventuals and declared the position of the religious heresy. Two of the leaders of the religious faction, the Minister General, **Michael of Cesena** *(1270-1342)* and **William of Oakham** *(c1285-c1349*) had to flee to Germany and take refuge with King Louis of Bavaria who was also in a power tussle with the pope.

These two events precipitated a flurry of literary controversies on the imperial versus papal and temporal versus spiritual powers and who wields what.

Pope John XXII believed in the supremacy of the papacy and never failed to stake the claim. However, this strained relationships between him and King Louis of Bavaria to the extent that the king supported the election of an anti-pope who assumed the name Nicholas V in 1328 AD.

In the latter end of his papacy, one of pope John XXII's earlier writing on the '***Beatific Vision'*** sparked controversy and accusations of heresy.

He had written that the just would see God only after the last judgment and not immediately after death. It was hotly debated by theologians and the consensus was that the just do see God immediately after death. He had to officially withdraw his earlier opinion and agreed with the consensus.

He was succeeded by **Pope Benedict XII (1334-1342 AD)** a Cistercian monk and theologian. He instituted a commission of theologians who settled once for all the issue of the Beatific Vision. He was reform oriented and tried to stem simony among the clergy. He advocated the use of the Inquisition to combat heresy.

He was succeeded by **Clement VI (1342-1352 AD),** a Benedictine monk. Pope Clement VI's papacy was bedeviled by arrant nepotism such that, out of twenty five cardinals he appointed, twelve were his relations. He permitted the king of France to receive the Communion in both kinds. He was profligate and worldly, living more like a temporal prince than an ecclesiastical ruler. He loved parties and banquets to which ladies were freely admitted and his life-style incurred higher taxes on the people which were greatly resented.

He was succeeded by **Pope Innocent VI (1352-1362 AD)** who deviated from the profligacy of his predecessor by banning luxury from the papal court.

He was succeeded by **Pope Urban V (1362-1370 AD),** a Benedictine monk and scholar of canon and civil laws. During his papacy, France and Italy were overrun by armed brigands, mercenaries called the ***"Free Companies"***. He tried to control them by using them to fight crusades against the Turks but failed; he then excommunicated them and asked the kings and the emperor to get rid of them but that too was fruitless.

He decided to return the papacy to Rome to secure the Papal States that had been taken back by a warlike cardinal. However, he had to return to Avignon because Rome remained riotous and the valiant cardinal died.

He was a lover of learning who founded many Universities and supported the older ones.

The last regular pope in Avignon was **Gregory XI (1370-1378 AD)** who succeeded Urban V. He was the nephew of Pope Clement VI who made him a Cardinal Deacon at the age of eighteen years; and he was not a priest at the time of his election as pope.

He was ordained priest the day before his consecration as Pope Gregory XI.

His effort to end the war between France and England was unsuccessful and some nobles in Italy continued to encroach on the Papal lands. One such noble was the Duke of Milan who Gregory XI had to excommunicate. However, the papal legate sent to present the Bull of excommunication was made to eat it. Therefore, the Pope put together a coalition of Germany, Hungary and Naples to fight him.

The problems in Italy were in part due to the resentment the Italians had for the appointment of French men as governors and legates over Papal States. He left Avignon for Rome in 1377 and returned the seat of the papacy to Rome. He condemned what he considered the errors of Wycliffe in five Bulls in 1377. He died in 1378.

The Avignon papacy was infamous for its corruption and avarice. During the period, various means were devised for increasing papal revenue including increasing **taxes on bishoprics**, collection of **annates** and the **sale of indulgence**s. In addition, the popes appropriated the possessions of dead bishops and institutionalized simony. Therefore the papacy was regarded as insensitive and greedy and it lost prestige.

The Western Schism (1378—1418 AD) [46, 47, 48]

After the death of Gregory XI, the restive Roman populace demanded a Roman or at least an Italian pope. As the sacred college of cardinals met, the people became unruly; eventually, the conclave elected Pope ***Urban VI (1378-1389)***.

However, within months of his election, he alienated the cardinals who elected him by his undiplomatic approach to reforms. A few months later, most of those who elected him reckoned that his election was uncanonical because it was 'under duress' by the Roman mobs. They therefore got together and elected another Pope, ***Clement VII (1378-1394)*** who moved his seat back to Avignon.

This divided the nations in western Christendom; Germany, England and most of Italy continued to recognize Urban VI as the Pope while France, Spain, Naples, Scotland and Sicily recognized Clement VII. Also divided were the religious communities and theologians.

The division continued for about forty years with Clement VII in Avignon succeeded by ***Benedict XIII (1394-1417)*** and Urban VI succeeded by ***Boniface IX (1389-1404), Innocent VII (1404-1406) and Gregory XII (1406-1415)***.

In 1409, an attempt was made to end the schism at the ***Council of Pisa*** by deposing all the existing popes and electing another. The Council elected ***Alexander V (1409-1410)*** but the previous rival popes refused to abdicate with the result that there was then three Popes all claiming to be the legitimate successor of Peter.

The issue was finally resolved at the ***Council of Constance (1414-1417)*** when Pope ***John XXIII (1410-1415),*** the successor of Alexander V and Benedict XIII were deposed and Gregory XII resigned. In 1417 AD, Pope ***Martin V (1417-1431)*** was elected, thus ending the schism.

The question for theologians and historians has been, 'which of the two, and later, three popes was the real pope considering that all were duly elected by the College of Cardinals?'

The schism, unlike the Eastern schism and others in the history of Christianity was, sadly, not doctrinal but political and about personalities and ambition.

As a result of the schism, there arose briefly the **"Conciliar Movement"** that attempted to supplant papal power with Church Councils following the efforts of Cardinals to resolve the schismatic impasse at the Council of Pisa.

The Conciliarists are of the view that the highest authority in the Church ought to be the Council rather than a single human being, the pope. They based their opinion on Scriptural example like the Council of Jerusalem in the apostolic era—Acts 15; and also the Council of Niceae in the early Church during the time of Emperor Constantine. However, though scripturally sound, the movement was effectively stifled by even the very pope the Council elected to end the Western Schism, Pope Martin V.

Instead, papal supremacy blossomed into Papal infallibility ex-cathedral just over a century later.

Chapter 10

Theologians, Philosophers and Reformers of the Middle Ages

Peter Damian (c.1007-1072 AD) [1, 2, 3, 4]

Peter Damian was an Italian Benedictine monk and Prior of a monastery who sought through his prodigious writings to effect reforms in the Catholic Church of his time. He was a rhetorician before he became a monk and afterwards became well versed in canon laws such that he served several popes as legate and ambassador.

He taught that philosophy is subsidiary to theology and that the study of philosophy was not necessary for salvation.

He was accused of violating the *"'universal' principle of non-contradiction"* when he defended God's Omnipotence and seemed to argue that God can bring it about that a past event did not happen. The two propositions were:

a) Can God restore virginity to a woman who has lost it?
b) Can God bring it about that what has been done has not been done?

Peter Damian's position was that dialectic principles do not always work in theology.

He also wrote about corruption, simony and sexual immorality in the Catholic Church in a book titled '***Liber Gommorrhianus***' dedicated to Pope Leo IX in which he documented, condemned and proffered solutions to rampant sexual immorality among the clergy, religious orders and the hierarchy.

He addressed such practices as homosexuality and pederasty among priests, sexual relations between priests and penitents, both male and female as well as between priests and "spiritual sons and spiritual daughters of priests" i.e. those preparing for Holy Orders. He identified four forms of the practice of homosexuality among the religious orders, namely:

(i) Self masturbation,

(ii) Mutual masturbation,
(iii) Femoral fornication and
(iv) Anal intercourse.

There were also references suggestive of group orgies.

He decried the practice of grading the offences and treating the first three categories as milder offences warranting lesser punishment. He posited that such an attitude allowed the sins to fester in religious communities while obfuscating the seriousness of the sins to those who were guilty. He had this to say about sodomy in general:

"Indeed this vice is the death of bodies, the destruction of souls. It pollutes the flesh; it extinguishes the light of the mind. It evicts the Holy Spirit from the temple of the human heart; it introduces the devil who incites to lust. It casts into error; it completely removes truth from the mind that has been deceived . . . It makes a citizen of the heavenly Jerusalem into an heir of infernal Babylon . . . It defiles everything, stains everything, pollutes everything . . . This vice casts men from the choir of ecclesiastical community and compels them to pray with the possessed and with those who work for the devil. It separates the soul from God to join it with devils . . ."

He condemned as dangerous invention of the devil the canons on sodomy which he said made a mockery of justice because they imposed severer penance on lay people convicted of sodomy and bestiality than on the clerics and religious who committed the same offence.

He also denounced as diabolical the practice by which the offending priests confess their sins to each other and then absolve themselves.

He believed that those with homosexual tendencies should not be ordained and if ordained should not be promoted and wrote to seek answers from the pope on whether any offending clergy should be defrocked.

He differed from St. Augustine of Hippo in his opinion about impious priests. He believed that—*"The service of an unworthy priest is the ruin of the people and God refuses to accept the sacrifice from the hands of the unclean".*

He also said: *"No holy offering which is soiled with crimes of impiety is received by God".*

His writings gave impetus to the ensuing Gregorian reforms.

Anselm of Canterbury (1033-1109 AD) [5, 6, 7]

Anselm was a monk who became the Archbishop of Canterbury, England. His tenure was plagued by the investiture controversy both with **William the Conqueror** and later **Henry I** of England until finally the **Concordat of London** was signed in 1107 AD.

He was a theologian and philosopher who sought to explain the Christian faith by reasoning and developed what was dubbed **"the Ontological Argument"** by later scholars. His works included the *'Proslogion' or 'Faith Seeking Understanding'*, *'Why God became man'*, *'On the Fall of the Devil'*, *'On freedom of choice, Sin and Grace'* and many others.

On the Existence of God:

As with many other philosophical approaches to issues of faith, his convoluted dialogues often raised more questions than they sought to answer or elucidate. For example, in his *'Proslogion' or 'Faith seeking understanding'* his proposition to prove the existence of God by reason was—**"that than which nothing greater can be thought"**.

He weaved a lot of complicated arguments around this and felt that he proved God's existence thereby. Anselm was challenged by one of his contemporaries named **Gaunilo** that his proposition and the argument proved something vague since to prove *"that which is greater than everything that can be thought"*, you need some knowledge of the thing itself. In addition, Gaunilo also averred that the proposition could be used to justify falsities.

Anselm did not address Gaunilo's objections directly but claimed that Gaunilo's **"that which is greater than everything that can be thought"** is different from his own proposition **"that than which nothing greater can be thought"**.

On Why God Became Man:

In *"Cur Deus Homo"* or *"Why God became Man"*, the basis of the work was to answer the objections of infidels who felt that the claim of Christians about God becoming man to redeem from sin was demeaning to God.

Anselm established that:
- Because God is just, sin cannot be remitted without punishment
- Complete satisfaction is necessary for sin
- Man, of himself, cannot make complete satisfaction for his sin

- No other being can pay for man otherwise man would be enslaved to such a being rather than to God
- Only a God-Man, Jesus Christ who is truly divine and truly human can redeem man; he said *"For only one who is divine can make satisfaction and only one who is truly human ought to make it. Therefore, since it is necessary to find a God-Man who retains the integrity of both natures, it is no less necessary that these two integral natures conjoin in one person (just as a body and a rational soul conjoin in one man); otherwise, it is impossible that one and the same individual be fully divine and fully human"*

Earlier, Boso, the student in the dialogue, charged that it was inconsistent with reason for an omnipotent God who could just cancel human sins if he chose to, or find some other means to save man, to choose to condescend so low as to become human and then suffer and die on the cross.

In answering, Anselm said *". . . the act of Christ's condescension which we speak of do not belong to His divinity, it yet seems improper to infidels that these things should be said of Him even as a man . . ."* and *"We affirm that the divine nature is beyond doubt impassible (that is, incapable of suffering, feeling or emotions) and that God cannot at all be brought down from His exaltation . . . But we say that the Lord Jesus Christ is very God and very man, one person in two natures and two natures in one person. When therefore we speak of God as enduring any humiliation or infirmity, we do not refer to the majesty of that nature, which cannot suffer; but to the feebleness of the human constitution which He assumed.*

COMMENT:

Anselm's explanations of how the divine and human natures are conjoined in Jesus Christ sounded more like *Appollinarianism* and his assertion that *only* the human nature that Christ assumed was humiliated because His divine nature was *"impassible"* was akin to *Nestorianism*. Incidentally Anselm was never challenged on these Christological positions which were considered heretic in the Roman Catholic Church.

Anselm, on faith and reason said: *"Nor do I seek to understand that I may believe, but I believe that I may understand. For this, too, I believe, that, unless I first believe, I shall not understand".*

On Original Sin:

Anselm's concept of the Original Sin was human nature without original justice and he separated Original Sin from the lust of sexual intercourse.

His concept of Sin was: "not rendering to God His due". He also said that in reality, no one can honor or dishonor God.

His concept of the Original Sin is a departure from the Augustinian position which dominated Catholic thoughts and doctrines for centuries but definitely more scriptural.

His conclusion or premise, that God is "impassible", (that is, devoid of feelings and emotions and that He cannot be honored or dishonored) contradict Scriptures and seem to negate his concept of sin.

Anselm, by a combination of Neo-Platonic, Aristotelian and Christian logic, is credited with laying the foundation of scholasticism. He is regarded as a Doctor of the Roman Catholic Church.

Comment:

In an attempt to understand God by philosophical reasoning, violence is often done to His character. When Anselm, just like the other Christian Philosophers before him realized this, they would sometimes back off. For example, when Anselm's student, Boso, suggested that, the idea that an omnipotent God would allow or desire the death of innocent Jesus Christ for man's salvation appeared unreasonable, unnecessary and unbecoming; Anselm declined "to ascribe to God anything unbecoming." He in essence merely dodged the question.

Anselm subscribed to the idea of God's "impassibility", that God cannot be honored or dishonored and yet defined sin as not rendering to God His due. The question is: *If God cannot be honored or dishonored, why count it as sin when something due to Him is not rendered? Why is anything due Him at all if nothing matters to Him?*

Throughout the Scriptures, it is clear that God is not indifferent. The Scriptures tell us that God loves, hates, gets angry, is pleased etc. God does expect honor from Believers and said so in many Scriptures, for example:—***1Samuel 2:30; Malachi 1:6.***

The fact is, while faith is not opposed to reason, understanding in faith comes through ***revelation*** by the Holy Spirit and not through ***reasoning***.

The Apostle Paul said ***"The natural man cannot receive the things of the Spirit of God: for they are foolishness to him: neither can he know them because they are spiritually discerned"—1Corinthians 2:14.***

Peter Abelard (1079-1142 AD) [8, 9, 10, 11, 12]

Abelard was a French dialectician, philosopher and theologian of the twelfth century. As a scholar-in-residence at Notre Dame, Paris, he became romantically involved with **Heloise**, the niece of Canon Fulbert of Notre Dame and had a child with her. The two got married secretly because an open marriage would have compromised his career which at the time was only possible through the Church.

However, when Heloise's uncle discovered the affair, he had Abelard castrated.

With this development, Abelard entered the monastery and became a monk while Heloise entered a convent and became a nun while their child was raised by a relation.

The two remained in love and exchanged love letters even as monk and nun and their lives inspired many literary and cultural works.

Abelard was controversial in his theological views and this pitched him against other monks, abbots and the powers that be in the Catholic Church of his day. He was tried for heresy on his ideas about Christology, the Trinity and a host of other issues.

On Sin, Original Sin and the Atonement:

Abelard defined *sin* as *"contempt for God or consent to known evil"*. According to Abelard, ignorance morally exculpate unless there is proof of negligence. He therefore concluded that: *"they did not sin who in ignorance crucified Christ..."* but since the deed was objectively wrong, punishment would have been reasonable. In other words something may be blameworthy but not necessarily or strictly sinful. He illustrated his point by the example of a set of fraternal twins, separated and kept in complete ignorance of each other, grew up, met and fell in love, got married and had sexual intercourse and thereby committed incest. Abelard felt there was no ground to lay blame and their ignorance was exculpatory.

Abelard also taught that "... ***on account of works (acts), neither better nor worse is brought about"***. That is to say, human actions are neutral and in themselves morally indifferent; that a man's merit or guilt is determined, not by what he does but by his intentions.

The issue of ***intentionalism*** in regard to guilt poses a problem in making ethical judgments since a man's intentions are known only to him. Abelard however posited that, since there is divine justice (as God has access to man's intentions); for the purposes of human justice, questions of intentions can be ignored, though that could mean that the innocent would be punished and the guilty freed. For Abelard, human justice functions primarily as deterrent.

He also said: *"that neither the deed, nor the will, nor the desire, nor the delight which moves it is a sin nor ought we to extinguish it"*. In other words merely *"wanting does not make sin, only acts do"; therefore he said; "lusting in the heart is not sin"*.

He illustrated this point with the case of a monk (with vow of celibacy/continence), forcibly chained between two women on a bed who involuntarily responded naturally and is 'brought to pleasure'. He said the monk would be blameless because in the situation he found himself, pleasure was natural and inevitable and that natural pleasure, weather for sexual intercourse or a delicious food are not sinful.

He was of the opinion that if sexual pleasure in marriage is not sinful, then the pleasure itself inside or outside of marriage is not sinful. He was of the opinion that if sexual pleasure is inherently sinful, marriage cannot sanctify it. Furthermore, he said, if it is concluded that such acts be performed without pleasure, that they cannot be done at all and that it would have been unreasonable of God to permit them only in a way they cannot be performed.

He differed from St. Augustine on the concept of Original Sin and guilt; Abelard believed what human beings inherit from Adam was a corrupted will and therefore inclination to sin but that no one inherited guilt on account of someone else's sin. Therefore he believed that children who die do not go to hell but to **limbo**, a place of natural happiness but not the ultimate happiness that comes with beholding the Creator.

Like Anselm, he believed that the ransom Christ paid to save man was to God and not to the devil; that *"Christ did not assume flesh to liberate us from the yoke of the devil"*.

He also believed that Christ's death achieved the liberation of man from subjection to sin by example; that Christ's exemplary obedience inspires love for God in human beings who then would merit God's forgiveness. This is known as the **Moral Theory of Atonement** as opposed to the **"Satisfaction Theory"** that views Christ's death as ransom paid for the redemption of man.

On Faith, Reason and the Trinity

Abelard disagreed with those who accepted only what they could prove by reasoning and berated them as mere solipsists who were contemptuous of authorities and believed such people were more prone to heresies. He believed there are vital truths beyond the limits of human reason but not beyond faith.

Abelard got into trouble on his views about the Trinity among other theological views he held. Abelard said the Holy Spirit is the "world soul"; this was considered as transporting Platonism into Christian theology and this prompted Bernard of Clairvaux, Abelard's most prominent opponent to say: *"The more Abelard sweats to make Plato a Christian, the more he becomes a pagan".*

He said the devil instigates suggestions (of lust, anger, etc), by the application of stones and herbs. For this he was charged with being a magician.

On Apostolic Succession:

He also taught that: *"the power of binding and loosing was given exclusively to the Apostles and not to their successors generally but only to those successors who share their worthiness".*

For his theological views, Abelard was tried at the **Council of Sens** in 1141 and convicted of a wide range of heresies including Nestorianism, Pelagianism and Arianism.

He died in 1142 and when Heloise died in 1164, she was buried beside Peter Abelard.

Comments:

Abelard's concept of Sin was more superficial than what is taught in the Scriptures. He considered Sin primarily from the standpoint of **man's blame-worthiness** rather than from **God's holiness** which is in fact the main issue. His idea that an action that may be blame-worthy may, on account of ignorance, not be sinful is in fact contrary to Scriptural concept of Sin. In the Old Testament, intention or deliberation was not a condition for the concept of sin. In fact the Sin Offering was for sins committed in ignorance—*Leviticus 4:1-35*. This is because sin, whether committed in ignorance or consciously violates God's holiness and has to be atoned for. However, there is mitigation for sin committed in non-negligent ignorance—*Luke 12:48*.

Abelard claimed that *"deeds, desires, wills and delights are not sinful, only actions"; but he also said that "deeds are inherently neutral";* if the two propositions are right, it's almost impossible to sin. However, Jesus Christ said that sins have their origin in thoughts; in fact Jesus said to look at a woman with lust is as bad as actual adultery—*Mark 5:27-28; Mark 7:20-23.*

The Scripture also differentiated between good and evil desires; James said wrong desires lead to temptations and finally to sin—*James 1:13-15* and Jesus warned that wrong desires would choke out the Word of God—*Mark 4:19*. Abelard's ideas that lustful thoughts are innocuous and that sexual pleasures cannot be wrong because they are natural are unbiblical and spiritually dangerous.

In addition, for Abelard, certifiable sin is acting against one's conscience. As earlier noted, it posed problems with making ethical judgment; it ignored the consequences of actions and 'opened morality to subjectivism'. Abelard tried to solve the problems by making obedience to God's will the bedrock of moral actions and the necessity to accept Christian beliefs in God and the afterlife.

Abelard's *"Moral theory of Atonement"* ignores the need for the Cross and the shedding of the Blood of Jesus Christ. This casts doubts on Abelard's understanding of God's plan of salvation as revealed in Scriptures. The Bible says there is no atonement for sin without the shedding of blood, not just any blood but that of the "Lamb of God, Jesus Christ". To talk of any atonement that discounts Christ's Blood is to either reject or display total ignorance of God's plan for the salvation of Mankind.

Arnold of Brescia (1090—1155 AD) [14, 15]

Arnold was an Italian reformer and a student of Peter Abelard. He preached against the corruption of the priests, bishops, cardinals and popes. He accused them all of simony and said the Church was no longer the true Church nor the pope the true Apostolicus because he did not exemplify the teachings of the Apostles in his life.

He therefore taught that people were not obliged to obey or respect him. He called for clerics to give up their properties, bishops their regalia and monks their possessions; essentially Arnold was calling the Church to give up *power and politics* and focus on ecclesiastical matters.

He was condemned at the *Second Lateran Council in 1139 AD* and sent on exile. He went to France where he continued his campaign against worldly ecclesiastics and monastics.

His teachings were considered erroneous, schismatic and heretical. He was tried at the *Council of Sens* with Abelard in 1141 for heresies and also condemned with him to perpetual silence in monasteries. However, while Abelard submitted to the decision, Arnold refused and went to France where he started a school of moral instructions. He was expelled from

France at the instigation of ***St. Bernard, the abbot of Clairvaux*** and he took refuge in Switzerland.

In 1145, he was in Rome where he got embroiled in a people's uprising calling for a republic. The incumbent **Pope Eugenius III** was exiled from 1146—1148 and Arnold was also excommunicated in 1148. The republic was destroyed when **Pope Adrian IV** sought the help of ***Frederick I Barbarossa (1152-1190)***, the German king, to crush the rebellion in 1155. Arnold was arrested, hanged, his body burned and the ashes cast into the river Tiber, so that his tomb would not become a martyr's shrine.

(Peter Lombard (1100—1164 AD) [16, 17, 18, 19]

Peter Lombard was a French scholastic theologian who was a professor at one time at the school of ***Notre Dame*** in Paris. He wrote sermons and commentaries but his most famous work was ***The Sentences"***. The Sentences covered a wide array of theological doctrines which he systematized in four volumes. The first dealt with God, the Trinity, the attributes of God, Providence, Predestination and evil; the second, the Creation, the Angels, the demons, the fall, grace and sin. The third dealt with the Incarnation, Redemption, the virtues and the Ten Commandments while the fourth treated the Sacraments, death, judgment, hell and heaven.

He drew on the works of the ante—and post-Nicene church Fathers as well as the '***Decretum of Gratian'*** of Bologna and also used the Bible and the work of Abelard.

He compiled and arranged doctrinal theories systematically by summarizing the theories and controversies and attempted to offer solutions to many questions which in turn raised questions and stimulated discussions.

He was not free of controversy, however, and even during his lifetime, his Christological proposition was condemned by Pope Alexander III.

Lombard conceded that man has free will but agreed with Augustine that it was not good or upright. He rejected Abelard's theory that the morality of actions depend on the intensions of the doer.

He viewed God's Grace as power which frees and heals the will of man to perform good and meritorious works.

In tackling the issue of Christ's atonement, he said His sacrificial death is sufficient for reconciliation, justification and freedom from eternal punishment. However, to set man free from temporal punishment, the penances laid on the penitents by the church require the addition of the merits of the penalty borne by Christ for sinners.

He was credited with being the first to clearly classify the seven sacraments.

Comment:
Peter Lombard struggled to explain or justify the Roman Catholic sacrament of penance by saying that Christ's atonement, though adequate for reconciliation, justification and satisfaction for eternal punishment; freedom from temporal punishment requires not just Christ atonement, but the addition of the penances that the clergy lay on penitents.

This is rather confusing as it seems to suggest that Christ's atonement is not sufficient to set man free totally from the penalties of sin which according to the Catholic doctrine include eternal and temporal punishments. He seems to be saying that while Christ's sacrifice suffices for eternal punishment, reconciliation and justification; somehow it is inadequate for temporal punishment and therefore man has to do some lifting too. It also suggests that temporal penalty is more serious than the eternal, which is quite preposterous.

St. Albertus Magnus (c. 1200-1280 AD) [20, 21, 22]

Albertus Magnus was a Dominican friar from a wealthy Bavarian family. He was a very intelligent man, a scientist, philosopher and theologian, who, because of the versatility of his works was called *"Doctor Universalis"* by the Church.

He was a lecturer of the Bible and Lombard's Sentences at the University of Paris. He studied Aristotle, Astronomy, Mathematics, Rhetoric, Ethics, Politics, Logic, Economics, Biology and other natural sciences. He saw no conflict between science and philosophy on the one hand and theology on the other but recognized the fact that knowledge gained through faith and revelation differ from that from scientific observations and philosophical enquiry.

Albert was the first chief Christian commentator on the works of Aristotle, the work he undertook to correct what he perceived as the errors of the Arabian philosopher, *Averroes (1126-1198)*, such as Rationalism, Pantheism and Averroeism.

He felt that Abelard and others had drawn false doctrines from the errors of Averroes in interpreting Aristotle and strove to reconcile apparent contradictions between Christian philosophy and Aristotelianism.

Averroes did not object to religion but considered it as the truth available to the unlettered while for him, philosophy is the real truth comprehensible only by the truly enlightened; therefore, for him, philosophy supersedes religion.

Albertus was recognized as an Alchemist and some legends even credited him with the discovery of the "philosopher's stone" while others believed he was involved in magical arts and crafts with the ability to turn the weather in midwinter to spring. He believed that various types of stones possess occult properties and that stars influence the lives of human beings.

Albertus was Thomas Aquinas' teacher in Paris and Cologne and was also an influence on other scholars of his day and later. He survived and defended his student and friend, Thomas Aquinas; he died in 1280. He was canonized and declared a Doctor of the Church by Pope Pius XI in 1931 and the Patron saint of the natural sciences by Pope Pius XII in 1941.

St. Thomas Aquinas (1225-1274 AD) [23, 24, 25]

Thomas Aquinas was a Dominican priest, scholastic philosopher and theologian of the thirteenth century who was a student of Albertus Magnus.

His works have been classified into three, namely—(1) exegetical, homiletical and liturgical, (2) dogmatic, apologetic and ethical and (3) Philosophical

His exegetical works included commentaries on the Psalms, the book of Job, the Gospels and others. His most famous work was the '*Summa Theologica*' which covered the dogmatic, apologetic and ethical subjects while his philosophical works were commentaries on Aristotle and others.

The Summa Theologica was in three parts; the first part dealt with God's existence and nature, the Trinity, Creation, Angels, Man and Government of creatures. The second part is in two parts; the first dealt with Eschatology, human acts, passions, habits, vice and sin, law and Grace. The second part dealt with Ethics and treated such topics as Faith, Hope, Charity (the supernatural virtues) and Prudence, Justice, Fortitude and Temperance (the natural cardinal virtues) which are biding on everyone.

The third part dealt with the Incarnation, Christ's life, the Sacraments and Penance.

On Epistemology

Thomas Aquinas believed that man needs divine help for the knowledge of the Truth and that God can move man's intellect to understand. However, he also believed that man has the natural capacity to know many things without divine revelation but in regards to faith, divine revelation is required.

On Faith and Reason

Thomas described two ways in which Truth can be known, namely, reason which he called natural revelation, and faith which requires supernatural revelation.

According to Thomas, the supernatural revelation is inspired by the Holy Spirit, made available through the teachings of the Prophets, summed up in the Scriptures and transmitted by the Magisterium. (The Magisterium is the teaching authority of the Catholic Church embodied in the episcopacy, that is, the current body of bishops led by the Pope). He however believed that the natural revelation (reason) and supernatural revelation (faith) are complementary and not contradictory.

On the Existence of God

Thomas tried to prove the existence of God from five arguments based on
  (i) The Unmoved mover
  (ii) the First Cause
  (iii) Contingency
  (iv) Goodness and
  (v) Intelligent Design.

He described the attributes of God as **_simplicity, unity, infinity, immutability, goodness, perfection, omnipotence and eternity._**

On Creation

Thomas was not opposed to the possibility of life emerging from inanimate or plant life in the course of creation. He said **_"it is not incompatible with the nature of things that from the corruption of the less perfect, the more perfect should be generated"._**

Aquinas' position seems not incompatible with evolution, though his position does not support random and mindless evolution.

He also described four kinds of laws—Eternal, natural, human and divine.

Eternal law is the decree of God that governs all creation; Natural law is the human participation in the eternal law which is discovered by reason and based on first principles.

The first precept, on which all other precepts of the natural law are based, is that ***"good is to be done and promoted and evil is to be avoided".*** He described human laws as positive laws which create new rights by legislation. (As opposed to natural laws which are inherent and not conferred by legislation).

He defined Divine laws as specially revealed laws in the Scripture.

On Sexuality

He considered the desire to live and procreate basic human values on which other human values are based. He opposed non-procreative sexual activities and condemned masturbation, oral sex, coitus interruptus and sexual positions other than the 'missionary position' because they are not conducive to conception.

On Theology

Thomas Aquinas considered Theology as a Science and was considered a proponent of '**Natural Theology'**, that is, theology based on reason. He believed that man can know some things about God based on reason and ordinary experience as distinguished from **'Revealed Theology'** based on Scriptures and religious experiences.

He affirmed the Nicene Creed of the Trinity and the Church's position on the nature of Jesus Christ.

On Heretics

Thomas Aquinas was very severe on perceived heretics; he said—***"With regards to heretics, two points must be observed, one on their own side and the other on the side of the Church. On their own side, there is the sin, whereby they deserve, not only to be separated from the Church by excommunication, but also to be severed from the world by death. For it is much graver matter to corrupt the faith which quicken the soul than to forge money, which supports temporal life . . ."***

He called on the Church to be merciful and admonish the heretics but if they remain stubborn, the Church should hand them over to the secular authorities.

On Evil, Sin, Predestination and Redemption
On the subject of evil, he rejected Dionysius' view that "evil would conduce to the perfection of the universe" as a reduction to an absurdity. His own position on the matter was that *"God neither wills evil to be done nor wills it not to be done; but wills to permit evil to be done; and this is good"*.

Thomas Aquinas, like St. Augustine believed in Original Sin through Adam by procreation. He defined sin as deviation from reason and divine moral laws originating from the will.

His position on the ultimate causation of sin is unclear. While he conceded that, on the one hand, God is not the cause of sin; on the other hand, he said that because God is the "cause of all things, ultimately and He is 'efficacious' also in sin". Furthermore, he said that the devil is not the direct cause of sin but only the inciter through man's desires and imaginations.

Aquinas believed that nothing in the world is free, by chance or by accident; and though he spoke about God's justice and mercy, he believed, like Augustine, that God predestined some people to eternal life and others to reprobation.

He believed that, although God could have forgiven man in a different way if He wanted to, He chose not to without satisfaction through Christ's obedience in suffering and death. Through Christ's atonement, man is delivered from the devil, obtained immunity from punishment, is reconciled to God and obtained eternal life.

Aquinas is regarded as a "*Doctor of the Church*"; he died in 1274 and was canonized fifty years later by Pope John XXII.

John Duns Scotus (1265-1308 AD) [26, 27, 28]

John Duns was a Scottish Franciscan philosopher and theologian. He was a lecturer of Peter Lombards Sentences in Paris and Cologne.

On theology, Duns Scotus agreed with Thomas Aquinas that one can know about God's existence from reason but not His essence which can only be known through revelation. He also agreed with Aquinas that what is known of God through reason begin with the creatures made by God, that is reasoning from the effect to the cause.

He however disagreed with Aquinas on the application of predicates. Whereas Aquinas had asserted that the same word cannot be applied to God with the same meaning with which it is applied to man, Duns Scotus maintained that for such predicates to be valid they had to be applied "univocally".

He tried to prove the existence and attributes of God from the *concept of infinity*. On this point also, he disagreed with Aquinas; while Aquinas' concept of infinity was *"negative and relational"*, Duns Scotus adopted the concept of infinity which is both *"positive and intrinsic"*. He contended that the concept of an "Infinite Being" simplified man's understanding of God, as such an infinite being would also possess all other infinite perfections.

He rejected *Skepticism* which held that nothing can be known with certainty; and *Illuminationalism* which held that certainty was only possible through divine illumination. He asserted that some truths can be known with certainty by reason.

He was an advocate of the literal sense in scriptural interpretation.

He argued for the *immaculate conception* of the Virgin Mary and posited that the grace of redemption was given to her in advance so that she was conceived without the taint of original sin. (*This doctrine of the immaculate conception of the Virgin Mary was later adopted by the Roman Catholic Church as dogma*).

Duns Scotus was unappreciated by many in his age and his critics accused him of sophistry. The term "Dunce" coined from his name was used to describe someone incapable of scholarship. This characterization is considered unfair and Duns has had influence on many subsequent scholars.

He was beatified by Pope John Paul II in 1993.

William of Ockham (1285-1349 AD) [29, 30, 31]

William of Ockham was an English Franciscan friar and scholastic philosopher. His writings were controversial and many were political. This landed him in trouble with the papacy which instituted a theological commission in Avignon to review his commentaries in 1324.

While still on this, the Minister General of his order asked him to review the position of Pope John XII on Apostolic poverty. When he did, they found that by Franciscan standards, the pope was a heretic on the issue. Fearing for their lives, they fled to Munich in 1328 and took refuge with Louis IV of Germany who was also in dispute with the pope. William was excommunicated for leaving Avignon without permission.

On Church—State Relations
He continued to write political treatises; he wrote that the Pope should not exercise temporal power or interfere in the affairs of the Empire and was an advocate of what was called *"secular absolutism"*. However, in spiritual matters he recognized and respected the authority of the Church.

On Papal Supremacy
He influenced the development of the principle of *"Conciliarism"*, which affirmed the representatives of the faithful as the last authority on spiritual matters rather than the pope. The idea gained traction for a while, especially during the Avignon papacy and shortly after but papal supremacy was quickly re-established.

On Theology
Ockham is considered a *fideist*, that is, he held that belief in God is predicated on faith rather than knowledge. On this issue, he differed from most of his predecessors who had tried to link faith and reason.

He considered the doctrine of the trinity a syllogical contradiction and held that theology is illogical and should not be mixed with philosophy.

He rejected both the ontological and cosmological proof of God's existence of Anselm and Aquinas respectively.

On Ethics and Morality
Ockham subscribed to the *"Divine Command"* theory of morality:

"That God does not command us to be kind because kindness is good; rather kindness is good because God commanded it". In other words, he believed that God is the standard of goodness rather than God conforming to a conceived standard of goodness. That God's will establishes right and wrong. Many of Ockham's contemporaries were uncomfortable with this theory but for him Divine freedom was paramount.

On Philosophy
In philosophy, Ockham was the proponent of what became known as the *"Ockham Razor"*—a concept that advocated not *"multiplying entities beyond necessity"*.

He also influenced the emergence of liberal democratic ideologies such as freedom of speech and the development of property rights through his influence on later political and theological thinkers like **Hobbes, Locke** and **Rousseau.**

He died in 1349 and was rehabilitated in 1359 by Pope Innocent VI.

John Wycliffe (1320-1384 AD) [32, 33, 34, 35, 36]

John Wycliffe was an English scholar, theologian and proponent of reform in the Roman Catholic Church in the fourteenth century.

A lecturer at the Oxford University, he entered the ecclesiastical political arena as a theological counsel to the English government in 1365.

That year Pope Urban V demanded the payment of the feudal tribute from England which King John (Lackland) had committed the nation to thirty five years earlier. The parliament refused to pay and told the Pope that neither King John nor anyone had the right to put England in subjection to a foreign power. The Pope wisely dropped the issue.

On State—Church Relations

John Wycliffe opposed the claim that St. Peter, and by extension the Popes, had united in their hands, both temporal and spiritual powers.

He considered as pernicious, the involvement of the clergy in temporal issues.

He taught that kings derive their authority from God and everyone, including the clergy should be subject to them; on the other hand, kings should align their laws with God's laws and rule with wisdom.

He contended that in temporal matters, the King was above the Pope and denounced the ownership of properties by the clergy. He believed the King should withdraw the property of any clergy who misused it.

On Church Corruption

He campaigned tirelessly against corruption in the Church and what he believed were wrong teachings and doctrines in the Roman Catholic Church.

His fundamental position is that the Church should be like Jesus Christ and the Apostles in regard to possessions.

He opposed the collection of annates and the sale of indulgences and considered the practice simony. He was fiercely opposed by the monks of the orders that owned properties who branded his ideas as dangerous; and the clergy who accused him of blasphemy, scandal, pride and heresy.

He called the cardinals *"the very synagogue and nest of Satan and heretics and the Pope the vicar of the devil"*.

The Church and Papal Supremacy

He corrected the pervasive but erroneous idea of the time that "the Church" consisted of the pope and the clergy and he defined the Church as consisting of all believers and that the pope, if not a true believer might not even be a member.

He also believed that Christ is the head of the Church and not the Pope; that the Church includes the ***'Church triumphant'*** in heaven and the ***'Church militant'*** on earth.

John Wycliffe believed that the Church did not need an earthly leader like the pope although the right kind of leader would do no harm. He criticized the mode of papal elections saying that if the electors were themselves not real Christians, they may in fact elect an anti-Christ.

On the Scripture and Christian Doctrines

Wycliffe believed that the Scripture is the basis of all Christian doctrines and faith as well as the only authority.

He believed everyone should have access to the Scriptures; therefore he teamed up with a friend to translate the bible from the Latin Vulgate to English.

The Church, strangely, vehemently opposed Wycliffe's effort to put the Bible in the laity's hands, saying: ***"The jewel of clergy has become the toy of the laity"*** and tried to destroy the manuscripts.

Wycliffe wrote persistently against the errors he observed in the monasteries, the clergy and the Church hierarchy.

In 1377, Pope Gregory XI published five Bulls to denounce Wycliffe's eighteen theses as erroneous and dangerous to the Church and the State and John Wycliffe used Scriptures to counter the entire papal and clerical onslaught.

From Pope Gregory's condemnation of Wycliffe, he was alleged to have denied the real presence of Christ in the Eucharist and that monasticism had no basis in the Scripture. Therefore, monks should earn their keep through working with their hands and that the practice of giving them alms should cease. He was also accused of saying that a clergy in mortal sin whatever the level in the hierarchy could not validly perform the function.

Philosophically, he believed the preexistence in thought of all reality; therefore he held that 'the free will of man is predetermined by God'. He was therefore a believer in predestination and election.

He advocated the study of logic which he believed essential in understanding Scripture and that ignorance of logic was the reason Scripture was misunderstood.

On Evangelism (Lollardy & Wycliffism) [37]

Wycliffe had many converts called '***Bible men***' but derisively '***Lollards***', by the papacy. These were itinerant preachers who lived simply but not bound by any vows.

Wycliffe died of stroke in 1384.

Wycliffism grew strong after Wycliffe's death in 1384 and by 1395; Wycliffites gained the cooperation of the parliament to which they forwarded *"Twelve Conclusions"* on which they sought Church reform. The twelve issues included:

- (i) the state of the Church,
- (ii) the Priesthood,
- (iii) Clerical celibacy,
- (iv) Transubstantiation,
- (v) Exorcism and Hallowings,
- (vi) Clerical secular offices,
- (vii) Prayers for the dead, (Chantries)
- (viii) Pilgrimages,
- (ix) Confessions,
- (x) Crusades and wars,
- (xi) Female vows of continence and Abortions and
- (xii) Arts and crafts in churches (icons).

The 'Conclusions':
- Denounced the decadence of the papacy, episcopate, monastics and the clergy.
- They felt that the vow of celibacy attached to the priesthood fostered homosexuality and that the same vows by nuns led to sins like abortions, infanticide and bestiality.
- They also said that prayer for the dead was simony,
- That confessions to priests were useless
- That a pilgrimage for the purpose of venerating icons was nothing but idolatry.

- Also denounced were the various forms of rituals in the Church and the practice of the clergy holding secular offices.

However, soon after, the Church and the State combined to persecute Wycliffites. In fact by 1408, laws were promulgated against the Wycliffite "heresy" and the translation of the Bible and other books was forbidden. Books considered heretical were to be submitted for burning and "heretics' were to be burnt at the stakes. Wycliffism became a capital offence in England and many, including the nobility such as *Sir John Oldcastle* were burnt at stake in 1417, while others fled the country. Wycliffism was not destroyed by persecution; it survived to merge with Protestantism in the sixteenth century.

Wycliffe was posthumously condemned as a heretic at the *Council of Constance in 1415*; his books were ordered burnt and his bones exhumed. In 1428, Pope Martin V carried out the Council's decree, Wycliffe's bones were exhumed, burnt and the ashes cast into the river.

John (Jan) Hus (1369-1415 AD) [38, 39, 40, 41]

Jan Hus, a priest, professor of theology and reformer, was born in Bohemia, present day Czech Republic in 1369.

Jan lived during the period of the Western schism and was influenced by the writings of John Wycliffe. He conducted his sermons in the local language like Wycliffe whose writings he continued to publicly affirm even after they were condemned in Bohemia.

Jan Hus, in his homilies, treatises and commentaries, criticized the Roman Catholic Church's doctrines and practices based on the Scripture.

On the Church
Jan Hus held that:
- The Church is made up of all who are predestined to blessedness (clergy and laity) and not only the Pope and the clergy as was widely held at the time.
- The Roman Catholic Church was not the Church but only a part of the Church militant which is not inerrant.
- That the Rock on which the Church is built is Jesus Christ and not the Apostle Peter.
- That to be in the Church is not the same as been of the Church. That there are many in the Church that are not predestinate to glory.

On the Pope, the Papacy, the Curia and the Clergy
Hus held:
- That the Pope is not the head of the Church but Jesus Christ. He chronicled a list of simoniacal, avaricious, adulterous and murderous popes to back his assertions.
- That the office of the pope is not of divine origin but a human invention for orderly administration of the Church
- That "the power of the keys", to loose and bind were not given exclusively to the Apostle Peter but to all the Apostles and the Church also—Mathew 16:19 and Mathew 18:18. That the "keys" given to the Church were *"Knowledge and Authority"* to preach, administer Sacraments and care for the sheep.
- That the Pope is not infallible and may err in matters of faith; may be a heretic or even a wicked person as attested to by history. He cited the cases of popes like ***Pope Benedict IX, Boniface VIII and his contemporary rival Popes Clement VII, Benedict XIII and Gregory XI***I who were declared heretics by the Council of Pisa. He argued that since a Judas made the list of Christ's Apostles, a reprobate or an anti-Christ may make the papacy.
- That the Church can exist without the pope and that in order to obey God, an erring pope or clergy should be disobeyed.
- That the Roman Catholic Church's concept of the Pope was unscriptural. That in the early Church, all the Bishops were called popes and that the bishop of Rome was just one of several.
- That the unity of the Church does not reside in the pope but in 'predestinating grace' manifesting in the exercise of Christian virtues.
- That priestly acts are valid only if the priest's life conform to the laws of Christ
- That not only the bishops, but all presbyters were successors of the Apostles.

On the Scripture, Salvation and the Eucharist
Jan Hus Held:
- That the Scripture is the supreme authority for faith and conduct.
- That Salvation is by divine predestination and not through the pope

- That it is impossible, without revelation, to know with certainty those who are members of Christ's mystical body (the real Church) on earth.
- That the laity should be given the Bread and the Wine in the celebration of the Eucharist as established by Jesus Christ and not the Bread alone as was being practiced by the Roman Catholic Church.

On the treatment of 'heretics'
Jan Hus believed:
- That censure should be used sparingly against heretics and that superior argument should be used to win them over.
- That those deemed heretics should not be killed since Jesus Christ did not call down fire on the Samaritan village that rejected his teachings—*Luke 9:51-56.*
- That sometimes, those who were called 'heretics' may actually be the ones holding the true doctrine.

On Corruption in the Church
Jan observed:
- That the luxury and pomp that surrounded the papacy, the Curia and the episcopacy were unscriptural and that Christ held no civil office.
- That both temporal and spiritual powers do not reside in the pope
- That it was presumptuous for any priest to claim to absolve anyone of sins.
- That the Scripture was being abused in the interest of clerical power

Jan Hus also condemned simony in the Church and wrote a tract in which he decried the sale of indulgences, baptisms, masses, confirmations, chrisms, parishes, episcopates, canonries and so on. He also decried the practice of placing a community or even a nation under interdict for the sake of one man.

Conflict with the Roman Catholic Hierarchy
His activities brought him into conflict with his archbishop and the papacy. To compound the problem, he supported a different rival pope from his archbishop who excommunicated him in 1412 for insubordination.

He was summoned to the **Council of Constance in 1414** to defend himself against charges of heresy with his safety guaranteed by the *Emperor Sigismund (1361-1437)* no matter the outcome. However, he was promptly arrested, tried and found guilty of heresy and was burnt at the stakes in 1415. **He refused to recant what he believed to be biblical truths even in the flames.**

With his last breath he prophesied that: *"In one hundred years, God will raise up a man whose calls for reforms cannot be suppressed".*

His ashes were thrown into the Rhine River.

The Hussites [42, 43, 44]

However, Jan Hus' ideas did not die with him; but spread to Poland, Hungary, Croatia and Austria. His supporters formed a movement that became a quasi political as well as religious resistance movement led by **Jakoubek Stribo** who was Hus' successor at the Bethlehem chapel in Prague.

The members of the movement, known as *Hussites,* rejected the verdict of the Council of Constance; evicted priests and monks and divested them of their possessions. They replaced the priests with *Ultraquist* priests, that is, priests who believed in the Eucharist in both kinds—the Bread and the Chalice—for the laity.

Between 1415 and 1420, there were skirmishes between the Roman Catholic loyalist nobles and priests and the Hussites.

In 1420, *Pope Martin V (1417-1431)* sent 'crusaders' to help Emperor Sigismund to exterminate the Hussites, the Wycliffites and other groups perceived as 'heretics'. The crusaders were defeated. In the ensuing negotiations, the Hussites drew up what became known as the "*Four Articles of Prague*" in which they stated their demands. The demands were for:

(i) The freedom of priests to preach from the Scripture
(ii) The Holy Communion for the laity to be in both kinds, the Chalice (wine) and the Bread.
(iii) The return of Church lands to secular owners and the return of the clergy to the precepts of Christ in regards to worldly possessions.

(iv) The prohibition of prostitution and the punishment of serious sinners by the laws of the land.

The Emperor, influenced by the papal legates who saw the demands as being prejudicial to the interest and authority of the papacy, rejected them and so the conflicts persisted.

Between 1420 and 1433, many crusades were launched against the Hussites but all failed and then the papacy agreed to negotiate. The demands of the Hussites were addressed at the ***Council of Basle*** and the agreement reached and finally signed in 1436 was called the '**Compactata of Basle'.** In substance, the Compactata was similar to the original 'Four articles of Prague'.

The moderate faction of the Hussites, the 'Ultraquists' accepted the agreement but the more radical 'Taborites' rejected it as they wanted more reforms.

This eventually caused a civil war between the Hussite factions with the defeat of the Taborites.

Relative peace was maintained until Pope Pius II (1458-1464) in 1462 declared the Compactata of Basle null and void. This rekindled religious and civil wars until equal rights were once again granted to Roman Catholic and Ultraquist factions.

In the cause of time, some of the Ultraquists by degrees became more Catholic except in the Chalice for the laity, while others later joined the Lutherans.

Chapter 11

Controversies, 'Heresies' and Schisms of the Middle Ages

The Eucharistic Controversy [1,2]
The controversy arose from the teachings of the theologian, **Berengarius (c.999-1088) of Tours**.

The doctrine of Transubstantiation of the Eucharist, (which stated that after consecration, the Bread and the Wine of the Eucharist are transformed literally into the real body and blood of Jesus Christ) had become accepted in the Roman Catholic Church. However, Berengarius taught that the bread and the wine do not literally turn to the body and blood of Jesus Christ after consecration, but that, while the bread and wine remain unchanged, they become for the believer the real body and blood of Jesus Christ in spiritual sense.

He was asked to recant this position and he complied to preserve his life but instantly reversed himself and continued to propagate his view among his students for years. One of them, Eusebius Bruno was condemned in absentia with him at the Synod of Paris.

In 1079, he was once again asked to recant by one of his friends in high places Hildebrand who had become Pope Gregory VII. He made his final retraction and retired to an Island to live in prayer and solitude, saddened according to some, that he had not had the steadfastness of heart to maintain his ground while others claimed he lived the rest of his life at peace with the Roman Catholic Church. He died in 1088.

The Cathari and Catharism [3,4,5]
Catharism was a dualistic Gnostic doctrine which surfaced in Europe in the eleventh century. It is believed to have come from the Byzantine Empire where it started as Manichaeism by way of the Balkans where it morphed into *Bogomilism* and finally into Europe.

The adherents of the faith are known as Cathari or Cathars which means 'The Pure'. They were also called *Albigenses* or *Albigensians* because the place where the religion first flourished in the South of France was *Albi*. There were two levels, 'the perfect' and 'believers'; the perfect were strictly ascetic and worked as artisans.

The Cathari believed that there is a good god, the creator and a bad god that is constantly trying to tempt and harm men. The group also believed in reincarnation, they were strictly vegetarian, did not lie, swear or take oaths and did not kill animals or men.

The people and the nobility supported them and they won many converts such that by the end of the thirteenth century, Catharism was the main religion in southern France. Many Catholics, including priests converted to Catharism.

In open debates, the unschooled Cathari embarrassed the Catholic theologians and the simplicity and honesty of the Cathari was in sharp contrast to the hypocrisy of the Catholic clergy that vowed poverty and preached poverty but lived in opulence.

The Cathari held the Catholic hierarchy in contempt and called them *"the church of wolves"* whilst the Catholics called the Cathari "the Synagogue of Satan". The papacy noticed what was happening and tried to oppose the Cathari with negative propaganda but it didn't work.

Therefore in 1208, Pope Innocent III called for a Crusade against the Cathari and declared indulgences for participants. Many knights and nobles signed up for the Crusade because participants could keep any conquered land.

The Crusade, called the *"Albigensian Crusade"*, was led by the papal legate, an Abbot of the Cistercian Order called *Arnaud Amaury*. The crusaders descended on the Cathari and massacred thousands of them; Amaury, when asked by a crusader how to differentiate Catholics from Cathari, was credited with the infamous statement—**"Kill them all, God will know His own"**.

The Albigensian Crusade continued on and off till 1255 when the last stronghold of the Cathari was conquered. Apart from the use of force, the Church also gave approbation to two mendicant orders, *the Franciscan* and *the Dominican Orders* who, ab-initio, were true to their vows of poverty. The Dominicans especially were instrumental in rooting out the Cathari in mop up operations after the crusade and they were specially trained as inquisitors and used by the Church for the Inquisition for centuries. The atrocities of the inquisitors was reported to have aroused popular revolt in 1235 which led to the inquisitors being run out of many towns, albeit, temporarily and some of them even killed.

The Waldenses [6, 7, 8]

The Waldenses or Waldensians were allegedly founded by Peter Waldo (c.999-1188), a rich merchant of Lyons. He used his influence and resources to get two priests to translate the four Gospels, some other biblical books and the works of the church fathers like Augustine and Jerome into the vernacular. As he read the bible, he became more fervent in faith and felt the need to live according to the teachings of Jesus Christ. When he enquired from his priest what he needed to do, Mathew 19:21 was quoted to him—*"If you want to be perfect, go sell your possessions and give to the poor . . ."* (NIV).

He obeyed promptly, provided for his wife and daughters and gave the rest to the poor.

Then he began to preach, and using the bible in the local language attracted many who were used to clerics who conducted mass and said prayers in Latin which they didn't understand. Many were attracted to the movement and those who would be preachers also took vows of poverty, chastity and obedience.

Waldo didn't want to form a church or leave the Catholic Church, he just wanted to live according to the Bible, and therefore, he asked his Archbishop for the permission to preach. His request was passed to Pope Alexander III who granted him permission but as granted by the local clerics.

The local clerics, out of envy refused to grant the movement permission to preach, so they disobeyed, choosing to obey God rather than man, and continued to preach.

Waldensians believed that preaching was necessary for salvation; and that salvation was not through the sacraments as taught by the Catholic Church.

In 1179, the ***Third Lateran Council*** prohibited the group from preaching; but again, the prohibition was ignored and in 1184, the movement was declared schismatic by Pope Lucius III.

In 1215, the movement was declared heretical by the ***Fourth Lateran Council*** because, among others, the Waldensians denied the doctrines of purgatory, indulgences and chantries (prayers for the dead).

- They believed that the Communion was a remembrance and not a sacrifice; were skeptical about the doctrine of transubstantiation of the bread and the wine and both kinds were given to all.
- They believed in the priesthood of all believers and the fact that the validity of the Sacrament depended on the worthiness of the minister.
- They doubted the validity of infant baptism
- They were opposed to lying, swearing and oath taking.
- They opposed wars and violence except in defense of self and family; they spoke against crusades against Jews and infidels and they were opposed to capital punishment and coercion in matters of faith.
- They did not engage in speculative theology on doctrinal issues but were advocates of spirituality, high ethical standards and personal integrity.
- They were modest in dressing and conduct and temperate in eating and drinking, keeping away from taverns, dances and other vanities. They worked as artisans and avoided trading because of its inevitable lies, oaths and frauds.

The movement's simplicity and honesty compared to the Roman Catholic clergy's opulence and corruption resonated well with the people and the sect grew fast, spreading to Italy, Spain, Switzerland and England.

In 1207, Pope Innocent III succeeded in making some members to return to the Catholic Church, these he organized into a religious order called the **"Poor Catholics"** with the express purpose of converting other Waldensians.

The Waldensians were also persecuted during the Albigensian crusade and were subjected to the Inquisition. Those found guilty were tortured, suffocated in caves, thrown to their death from cliffs or burnt at the stakes.

In spite of the persecutions, the Roman Catholic Church did not succeed in exterminating the movement and they persisted until the reformation in the sixteenth century when they merged with other groups.

The Inquisition [9, 10, 11, 12]

The Inquisition was an institution in the Catholic Church charged with the discovery, trial, punishment and eradication of 'heresies'; that is, any religious opinion other than that held by the Roman Catholic Church.

It was initiated informally by ***Pope Innocent III (1198-1216)*** as a mop up instrument after the Albigensian crusades but it was formalized by his successors.

The formal Inquisition was instituted by ***Pope Gregory IX (1227-1241 AD)*** in 1233 to deal with the remnants of the Albigensian sect in southern France. The inquisitors were mainly drawn from the Dominican friars but frequently supported by the Franciscan friars.

The process:

The Inquisition in a community usually begins with a 'period of grace' of thirty to forty days in which those who considered themselves 'heretics' could voluntarily confess.

When a heretic failed to self report during the period of grace;
- Questioning occurred upon the testimony of at least two or more witnesses. However, the accused was not allowed to personally meet his accusers, neither were their names revealed to him. This was legalized by ***Popes Gregory IX, Innocent IV and Alexander IV*** but set aside partly by ***Pope Boniface VIII*** who allowed witnesses to be named although there was still no cross examination of accusers
- The testimonies of known heretics, perjurers, excommunicated persons and other infamous persons were admissible in Inquisitorial courts. (Ironically, the testimonies of such people were not admissible in civil courts in the interest of justice)! The inquisitors were initially disturbed about this provision but Pope Alexander IV silenced their scruples.
- There were no legal representations allowed for the accused; in fact Pope Innocent III in 1205 prohibited, on threat of excommunication, any legal representation for 'heretics'.
- There were usually no witnesses for the accused because such witnesses would immediately come under suspicion of heresy themselves.
- The use of various forms of torture to extract a confession was authorized in 1252 by Pope Innocent IV with the proviso that the

torture must not cause loss of life or limb. The techniques of torture included: ***imprisonment with starvation, threats of torture and death, false promise of leniency and use of torture instruments like the rack, Judas' chair, skinning, torture chair, strappado, burning, thumb screws, the wheel, water-boarding*** and so on.
- Again, when inquisitors felt appalled by this provision because it caused "irregularity" in the inquisitors' offices, the Pope granted them the power to absolve themselves.
- The accused was required to swear before the inquisitor to accept the sentence, whatever it might be with good grace, (this created a problem for sects whose beliefs forbid oath taking but helped the inquisitors to quickly separate them out on suspicion of heresy).

The penalties:
- Those who availed themselves of the period of grace were sentenced according to whether they were secretive or open in their heresy. A secret heretic is sentenced to secret penance while open heretics were given light canonical penance like short pilgrimages in the locality and the wearing of the *'cross of infamy'*—yellow crosses sewn to the clothing. Others were required to perform longer pilgrimages or participation in a crusade.
- For those prosecuted and found guilty but repentant, the sentence included Imprisonment for life and forfeiture of properties, a third of which accrued to the convicting court, a third to the accuser and a third to the state for the upkeep of the accused in jail. Another penalty for this category was banishment, also with confiscation of property.
- Those who were unrepentant were handed over to the temporal powers for execution, usually by burning at the stake; in addition to confiscation of properties and razing down of the houses.

The Purpose:
The purpose of the penalties for the repentant was for correction and to serve as deterrent for future infringement for the accused as well as a warning for others.

The purpose of the inquisitional penalties for the unrepentant was 'for the public good' and not for the correction or the good of the 'heretic'; but designed to terrify others into submission and return to the Catholic faith.

The Inquisition was not applied only to the living, it was often used against the dead and if found guilty, their bones were exhumed and burned and their properties confiscated with no thought for the children or other dependants.

One such case pitted the Franciscan order against the Dominicans who were the major inquisitors. A rich patron of the Franciscan order, **Castel Fabre** had died and endowed the order with his property. However, he was posthumously accused of heresy; if convicted, his property would be appropriated by the Dominicans.

A Franciscan friar, **Bernard Delicieux** appeared in his defense and he was cleared. Bernard Delicieux was a critic of the Inquisition and was reputed to have said that, "were Saints Peter and Paul to be subjected to the inquisition, they would not escape". It was therefore not surprising that he was implicated in a political plot, tried by the Inquisition and sent to prison where he later died.

The Inquisition was not applied only in cases of frank or pure heresy; it was used on Catholics who became social critics of the papacy like Bernard Delicieux. Popes Clement V and John XXII persecuted and turned the Inquisition on the Franciscan 'Spirituals' and sided with the 'Conventuals' who preferred a less ascetic lifestyle. Many of the 'Spirituals' and the Franciscan Third order were tried by the Inquisition for their preference of asceticism and criticism of the flamboyant lifestyles of the clergy and church hierarchy.

The Spanish / Portuguese Inquisitions (1478-1834 AD) [13, 14, 15]

In 1478, *King Ferdinand (1452-1516)* and *Queen Isabella (1451-1504)* sought and obtained permission from *Pope Sixtus IV (1471-1484*) to institute the Inquisition in Spain.

Initially, the Spanish Inquisition was instituted against suspected 'false Jewish (marranos) and Moslem (moriscos) converts'; that is those who pretended to be Catholics but were still practicing Judaism or Islam secretly. In 1483, Pope Sixtus IV appointed a Dominican monk, **Tomas de Torquemada** as the Inquisitor General for Spain.

In 1492, the Jews were expelled from Spain to prevent them from polluting Jewish converts; they moved to Morocco in North Africa, to Portugal and other countries.

In 1497, most were again expelled from Portugal.

In the sixteenth century, after almost eight centuries in most of Spain, the Moslems were driven out. Those who converted, like the Jews, also came under suspicion of clandestinely practicing Islam and were subjected to the inquisition.

The Inquisition virtually kept Protestantism out of Spain after the reformation in the sixteenth century. Apart from the 'heretics', Jews and Moslems; the various Inquisitions also targeted alleged witches, wizards and sorcerers many of whom were burnt at the stake over many centuries.

The Inquisition went international when Queen Isabella and King Ferdinand) of Spain authorized the use of the Inquisition in the Americas and in Asia even as efforts were being made to convert the natives to the Catholic faith. The Inquisition was directed mainly at the same group of people that were more vulnerable in Europe but who fled to the New World to seek respite from the heat of religious fervor at home.

In 1542, *Pope Paul III (1534-1549 AD)* created in the Papacy, a permanent department called the **'Holy Office of the Inquisition'**, fully staffed with Cardinals and other officials to deal with heresy and defend the faith.

Intellectuals were not spared; *Copernicus*' book was forbidden and *Galileo Galilei (1564-1642)* an Italian Physicist and Astronomer got into trouble with the Church for his heliocentric theory of the universe as opposed to the geocentric view held by the Church. In 1633, he was made to face the Inquisition on suspicion of heresy and was found guilty. He was forced to recant and was, on account of his age, placed under house arrest until he died in 1642.

In 1992, Pope John Paul II expressed regret for how the Roman Catholic Church handled Galileo's case and acknowledged the errors of the Church in her evaluation of his scientific positions.

The Inquisition was responsible for the death of thousands and the displacement of hundreds of thousands.

One historian wondered whether "**the stimulant of pillage (of properties) lent the Inquisition the good will of the princes and the Church**".

The people of the time thought so, for some were on record as saying that **"The Inquisition was designed to rob people; they were burnt for their money . . . and only the rich were burnt"**.

COMMENT

The Bible, in particular, the New Testament is replete with warnings about false teachers and false teachings. Jesus Christ constantly warned believers about them—*Mathew 7:15; Mathew 24:11, 24;*

And His recipe for dealing with the issue was correct knowledge and watchfulness.

Even for those who rejected His teachings, His instruction to the apostles was to leave them alone—*Luke 10:10-12.* When James and John took umbrage at a Samaritan village that would not give them audience and asked that they be allowed to call down fire on the villagers, Jesus scolded them saying: "You do not know what kind of Spirit you are of, for the Son of Man did not come to destroy men's lives but to save them"—*Luke 9:55-56 (51-56).*

The Apostles also warned about false teachers and their heresies—*(Acts 20:29; 2Corinthians 11:13-15; 1Timothy 4:1-3; 2Peter 2:1-3; 1John 4:1-6.* Again their prescription is for believers to be watchful, to patiently admonish, instruct and correct *(2Timothy 4:2, Titus 1:10-11, 13)*; to excommunicate unrepentant heretics so that they would not infect the whole body—*(Romans 16:17; Titus 3:10-11;* and to commend the believers to God for safe keeping—*Jude 17-24.*

Therefore, during the apostolic era, force or violence against unbelievers or heretics was unheard of.

In the first three centuries AD, the early 'Church Fathers' were opposed to the use of force against those perceived as 'heretics'; instead many of them were 'apologists' who defended the faith with arguments.

Here are some of the early Fathers in their own words:

Tertullian (c.160-c.225) [16] who did not believe that a Christian should serve in the military said:

"If a Christian has no right to use force, even in the name of the State, he is all the more bound not to use it against his dissenting brethren in the name of the Gospel, which is a law of gentleness . . . It is a fundamental human right, a privilege of nature that every man should worship according to his convictions. It is assuredly no part of religion to compel religion. It must be embraced freely, not forced".

Cyprian (c.200-c.258) [16] **said:**

"God commanded that those who did not obey his priests or hearken to his judges, appointed for the time, should be slain. Then indeed they were slain with the sword, while the circumcision of the flesh was yet in force; but now that circumcision has begun to be of the Spirit among God's faithful servants, the proud and contumacious are slain with the sword of the Spirit by being cast out of the Church".

Lactantius (c.250-c.325) [16] wrote:

"There is no justification for violence and injury, for religion cannot be imposed by force. It is a matter of the will which must be influenced by words not blows ... Why then do they rage, and increase, instead of lessening their folly? Torture and piety have nothing in common; there is no union possible between truth and violence, justice and cruelty ... For religion is to be defended, not by putting to death, but by dying; not by cruelty, but by patient endurance; not by crime but by faith ... If you wish to defend religion by bloodshed, by tortures and by crime, you no longer defend it, but pollute and profane it. For nothing is so much a matter of free will as religion".

St. Hilary of Poitiers (c.300-c.368) [16] said:

"I ask you bishops to tell me, whose favor did the Apostles seek in preaching the Gospel and on whose power did they rely to preach Jesus Christ? Today, alas, while the power of the State enforces divine faith, men say that Christ is powerless. The Church threatens exile and imprisonment; she in whom men formerly believed while in exile and prison, now wishes to make men believe her by force ... She is now exiling the very priests who once spread her gospel. What a striking contrast between the Church of the past and the Church of today".

St. Chrysostom (347-407)

"For Christians above all men are forbidden to correct the stumbling of sinners by force ... It is necessary to make a man better, not by force but by persuasion. We neither have authority granted us by law to restrain sinners, nor, if it were, should we know how to use it, since God gives the crown to those who are kept from evil, not by force but by choice". [17]

In spite of the virtual unanimity of the Church fathers in opposition to the use of force or violence against heretics up to the end of the third century, by the middle of the fourth century, divergent views were emerging.

St. Optatus (d. 385) [16] **Bishop of Milevis said:**

'Will you tell me that it is not lawful to defend the rights of God by the death penalty? ... If killing is an evil, the guilty ones are themselves the cause of it. It is impossible, you say, for the State to inflict the death penalty in the name of God; but was it not in the name of God that Moses, Phineas and Elijah put to death the worshippers of the golden calf and the apostates of the old law? ... 'These times are altogether different' you reply, 'the New Law must not be confounded with the Old. Did not Christ forbid St. Peter to use the sword?'

Yes, undoubtedly, but Christ came to suffer, not to defend Himself. The lot of Christians is different from that of Christ".

St Augustine (354-430)

St. Augustine evolved from a position of absolute toleration of heretics to that of approval of coercion for the purpose of changing heretics but not the death penalty. He also subscribed to the use of civil authorities to bring heretics in line with what is considered the true doctrine.

It is obvious that over time, even though the Roman Catholic Church pride itself on tradition, on the issue of force and violence against heretics, it did not adhere to the oldest and the more Christian tradition but rather the tradition that was based on the Old Testament.

The doctrine of violence against heretics developed after Emperor Constantine's conversion to Christianity. He considered himself as the *"Bishop of the Externals" of religion* with the duty of protecting the true religion. His successors felt the same way and therefore promulgated scores of edicts over a period of six decades to punish every form of perceived heresy with increasing severity until the death penalties were prescribed ostensibly in the interest of public peace.

With opinions like those of St. Optatus, it is not surprising that over time, force and violence against perceived heresy became the norm.

In the Middle Ages, the position found support by respected apologists and theologians like Thomas Aquinas.

Many commentators have tried to exonerate the Roman Catholic Church from blame of the horrors of the Inquisition on the grounds that it was the emperors or the civil authorities that were usually responsible. However, the fact of the matter is that, even before it became an institution of the papacy, violence against heretics had the full support and cooperation of the Roman Catholic Church and it would be duplicitous to absolve the Church hierarchy from responsibility given the kind of influence they welded over the lives of the people and the civil authorities. Even at the time of the Roman Empire, if the Church showed her displeasure, the civil authorities would likely have acquiesced, after all St. Ambrose the bishop of Milan got Emperor Theodosius to do public penance.

The verdict of history on the Inquisition, both from within and without the Roman Catholic Church is encapsulated by the comments of these historians:

Henry Charles Lea—(1825-1909) [18]: *"The judgment of impartial history must be that the Inquisition was the monstrous offspring of mistaken zeal utilized by selfish greed and lust of power to smother the higher aspirations of humanity and stimulate the baser appetite".*

"The Inquisition in the Middle Ages was a massacre almost without parallel in human history".

Lord Acton (1834-1902) [18] **a Catholic historian:** *"The Inquisition is peculiarly the weapon and peculiarly the work of the popes . . . The principle of the Inquisition is the pope's sovereign power over life and death"*

Peter de Rosa (1932—*) [18] *a former Jesuit priest: "In the age of barbarism, the popes led the pack, in an age of enlightenment, they trailed the field".*

No matter how it is considered, the Inquisition represented a very dark spot in the history of the Roman Catholic Church and cast opprobrium on Christianity. The unjust and definitely unholy concept called the Inquisition was patently unchristian.

Chapter 12

Monastic Movements of the Middle Ages

The Cluniac Order [1,2]
The Cluniac Order was founded in 910 at Cluny by a grant from ***Duke William of Aquitaine*** as a reformist offshoot of the Benedictine Order.

The benefactor released the Order from all military services and other diocesan interference and was made answerable only to the Pope. The order followed the strict Benedictine rule and became the agent for reforming the other monastic houses.

The order is noted for elaborate liturgical ceremonies which left little time for the pursuit of scholarship or manual labor. The order also emphasized silence and encouraged the use of signs when communication was unavoidable and conversation of any kind was discouraged within certain areas of the house such as the church, the dormitory and the refectory.

The order produced intellectuals who served as bishops in many places and produced four Popes—***Gregory VII, Paschal II, Urban II and Urban V.*** The Cluniac monks backed the reform efforts of Pope Gregory VII and his successors.

However, by the twelfth century, the Cluniac Order became a victim of its success, becoming wealthy and decadent from various donations, it lost favor with both the clergy and the laity.

The Cistercian Order [3,4]
The Cistercian Order was founded in 1098 by St. Robert, originally a Benedictine monk who on account of poor observance of the Benedictine rule by his cloister broke away to found a new order. The new Order struggled until it was joined in 1112 by ***St. Bernard of Clairvaux (1090-1153).***

The order engaged in manual labor as agriculturists and horse and cattle breeding. Initially, the order renounced all sources of income arising from benefices, tithes, tolls and rents, depending only on revenues from the commerce of the produce of their labor and the land. In this way, they contributed to the economy of their communities. They introduced the idea of lay brothers who helped with the labor.

By the Cistercian Charter, each house was autonomous in administration and finance and is headed by an abbot. However, there was uniformity of rules enforceable by the abbot of Citeaux who presided over the annual meetings of abbots of all the affiliated houses. Soon, their influence eclipsed that of Cluny which they supplanted as a force for reforms.

They influenced the Church positively and produced Popes like ***Eugenius III (1145-1153)***.

However, they too succumbed to the same laxity that destroyed the Cluniac Order. The lifestyle of simplicity and austerity were relaxed and sources of income previously renounced were accepted. The farming operations became purely commercial ventures bringing in wealth for the monks. As the number of houses grew exponentially, the attitude of the monks changed, discipline declined and dissensions occurred among the superiors. Efforts to reform the Order did not reverse the secular trend. Later attempts at reform led to an offshoot of the order called the ***Trappists***.

The Franciscan Order [5, 6, 7, 8, 9]

The Franciscan order was a ***Mendicant Order*** founded in 1209 by ***St. Francis of Assisi (1182-1226 AD)***. St. Francis sought and received oral approbation from Pope Innocent III in 1209 after which the Order grew very rapidly and a formal approbation was given in 1223 by Pope Honorius III.

The order was different from the existing Orders in that the vow of poverty not only applied to the individuals but also applied collectively. They were given the right to preach, hear confessions and dispense papal pardon for a fee. They were not confined to particular monasteries or subject to Episcopal control anywhere. Members took the vows of obedience, poverty and chastity, pledge obedience to the Pope and the Roman Catholic Church and lived by the rules of the founder.

This placed them on collision course with local curates and others like Wycliffe who felt the mendicant orders were '***peddlers of phony pardons on behalf of the pope***' and therefore dangerous for the spiritual wellbeing of the people. An archbishop in England dubbed them a *"pestiferous canker"*.

Members could not defect after admittance following probation and members were forbidden from receiving money as gifts or even as payment for work done; payment could only be in kind and not money. Members were free to accept alms. The men were forbidden from entering the Convents of nuns.

St. Francis founded three orders, namely, the **Friars Minor**, the **Poor Ladies or Clares** and the **Third Order or Tertiaries**. The poor ladies or Clares were the nuns who took vows just as the men of the friars minor. The Tertiaries were the men and women in the world who wanted to live the higher spiritual standard advocated by Francis but could not be nuns or monks for various reasons.

The call for the relaxation of the vow of poverty espoused by the order started before the death of the founder but became more strident afterwards such that by 1415, formal sanction was given by the Council of Constance for the division of the Friar Minor order into the **Observants**—(strict observers) and the **Conventuals**—(relaxed observers).

Both factions continued under one head until 1517 when Pope Leo X called a general chapter of the Order with a view at reuniting them. The Observants declined papal dispensation to relax the rule of poverty while the Conventuals rejected reunification if it entailed giving up the papal dispensation for the relaxation of the rule of poverty.

Therefore, the Pope incorporated them into independent orders with the Observants having precedence over the Conventuals and regarded as the original Friars Minor retaining the seal of the founder and their leader regarded as the successor of Francis of Assisi. The Conventuals contested this arrangement until 1728 when Benedict XIII imposed perpetual silence on the matter on them.

In 1619, yet another order, the **Friar Minor Capuchins** started as a reformist offshoot of the Observants.

The Franciscans produced many intellectuals like *Duns Scotus and William of Ockham as well as popes such as Nicholas IV, Sixtus IV, Sixtus V and Clement XIV.*

The Dominican Order [5, 7, 8, 10]

The Dominican Order was founded by **St. Dominic of Navarrese (1170-1221)** a Spanish cleric, who in 1216 AD received approbation from Pope Honorius III.

The order was organized under the Augustinian rule and was known as the **'Order of Preachers'**. It was established to preach the Gospel and to combat perceived heresies, schisms and paganism; in particular Catharism.

Initially, members of the order, like the Franciscans, took the vow of poverty individually and collectively in addition to vows of obedience and chastity. They went about in pairs to preach in vernacular like the Albigensians and Waldensians and got sustenance from alms from the laity. In addition to preaching and work of Charity, the order also engaged in contemplation, prayer and meditation. The **'Rosary'** is usually attributed to the founder, St. Dominic who allegedly received it during a **Marian apparition** in 1208 at the church of Prouille. The order has been an ardent promoter of the use of the Rosary in prayer.

The order made intellectual pursuit by members a requirement; therefore, they set up training centers and were students and faculty members in the Universities. The order engaged in social services in urban areas; attending to the sick and helping the poor. They were exempted from the jurisdiction of the bishops, allowed to preach, hear confessions and have their own churches with rights of burial. These privileges attracted opposition from the secular clergy whose sources of revenue were being encroached upon, because, as the order grew in popularity, the laity began to endow them with property and wealth.

The Dominicans were the Roman Catholic Church's instrument of the Inquisition; the members were trained to recognize heresy and prosecute them all over Europe. It is believed that means amounting to torture were used to extract confessions from suspects. Those found guilty had their properties confiscated, and penalties for those who abjured included pilgrimages, wearing the cross of infamy or imprisonment for life. For those who refused to abjure, the penalty was death by burning at the stake carried out by the secular authorities.

The order grew rapidly and was highly respected, producing intellectual giants like **Albertus Magnus and Thomas Aquinas**. Many members also served as cardinals, legates, ambassadors and popes. Attempts to separate members of the order from the management of the properties were unsuccessful and by the end of the thirteenth century, the order had become wealthy and was attracting members on account of its wealth and success rather than from the original principles.

Both the Franciscan and the Dominican orders were involved in international missions to Africa, Asia and the Americas in later centuries.

The Augustinian Order [7, 11]

The Augustinian order came into being as a result of the amalgamation of separate groups of hermits by Pope Alexander IV in 1256 AD although the enabling decree was promulgated by Pope Innocent IV in 1243 AD.

At inception, the order was under the presidency of a cardinal and therefore more directly under papal supervision and control generally believed to be in order to counterbalance the power of the Franciscans and Dominicans who had become influential.

The order, international in nature from the beginning, was inaugurated under what was known as the "Augustinian Rule"

Notable members of the order include: ***Popes Adrian IV and Eugenius IV, humanist Desiderius Erasmus, reformer Martin Luther, mystic Thomas a Kempis and geneticist Gregor Mendel.***

Chapter 13

Renaissance and Renaissance Humanism

Renaissance is a French word meaning "rebirth". It is defined as "a movement of cultural and educational reform led by scholars, writers and civic leaders". Developed in the latter end of the thirteenth to the sixteenth centuries, it is generally regarded as the bridge between the Middle Ages and the beginning of the Modern time.

Renaissance Humanism is defined as "the spirit of learning that developed at the end of the middle ages with the revival of classical studies and a renewed confidence in the ability of human beings to determine truth and falsehood for themselves".

Other forms of humanism have been described, namely, cultural, literary, philosophical, Christian, religious, and secular; but all of these are essentially aspects of the Renaissance Humanism.

Generally, during the Renaissance, religious beliefs and social norms were questioned and challenged; the appreciation of worldly pleasures, personal independence and individual expressions were stimulated. Medieval Christianity had fostered self abnegation, restricted self expression and demanded unquestioning faith while individualism was branded as arrogance, rebellion and sin.

However, as the humanistic spirit flourished, faith gave way to reason, providence to chance, afterlife to 'presentism' (the here and now) and unreasoning faith to honest doubt. The ideal life ceased to be found in monastic escape from society but the full exploration and participation in all that life had to offer.

The humanists tried to graft classical pagan values unto Christian values and many actually felt that the two were in harmony. Renaissance humanism produced three streams:
- (i) Those who believed that philosophers like Plato basically agreed with Christianity and that Platonism contained lessons effective

for morality and who criticized important Church doctrines and institutions that lacked biblical and historical support; these tended towards a syncretic religious view.
- (ii) Those who subscribe to the idea of Natural Religion, that is, religion based on reason and the rational rather than faith and the supernatural and
- (iii) Those moved towards agnosticism or frank atheism.

The humanistic movement sought to base every branch of learning on the literature and culture of classical antiquity. The groundwork for humanism was laid by **Dante** and **Petrarch** and it was promoted by **Erasmus** and others.

Unfortunately, as Humanism flourished, Christian ethics suffered because humanists were morally deficient in their private lives and the upper class of the society became morally bankrupt. The political standard was defined by **Nicolo Machiavelli's** book **"The Prince"** with its message of brute force, contempt for all morality and cynical selfishness.

Renaissance Humanism found advocates and patrons in the papacy; *Popes Pius II (1458—1464), Sixtus IV (1471—1484), Alexander VI (1492-1503) and Leo X (1513-1521)* were all humanists.

Dante Alighieri (c1265-1321 AD) [4, 5]

Dante was an Italian poet of noble birth from Florence. He criticized the involvement of popes in politics and vehemently denounced ecclesiastical corruption.

He was exiled by Pope Boniface VIII who supported his political opponents.

Dante is best known for his allegorical poem about heaven, purgatory and hell, the famous **"Divine Comedy"** which is considered a concise summary of the knowledge and intellectual attainment from the fall of Rome to the beginning of the Renaissance. It is also believed to have given the complete picture of Catholicism in Italy of the thirteenth century.

In the Divine Comedy, Dante traveled through hell, purgatory and finished in paradise and he consigned all his contemporary popes to hell. Unlike the usual practice of writing serious books in Latin, the book was written in the Italian dialects and this made it an instant success with an expanded readership and set a precedent for other writers.

A Dante quote: *"The hottest places in hell are reserved for those, who in the time of great moral crisis maintain their neutrality".*

Francesco Petrarch (1304-1374 AD) [6, 7]

Francesco Petrarch was a poet, scholar and humanist. He was one of the architects of the Renaissance. He entered the minor orders and was a prolific writer in both Latin and Italian.

He fell in love with a married woman named Laura and wrote sonnets for her throughout his lifetime both before and after her death—(it was an impossible situation as she was married and he had a career in the Church). His work became widely known and he was crowned the **"poet laureate"** in Rome in 1341. He became a celebrity and was sought after by kings, nobles and Cardinals, traveling throughout Europe as an ambassador.

He had two children out of wedlock and legitimized them in 1343.

Though a devout catholic, he counseled a friend against unquestioning believe in prophesy. He said fabrications were often attributed to Christ to ensure acceptance and that it was "an old device to drape lying inventions with the veil of religion and sanctity in order to give the appearance of divine sanction to human fraud".

While Dante was regarded as the initiator of the Renaissance, Petrarch was regarded as the launcher.

Lorenzo Valla (1406—1457 AD) [8, 9]

Lorenzo Valla was an Italian priest, rhetorician and humanist. He compared and contrasted the Stoic and Epicurean philosophies and declared his sympathy with the latter, admitting natural man's right to indulge his appetites freely.

He used textual analysis (*philology*) to convincingly prove that the documents on which some Church dogmas were based were forgeries. The most famous of this was the ***"Donation of Constantine"*** on which the papacy had based its claim to temporal power over the nations of the western half of the old Roman Empire.

He proved that the document was not written during the time of the Emperor Constantine and Pope Sylvester I as alleged but sometime during the eighth century AD. He said the document contained **contradictions, impossibilities, stupidities, barbarisms and absurdities**. He wondered how the popes could have been ignorant of the forgery or whether they simply chose to ignore the truth out of avarice, pride or plain deceit.

He felt that the papacy's defense of the document dishonored the office, their predecessors and the Christian religion. He also accused the papacy of planning to hold the nations in vassalage contrary to the teachings of Jesus Christ.

Another document Valla debunked was the purported "***Letter of Christ to King Abgarus of Edessa***" which was said to have produced the first non human made image (acheiropoeta) of Christ.

He compared St. Jerome's Latin translation of the New Testament with the Greek Text and helped subsequent translators and scholars to better understand the texts.

His writings and disposition made him many enemies and he was described as an acute critic and venomous writer.

His dream of working at the papacy was realized under Pope Nicholas V and Calixtus III. His work, especially on Latin grammar and Greek was praised by younger writers like Erasmus and was useful in the translation of the bible.

Desiderius Erasmus (1466-1536 AD) [10, 11, 12]

Erasmus was a scholar, theologian and humanist; born at Rotterdam and educated in Augustinian monastic and semi-monastic schools. At the age of twenty-five years he entered into a monastery and became a priest.

He left the monastery when he became the secretary of a bishop and went to the University of Paris for further studies with the permission of the bishop. An independent spirit, Erasmus' intellectual and literary pursuits were made free from country or academic ties or religious allegiance.

He felt that the evil of his day was 'formalism', respect for tradition and a regard for what others thought rather than the true teachings of Christ. He rejected many lucrative positions to maintain his literary and intellectual independence and expressions.

Erasmus produced a new Latin edition of the New Testament and studied Greek to produce the Greek New Testament on which the King James' New Testament was based. He also published a parallel Latin-Greek New Testament which was used by Martin Luther to translate the New Testament into the German language for the first time in 1522.

In his famous book, *"In praise of Folly",* Erasmus satirized the society, the Church and their institutions.

- ➢ Of *the merchants* he said: they did business using corrupt methods, lied, stole, perjured, misled and cheated people; yet they were highly regarded in the society and even by the religious who he said were only interested in their share of the loot.

- ➢ ***The philosophers*** he said were conceited and thought no one apart from them knew anything. However, he said the fact that they constantly disagreed among themselves was proof that they didn't know the truth about anything though they profess to know everything.
- ➢ ***The theologians*** he described as supercilious, conceited and bombastic; that "they walled themselves behind ***imposing definitions, conclusions, corollaries and propositions*** both explicit and implicit and threaten the voices of dissent with the label of 'heresy'".
- ➢ He said: ***"our young divines, by leaving out four or five words in a place and putting a false construction on the rest, can make any passage serviceable to their own purpose; though from the coherence of what went before or follow after, the genuine meaning appear to be either wide enough or perhaps quite contradictory to what they would thrust or impose upon it"***.
- ➢ ***The monks*** and ***the religious*** he said were misnomers as they had no religion in them nor led solitary lives. He said they celebrated ignorance, capitalized on dirt and poverty and whine for food from door to door. He said they sang the Psalms only by rote and had no understanding. He derided some Orders' supposed hatred of money but not wine or women. He said the Orders engaged in bickering and rivalry among themselves, **striving more to be unlike one another than to be like Christ**. He mocked the regimentation of their lives in inconsequential things like the style or color of habits and said they based their salvation on foppish ceremonies and strict conformity to traditions.
- ➢ ***The Doctors*** of the Church he derided for their ***allegories, tropologies and analogies***. He said they were buffoonish and ridiculous, thought many were impostors and that their profession of piety was only contrived.
- ➢ Of the ***Cardinal's Conclave***, he alleged simony and bribery in the election of popes.
- ➢ ***The popes*** he said **secured their positions by pistol, poison, force and violence. He said popes thrust their sickle only into the harvest of profit and take advantage of their flocks by the benefit of their fleece.** *"Though indeed, the Church has no enemies more bloody and tyrannical than such impious popes, who give*

dispensation for the not preaching of Christ; evacuate the main effect and design of our redemption by their pecuniary bribes and sales; adulterate the gospel by their forced interpretation and undermining traditions; and lastly by their lusts and wickedness, grieve the Holy Spirit and make their Savior's wounds to bleed anew".

- ➤ ***The priests**, he said, "blacken the darkness and promote delusion thereby enslaving the people to ignorance and blindness."*
- ➤ ***The people** he derided **for their superstitious believe in saints and even the Virgin Mary as well as their faith in the sale of indulgences to cleanse them of their sins.***

Erasmus considered ***scholasticism the greatest perversion of the religious spirit; this, he said dated back to the primitive Christological controversies which caused the Church to lose its evangelical simplicity to become a hair-splitting philosophy.***

The Roman Catholic Church considered the book a cold blooded deliberate attempt to discredit the Church.

He was accused of *"laying the egg that Luther hatched" to which he responded that "he had expected another kind of bird".*

Although Erasmus lived through the reformation, he refused to identify with it; he wanted only to reform the Roman Catholic Church from within.

Thomas More (1478-1535 AD) [13, 14]

Thomas More was an English statesman, renaissance writer and philosopher who gave up the monastic life to marry and enter politics. His first act in parliament was to propose a reduction of the appropriation to King Henry VII, an action the king responded to by imprisoning Thomas More's father until a ransom was paid.

He was King Henry VIII's adviser and he wrote many treatises to refute the writings of Martin Luther and William Tyndale who were opposed to the Roman Catholic Church. He was responsible for the execution of many people found reading Tyndale's English translation of the Bible.

He fell out with King ***Henry VIII (1491-1547 AD)*** by his refusal to agree with the King's intention to divorce Catherine of Aragon. He did not attend the coronation of Queen Anne Boleyn as well and refused to swear allegiance to the parliament's **"Acts of Succession"** and **"Oath of Supremacy"** which stipulated that the King was the head of the **Church** of **England** and not the pope. He was charged with treason, arrested and finally beheaded in 1535.

He was a life-long friend of Erasmus who dedicated the book "In Praise of Folly" to him.

Thomas More wrote **"Utopia"** a book about a fictional Island of a 'perfect society' where everything is orderly. Utopia was a pun on the Greek words "Ou-topos" meaning (no place) and "Eu-topos" which means (good place).

In Utopia:
- The leaders, though excused by law, worked.
- The society had a good maintenance culture
- The family size was regulated and children re-distribution was practiced from those who had many to those who had none or fewer.
- No one had anything more than needed and supply was assured because wealth re-distribution was practiced.
- Wars were fought with mercenaries rather than exposing citizens to the dangers of war.
- Adults led simple lives, not vainglorious and adornment with jewelry reserved only for children.
- The society did not engage in hunting except for food by the slaves and the butchers.
- Only criminals were enslaved and
- Children of slaves were freed.
- Priests 'encouraged' the terminally ill to commit suicide either by taking opium or starving to death—no one was forced, just 'persuaded' to die 'without pain' and with 'dignity'.

Thomas More is admired by modern socialists and his Utopian ideals are found in communist, socialist, welfare and humanist States today. He was canonized in 1935 by Pope Pius XI.

The spiritual rot of the Dark Ages continued unabated in the Middle Ages. The episcopate and the papacy, instead of seeking spiritual revival, expended all their energy is efforts to preserve or wrest temporal power from their self imposed "protectors"—the 'Holy Roman Emperors'. The popes and bishops led troops all across Europe and beyond in crusades to defend temporal gains while the welfare of souls were neglected or preyed upon through ungodly canons or dogma. The priests and friars were largely theologically illiterate; therefore what they lacked in knowledge, they made for in superstitions; peddling icons, relics and papal indulgences and other confessionalia.

The rot in the Church was all encompassing and no soundness was found anywhere as the comments of people mostly from within the Church like St. Peter Damian, Wycliffe, Jan Hus, Erasmus and others about the period, itself attests.

Here are some other comments from the Middle Ages:

Pope Gregory VII (1073-1085) [15, 16] —About bishops

> *"The time is come that judgment should begin with the House of God, in order to separate from the House of God all that work iniquity, prepare to punish those, who being bound by their office to correct the sins of others, sinned worse than the rest, being themselves blind leaders of the blind, in morals Pharisees, in works Sadducees, in vileness, Nicholaites, in avarice, Simoniacs*
>
> *". . . I scarcely discover any bishops who are lawful either in their entrance or mode of life; who govern the Christian people from the love of Christ and not from secular ambition; and among all secular princes, I know of none who prefer God's honor to their own, or who prefer righteousness to gain".*

Hildebert—Bishop of Mans (1090) [15, 16]

> *"There are those who purchase litigation and sell intercessions, and who have no regard for any kind of men, order or times. In the forum, they are Scythians, in the chamber vipers and at the banquet buffoons, in their exactions, harpies . . ."*

Honorius of Autun (1120) [15, 16] —12th Century
Honorius was a Benedictine monk, theologian and philosopher whose views about the Church leaders of his time were expressed as follows:

> "Turn to the citizens of Babylon . . . , look upon her princes and judges, cardinals and archbishops; the very seat of the beast is placed in them. All days they are intent on doing evil, ever insatiably occupied in works of iniquity. They not only themselves perform, but instruct others in flagitious wickedness. They offer things sacred for sale; they purchase iniquity and labor with their might that they may not descend alone to hell".

St. Bernard of Clairvaux—1140 [15]

> "The contagion spreads through the whole church and the wider it spreads the more hopeless the remedy; the more deeply it penetrates, the more fatal the disease. A meretricious splendor is everywhere visible . . . . The vestment of actors, the parade of kings, they are ministers of Christ but servants of the Antichrist . . ."

Giraldus Cambrensis [17] —on the menu of the monks of Canterbury in the 12th Century

> "It is curious as a picture of the times: sixteen lordly dishes and upwards, besides a course of herbs which latter, however, were not in much request; fish of diverse kinds—roast and boiled, atewed and fried, omelets, seasoned meats and sundry provocatives of the palate, prepared by cunning cooks. Wines in ample profusion, sicera, pimea, claret, must, Mede and moretum, anything and everything but ale, the boast of England . . . What would Paul the Hermit have said to all these . . . . or St. Benedict the founder of the order?

Pope Innocent III (1198-1216) [15, 16] at the Fourth Lateran Council

> ". . . hence evils have entered into the Christian world. Faith perishes, religion is disfigured, liberty is confounded, justice is trodden underfoot, heretics spring up, and schismatics gather strength, the wicked rage . . . It is the time as the

apostle said: 'that judgment should begin at the house of God'. For all corruption which is in the world chiefly proceed from the clergy".

Thomas Aquinas (1225-1274) [18] and a Pope on the Power of the Church

On his first visit to Rome, the conversation below reportedly took place between Thomas Aquinas and the pope.

While the pope was giving him a guided tour of the gilded treasures of the Papal Palace:

Pope—*"We cannot say with Peter of old 'Silver and Gold have I none . . ."*—*(Acts 3:6)*
Thomas Aquinas—*"No indeed" . . . "Nor can we now say, 'such as I have I give to thee: in the Name of Jesus Christ, rise up and walk'".*

Pope Gregory X to the Bishop of Liege, 1274 [15]

> *"We hear with great concern that you are abandoned to incontinence and simony, and are the father of many children, some born before and some after your promotion to the Episcopal dignity. You have taken an Abbess of the order of St. Benedict for your concubine, and have boasted at a public entertainment of having fourteen children in the space of twenty months. To some of your children you have given benefices and even trusted them, though underage with the cure of souls . . . You do not say, nor do you understand, being quite illiterate, your office, the prayer which every priest is bound to say daily . . ."*

William Palmer (1803-1885) on Monasteries in the 13th and 14th Centuries

> *"The monasteries which had been originally intended to afford example of perfect purity, devotion toward God and deadness to the world, were polluted by gross sins . . . The bishops and clergy themselves shared but too often in the*

> evils of the times . . . Archbishops and bishops engaged in wars and crusades and other temporal vocations . . . They were involved more in temporal than spiritual affairs".

Soames (1785-1860) [15]—Historian of the English Church on medieval monks and nuns

> "Pretenders as all these recluses necessarily were, to the most scrupulous chastity and purity, whole societies of them were found to be abandoned to lewdness, debauchery and even viler abominations".

John Gerson—Chancellor of Paris at the Council of Pisa (1409) [16]

> **"For whom will you find among the priests, who is not ignorant of the law of Christ? . . . I grieved also, beholding others with rapacious avarice spoiling the sheep by exactions, heaping up extortions, laying accusations, sowing dissensions, falsely accusing the innocent, heaping up money, intent only on worldly affairs . . ."**

Nicholas De Clemangis (1360-1437) [15] on Corruption in the Church

Nicholas de Clemangis was a French divine who in 1414 wrote about the corruption in the Church thus:

> "Whence come s the indevotion of the people, the contempt of the priests, the loss of the Church's rights and liberties but because it is full of contemptible persons, unworthy of their ministrations? Whence comes it to pass that an infinite number of ignorant persons are admitted to the priesthood, who understand no Latin and can scarcely read; who repeating or singing the prayers know not whether they bless or curse the Lord; and so many others of bad morals, who live all sorts of debauchery? The bishops are the chief cause of these disorders . . ."

John James Blunt (1794-1855) [17] —about Medieval Secular Clergy and Friars

John James Blunt, English divine and historian had this to say about medieval clergy and friars:

> *"In those days, men seem to have received ordination without any adequate examination either as to learning or character; . . . persons of the lowest of the people, with all gross habits of the class from which they spring; loiterers of ale house bench, dicers, scarcely able to say their paternoster, often actually unable to repeat the Commandments. Such were the ministers to whom was consigned a very large proportion of the parishes of England before the Reformation. With what effect, the ignorance, the superstition, the vices which then spread themselves over the whole country sufficiently testify. 'The prayers of the Church, being in Latin, tended little or nothing to edification . . . ' The friars . . . most constant hearers were at a loss to distinguish between the deadly sins and the Ten Commandments of which latter, indeed the people were entirely ignorant, being wholly given to superstitions. They hastened to the church for holy water, of which the devil was said to be afraid . . ."*

About Friars

> *"The vows of voluntary poverty only led to Jesuitical expedients for evading it; a straining at gnats and swallowing of camels. The populace were to be alarmed or caressed or cajoled out of subsistence. A deathbed was a friar's harvest; then were suggested the foundation of chantries and provision for masses and wax-lights. The confessional was his exchequer; there, hints were dropped that the convent needed a new window or that it owed 'forty pounds' for stone . . . The friar had the art of leading women captive and reaching the family purse by means of the wife . . ."*

> *"Rival relics were set up, and impostors of all kinds multiplied without shame, to the impoverishment of the people, the disgrace of the Church and the scandal of Christianity".*

It was not surprising that during the Middle Ages, many lost faith and sought spiritual fulfillment from resuscitating pre-Christian philosophies like Platonism; while others rejected Christianity and sought meaning in nature and reason culminating in the Humanist and Enlightenment movements.

However, others like Damian, Wycliffe and Hus challenged the Church authority to bring the truth to the people, reform the Church and revive the faith.

Their efforts eventually found fruition in the Reformation midwifed by Martin Luther.

Chapter 14

The Reformation and the Reformers—1450-1750 AD

Jacques Lefevre d'Etaples (1455-1536 AD) [1]

Jacques d'Etaples was a French priest, theologian and humanist and the forerunner of the protestant movement in France. He was a professor at the University of Paris and one of his students was **Guillaume Farel (1489-1565),** an associate and host of Calvin in Geneva and co-founder of the Reformed Churches in Switzerland.

He believed in the Holy Scripture as the sole basis for doctrine and justification by faith alone. His views engendered opposition from the Roman Catholic establishment but he was protected by the king.

He translated the Latin Vulgate Bible into French and the revised editions from the Greek and Hebrew texts. Like Erasmus, although he observed the need for reform in the Roman Catholic Church, he did not subscribe to schism but believed in reformation from within.

Martin Luther (1483-1546 AD) [2,3]

Martin Luther was born in Eisleben, Germany in 1483. He was a brilliant young man who obtained his Bachelor's degree in 1502 and Masters in 1505 and was set on a career in law but dropped out of law school after a spiritual experience to become an Augustinian monk. He devoted himself to monastic life but found no peace or fulfillment in confessions, good works, fasting, long hours of prayer and flagellations.

His superior thought he needed to be distracted from too much introspection and ordered him to pursue an academic career in theology. He was ordained into the priesthood in 1507 and earned his Bachelor's degree in Biblical Studies in 1508. He started teaching at the University of Wittenberg and studying for his doctorate in theology which he earned in 1512.

The demands of teaching and studying drove him to study the Scripture in depth. His study of Scripture convinced him that the Roman Catholic Church had lost sight of many core truths of the Christian faith.

He rejected the philosophical approach to theology and believed that God can be known only by revelation and felt that logic and reason could in fact be stumbling blocks to understanding God.

Luther was not anti-intellectual and believed that philosophy and reason have their usage in areas of human interactions and governance but not in theology.

He discovered and taught that salvation is a gift of God's grace, received by faith and trust in God's promise to forgive sins for the sake of Christ's death on the Cross. He rejected the Roman Catholic sacerdotal doctrine of salvation and considered salvation as God's work from beginning to the end. He opposed the doctrine of indulgences which suggested that man had to do something to merit forgiveness and considered it a confusion of the laws and the Gospel.

Jan Hus's prophesy was fulfilled almost to the date when in 1517, Martin Luther nailed his **95 theses on indulgences** to the door of the church at Wittenberg. The 95 theses charged the Roman Catholic Church with heresy.

His views in turn were considered heresy by Pope Leo X and he was summoned to the **Diet of Worms in 1521** and asked to recant but he refused.

He was declared an outlaw with a price on his head but was protected in a friend's castle where he worked on the translation of the Bible into the German dialect from Erasmus' Greek translation.

Although Martin Luther's 95 theses on indulgences were the lightening rod, his call for reform covered a wide range of social, political, educational and religious issues. He not only highlighted the problems and abuses in the Church and the society in general, he also proffered what he thought the solutions should be.

On Universal Priesthood of Believers [4*]
In his treatise on *"The Three Walls of the Romanists"*, Martin Luther:

Rejected the idea of two separate estates within the Church; a *'spiritual estate'* (comprising the pope, bishops, priests and the monks) as separate from a *'temporal estate'* (comprising the princes, lords, farmers, artisans and other laity). He believed that Christ has only one Body and not two.

He also rejected the Roman Catholic Church's belief that the 'spiritual estate' is superior to the 'temporal estate'. He averred that a priest and an artisan had the same baptism and that "a priest in Christendom is nothing more than an office holder". That there is no difference between the priest and the layman or a bishop and a prince.

He debunked the Roman Catholic dogma that only the **Magisterium** has the authority to interpret Scripture and rejected the doctrine of '*papal infallibility*' and said that such a notion reduces the Church to a single individual, contrary to the Creed.

Finally he rejected the papacy's claim that only the pope can call for a Council and confirm its actions; he contended that the first Christian Council at Jerusalem was not called by Peter but by the elders and the Apostles. That the Council of Niceae was called, not by the bishop of Rome but by the Emperor Constantine. He pointed out that if the papal claim were true, previous Councils in the history of the Church would have to be considered heretical.

In his own words, the following are quotes from Martin Luther on various subjects—

On Canon Laws [4, 5*]
Martin Luther said:
- "The bible contains more than enough directions for all our living and so the study of the canon law only stands in the way of the Holy Scriptures; moreover, for the most part, it smacks of mere avarice and pride . . . Even though there were much in it that is good, it might as well be destroyed, for the pope has taken the whole canon law captive and imprisoned it in the chamber of his heart that the study of it is a waste of time and a farce."
- *"It looks as though all the laws of the Church were made for one purpose only . . . to be nothing but so many money snares, from which a man must extricate himself if he would be a Christian. Yea, here the devil becomes a saint and a god to boot".* "The canon law is not what is in the books but what is in the sweet will of the pope and his flatterers".
- "At Rome, everything goes as the devil wills . . . justice had either to be bought or else suppressed with money . . ."

- *"Certain penalties or punishment of the canon law should also be abolished especially the interdict which is beyond all doubt, an invention of the evil spirit".*
- "The ban is to be used in no case except where the Scripture prescribe its use, that is, against those who do not hold the true faith or those who live in open sin . . ."
- *". . . Would to God that all the things we must buy at Rome to free ourselves from that money snare, the canon law . . . such things as indulgences, butter-letters, mass-letters and all the rest of the 'confessionalia' . . . with which the poor folks are deceived and robbed of their money . . ."*
- "It must therefore have been the very prince of devils who said what is written in the canon law: 'if the popes were so scandalously bad as to lead souls in crowds to the devil, yet he could not be deposed'".
- *"But they have caught us with their canon laws and stolen our rights from us, so that we may have to buy them back with money. Thus they have made our consciences so timid and shy that it is no longer easy to preach about this liberty because the common people take such great offense, thinking it is a greater sin to eat butter than to lie, to swear or even to live unchastely".*

On Canonization of Saints, Feast Days and Pilgrimages [5, 6*]
- *"The forest chapels and rustic churches must be utterly destroyed, those to which recent pilgrimages have been directed . . . and a number of others . . . what a terrible and heavy account will the bishops have to render who permit this devilish deceit and receive its profits. They should be the first to forbid it, and yet, they think it a divine and holy thing and do not see that it is the devil's doing, to strengthen avarice, to create a false, feigned faith, to weaken parish churches, to multiply taverns and harlotry, to waste money and labor and lead the poor folks by the nose"*
- ". . . Everyone plans only how he may establish and maintain such a place of pilgrimage in his diocese and is not at all concerned to have the people believe and live aright".
- 'That miracles are done at these places does not help things, for the evil spirit can do miracles"—Mathew 24:24.

- "... where pilgrimages are unsuccessful, they begin to canonize saints, not in honor of the saints ... but in order to draw crowds and bring in money".

"*... all festival should be abolished and Sunday alone retained ... the feast days are now abused by drinking, gaming, idleness and all manner of sins, so that on the holy days we anger God more than on other days*"

Cardinals, Papal Legates and Theologians [5, 7*]

- "... we should drive out of German lands the papal legates with their 'faculties' which they sell us for large sums of money, ... for example, in return for money, they legalize unjust gains, dissolve oaths, vows and agreements, break and teach men to break the faith and fealty which they have pledged to one another; and they say the pope has authority to do this ... thus they sell us a doctrine of devils, and take money for teaching sin and leading us to hell".
- "*... for those people are utter ignoramuses as regards things Christian, they seek not the welfare of souls but, like all the pope's hypocrites, only their own power, profit and glory ...*"
- "The nearer Rome, the worse Christians, men bring back with them contempt for God and His Commandments".
- "*... The theologians have spared themselves pains and labors; they leave the bible in peace and read the Sentences ... Moreover, the pope commands, with many severe words, that his laws are to be read and used in the schools and the courts, but little is said of the Gospel ... the Gospel lies idle in the dust under the bench, to the end that the pope's harmful laws may rule alone*".
- "If we are called by the title of teachers of Holy Scripture, then we ought to be compelled in accordance to our name, to teach the Holy Scriptures and nothing else, ... but now, under the despotism of the Sentences, we find among theologians, more of heathen and human opinions than of the holy and certain doctrine of Scripture".
- "*The writings of the holy fathers should be read only for a time, in order that through them we may be led to the Holy Scriptures. As it is, however, we read them only to be absorbed in them and never come to the Scriptures.* **We are like men who study the sign-posts and never travel the road**".

The Clergy, the Monks and Celibacy [6, 7*]
- "Now, everyone is drawn to the priesthood or monastic life, and among them, I fear, there is not one in a hundred who has any other reason than that he seeks a living . . . despair makes most of the monks and priests and so things are as we see them."
- *"I fear that greed has been the cause of this wretched unchaste chastity . . . and as a result of greed, every man has wished to become a priest and everyone wants his son to study for the priesthood, not with the idea of living in chastity, . . . but of being supported in temporal things without care or labor contrary to the command of God"*
- ". . . when there were many persecutions and controversies with heretics, there were many holy fathers who of their own accord abstained from matrimony, to the end that they might the better devote themselves to study and be prepared at any time for death or for controversy. Then the Roman See interfered out of sheer wantonness and made a universal commandment forbidding priests to marry".
- *"I see how the vows are kept, especially the vow of chastity which has become so universal through these monasteries and yet is not commanded by Christ; . . ."*
- "We also see how the priesthood has fallen, and how many a poor priest is overburdened with wife and child and his conscience troubled; yet no one does anything to help him though he might easily be helped . . ."
- "My faithful counsel is that, in order to avoid many sins which have become very common, neither boy nor maid should take the vow of chastity or of the spiritual life before the age of thirty years. It is, as St. Paul said, a peculiar gift".

Education and the Universities [7*]
- "Above all, the foremost and most general subject of study, both in the lower and the higher schools should be the Holy Scriptures, and for the young boys, the Gospel. And would to God that every town had a girl's school also in which the girls were taught the Gospel . . ."
- *". . . The Christian youth and the best of our people, with whom the future of Christendom lies, are to be educated and trained.*

> *Therefore I consider that there is no work more worthy of pope or emperor than a thorough reformation of the Universities, and there is nothing worse or more worthy of the devil than unreformed Universities".*

- "The Universities also need a good, thorough reformation . . . I must say it, no matter whom it vexes . . . **for everything which the papacy has instituted and ordered is directed only towards the increasing of sin and error . . . loose living prevails, the Holy Scripture and the Christian faith are little taught and the blind, heathen master, Aristotle, rules alone even more than Christ**".

- *"But where the Holy Scripture does not rule, there I advise no one to send his son. Everyone not unceasingly busy with the Word of God must become corrupt; that is why the people who are in the universities and who are trained there are the kind of people they are . . . I greatly fear that the universities are wide gates of hell, if they do not diligently teach the Holy Scriptures and impress them on the youth".*

Martin Luther called Aristotle a wretch and had no use for Aristotelian ideas and ideals on ethics which he considered opposed to Christian virtues and divine grace because he taught the death of souls with the body.

On the Pope and the Papacy [4, 5, 6, 7, 8, 9*]

- *"It is a horrible and frightful thing that the ruler of Christendom, who boasts himself the Vicar of Christ and successor of St. Peter lives in such splendor that in this regard no king or emperor can equal or approach him and that he who claims the title of 'most holy' and 'most spiritual' is more worldly than the world itself. He wears the Triple Crown when the greatest king wears but a single crown; if that is like the poverty of Christ and of St. Peter, then it is a new kind of likeness. When a word is said against it, they cry out—'heresy'".*

- "He (the pope) suppresses God's commandment and exalts his own commandment over it; if he is not the antichrist, then let someone else tell who he can be".

- *"They assumed for themselves sole authority and insolent juggling of words, they would persuade us that the pope, whether he be a bad or a good man, cannot err in matters of faith . . . hence it*

came about that so many heretic and unchristian, nay unnatural ordinances have a place in the canon law . . ."
- "God had commanded to keep oath and faith even with an enemy, and thou undertakest to loose this His commandment, and ordainest in thine heretical antichristian decretals that thou has His power . . .".
- *"For many years now, nothing has overflowed from Rome into the world . . . than the laying waste of goods, of bodies, of souls and the worst examples of the worst things. These things are clearer than light to all men; and the Church of Rome, formerly the most holy of all churches, has become the most lawless den of thieves, the most shameless of all brothels, the very kingdom of sin, death and hell; so that not even the antichrist, if he were to come could devise any addition to its wickedness".*
- "Is it not true, that there is nothing under the vast heavens more corrupt, more pestilential; more hateful than the court of Rome? She incomparably surpasses the impiety of the Turks . . ."
- *"Christ also whose vicar he boasts himself to be, was never willing to have aught to do with temporal rule . . . But the pope rushes in unbidden, and boldly takes hold of everything as though he were a god, until he no longer knows what Christ is, whose vicar he pretends to be".*
- "This arbitrary will and lying "reservation" of the pope creates in Rome a state of affairs which is unspeakable. There is buying, selling, bartering, trafficking, lying, deceiving, robbing, stealing, luxury, harlotry, knavery and every sort of contempt of God, and even the rule of the antichrist could not be more scandalous".
- *"If we justly hang thieves and behead robbers, why should we let Roman avarice go free? For he is the greatest thief and robber that has come or can ever come into the world, and all in the holy name of St. Peter! . . . almost everything he owns has been gotten by theft and robbery; that is the truth, and all history shows it".*
- "The pope leads you away from the gifts of God, which you have without pay, to his gifts which you must buy; and he gives you lead for gold, hide for meat, wax for honey, words for goods and letters for the spirit".

- *He leaves to bishops, archbishops and primates no regular authority or office, usurps everything for himself and lets them keep only the name and empty title. It has gone so far that by his "exemptions", the monasteries, the abbots and the prelates are withdrawn from the regular authority of the bishops so that there is no longer any order in Christendom. From this must follow what has followed . . . relaxation of discipline and license to do evil everywhere.*
- *"In short, in Rome, Christ counts for nothing, the pope counts for everything; and yet, they would compel us with threats to approve and praise and honor such antichristian doctrine"*

***Note:—All quotations from the Project Wittenberg—www.iclnet. org/pub/resources/text/wittenberg**

Martin Luther compiled the abuses he wanted discussed in council and sent these together with his proposed reforms to the German nobility. He reminded and counseled the nobility:
- That it was their duty to seek the highest good for their subjects.
- That the German nation, the princes and the bishops were also Christians and ought to protect the people over whom they ruled in things spiritual and temporal from ravening wolves in sheep clothing.
- That the princes, nobles and cities should boldly forbid and in fact abolish the payment of annates by their subjects to Rome as the pope had broken the compact and made annates robbery.
- That the Christian nobility should stand as one against the pope who he said had become tyrannical and the common enemy and destroyer of Christendom.
- That no temporal matter should be taken to Rome and that such cases should be adjudicated by the temporal authorities.
- That the pope should have no authority over the emperor and that the practice of the emperor kissing or sitting at the feet of the pope should be abolished and that the emperor should not swear allegiance to the pope.
- That there should be a restriction in the traffic of spices
- That there should be a decree against extravagance and excesses in dressing.

- That imports be minimized and consumption of locally produced goods be encouraged.
- That the common houses of prostitution be closed

Apart from the social, cultural, legal and national issues and how religious practices impacted them, Martin Luther wrote extensively on doctrinal issues. He wrote long and short catechisms on the sacraments and treatises on good works and Christian liberty.

On Baptism and Infant Baptism: [10, 11]

Martin Luther considered baptism to be sacramental, that is, it was ordained by Jesus Christ and necessary for salvation and not just a mere symbol. This belief he based on Mark 16:16 and Mathew 28:19-20. He contended that:

(i) What God commanded and instituted cannot be a vain thing or of no consequence even though it may appear ordinary

(ii) He believed that, to be baptized in the Name of God is to be baptized by God Himself

(iii) That the baptismal water ceases to be natural once God's Word, command and Name are added. That when the Word is joined to natural substance, it becomes a holy or divine matter or sign.

(iv) That the power, work, profit, fruit and end of baptism is to save and that to be saved is to be delivered from sin, death, and the devil and to enter the kingdom of Christ and live with him for ever.

(v) He believed that in baptism, believers enter into a fraternity with Christ, all the angels, saints and Christians on earth.

(vi) He disagreed with St. Jerome's teaching that the "ship of Baptism" can be broken leaving only repentance for the believer to re-enter the Church. (*It was believed in the early Church that it was fatal to salvation to sin after Baptism; allowance being made for only one canonical penance for sin after Baptism*). Luther's position was that Baptism abides forever and that though the believer may slip and fall off the ship, through repentance he can swim back and cling on until he re-enters and lives in it.

(vii) That faith alone makes a person worthy to receive profitably the saving, divine water; that without faith, it profits nothing. That **'baptism benefits only he who believes'.**

Martin Luther supported Infant Baptism and dismissed the misgivings of objectors. He predicated his belief in Infant Baptism basically on tradition; he contended that it must be pleasing to God because the gift of the Holy Spirit was perceptible in some of the Church Fathers and others such as St. Bernard and John Hus who were baptized as infants.

He further defended his position by stating that: *"Further, we say that we are not so much concerned to know whether the person baptized believes or not; for on that account Baptism does not become invalid; but everything depends upon the Word and command of God".* He went on to say: *"Baptism is valid even though faith be wanting; for my faith does not make Baptism but receives it. Now, Baptism does not become invalid even though it be wrongly received or employed; since it is not bound (as stated) to our faith but to the Word".*

COMMENT:

On this issue, Luther contradicted himself and engaged in intellectual acrobatics.

He had stated that:

"Faith alone makes a person worthy to receive baptism" and that *"without faith baptism profits nothing"*, that *"it has benefit for only those who believe"*.

The question in regard to infant baptism is:

Do infants and young children have understanding and therefore '<u>faith</u>' to be '<u>worthy to receive</u>' and to '<u>benefit</u>' from the ordinance?

To this, Luther replied, strangely, *"we are not so much concerned to know whether the person baptized believes or not (?!); for on that account, baptism does not become invalid . . . baptism is valid even though faith be wanting; for my faith does not make baptism but receives it"*.

Luther's positions on adult and infant baptism are irreconcilable.

If, as he posited, <u>**baptism cannot not be worthily received and does not profit where there is no faith;**</u> it stands to reason that, in Infant Baptism, even though baptism may be valid, it cannot be worthily received and will not profit the children who are too young to exercise faith.

The question then is:

If infants can neither worthily receive nor profit from baptism, should they be baptized?

On this question, Martin Luther, like Augustine obfuscates the issue and their arguments for the practice are unconvincing.

On the Sacrament of the Altar [12, 13]

(i) Martin Luther believed that the Roman Catholic doctrine of transubstantiation, which essentially stated that the consecrated Bread and the Wine are changed in such a way that they are no longer naturally in the sacrament is the opinion of St. Thomas Aquinas and the pope and not an article of faith. He however believed as an article of faith, that the Body and the Blood of Jesus Christ are truly present in the consecrated natural bread and wine. As with Baptism, he believed that when the Word joined with the Bread and the Wine, they are converted to the sacrament and no longer just natural bread and wine.

(ii) He believed that sharing the Bread and the Wine in communion is for the forgiveness of sins based on ***Mathew 26:28***.

(iii) He believed that the Holy Communion is food for the soul and that it nourishes and strengthens the believer. He therefore recommended that it be taken regularly by all except those who had committed excommunicable sins.

(iv) He held that only those who have faith can receive the benefit of the sacrament because *"whoever believes has what the Word declares and brings"*.

(v) He believed, like Augustine, that even if a foolish or a wicked priest handles or dispenses the sacrament; or if it is received by a worthy or unworthy person; the character of the sacrament is not changed because *"The word by which the element becomes a sacrament and was instituted does not become false because of the person or his unbelief. That the sacrament was not founded on the holiness of men but upon the Word of God"*.

COMMENT:

On this last point, Luther was merely reiterating the Roman Catholic position since the days of St. Augustine. Luther in fact contradicted himself again because in his treatise on *"Concerning Christian Liberty"*, he had said: *"But to an unbelieving person nothing renders service or work for good . . . he is not a priest, but a profane person whose prayers are turned into sin, nor does he ever appear in the presence of God, because God does not hear sinners"*.

If a wicked priest's prayer is turned to sin, it is clear that he cannot minister the sacrament, if he ministers, he is ministering sin. That this is so can be examined in the light of the Scriptures with the following questions:

i) Will God accept a wicked priest?

God said He hides his face from unrepentant sinners and will not listen to their prayers—*Isaiah 1:12 (10-20; Psalms 66:18)*.

* A wicked priest is not acceptable to God.

ii) Is a wicked priest qualified to speak God's Word? And if he does speak God's words, does God honor His word spoken by a wicked priest?

In **Psalm 50:16**, God said that the wicked has no right to declare His statutes or take His covenant in his mouth. God also said He confirms only the word of His servants and performs the counsel of His messengers but acts contrary to the false prophets and frustrates the rebellious—*Isaiah 44:25-26.*

* God forbids the wicked from speaking His Word and if the wicked does speak God's Word, God will not honor or confirm it.

iii) The Communion is called a 'sacrifice'; if this is so, does God accept the sacrifice of a wicked priest?

The Scriptures say that "God is far from the wicked and that the sacrifice of the wicked is an abomination to the Lord"—***Proverbs 15:8, 29; Proverbs 21:27.***

* God will not accept the sacrifice from the hand of a wicked priest; what He called in His Word, an abomination.

iv) Does anyone benefit from the ministry of a wicked priest? Can a cursed person or priest minister blessings to others?

God says a sinning priest causes the people to sin, brings guilt on the entire congregation and corrupts God's covenant—***Leviticus 4:3 (NIV); Malachi 2:7-8.***

In addition, God said that a priest who fails to glorify Him is cursed and his blessings will be cursed—***Malachi 2:1-2.***

* An unrepentant or a wicked priest who nonetheless chooses to approach God is not glorifying God, in fact he is being irreverent and God said he is cursed.

Therefore, based on the Scriptures, a wicked priest is not acceptable to God and he has no right to speak the word of God; and if he does speak it, God will not confirm it.

A wicked priest therefore cannot effectively confect the Sacrament because God will not confirm his word. In other words, a wicked priest cannot invoke the Body and the Blood of Jesus into the natural bread and wine of the sacrament; at best he can only give to Communicants ordinary and unchanged bread and wine. Moreover, since the Scriptures say the sacrifice of the wicked is an abomination to the Lord, it follows that a wicked priest, trying to minister the sacrament is an abomination.

Lastly, the Scriptures say that a wicked priest is cursed; therefore no one can get any benefit from the ministration of such a priest. In fact, according to the Scriptures, he makes people to sin, brings guilt on them and brings them under a curse because God has cursed his blessings.

God said "By those who come near Me, I must be regarded as holy; And before all the people, I must be glorified . . ."—Leviticus 10: 1-11.

When Nadab and Abihu approached God irreverently, they were consumed by fire—**Leviticus 10:1-3.**

In situations where the Spirit of God operates in truth, no wickedness can exist; talk less of ministering before God! Ananias and Sapphira learnt that they could not lie to the Holy Spirit and were struck down dead upon discovery—**Acts 5**

As for Communicants who eat the sacrament 'unworthily', the Scriptures say they are ***"guilty of the Body and Blood of Jesus Christ and are eating and drinking damnation to themselves";*** that those who do so might become weak or sick or even die—**1Corinthians 11: 27-30.**

It would appear, therefore, that Martin Luther's position (as well as the Roman Catholic Church), that the wicked can administer the sacraments and that the unworthy can receive it is erroneous, unscriptural and a dangerous doctrine spiritually.

On the Creed and the Ten Commandments [14]

The Creed, (the Nicene Creed), according to Martin Luther, teaches us to know God fully because it sets forth everything that is expected and is received from Him. He divided the Creed into three articles:

The first article, the Father, explained creation,
The second article, the Son, explained Redemption and
The third article, the Holy Spirit, is the Sanctifier.

He said the Ten Commandments teach us what we ought to do; but the Creed tells us what God does and gives to us. ***That God gives Himself entirely to us with all that He has and is able to do, to aid and direct us in keeping the Ten Commandments***.

On the Law and the Gospel [15]

Martin Luther views the law as that which tells us what we ought to do as in the Ten Commandments. He divided the whole Scripture into two; the precepts (the law) and the Promises (the Gospel). The precepts he said teaches us what is good and ought to do but do not give the power to do them. The purpose of the law, he believed, was to reveal to man his impotence for doing good and cause him to despair of his own strength.

Martin Luther believed that obeying the Law for rewards or the fear of the evil consequences from disobeying is hypocritical; and held that real obedience of the Law should spring from the Love of God without any consideration of reward or punishment.

He believed that without the grace of God, the Law cannot be kept and to fulfill the law, faith in Jesus Christ is required because it is in Him that grace, justification, peace and liberty are promised by God.

Faith, he said, involve believing God's promises and holding Him to be true, just, wise and righteous and consequently live in obedience to Him in all things.

Therefore, God's promises (the Gospel) fulfill what God commands (the law). ***Anyone who believes the Gospel receives God's grace and the Holy Spirit whereby the law can be kept gladly and freely without fear of punishment or expectation of reward.***

On Good Works, Faith, Freewill and Salvation [16, 17]

Martin Luther rejected the Roman Catholic Church's notion of good works, when devoid of faith and confidence in God and stated that:

"There is no good work except that which God has commanded..."—**Mathew 19:16-18.**

Good works, as defined by the papacy during Luther's time consisted of such things as fasting, prayers, buying indulgences, giving alms or pilgrimages to pay off debts incurred in sinning against God.

He stated that what qualified work as 'good' was not the number, the appearance or the magnitude as judged by human laws or custom and that the most precious of good works is faith in Jesus Christ—*John 6:28-29*.

He said works done outside of faith were dead and that if every man had faith, there would be no need for the law because every one would at all times do good works—*1Timothy 1:8-11.*

However, because not every one has faith, there are four categories of people, namely:

    i   **Believers who live in the favor and grace of God and therefore do what is right.**

    ii   **Those who abuse or think they can abuse the freedom that is in Christ—1Peter 2:16; Galatians 5:13. To these people he** said: **"The freedom of faith does not permit sins nor will it cover them . . ."**

ii) Young believers who need further teachings and nurturing to mature.

i) Unbelievers who need to be constrained by spiritual and temporal laws like wild horses and dogs.

Martin Luther believed that man has freewill in 'civil righteousness' that is in things subject to reason but does not believe man has freewill in 'spiritual righteousness'. In other words, man has free choice in everything except in regard to salvation because faith is the work of the Holy Spirit and not man.

He believed that faith alone suffices for salvation and that works is not required. He believed that good works is the result of and not the requirement for Salvation.

He said: *"Works, since they are irrational things cannot glorify God, although they may be done to the glory of God if faith be present".*

He concluded: *"It is clear then that to a Christian man his faith suffices for everything, and that he has no need of works for justification. But if he has no need of works, neither has he need of the law; and if he has no need of the law, he is certainly free from the law, and the saying is true, 'The law is not made for a righteous man' (1Timothy 1:9). This is that Christian liberty, our faith, the effect of which is, not that we should be careless or lead a bad life, but that no one should need the law or works for salvation".*

On Christian Liberty, Sin and Forgiveness [14, 16, 17, 18, 19]

The Christian liberty, he said was not for a careless or bad life but simply that the law and works are not necessary for salvation.

He said: *"Since then this faith, can reign only in the inward man, as it is said: 'With the heart man believeth unto righteousness' (Rom. x. 10); and since it alone justifies, it is evident that by no outward work or labor can the inward man be at all justified, made free and saved; and that no works whatever have any relation to him. And so, on the other hand, it is solely by impiety and incredulity of heart that he becomes guilty and a slave of sin, deserving condemnation, not by any outward sin or work".*

He however advocated good works for its own sake to please God but not to trust in good works for justification or expect merit or reward from God.

Martin Luther believed that the forgiveness of sins is wrought through the Holy Sacrament, absolution and the consolatory promises of the entire Gospel through the Christian Church.

He also believed that, though the grace of God is secured through Christ and sanctification is wrought by the Holy Spirit through the Word of God in unity with the Christian Church; yet, on account of the flesh, man can never be without sin.

He said: *"A believer can never be free from sin nor live outside the grace of God"*.

Also that: *"although we have sins, the Holy Spirit does not allow them to injure us because we are the Christian Church where there is nothing but continuous, uninterrupted forgiveness of sin . . ."* (?)

He said that: *"the believing soul, by its pledge of faith in Christ, becomes free from all sin, fearless of death, safe from hell, and endowed with eternal righteousness, life and salvation of it s Husband, Christ"*.

Martin Luther further said: *"For it (faith), is the highest work for this very reason, because it remains and blots out these daily sins by <u>not doubting that God is so kind to you as to wink at such daily transgression and weakness</u>. Aye, even if a deadly sin should occur (which never or rarely happens to those who live in faith and trust towards God), yet faith rises again and does not doubt that its sin is already gone . . ."* Faith, he said, *". . . looks for no judgment, but only for pure grace, favor, kindness and mercy"*.

In his letter to Melanchton, Luther said: *"If you are a preacher of mercy, do not preach imaginary but true mercy. If mercy is true, you must therefore bear the true, not imaginary sin. God does not save those who are only imaginary sinners. <u>Be a sinner and let your sins be strong but let your trust in Christ be stronger, and rejoice in Christ who is victor over sin, death and the world</u>". We will commit sins while we are here, for this life is not a place where justice resides . . . It suffices that through God's glory we have recognized the Lamb who takes away the sin of the world. <u>No sin can separate us from Jesus Christ even if we were to kill or commit adultery thousands of times each day"</u> (!?!)*

This conclusion suggests (and in fact led some of Luther's followers, including his friend **Johannes Agricola (1494-1566 AD)** to believe) that

Christians are exempted from Mosaic moral laws. Martin Luther disclaimed this **"Antinomian"** doctrine and it caused a rift between him and Agricola. His assertions on sin and forgiveness have also led his opponents (with good reasons) to suggest that his doctrines support licentiousness.

Comments:

Martin Luther's assertions on sin, faith, grace and forgiveness contradict his belief that *"faith does not excuse nor will it cover sin"*.

Luther, like Augustine concluded that man cannot be without sin while on earth; he believed that faith in God's grace and mercy removed the sins committed daily or that God overlooks sin because of a believer's faith.

Luther misrepresented the Scripture by suggesting that because of a believer's faith, God would wink at sin. **What God winks at is "the time of ignorance" after which "He expects all men to repent, turn to Him and do works worthy of repentance . . ."—Acts 17:30; Acts 26:20.**

The Bible made it clear that a true Christian does not make a habit of sinning and stated that: **"No one who lives in Him (Jesus Christ) keeps on sinning. Anyone who continues to sin has neither seen Him nor known Him"—1John 3:6.**

Martin Luther was also wrong and he directly contradicted the Bible when he stated that: *"No sin can separate us from Him, even if we were to kill or commit adultery thousands of times each day"*.

The Bible clearly stated that Sin separates us from God—**Isaiah 59:1-2**. Jesus also said there is an unforgivable sin that can separate man from God here and in the hereafter—**Mathew 12:31-32.**

Luther's assertions that believers cannot be free from sin also contradicts Jesus Christ who said anyone who sins is a slave of sin but those He sets free are free indeed—**John 8: 34-36**.

Moreover, the Bible says that to keep on sinning after coming to the saving knowledge of Jesus Christ is "to hold His Blood in contempt, trample Him underfoot and to insult the Holy Spirit of Grace". The Bible says Christ's sacrifice does not cover such willful sins and that the punishment for such sinners will be much worse than for those who broke the laws of Moses—**Hebrews 10:26-31**.

Actually, Christians, rather than sinning robustly and trusting God to "wink" at their sins are enjoined to espouse holiness and eschew sin. **Titus 2:11-14.**

Martin Luther's position on the issues of sin and faith contradicts his exposition on the Creed where he said that *"God gave Himself to us with all that He has and is able to do to aid us in keeping His moral laws, the Ten Commandments"*. It also contradicts his exposition on the Gospel where he averred *that "the Gospel is God's promises which fulfils the law and that those who believe receive God's grace and the Holy Spirit whereby the law can be kept gladly . . ."*

Therefore, Martin Luther, in concluding that "*A believer can never be without sin or live outside the grace of God*" remained faithful to St. Augustine who had posited that 'sin is required to treat sin', rather than to God's revelation that he got from the Scriptures about faith, grace and the Holy Spirit.

Such a conclusion suggests that in spite of the fact that God, who ('had given Himself with all that He has, and is able to do), the Holy Spirit and grace (that He also gave to believers) are all no match for the flesh sin and Satan, which is blasphemous!

To be Holy or live without sin is not to live 'outside the grace of God'; it is to thrive in it.

The apostle Paul made it clear that it is erroneous to think that God's grace abound only when or where sins abound—**Romans 3:8; Romans 6:1-2, 15**

Martin Luther's position that believers can sin with impunity but would be exonerated on account of faith is somewhat a kind of "faith in faith" rather than faith in Jesus Christ. The Scripture says that Jesus destroyed the power of sin and sin should not have dominion over the believer—**Romans 8:3 (NLT)**. Again, believers are new creatures, created in the likeness of God in righteousness and true holiness—**2Corinthians 5:17; Ephesians 4:24;** and are called to cleanse themselves of all the filthiness of the flesh and spirit and to perfect holiness in the fear of God—*2Corinthians 7:1.*

'The **grace** of God that **brings** salvation **teaches** believers to say **"No"** to ungodliness and worldly passions . . . ', not to revel in them in the erroneous and vain hope of automatic forgiveness—***Titus 2:11-14 (NIV).***

On Jews [20]

Martin Luther initially tried to convert the Jews in Germany but after his attempts failed, he wrote a treatise, **"On the Jews and their lies"** in which he traced the history of the Jews and documented their attitude towards Jesus Christ, the Virgin Mary and Christians in general.

- Luther accused the Jews of being arrogant because of their heritage from the patriarchs and their pride as the chosen people of God.
- He alleged that they held Jesus, Mary and Christians in contempt and called them derogatory names in an attempt to weaken and destroy the faith of Christians.
- He accused them of avarice and of defrauding the German people of their wealth and properties through usury.

- He called them a rejected and condemned people and called for the burning of their synagogues and schools as they neither obeyed Moses nor follow Jesus Christ.
- He advocated restrictions on the movements and commerce of Jews in the country as well as confiscation of their properties and putting them to labor.
- He admonished preachers to instruct the parishioners not to deal with the Jews whom he called "venomous, bitter, vindictive, tricky serpents, assassins and children of the devil"
- As a last resort, he called for the expulsion of the Jews from Germany as had been done from other countries as the nation's Christian duty.

Martin Luther's writing and opinion of Jews was so controversial and patently anti-Semitic that many have dissociated themselves from it. It is alleged that the Nazis used the document in their propaganda against Jews.

Martin Luther left the monastery in 1524 and got married in 1525 to **Katharina Von Bora (c1499-1552),** a former nun and they had six children. He continued to teach theology at Wittenberg until his death from natural causes in 1546.

Martin Luther's intention was to reform the Roman Catholic Church from within; he failed in this regard but his ideas fundamentally changed the world. His doctrines gave rise to Protestantism and his idea of individual freedom and liberation from religious tyranny later informed political and social systems that seek individual, political, economic and other freedoms. The **"Protestant Church",** of which the Lutheran Church was the pioneer, has splintered into numerous pieces over the ages such that there are currently literally thousands of denominations each with its own peculiar doctrinal beliefs.

Ulrich Zwingli (1484-1531 AD) [21, 22]

Ulrich Zwingli was a Swiss secular priest, theologian and humanist who was influenced by humanist teachers and friends like Erasmus. Ulrich Zwingli converted to the Protestant point of view and led a movement that systematically dismantled the Roman Catholic ways in Zurich. He had disputations against many Roman Catholic doctrines in sixty-seven articles of faith among which were that:

- Christ is the only way to salvation
- Christ is the head of the Church
- The mass (Eucharist) as a sacrifice offered to God for the living and the dead was unscriptural
- Christ is the only mediator between God and man
- The doctrine of purgatory was unscriptural
- Worship of images was unscriptural
- Clerical celibacy was unscriptural

As his message of reform caught on, images were removed from the churches, Communion was given in bread and wine, lentine fasts were declared unscriptural and he removed from worship anything that was not expressly in the bible.

He disputed the nature of Christ's presence in the Eucharist with Martin Luther at a castle in Marburg; while Luther subscribed to the doctrine of *consubstantiation* which is essentially similar to the Roman Catholic *transubstantiation*, Zwingli denied the real presence of Christ in the Eucharist. The difference of opinion regarding the Eucharist foreclosed the possibility of a merger of the German and Swiss streams of Reformation. Zwingli also disagreed with the Anabaptists over their rejection of infant baptism. He renounced his vow of celibacy and got married in 1524.

The Holy Roman Emperor attacked Zurich on behalf of the Roman Catholic Church and Zwingli went into battle with the people to defend his land and faith and was killed in 1531.

He was succeeded by **Heinrich Bullinger (1504-1575 AD),** [23, 24] the fifth son of a Roman Catholic priest living in concubinage who was raised for a career in the Church. Bullinger consolidated Zwingli's doctrines and as an architect of the *Second Helvetic Confession* which was adopted in Switzerland, Hungary and Bohemia as well as elsewhere, shaped the beliefs of the Presbyterians and the Puritans. He renounced celibacy, married a former nun and had eleven children. He died in 1575.

William Tyndale (1494-1536 AD) [25, 26]

William Tyndale was an English scholar, theologian and polyglot who translated the Bible from Greek and Hebrew text into English. The project was facilitated by the invention of the printing press. His passion was to give the common man (even the boy that drove the plow) access to the Scriptures.

The Roman Catholic Church was opposed to the translation of the Bible into any vernacular. In his treatise ***"The Obedience of a Christian Man"***, Tyndale answered the Roman Catholic objections to Bible translations as follows:
- On the objection that the Bible ought not to be in the mother tongue; he answered that it was because they feared the light and desired to lead people blindfolded and keep them captive.
- On the assertion that the Scripture needs a pure and quiet mind and laymen are too encumbered with worldly business to understand it he replied that this also applied to the prelates even more as they were all more entangled in worldly affairs than the ordinary people.
- That the laymen would misinterpret the bible—he said the way to deal with this was to teach them the right way to interpret it. That the lives and teachings of the clergy were so contrary that even when they preached the truth, they were no longer credible.
- That the other 'tongues' were too rude and crude—Tyndale said, God made all tongues; that the Church allowed the translation of ribald and filthy classic tales but forbid the translation of the Bible.
- That the Scripture was too hard and needed 'doctors' to interpret it—Tyndale contended that even Origen and Augustine made mistakes and that the Scripture is required to correct them and if the curate would not teach the people, they should be allowed to read it themselves and let God be their teacher.

Tyndale called the Roman Catholic clergy—***"wicked and damnable servants of mammon".***

William Tyndale differed doctrinally from the Roman Catholic Church in many important areas. For example:
- he did not believe in 'freewill'
- He was of the opinion that baptism was just a sign with no intrinsic spiritual significance.
- Similarly, he did not believe the Catholic teaching that the Eucharist was a sacrifice instituted by God to help souls in purgatory or promote men and make them rich.
- He believed the Eucharist was instituted to seek absolution of sins with the set purpose to sin no more as much as possible, call to

memory the passion of Christ, meditate to weaken the flesh and strengthen the spirit and to give thanks.

His ideas were considered heretical by both the Catholic and the Church of England and his Bible translations, which he ran to Germany to print and publish, were banned from circulation. He was betrayed by someone he considered a friend, was arrested, tried, convicted of heresy and strangled before he was burnt at the stake in 1536 by King Henry VIII and the Anglican Church. ***His dying prayer was "Lord, open the king of England's eyes".***

His prayers were answered within three years when the king commissioned the publication of the "Great Bible", which he instructed to be placed in every church in the land and made accessible to all. The Great Bible was compiled from the 'Mathew Bible and the Coverdale Bible both of which had heavily relied on William Tyndale's translations.

The King James' Authorized Version was mainly dependent on Tyndale's translations. Modern translations that owe a lot to William Tyndale include the Revised Standard Version, the American Standard Bible and the Living Bible versions.

He is revered as the "Father of the English Reformation" and "The Apostle of England".

John Calvin (1509-1564 AD) and Calvinism [27, 28, 29, 30]

John Calvin was a French theologian whose father was a lawyer. He studied theology and law and was influenced by humanist teachers and friends such as Erasmus. After what was described as a sudden 'conversion', he became a critic of the Catholic Church and had to leave France where his views were considered heresy.

He eventually settled in Geneva which became a Protestant city in 1536; renouncing papal authority, dissolving monasteries and abolishing Mass. However, there were two factions; those who favored the control of the clergy by temporal powers—(the Libertines) and those who favored civil governance by the Church or Theocracy. The Libertines won and John Calvin and his companion, **Guillaume Farel (1489-1565),** had to leave Geneva for Strasbourg.

Church Government:

He returned in 1541 after the Libertines lost power and introduced his own liturgy, doctrines and social organization. The hierarchy consisted of pastors or ministers, teachers, elders and deacons; the pastors exercised authority on religious matters, the teachers taught doctrine, the elders, usually twelve in number were elected by the municipal council and were responsible for visiting every sector of the city to ensure that things were in order and the deacons were in charge of the widows, the poor, the sick and the elderly. Discipline was strict and in 1555, draconian moral laws were enacted; lewd singing was punishable by tongue piercing and blasphemy by death. The taverns were closed down and replaced with "Evangelical Refreshment Places" where the drinking of alcohol, though allowed, was preceded by bible reading and every meal in public eateries with grace.

These reforms were however speedily repealed when Calvin realized they were very unpopular. Nonetheless, Calvin built a Church Structure that he thought was infallible and would brook no indiscipline or delinquency; the **Church Consistory** had the power to excommunicate offenders and those considered heretics were imprisoned, exiled or executed.

A prominent case was that of a Spanish scholar, **Michael Severtus** who questioned the doctrine of the Trinity and also criticized Calvin's **"Institutes of the Christian Religion"**, written in 1536 with several updates, and which had been as a "holy doctrine" which no man could speak against. Unwittingly, Severtus therefore committed 'heresy' and when he visited Geneva in 1553; he was tried for heresy, condemned and burnt at the stake.

Calvin had considered the criticism of the 'Institutes' as a charge and stigma of heresy on all Protestants. The Consistory recommended the capital punishment to the civil authorities which then carried it out just as in the Roman Catholic Church system.

Sebastian Castellio (1515-1563), a moderate contemporary of Calvin called him the *"Pope of Geneva"*. Castellio suffered persecution from Calvin and his clergy, left Geneva for Basle but never stopped advocating freedom of conscience in believing and opposing Calvin's position of executing perceived heretics. He died at the young age of forty eight years in 1563. His body was exhumed, burnt and the ashes scattered

Calvin's autocratic style was resented by many who felt that his intolerance of dissent and the execution of dissenters were no better than what obtained under the papacy.

Calvin was the first political thinker to incorporate the Church into city Government and employ biblical principles in social organization.

Geneva became the hub for exiles from other European countries where Protestants were facing persecution. It therefore became the center of the Reformation in Europe and the Academy for teaching missionaries became the University of Geneva which trained missionaries from all over Europe.

Calvin's Doctrines

Calvin's doctrines are encapsulated in what is commonly called the "*Five Points of Calvinism*" with the acronym **TULIP**; namely—
- **T**otal Depravity
- **U**nconditional Election
- **L**imited Atonement
- **I**rresistible Grace
- **P**erseverance of the Saints

The essence of Calvinism is ***Predestination***; that salvation as well as reprobation is predestined by God and no human being can influence it in any way. God has fore-knowledge of those He would save and those who would be lost and Christ died only for the elect who in turn respond to His call irresistibly. Therefore the elects cannot lose their salvation while the reprobates are irrevocably doomed.

Critics have labeled Calvinism a great obstacle to evangelism because if predestination holds true, what is the use of evangelism or holy living?

Calvin recognized only two sacraments, the Holy Communion and Baptism but did not subscribe to the real corporeal presence of Christ in the bread and the wine.

From Geneva, Calvinism spread as the exiles returned home as missionaries to their own countries and Calvinism today has many shades found in many Protestant groups such as the Reformed Churches, Presbyterians, Puritans and some Baptists.

He was succeeded by his lifelong friend, ***Theodore Beza (1519-1605)***.

Comment:

Calvin, like Augustine before him did violence to God's character in many ways by the doctrine of predestination and limited election. He sacrificed all the other attributes of God like justice, love, mercy etc on the altar of His sovereignty by which it is implied that ultimately God is responsible for sin and evil in the world.

Why would a just and merciful God command all to repent of their sins (Acts 17:30) then give only a few the grace to do so and then turn around and punish those he did not give the grace to obey His command?

A doctrine that holds that a loving, merciful God would create man, destine him to fail and fall and yet hold him responsible by punishing him with eternal fire in hell is totally repugnant and irreconcilable with many scriptural texts to the contrary—**(Mathew 26:51-53; John 3:16-18; 1Timothy 2:1-4; 2Peter 3:9; Ezekiel 18:23; Jonah 1:1-4:11. etc)**

Calvin's tyrannical Government with its intolerance of dissent and executions was also unbiblical and the criticisms leveled against it were well deserved.

Jesus never taught that those who refuse his message should be tortured or killed—***Mark 6:7-11; Luke 9:5, 49-56; Luke 10:1-11;*** and He never imposes Himself on anyone—***Revelations 3:20***

Jacobus Arminius (1560-1609 AD) and Arminianism [31, 32, 33]

Jacobus Arminius was a Dutch scholar, theologian and Remonstrant Reformer. He lost his father in infancy and the rest of his family as an adolescent during the ***Spanish massacre of Oudewater of 1575*** when the city joined in a call for independence from Spain. He was raised by family friends and he studied under scholars with humanist views and later under Theodore Beza, Calvin's successor in Geneva. He returned to Amsterdam and was ordained as a pastor and was later a professor of theology at Leiden University.

Although he appreciated Calvin's commentaries and considered them as "above those of all the fathers"; nevertheless, he differed from him in many essential points considered central to Calvinism.

- He rejected Calvin's absolute sovereignty of God in preordination and fore-ordination of salvation and held the view that man responds to God in salvation.
- He averred that Calvinists reversed the order of things by stating that adoption was prepared for those who would believe rather than what the Scripture says that those who believe are adopted; and that the adopted person is justified rather than that the justified is adopted.

On this position, he was accused of making God's sovereignty subservient to Man's action and was accused of Pelagianism but denied it. He countered that the Calvinist's doctrine of predestination makes God the author of Sin and Man's arbitrary condemnation; ***that Calvinism makes***

God "a tyrant and an executioner" and that it dishonors Him. In a series of lectures on the book of Romans; Arminius maintained that:
- Romans 7 referred to the Apostle's pre-Christian period
- God predestinates those He fore-knows would of their own freewill respond to His call
- In exercise of freewill, a person can reject the faith, fall away and lose their salvation

At the **Synod of Dordt (1618-1619),** Arminius' views were condemned and the five points of Calvinism defined in response to the followers of Arminius' points of Remonstrance.

The 'Remonstrants' were purged from the Reformed churches and they became a separate movement.

One of the strongest torch bearers of Arminianism was **John Wesley**, who, with his brother **Charles Wesley** started the **Methodist** denomination. Other groups that subscribe largely to the doctrines of Arminianism include Pentecostals, Assembly of God, the Nazarene, the Mennonites, Charismatics and many Baptists.

The Anabaptists [34, 35, 36]

'Anabaptism' means re-baptism, a term that is used to describe a disparate group of Christians outside the main stream of Reformers during the Reformation. However, the beginning of the re-baptism movements has been traced to **Simon Mennon, Feliz Manz and Conrad Grebel** who in 1525 re-baptized one another as adults.

Manz and Grebel were associates of Zwingli who, on studying the Bible in Greek, Hebrew and Latin found no Biblical foundation for infant baptism. The two grew apart from Zwingli and were joined by Simon Mennon, a Roman Catholic priest who renounced his allegiance to Rome upon conviction of the Reformers point of view.

The Anabaptist articles of faith include:
- **Sola Scriptura**—they were more consistent than the Magisterial Reformers (Calvinists) in their application of Scriptural authority to matters of church operations and worship.
- **Believers' Baptism**—they believed baptism is only for those old enough to understand and personally believe that their sins have been taken away by Christ. They pointed out that there was no Biblical basis for infant baptism. The Anabaptists opposed infant baptism on the ground that it entraps the soul of the subject and

impede such a person from experiencing the joy of salvation through personal repentance and regeneration. Re-baptizing rectifies the situation, giving people the freedom to experience the saving grace of Christ.
- **The Holy Communion**—The Anabaptists believed the communion should be taken by baptized believers only.
- **Separation of Church and State**—Anabaptist considered the Church as the assembly of the redeemed who are opposed to the world. They rejected State religions
- **Freedom of Conscience**—They were consistently opposed to persecution and did not support the idea of the State to punish or execute anyone for their religious beliefs.
- **Holiness**—they emphasized spiritual experience and obedience to divine standards and did not tolerate licentiousness based on the claim of justification by faith.
- **The Civil Authority**—they accepted the authority of the civil authorities to wield the sword against evil doers but held that Christians cannot wield the sword even in defense of the good; therefore they do not serve in the military. They also held that Christians cannot be magistrates.
- **Oaths**—all oaths were forbidden
- **The Ban**—they held that the ultimate disciplinary action is excommunication of erring members after two private and one public warning.

The Anabaptists rejected the Roman Catholic sacramental/sacerdotal system of soteriology and held that it was being manipulated to keep people captive in direct contradiction to what salvation is supposed to be.

They believe that salvation sets free from bondage to sin and that this fact is to be celebrated by the redeemed. They held that the Roman Catholic Church had made salvation a regulated state of existence instead of a divine particular event to be celebrated and that the sacraments were being used as weapons of ecclesiastical manipulation of the people instead of joyous celebration.

They also rejected Luther's concept of justification by faith irrespective of conduct because they felt it had a tendency to antinomianism and licentiousness. They believed that the Church had fallen since the time of the Emperor Constantine and that radical reform was needed not the palliative measures advocated by Luther and the Reformed churches.

They comprised a number of groups with differing doctrines and beliefs and were not confined to any particular geopolitical area. While some were militant, many rejected war or violence even for self defense.

The Anabaptists were considered the *"**Radical Reformers**"* and were therefore persecuted by the State as well as the Roman Catholic, the Reformed and the Lutheran Churches for their religious beliefs. Many of the leaders were incarcerated and left to rot in prison, drowned or burnt at the stake between 1520 and 1580. With time, the more peaceful groups were tolerated and although they had no prominent theologian or academic to champion their cause, they increased and flourished. Many emigrated to North America and contemporary groups that evolved from them include: the Mennonites, various Brethren groups and the Amish.

Chapter 15

European Wars of Religion

Germany
The Schmalkaldic War (1546-1547) [1,2]

Many German princes converted to Luther's religious views, therefore the Holy Roman Emperor (HRE) Charles V, in an effort to preserve religious and political unity in his realm requested the Lutheran princes to present the articles of their faith at the ***Diet of Augsburg*** in June 1530 AD.

Martin Luther, Melanchton and other Lutheran theologians prepared a summary of the Lutheran faith in form of twenty-eight articles presented at the Diet of Augsburg and it became known as the "***Augsburg Confession***". It was considered by representatives of the Emperor and the papal legates who later wrote a poorly prepared "***Pontifical Confutation of the Augsburg Confession***" to which Philip Melancthon made a reply in the "***Apology of the Augsburg Confession***" in which he refuted the arguments in the confutation. Anticipating a reaction from the Emperor, the princes formed a military alliance, "***The Schmalkaldic League***" and admitted other states and cities that officially assented to the Augsburg Confession and the Apology.

The tension between the German princes and the Emperor with the papacy grew and eventually the "***Schmalkaldic War***" broke out between 1546 and 1547 AD. The Emperor won but the religious and political problems remained unsolved.

Augsburg and Leipzig Interims [3,4]

In 1548, following the defeat of the German princes in the Schmalkaldic war, the HRE Charles V enacted an imperial decree called the "***Augsburg Interim***" intended to guide religious observance before a final resolution at a general council. The Interim ordered Protestants to re-adopt the

Catholic beliefs and practices including the seven sacraments but gave some concessions such as the administration of the Eucharist in both kinds of bread and wine and allowing clerical marriage.

Many Lutheran pastors and theologians opposed the Interim and were removed from office, imprisoned, banished or even executed.

Philip Melanchton, for the sake of peace worked with the protestant collaborator of the Emperor, Maurice of Saxony the Protestant Elector, to improve the terms of the Interim in favor of Lutherans. The result was the *"Leipzig Interim"* which gave more concessions on doctrinal issues considered essential by Lutherans such as justification by faith alone. Melanchton and the negotiating party were willing to compromise on issues deemed to be *"Adiaphora"* or non-essential such as clerical vestments, mass, confirmation or the holy days. Many still refused to abide by the Leipzig Interim and were called the *Gnesio-Lutherans* (genuine Lutherans) while those who accepted the Interim were called Philipists.

The **"Adiaphoristic Controversy"** followed and this was finally resolved by the **"Formula of Concord"** which defined adiaphora as *"church rites which are neither commanded nor forbidden in the Word of God"*.

The two Interims did not result in lasting peace.

The Peace of Augsburg (1555) [5]

Maurice of Saxony, the Protestant Elector overthrew the Interim in 1552 and turned against the Emperor. Eventually in 1555, the *"Peace of Augsburg"* was negotiated and signed. The treaty gave Lutheranism an official status in the Holy Roman Empire and the princes were allowed to determine the religion of their domains on the principle of *"Cuius regio, eius religio"* that is *"He who rules, his the religion"*. The religion of the ruler therefore determined the religion of the people of the domain.

Under this arrangement, dissenters were given a period of grace within which to leave the domain for a place where their religion is practiced or face persecution. The Peace of Augsburg proved to be inadequate as it recognized only Roman Catholicism and Lutheranism and did not accommodate other Protestant groups like the Calvinists.

The Thirty Years War—(1618-1648) [6,7]

The Thirty years war was essentially a German religious cum political civil war with international dimensions involving many European countries such as Austria, Netherlands, Denmark, Sweden, Spain and France.

The religious aspect involved Catholics, Lutherans and Calvinists but compounded by dynastic ambitions of the secular leaders.

There were several phases to the war which was triggered in Bohemia, a predominantly Hussite nation in 1618 when a Catholic prince became the king and HRE with the implication that the people had to embrace Catholicism based on the Peace of Augsburg. The people resented this, and, supported by some Protestant German princes, revolted. The revolt was crushed by the imperial army supported by Spain and Catholicism was re-imposed on the people of Bohemia.

Historians have identified other phases in the war, namely:
- The Danish phase—involving Denmark, Norway and England against Germany—1625-1629.
- The Swedish Phase—involving Sweden and France against Germany—1630-1635.
- The French phase—with France declaring war on Spain the constant acolyte of the HRE.

The war devastated many countries in Europe and by 1648 most of them were weary and ready for peace.

'**The Peace of Westphalia**' was negotiated and signed in 1648 and by the terms of the treaty:
- German principalities gained sovereignty and the ability to make treaties with foreign nations.
- Calvinism was recognized with Lutheranism and Catholicism as an official religion.
- Secular kingship was recognized as the legitimate and dominant form of government.
- Switzerland and the Netherlands were recognized as Sovereign States
- Sweden gained strategic areas and expanded its territory.
- France became the dominant power in continental Europe
- Spain lost power in Europe and abroad.

In general, nationalism prevailed over universalism favored by Roman Catholicism and the need for religious tolerance became apparent.

England
The English Reformation and the English Civil War [8, 9, 10, 11]

The Reformation in England was gradual. Though the crystallization began during the reign of *Henry VIII (1491-1547)*, the root of England's fray with the papacy went further to the twelfth century and the Conflicts of Investiture and the Wycliffite Lollardism of the fourteenth century.

The reformation was not a result of doctrinal differences per se but rather the application of doctrine. Although Martin Luther's writings in English were already circulating and the wind of Protestantism was blowing in England by 1521, the break with Rome was more political than religious.

In 1521, King Henry VIII, with the help of *Thomas More* wrote a treatise defending the Seven Sacraments of the Roman Catholic Church in a rebuttal of Martin Luther's writing on the subject. For this, the king was recognized by the papacy and given a **"Golden Rose"** and the title of the **"Defender of the Faith"**. In 1526, the Papal legate in England, *Cardinal Wolsey (1473-1530),* presided over the burning of Martin Luther's books.

The precipitating factor initiating the break from Rome was the lack of response by the papacy to King Henry VIII's request in 1527 to have his marriage to *Catherine of Aragon* annulled because she had not given birth to a male heir. However, this was a problem for the papacy because the marriage with Catherine had been allowed due to a special papal dispensation as she was the widow of Henry's late brother. To grant another dispensation would have been to regard as erroneous the first dispensation.

Apart from doctrinal and canonical issues, the pope feared Emperor Charles V who happened to be Catherine of Aragon's nephew and had earlier invaded Italy, abducted and briefly imprisoned the pope. Therefore the discussion on the possibility of another dispensation dragged on until King Henry got impatient and dismissed Cardinal Wolsey, replacing him with Thomas More as the archbishop and the chief minister in 1529. The king then hatched the idea of securing the annulment without the pope. He called the parliament which between 1529 and 1536 AD, passed a series of legislations that gradually severed connection of the clergy, the people and the king of England from Rome.

King Henry VIII married Anne Boleyn in 1533 and in 1534, the *"Act of Supremacy'* was passed which required all citizens in England to recognize King Henry as the supreme head of the **Church of England** on earth.

Thomas More refused and resigned and he was replaced by ***Thomas Cranmer (1489-1556)***.

The king and his new archbishop, Cranmer were excommunicated by the Pope.

In 1536, the *"Act against the Pope's Authority"* was passed; removing the pope as the final arbiter in things pertaining to the Scriptures. Other steps taken to disengage England from the papacy include: abolition of feast days, (considered occasions for vice and idleness), prohibition of image veneration, (images being considered objects of superstition) and prohibition of lighting candles before images.

King Henry also moved against the monasteries on the allegations that the monks were corrupt or sexually immoral. The monasteries were closed down and the properties appropriated by the Crown or sold to the nobles. The various reforms were generally received by the people with equanimity because Church corruption was common knowledge but there were some pockets of tension and violent revolts in some communities.

In 1539, Henry passed the *"**Acts of the Six Articles**"* which reaffirmed the doctrines of transubstantiation, Eucharist in one kind to the laity, clerical celibacy, private masses and confession as well as restrictions on the reading of the Bible. In essence, the Church of England was still essentially Catholic except for the headship.

The Anabaptists and others with protestant views were given ten days of grace within which to leave the country; and many were arrested and executed. For reasons that were not entirely clear to historians, Henry had his chief minister, ***Thomas Cromwell (1485-1540),*** who coordinated the reforms, arrested and beheaded in 1540. He apparently regretted this immediately and was said to have mourned him for two weeks.

Henry VIII died in 1547 and was succeeded by his son, nine year old ***Edward VI (1547-1553)***. King Edward VI was fervently protestant and with the help of the archbishop Cranmer, advanced the cause of the reformers. He repealed the Six Articles Act of his father, allowed the clergy to marry, ordered the removal of all images from churches and decreed the use of the Book of Common Prayer, written by Cranmer in all churches. Unfortunately, Edward was sickly and died young in 1553 AD.

He was succeeded by ***Queen Mary (1553-1558 AD)*** the daughter of Catherine of Aragon, a devout Catholic who reversed the protestant reformation of her father and half brother. She declared England a Catholic country subject to the pope and moved to restore Roman Catholic worship style to churches by dismissing married priests, restoring clerical celibacy and images.

Her attempt to restore monasticism failed because less than one per cent of the monks and nuns were willing to return to a life of celibacy. She persecuted and burnt at the stake the archbishop Cranmer, bishops, priests and ordinary men and women who were Protestants; this earned her the sobriquet of "**Bloody Mary**".

However, Queen Mary died after only five years on the throne and was succeeded by her half sister, **Queen Elizabeth I (1558-1603 AD)**.

Queen Elizabeth I was a staunch Protestant but pursued a course of religious tolerance and compromise to bring peace to her country. Although she repealed Mary's Catholic laws, she retained some of the Catholic mode of worship like the vestments and Saints' days. She however re-enacted the "Supremacy Act" and was excommunicated by the pope.

The excommunication made her an open target for Catholics in England who had the religious obligation to kill her. She was the target of several assassination plots but survived all. Her cousin, Mary of Scots was involved in one such plot and had to be executed in 1587. She allowed the "**Puritans**", the Protestant faction that wanted no Roman Catholic relic in worship to operate freely and participate in parliament but they had to recognize her as the head of the church.

Queen Elizabeth I's long reign ensured that Protestantism became entrenched in England. She is considered one of England's greatest and politically adroit monarchs.

Elizabeth I was succeeded by James I (James VI of Scotland—1603-1625), who, though raised in the Scottish Calvinist tradition, hated the Puritan idea of equality before the law and believed in the divine rights of Kings to rule their subjects.

The Puritans wanted political and Church reforms and were backed by Parliament. Tired of the wrangling, James I suspended the parliament in 1611 and ruled alone until 1621.

King James I commissioned the translation of the popular "**King James' Authorized Version**" of the bible from original texts and existing translations by a group of scholars. King James I died in 1625 and was succeeded by his son, **Charles I (1625-1649)**.

Charles I also believed in the divine rights of kings to rule and like his father got into conflicts over political and Church reforms with the parliament. The situation was not helped by the fact that he was married to a pro-Catholic French lady and his ecclesiastical policies increased Catholic flavor in the Church of England while the Puritans were persecuted. As the differences between the king and parliament increased, he dissolved parliament in 1629 and governed alone until he had to reconvene parliament in 1640 in order to get authorization to raise money to finance the war with Scotland.

The parliament also passed the *"Triennial Act"* making it mandatory to call the parliament into session at least once every three years.

In 1641, the parliament also compiled a list of grievances against King Charles I's rule and demanded Church reforms as well as parliamentary control over the army and royal appointments. Eventually, a civil war, essentially religious but with social and political colorings, broke out in 1642. After initial setbacks, the parliament's forces won in 1649 and Charles I was tried as a tyrant, traitor and murderer and was sentenced to death by beheading.

A Commonwealth/Republic was declared with *Oliver Cromwell (1599-1658)* as the Lord Protector. Unfortunately, under Cromwell, apparently, no one was happy, civil liberties were subordinated to the liberty of the few "elect people of God" and many considered his administration another form of tyranny. He died in 1658 and was succeeded by his son. However, the people had had enough of the Commonwealth experiment and in 1660, the Presbyterians and royalists combined to restore the monarchy in the person of *Charles II (1630-1685),* one of Charles I's sons.

The restoration of the monarchy resulted in Anglicanism being favored over other sects and legislations were passed against dissenters. It was during this time that *John Bunyan (1628-1688)*, a popular puritan preacher, wrote the *"Pilgrim Progress"* while in jail and *John Milton (1608-1674),* renowned poet and polemicist wrote *"Paradise Lost".*

Religious tolerance was restored partially with the passage of the *"First Toleration Act"* in 1689 which allowed nonconformists to worship publicly but full rights were not gained until 1828 when the *'Test and Corporation Acts'* were repealed.

France
The French Reformation [12]

The forerunner of reformation in France was **Jacques Lefevre d'Etaples (1455-1536)**, a French priest, humanist and theologian. Guillaume Farel, one of his students hosted Calvin in Switzerland when he fled from persecution in France.

Calvin later developed Calvinism and students and missionaries from Calvin's Academy in Geneva flooded France and made converts, including some nobles, to Calvinism in sections of the country. The Calvinists were called Huguenots, a derogatory term of uncertain origin.

French Wars of Religion (1562-1598) [13, 14, 15]

As in many European nations, the mixture of politics and religion also produced communal and national tensions in France. Violence frequently erupted between rival noble families one of which was catholic and two prominent Huguenots.

The French religious wars began in 1562 when the powerful Catholic Guises noble family, seeking to assert its control over the nation's politics, attacked unarmed Protestants at a church service and killed everyone present. The carnage was dubbed the *"Massacre of Vassy"*, and it set off a series of communal violent conflicts and assassinations which continued on and off for decades.

In 1572, the royal troops were instigated to slaughter thousands of Protestants on St. Bartholomew Day, to cover up a botched intrigue by the Queen Mother. The Royal troops and the Catholic political faction slaughtered thousands of Huguenots in several towns over several weeks, beginning from St Bartholomew's day. The Pope, Gregory XIII, celebrated the massacre and awarded the *"Golden Rose"* to the French King in recognition of his role as a *"Defender of the Faith"*.

The *"St. Bartholomew Day Massacre"* as it came to be known, appalled Protestants all over Europe as well as moderate Catholics in France. The Guises formed a *Catholic League* which was supported by **King Philip II (1556-1598)** of Spain whose passion was to rid Europe of Protestantism. This changed the perception of Protestants about Catholics from being mere misguided Christians to be reformed to being actually a malevolent force to be resisted and overcome. Therefore the Protestants slowly evolved into militant groups engaged in wars of survival with the Catholic monarchies and the Roman Catholic Church.

The religious/political wars continued until 1598 when **King Henry IV (1589-1610)** promulgated the *"Edict of Nantes"* which gave the Huguenots the right to worship publicly, occupy public office and administer their towns but with certain restrictions.

The Edict of Nantes did not totally end the oppression of the Protestants which continued in one form or the other until the Edict of Nantes was repealed by King Louis XIV in 1685. The resumption of vigorous persecutions led to the emigration of many Protestants to other European countries and British colonies in America and South Africa.

Spain [7, 15]

Spain, since the beginning of the Spanish Inquisition in 1478 had been intolerant of anything that was not Roman Catholicism.

In the sixteenth century, in addition to Moslems and Jews, Protestants were also persecuted.

Apart from Protestants within its borders, Spain was dedicated to rooting out Protestantism from other European nations. Spain was a major player in the Thirty Year War (1618-1648) and it allied with the Catholic league in the wars of religion in France. She sent an inquisitor to the Netherlands with the subsequent execution of thousands of Protestants while others were exiled. Spain also invaded England to execute the Pope's excommunication on Queen Elizabeth I and revenge the execution of Mary, Queen of Scots, a Catholic, for her part in the conspiracy to assassinate Queen Elizabeth I.

The Spanish Inquisition against anything that is not Roman Catholic continued until 1834.

Chapter 16

The Roman Catholic Counter-Reformation

The Council of Trent (1545-1563) [1, 2, 3]

The Roman Catholic Church responded to the spread of Protestantism with attempts to reform itself by curbing the abuses within the Church hierarchy. A General Council was finally called to address various issues and new religious orders were approved and old ones were reformed.

The Council of Trent was convoked by ***Pope Paul III (1534-1549)*** in 1545; the council met intermittently in three stages, under three popes—(***Paul III, Julius III (1550-1555) and Pius IV (1559-1565)*** over a period of eighteen years—*1545-47; 1551-1552* and *1562-63*.

The Church was divided before the Council met between those who wanted the Protestant doctrines to be considered for the sake of unifying the Church and those who remained uncompromising and felt that the Roman Catholic doctrines must be preserved at all costs and dissent to be suppressed with force. There were also factions that hoped for the conciliar system of Church government as happened during the Great Schism. The Italian bishops at the Council outnumbered those of Germany, Spain and France combined, therefore, the tone and the conclusions favored those who wanted to maintain much of the status quo especially as regards papal powers.

At the first meeting in 1545-1547, the decisions included:
- The adoption of the Latin Vulgate Bible as the official text and all its books declared canonical despite the apocryphal label on some books that were absent from the original Hebrew versions.
- The rejection of the Protestant position on Scriptures as the sole authority on faith
- The affirmation of Traditions as co-ordinate in authority with Scriptures.

- The rejection of the Protestant position on justification by faith alone and the affirmation of the necessity of both faith and good works for salvation.
- The rejection of the Calvinists' doctrines of bondage of the will, total depravity and predestination
- The affirmation of the validity of all the seven sacraments

The second meeting between 1551 and 1552 was cut short but before adjourning, it—
- affirmed the doctrine of transubstantiation of the Eucharist
- affirmed that the bread contained the entire sacrament and rejected the call to give the chalice to the laity, despite the fact that this had been previously granted to the Hussites

At the last meeting between 1562 and 1563, the Council decided:
- That bishops should reside in their dioceses and not to be absent for more than three months in a year. They were to be at their diocese at Lent and Advent and visit every church in the diocese at least once a year. They were to preach every Sunday and maintain discipline among the clergy in their jurisdiction.
- The priests were to preach and instruct the laity on Church doctrines, liturgy and sacrament.

The proceedings of the Council were submitted to the Pope for ratification which he did in 1564.

An index of books to be prohibited was compiled and this was to be enforced at every level of the Church.

Other measures in the counter-reformation included the restoration of the office of the Inquisition and the founding of new religious orders—the *"Society of Jesus" (or the Jesuits)* to combat the spread of Protestantism and the *Oratory of Divine Love* to restore piety.

The Jesuits [3, 4, 5, 6, 7, 8]

The founding of the "**The Jesuits**" **Order** by **Ignatius Loyola** in 1540 is considered as another important development in the Counter-reformation.

Loyola was a Spanish Soldier turned priest who, after a religious experience during his convalescence from war wounds decided to devote himself to the service of the Church. He and others of like mind gathered together to found an order that was unlike the previous ones as they did not live in monasteries or adopt any particular form of uniform but live and work among the people. Members took the traditional vows of poverty, chastity and obedience plus a fourth and special vow of obedience to the pope. The order taught its members to become like an inanimate object or a corpse, having no self will and to be ready to obey the pope. The distinctive characteristic of the order was its unquestioning obedience to the hierarchy, in fact one of its tenets says that: *"if the Church hierarchy says something black is white, members are bound to believe that it is white without question."*

Every member followed a training based on the founder's book on **"Spiritual Exercises"** which taught members how to empty themselves of self.

The order grew very fast and its original purpose was to win back to the Catholic faith those who had strayed into Protestantism.

The Jesuits were very involved in intellectual pursuits, science and exploration.

The Gregorian calendar was developed by a member of the Order and five of the eight major rivers in the world were charted by Jesuits. They dominated Universities and Seminaries, their goal being more the making of good Catholics than the dissemination of knowledge.

The Jesuits helped to re-establish Catholicism in Eastern Europe—Poland Hungary etc; and they served as missionaries to the Far East and the New World. Francis Xavier, a founding member of the Order was a missionary to Japan and India, dying in his attempt to reach China. Matteo Ricci evangelized China, focusing mainly on the nobility. The methods of evangelization by the Jesuits were criticized by other orders on the field, the Franciscans and the Dominicans. For example Francis Xavier was reputed to have baptized thousands in India without any catechism, telling them that others would follow later to teach them about the religion.

In China, Matteo Ricci was said to have been so accommodating that he allowed converts to practice Confucian rituals dismissing them as social rather than religious.

The disagreement between the Jesuits and the other Orders was so sharp it precipitated what was called the *"Rites Controversy"* which had to be referred to Rome for arbitration and more significantly caused disenchantment of the Japanese who decided to ban the Christian religion. The decision of the papacy to ban Chinese rites also led to the banning of Christianity by the Chinese Emperor.

The Jesuits have had a checkered history; at its inception, the Jesuit Order was favored above the older Orders: members could celebrate Mass anywhere, hear confessions and grant absolution, sometimes even for cases usually reserved for the Pope and administer sacraments without necessarily obtaining permission from the local bishop or priest. These privileges were expanded by Pope Paul's papal Bull *"Injunctum Nobis,"* (1543), by which the General of the Jesuits and his Council were granted permission to alter, expunge and make additions to the Order's rules or make new rules for the society without recourse to the papacy. Also:

- The members of the society, their goods, incomes and possessions were exempted from the jurisdiction or control of the local episcopate but solely under the protection of the Pope.
- Members who were priests could have their own houses of prayer anywhere they reside and were exempt from papal interdicts; that is they could say Mass behind closed doors and administer sacraments during an interdict provided those ministered to excluded the excommunicated and heretics.
- No bishop could excommunicate any member of the Society or laymen friendly to the Society
- Those in the employment of the Society were also exempt from interdicts
- Members were allowed to live and communicate with excommunicants and schismatics and live in countries of heretics and unbelievers.
- Members were exempted from paying taxes, tithes or dues of any kind
- Donations by princes, such as houses, churches, colleges etc were deemed ratified by the Pope upon delivery without the need for special deeds.
- Bishops were required to consecrate without much ado, all Jesuits' places of interment
- The Society could admit all and sundry even offspring of incest (except murderers and bigamists) and consecrate them.

The Jesuits, apart from being lax in evangelizing 'heathens' were also known to be very lenient with penitents and did not give severe punishment for grave or mortal sins. This had the effect of making them popular with penitents and eroding the influence of regular priests thereby reducing their revenue.

Blaise Pascal (1623-1662), a French theologian, philosopher, mathematician and physicist, satirized the Jesuits' use of ***casuistry*** to be all things to all people in his ***"Provincial Letters"***. This led to accusations of serious crimes like regicide, idolatry, and moral laxity against the order. In the '***Provincial Letters'***, Blaise Pascal revealed how the Jesuits:
- Excused sin and promoted licentiousness by dissembling on the facts and circumstances of sin
- Excused sin if it was to protect self or neighbor and promoted idolatry on the grounds of "***probable opinion***".
- Condoned clerical fornication as long as the priest was temporarily defrocked
- Condoned homicides as long as it was not mercenary or vengeful.
- Excused the corruption of judges and usury
- Excused robbery and stealing by servants from their masters
- Condoned lying through the so called ***'mental reservation'*** and equivocations.
- Condoned dishonest gains by merchants through adulteration of goods
- Taught that ***'contrition'*** is not necessary and that ***'attrition'*** alone plus penance suffice.
- Legitimized tyrannicides and abortions.

In fact critics have accused them of subversive activities in nations, of setting at naught divine, human and natural laws and that they are in fact ***moral assassins.***

The Jesuits have been implicated in many intrigues and controversies.

In 1605, ***Henry Garnet (1553-1606)***, an English Jesuit was implicated and hanged for his involvement in the '**Gunpowder Plot'** to assassinate King James I and members of the English Parliament although his knowledge of the plot was said to have been through confessional statements which were considered strictly confidential.

The Society fell into disfavor all across Europe in the mid-eighteenth century and the members were expelled from many countries and their assets confiscated. In 1773, Pope Clement XIV passed the decree suppressing the Society worldwide but this was reversed in 1814 by Pope Pius VII.

It is surprising, given the founders' commitment to the papacy, that over time, many members of the Order had apparently progressively become openly defiant of the papacy on issues such as clerical celibacy, homosexuality, abortion and Liberation theology which is a mixture of Scripture and Marxist ideology developed by Jesuits in South America.

The Holy Office of the Inquisition

Another important instrument in the Catholic counter-reformation was the revival of the "Holy Office of the Inquisition"; which tried those considered heretics and handed them over to civil authorities to be burnt at the stake.

Chapter 17

The Enlightenment and Enlightenment Philosophers
—17th & 18th Centuries

Enlightenment [1]

The Enlightenment was a philosophical, intellectual and cultural movement in which reason was advocated as the legitimate source of authority. Previously accepted ideas, traditions and doctrines about God, nature and man were scrutinized and subjected to reason with resultant revolutionary reforms in art, philosophy, religion and politics.

Essentially, Enlightenment was a product of the humanistic philosophies of the Renaissance and the Reformation but both the Greco-Roman and the Judeo-Christian sources of intellectual authorities were overthrown.

Natural Religion and Deism [2,3]

Natural Religion is religion based on reason and ordinary experience rather than faith and supernatural revelation. "Natural Religion" is exemplified by Deism but also include in its spectrum those who equate nature with God.

Deism

Deists hold that:
- There is a God who created the Universe which is governed by unchangeable laws inherent in its structure. Therefore deists reject the idea of the supernatural in which there are departures from the natural laws as in miracles claimed by Christians.
- There is need for repentance
- There is an afterlife with rewards and punishments based on how life is lived on earth.
- "Revealed religion" such as found in Christianity, Judaism and Islam are products of self-interested priests using "priest-craft"

- By the use of reason and experience, man can achieve the perfect society and they rejected the total depravity doctrine of Calvinists

The deist ideas seeped down into both the Catholic and Protestant Churches in Europe and morality based on reason replaced religious experience.

Natural Religion
- Natural religion is described by adherents as 'fact religion' rather than 'faith religion'; it deals in the natural rather than the supernatural.
- Subscribe to ethics and morals because it makes sense; (crimes hurt the society, promiscuity is inimical to health etc.) and not out of religious convictions.
- Religion is viewed as a means to improve the quality of life and the human condition individually and globally through human knowledge and idealism. It therefore focuses on global economic trends, population growth and poverty and its alleviation.
- For devotees of Natural religion, "Nature is God" and they believe it can provide meaning and ethical guidance.
- Advocates of Natural Religion are consecrating Darwin's theory of evolution as a sacred story of human origin.
- Aspects of Natural religion are found in Conservationist Movements, Ecotourism and Vegetarianism.
- Its spirituality consists of earth veneration and sometimes, devotees seek to graft it to existing long standing religious traditions and hope it will evolve into an Earth Religion that will unite humanity in a civil Eldorado.
- Nature spirituality is being pushed at global forums like the United Nations and events like the Olympics.

Thomas Hobbes (1588-1679 AD) [4, 5, 6]

Thomas Hobbes was an English Philosopher born in 1588. He studied Classics at Oxford and traveled widely in Europe to see how people were governed and their acceptance of the government.

He concluded that human beings operating under the 'state of nature' would be in perpetual state of war because human beings are naturally selfish. That each individual would be a law to himself; determining what he needs, what is respectful or pious, foolish or prudent etc. He would also seek to impose his ideas on others and others would do exactly the same to him. In order to maintain peace and solve the problems of the 'state of nature', rational beings, he believed understand the "laws of nature" which is treating others as we would be treated. To this end, rational human beings are able to form alliances with others by relinquishing their rights to a sovereign authority.

He said the *"social covenant"* entered involved the transfer of rights and the authorization of power to the sovereign. To be effective, he believed that government must have absolute authority, not divided or limited because the power of legislation, adjudication, taxation and executing wars are so interconnected that the loss of one could thwart the effectiveness of the others.

He believed that the sharing of power between different bodies lead to paralysis of government because the different bodies tend to disagree about not only what should be done but how to do it. Hobbes' contribution to the development of systems of government was his idea of voluntary **"social contract"** or covenant between the ruled and the ruler; and the powers of rulers being derived from the ruled rather than from divine endowment.

Baruch Spinoza (1632-1677 AD) [7, 8]

Baruch Spinoza was a Portuguese Jewish philosopher born in Amsterdam in 1632 AD. He was excommunicated from the Jewish community in 1656 most probably for his religious beliefs.

Baruch Spinoza:
- Believed that God exists only in philosophical sense and rejected any idea of anthropomorphism.
- Held that the way to know God is through philosophy and science as these lead to enlightenment; not through religious worship which he said leads to superstitious behavior and subservience to ecclesiastical authority.
- Identified God with nature and does not believe in God outside of nature. The idea of a supernatural God he said belong in the realm of superstition.
- Held that there was no purpose in nature and that *"the will of God" is the 'sanctuary of ignorance'*.
- Rejected the idea of a goal oriented God who plans and judges things by how they conform to His purposes.

- Did not believe in miracles and held that things happen only according to the laws of nature. He held that 'miracles' were stories calculated to move the uneducated to devotion and that no matter how extraordinary an event might be, there must be a natural cause and rational explanation even though it may not yet be known.
- Believed that the law of God "commands only the love of God and the actions required to attain that condition. That such love must not spring from fear of punishment or hope of any rewards but only from the goodness of the object".
- Held that "the divine law does not require any particular rite or ceremony" and that true piety and blessedness are universal and accessible to all regardless of creed.
- Did not believe in prophecy and held that it resulted from vivid imagination. That the idea of the election of the Jewish people was only for social and political expediency.
- Denied that Moses wrote most, if any of the Torah and that the 613 precepts of the Torah have nothing to do with virtue or blessedness. That they were directed only at the Hebrews to help them govern themselves in an autonomous state and preserve their kingdom. He held that they were valid only as long as the political entity lasted and not binding on all Jews under all circumstances.
- Held that, as the Bible was written by several authors and compiled by fallible human beings, it should be treated like any other book and studied rationally.
- Opined that the universal message of Scripture is "to know God and to love one's neighbor as oneself".
- Argued that familiarity with Scriptures was for piety, that the message can be known through rational faculties alone with the conferment of the same blessedness.
- Held that preachers were opportunistic and play on peoples' fears and hopes in the belief that a judging God needed to be placated and obeyed.
- Advocated that a "Catholic faith" should contain only dogmas in which obedience to God is absolutely necessary and held that beyond these, individuals should be free to embrace the dogmas they believe would best strengthen them in love and justice.

- Advocated a democratic sovereign rule for the 'externals' of religious observance and state regulation of the external practices of religion.
- Agreed that life in the Hobbesian state of nature would be nasty, brutish and short and though he also believed, like Hobbes, that the authority of government is derived from the people who are in a 'social contract' with it; he did not subscribe to the violation of individual autonomy which Hobbes sovereign absolutism might allow.
- Held that monarchies were less stable and prone to degeneration into tyranny.
- Advocated freedom of beliefs, inward piety and freedom of speech except seditious speech.

Spinoza's views were, for his time revolutionary and clearly rebellious against established religion. He reduced the message of the Scripture to a simple maxim and seemed to believe that it matters little what is believed about God so long as such beliefs do not predispose to sinning against God. He stripped religion of *"multitudes of prescriptive and proscriptive observances and gave individuals a lot of latitude to interpret religion as they choose"*.

He naturalized and demystified the fundamentals of Judaism and of Christianity which sprang from it.

John Locke (1632-1704 AD) [9, 10, 11]

John Locke was an English Enlightenment philosopher, rationalist theologian and Medical researcher born to Puritan parents. He was a contemporary of scientists like Isaac Newton.

John Locke:
- Believed that an individual should use reason to search for truth rather than docile acceptance of the opinion of authorities. That truth has the capacity to be understood by its own light without the use of force and cannot be taught by laws.
- Believed in reason as the basis for faith and not unquestioning acceptance of the word of authority.
- Believed that assent should be proportional to the evidence and rejected faith based on revelation and insisted that revelation be judged by reason.

- Held that a church is a free and voluntary society and that the Scriptures are the reference point in spiritual matters. He advocated simplicity in religion and was dismissive of dogmas.
- Advocated religious tolerance and the separation of the Church and the State but did not extend toleration to Catholics and atheists on the grounds that the former held allegiance to a foreign prince and the latter nothing to swear on to make them accountable.
- Argued against the prevalent notion of the divine rights of kings to rule and advanced the concept of individual natural rights.
- Believed that man's survival is God's purpose and ***to achieve survival, man needs life, liberty, health and property.*** He considered these basic and natural rights common to all men equally and preceded governments.
- Believed that the natural rights of a man should not be violated by others and vice versa.
- Believed that ***'the function of a legitimate government is the preservation of the rights to life, liberty, health and property of the citizens', and to prosecute and punish those who violate the rights of others***.
- Believed that government should pursue the public good even when this may conflict with the rights of individuals.
- Believed that relationship with others in a community or nation is based on "social contract" from which political obligation and private property are derived.
- Believed that rulers get legitimacy to govern only through the consent of the governed and that rulers execute the derived power to govern from the transferred power from the people.
- Held that rebellion and regicide were legitimate to terminate an illegitimate government.
- Believed that man is the property of God, therefore murder and suicide violate the purpose of God.
- Held that the human mind is "Tabula Rasa", that is, a blank slate in which ideas accumulate and that knowledge is gained through experience.

In his treatise on *"The Reasonableness of Christianity,* John Locke seemed to have realized the limitations of reason in morals and religion when he wrote: *"It should seem by the little that has hitherto been done in it, that it is too hard a task for unassisted reason to establish morality in all its parts upon its true foundation, with clear and convincing light . . . It is plain, in fact that human reason unassisted failed men in its great and proper business of morality."*

He believed that those who profess to be Christians ought to live it saying: *"It would indeed be very hard for one that appears careless about his own salvation to persuade me that he were extremely concerned for mine. For it is impossible that those should sincerely and heartily apply themselves to make other people Christians, who have not embraced the Christian religion in their own hearts."*

He also believed that Christians should live by a minimum standard code of conduct otherwise they should not be so called; he said: *"It is vain to usurp the name of Christian without holiness of life, purity of manners, benignity and meekness of spirit.* **'Let everyone that nameth the Name of Christ, depart from iniquity'"**—2Timothy 2:19.

John Locke is called the **'father of liberalism'** and his ideas and concepts of individual rights, governments and the interactions between the two influenced the development of political systems in Europe and the United States. In fact his idea of 'rights' is very prominent in the American ***"Declaration of Independence"***.

David Hume (1711-1776 AD) [12, 13]

David Hume was a Scottish philosopher and historian and a notable figure in the Age of Enlightenment. Hume was at best a skeptic, in fact to most of his critics, he was an atheist. He had very unflattering views of religions in general and probably Christianity in particular.

Hume believed:
- That religion is not based on reason but originated from human ignorance, weaknesses, fears and vulnerability. He considered the principles prevailing in the religions of the world as no more than "sick men's dreams". He was of the opinion that the scrutiny of religion produce only doubts, uncertainty and suspense of judgment.
- That religion has a corrupting and disturbing influence on morality and social stability.
- That monotheism produces intolerance and persecution of opponents and encourages unnecessary self denial and self abasement.

- That monotheism breeds serious moral vices like fraud, cruelty and hypocrisy; that it sanctions the greatest crimes in the name of piety and devotion.
- That religion is in fact a major source of moral sickness in the world.
- That monotheism corrupts and perverts philosophy.
- That Judaism and Christianity are permeated with philosophical absurdities as well as corrupt and confused practices.
- That religious people are less trustworthy than those without religious pretensions; the religious, he said, put people on guard for fear of being cheated.
- That the most ethical response to religion is to expose its frauds and corruption and oppose its influence over man.
- He rejected the design argument of creation as proof of the existence of God on the grounds that Epicurus' questions remain unanswered. *[Epicurus had posed the question as to whether God was willing to prevent evil but unable, in which case He is impotent (not omnipotent); or able but not willing, in which case He would be malevolent (not benevolent); or if He is both willing and able, why is there still evil in the world?].*
- While he did not deny the existence of God on the failure of an answer to Epicurus' question, he considered that without an answer, it was impossible to attribute to God omnipotence and goodness.

David Hume made it his life ambition to expose what he believed was the groundlessness of the Judeo-Christian doctrines as well as their 'destructiveness' on human life. He rejected the notion that morals would collapse in the absence of religion.

He believed that with reason, people would choose virtues that produce happiness and eschew vices. He also rejected the notion that the human nature is wholly selfish though he agreed that human benevolent tendencies are limited and egocentric and therefore prone to engendering conflict and competition.

Hume did not believe in the intelligent design of the Universe and did not believe in miracles or the immortality of the soul and was a supporter of suicide.

He was as controversial in life as in death. While his friends, to the chagrin of Christians extolled his peace when facing death, it was reported that his house keeper in fact said the peace was a mere façade and that he in fact was terrified of dying.

David Hume's writings on economics influenced notable economists like **Keynes** and his writings on religion and politics influenced other thinkers like ***Adam Smith.***

Jean-Jacques Rousseau (1712-1778 AD) [14, 15]

Jean-Jacques Rousseau was one of the most influential thinkers of the Enlightenment era. Born in Geneva, he was brilliant but unconventional to the point of irresponsibility. He was controversial and lived in constant conflict with friends, peers and both secular and religious authorities. He had many extra-marital relationships and had children that he did not raise but left in the care of an orphanage. Raised a Calvinist, he converted to Catholicism at an impressionable age when he found himself alone and under the auspices of an older lady who was on contract by the Catholic Church to convert Protestants to Catholicism.

He wrote about political and social systems, religion and methods of education. In his first work, an essay titled "*A Discourse on the Sciences and the Arts*" he argued that advances in the arts and sciences did not enhance but rather had caused a decline in morality and backed up his argument with the examples of previous civilizations like Greece, Rome and even China.

In *"The Discourse about the origin of Inequality among Men"*, Rousseau portrayed the natural man as "isolated, timid, peaceful and mute without the foresight to worry about the future". This is contrary to the ***Hobbesian*** natural man who was a nasty, selfish brute. Although Rousseau admitted that the natural man is driven by the principle of self preservation, he believed there was a second innate principle of "Pity" which is repulsed by the suffering of his fellow human being.

He said the natural man is amoral, that is, neither virtuous nor vicious but with socialization, he became moral. He argued that reason, though dormant in the natural man differentiates him from beasts and that circumstances act as the trigger for development and advancement.

He considered the "social contract" as applied to the society of his days as specious and merely designed by those who had the most to lose to hold on to power but sold to those with less as in their best interest.

He saw the existing system as enslaving saying: ***"All ran to meet their chains, thinking they secured their freedom; for though they had enough*** *reason to feel the disadvantages of the political establishment, they did not have enough experience to foresee its dangers".*

In his writings on *"The Political Economy",* he advanced the concept of the *"General will".* He saw the society as a unified entity though with many parts much like the human body; the politically virtuous State therefore would follow the three maxims:

(1.) Follow the *general will (general interest)* in every action

(2.) Ensure that every *particular will* is in accordance with the *general will* and

(3.) Ensure that the public needs are met regardless of the will of the majority, (that is the aggregate of individual wills or private interests).

He believed that citizens would comply with rules, have a genuine respect and love for the law when they have a sense of equality. In this respect he also differed from Hobbes who had posited that man would only obey laws out of fear for punishments and therefore had recommended that penalties be severe enough to serve as deterrent to breaking the law.

Rousseau believed that political conflicts arise from conflicts between the general will and individual wills.

Even to his contemporaries, the conflicting concepts of individual freedom or will and the subjugation of same for the "general will" for the well-being of the whole society was obvious and hardly reconcilable. His *"Legitimate Social Contract"* called for the overriding of the *individual will* by those with *'sovereign authority'* to protect the *general will*; a situation that is bound to undermine the individual freedom he seemed to champion. His concepts have been criticized as confusing; on the one hand advocating **liberalism** and on the other **totalitarianism.**

On religion, though he was a Calvinist turned Catholic and back again to Calvinism, he seemed to have embraced Deism and natural religion. He opposed orthodox Christianity's claim as the only true religion and believed that any organized religion that identifies God as Creator and preaches virtue and morality is true and could be adopted by citizens. He believed that "the will is known in its actions and not in its nature".

Rousseau advocated a method of education that develops character by presenting the student with experiences that teach moral lessons, sometimes by manipulating the environment but ensuring that harm is prevented. He also advocated gender oriented education, by subscribing to an education of women that favor domesticism. This is not to say that Rousseau was a chauvinist, he actually believed that women are smarter than men.

Rousseau influenced people like ***Immanuel Kant, Robespierre and Karl Marx.***

Thomas Malthus (1766-1834)
Reverend Thomas Malthus was an Anglican priest and English scholar. He was a professor of Economics and Human populations.

He showed that while populations grow geometrically, food production grow arithmetically and postulated a cycle of plenty and poverty which keeps human populations in check through famine, diseases and wars.

Among the measures he proposed for social and economic improvement especially among the lower social classes were:
- Delaying marriage till economically ready to sustain a family
- Strict moral restraint with strict abstinence before marriage (he believed this to be consistent with virtue and socio-economic improvement)
- Gradual abolition of "Poor Laws" by decreasing the number of persons qualifying for relief (He believed that charity would take care of real distress)

He believed that the "Poor Laws" were detrimental to the interest of the poor in the long run as it tends to undermine their independence and resilience and the ***"the Poor laws tended to create the poor that the laws maintain"***

He believed that privations teach hard work and virtuous habits.

His theory gave impetus for the National population census of 1801 in the United Kingdom and the "Poor Law Amendment Act" of 1834.

Malthus views and theory caused political, social, economics and scientific controversies. His critics made his theory the harbinger of Eugenics and Darwin's theory of Evolution.

He was viciously vilified by virtually across all political, social, scientific and religious spectra. His supporters believe he was largely misunderstood.

He died in 1834.

Chapter 18

Global Evangelization and Re-Evangelization

Evangelization of Africa [1,2]

Christianity in North Africa is as old as Christianity. There are accounts in the Gospels about Africa, Africans and Jews from Africa at events during the time of Jesus Christ. The infant Jesus was taken to Egypt by His parents, Simon from Cyrene helped to carry the Cross of Jesus Christ, Pilgrims from Egypt and Libya were present at Pentecost and the Ethiopian eunuch, the official from Candace, queen of Ethiopia was baptized by Philip one of the seven deacons. In addition, tradition credited the Apostle Mark and /or Mathew with the evangelization of North Africa.

Christianity was vibrant in North Africa from Egypt through Algeria, Tunisia, Libya, Morocco and Mauritania till the end of the 7th century. Many of the early notable Church divines and saints of the early Catholic Church like Origen, Tertulian, Clement of Alexandria, Cyprian of Carthage and Augustine of Hippo were Africans and contributed immensely to the shaping of the early Roman Catholic Church dogmas.

The early African Christians, like all Christians elsewhere, suffered persecutions under successive Roman Emperors before Constantine. Unfortunately, even after Constantine embraced Christianity, African Christians were targets of persecution from other Christians supported by the State on accusations of heresy. Constantine, Theodosius and other Byzantine Emperors subjected them to so much persecution that these African Christians welcomed the early Moslem invaders who were initially more tolerant than their Christian brethren. However, Christianity dwindled in North Africa after the Moslem invasions but has survived as a minority religion in Egypt.

Evangelization of Africa South of the Sahara

Although Christianity was vibrant in North Africa in the early Church, Africa South of the Sahara largely did not have contact with Christianity until the *Age of Exploration and Discovery* except for Ethiopia.

Pre-Colonial (1450-1890) [3, 4, 5]

The exploration of Africa South of the Sahara was pioneered by the Portuguese explorers who were often accompanied by Catholic priests. The Portuguese had many trade posts for slaves along the west and South African coasts but were not, unlike the Spanish, involved in any major missionary activity.

By 1486, the Dominican priests were among the Sene-Gambians and Dominican and Franciscan priests were in the Congo by 1491. However, these early efforts were largely unsuccessful because of the slave trade and the fact that some of the clergy spent more time in trading than in preaching while others got embroiled in the local politics.

The abolition of the slave trade and slavery by Britain in 1807 and 1834 respectively opened a more conducive portal of evangelization in the region. Prior to the end of the slave trade, European presence had been mainly along the coastal areas where goods were exchanged for slaves. Following the abolition of the slave trade, many Protestant Church Missionary Societies sent missionaries to people groups in Sub-Saharan Africa.

The colony of Sierra Leone, established for freed slaves by Britain, served as the source of indigenous missionaries to the interior prior to the colonial era.

Bishop Ajayi Crowther (1809-1891) of the Anglican Church Missionary Society's *Niger Mission* was an example of how effective the natives were in evangelizing their own people with the support of the foreign Missionary Societies. He translated the Bible into the Yoruba language, compiled a Yoruba dictionary and produced primers for Igbo and Nupe languages.

David Livingstone (1813-1873), the British missionary and explorer, reacting to the continuation of slavery that he witnessed in the inland areas of South and East Africa called for Europeans to bring ***Christianity, Commerce and Civilization*** to fully stamp out slavery which he described as "an open wound".

Europe responded with the Scramble for Africa.

Colonial (1880-1900) [6, 7, 8, 9, 10, 11, 12, 13, 14]

The *"Scramble for Africa"* ensued in the 1880s and by the time of the First World War in 1914, Africa had been carved up and colonized by various European nations without regard to existing ethnic or cultural affiliations.

Prior to the Scramble for Africa, colonial holdings in Africa were few and limited to Angola, Mozambique and Guinea by the Portuguese, Cape Colony by the Dutch and the Spanish Equatorial Guinea, with British trading posts in Gold Coast and Lagos.

With France taking over Tunisia, Britain occupying Egypt and the Suez Canal and the Belgian King Leopold II's massive land grab around the Congo River, the scramble had begun in earnest.

The Berlin Conference of 1884-1885 was called by the German Chancellor, **Bismarck** *(1815-1898)* to ensure civility in the process of staking claims to lands in Africa by European nations. The conference agreed to free navigation among the nations present along the Niger and Congo Rivers. France had most of West Africa pushing east, while Britain was virtually from Cairo in the north to the Cape in South Africa, interrupted only by the German colony of Tangayika. The Gambia, Sierra Leone, Gold Coast and Nigeria were also British colonies in the West. Germany colonized Togo, Cameroon, Southwest Africa and Tangayika while Italy had Libya, Eritrea and part of Somaliland. Portugal regained its stake on Angola and Mozambique. King Leopold II was allowed to keep the Congo Free State as his personal colony.

Colonialism introduced frictions and sometimes even animosity between the indigenous and the expatriate missionaries. Some expatriate missionaries did not believe the natives had the capacity to hold leadership positions. This situation was exemplified by the experience of Bishop Ajayi Crowther and some expatriate missionaries. The Rev. Henry Townsend resisted to the end the idea of Ajayi Crowther as a bishop; he believed the natives were under the illusion that the white man was superior and felt it should remain so. He and other missionaries of like mind therefore never really submitted to Crowther's leadership and did all in their power to undermine him. Eventually, on the death of Crowther, he was replaced by an expatriate missionary.

In the Kongo, the Portuguese priests rejected the authority of the son of the Manikongo who joined the priesthood and became a bishop. He had to leave the Kongo for Portugal and was a bishop in Utica, Tunis in North Africa. There was no other black bishop in the Kongo until 1970.

The impact of the missionaries vary, while some with colonist mentality were contemptuous of the people they sought to convert, others, like ***Mary Slessor (1848-1915)*** were extremely dedicated. Mary Slessor, a Scottish Presbyterian missionary to South East Nigeria was instrumental in the abolition of the custom of throwing twins away at birth and cannibalism among the Calabar people. However, some missionaries connived with the colonial powers to subvert the interests of the indigenous people.

In the *'Hall of Infamy'* were missionaries like the **Reverend Helm** of the **London Missionary Society (LMS)** who deliberately mistranslated a document of agreement between ***King Lobengula of Ndebele*** (present day Zimbabwe) and the ***British South Africa Company of Cecil Rhodes***. This act of duplicity resulted in the king signing away all his lands to speculators while thinking he had only signed a limited mining concession. This not only resulted in the king rejecting Christianity but also created an enduring distrust between generations of colonists and indigenous people that persisted till today.

Another missionary contender in the Hall of Infamy was ***Friar Anthonio Barroso*** who made ***King Dom Pedro V*** of the Congo to sign off his sovereignty thinking he was signing a 'thank you' note for the gift of a gilded Chair.

Generally, the Protestant missionaries had a policy of educating the indigenous peoples because the goal was to make converts literate so that they can read the Bible. On the other hand, the Catholics were more concerned about making the converts faithful to Rome; in fact the goal was to discourage the wish to read the Bible which they thought would be misinterpreted if read by the people.

Evangelization of Asia & Southeast Asia [15, 16]

The roots of Christianity in Asia go right to the early Church in Palestine. Early traditions and chronicles traced the introduction of Christianity to parts of Asia to some of the Apostles of Jesus Christ.

Saint Thomas is credited with evangelizing Persia (Iran), the North West and the South of India, while the Apostles Thaddeus and Bartholomew are credited with evangelizing the regions of Armenia, Albania and Georgia; and the region in present day Turkey by the Apostles Simon Peter and

Paul. The evangelical activities of Jewish Christian merchants and later, Nestorian Christians help to spread Christianity further into Asia.

China [15, 17, 18, 19]

Archeological findings in China revealed that Patriarch Yeshuyab II sent missionaries to China in 635AD.

By the 9th century, the regime in power in China perceived the many Christian and Buddhist monasteries in the empire as a drag on the economy and as systems causing social dislocations. Therefore, all religions other than Confucianism were persecuted and suppressed. The persecution eased in the following centuries until the Mongols conquered China in the 13th century.

Under the Mongol ruler ***Kublai Khan (1215-1294)*** who was tolerant of Christianity, the Italian merchant, ***Marco Polo (1254-1324)*** traveled extensively in China and Southeast Asia and reportedly encountered pockets of Christian communities. Christianity was tolerated by the Mongols until the rule of ***Tamerlane (Timur the Lame) (1336-1405)*** when persecution resumed and Christianity was eclipsed in Asia by 1500 AD.

The various reasons adduced for the virtual disappearance of Christianity in Asia include the minority status for fifteen centuries, the fact that Christianity never really made inroads into the higher social class of Hindus and Buddhists and the geographical separation from other Christians. One historian pointed out that *"Asia never had an Emperor Constantine"* as the West had. However, it was, perhaps, a case of missed opportunity.

It is reported that Kublai Khan refused to convert to Christianity because he perceived it as a powerless religion. He told Marco Polo's uncles who had wanted him to convert to Christianity that he couldn't, living as he was among idolaters who could make objects move without being touched and who seemingly control the wind and the weather. He agreed to convert on the condition that the pope sent to his kingdom one hundred priests who could take on the idolaters and counteract their powers so that they would not be able to do the wonders they were doing. He felt that without the protection of a superior power, the idolaters could easily kill him; therefore, the only condition on which he would agree to be baptized was if and when the Christians prove the superiority of their power over the pagan arts. It is not known if the Christians ever took up the challenge.

Catholic missions to Asia and Southeast Asia followed the voyages of exploration and discovery of men like ***Vasco Da Gama (1460-1524) and Magellan (1480-1521).***

Catholic Missions to China began in the 16th century with the age of Discovery and exploration. A new wave of Franciscan, Dominican and Jesuit missionaries accompanied the Portuguese and Spanish explorers to China, India, Japan and the Philippines.

The efforts of many missionaries to evangelize China proved difficult until the Jesuit missionary **Matteo Ricci (1552-1610)** arrived in China in 1582. He took time to study the Chinese culture, traditions and beliefs and decided on a strategy of adaptation of Christianity to the Chinese culture in order to open doors for evangelism. By this approach, he allowed the Chinese converts to continue venerating ancestors and Confucius considering the rites as mere social and political ceremonies with no idolatrous intent. He also accepted the Chinese terms meaning "Lord of heaven" as the same with the Christian God. He reckoned that the approach would produce better Chinese Christians rather than Europeanized but indifferent Chinese Christians. His approach indeed opened the door of the Chinese elite society including the imperial court to the Jesuits' message and the ***Emperor K'ang-xi (1654-1722)*** decreed that Christians be tolerated in the empire in 1692.

Chinese Rites Controversy

However, the Dominican and Franciscan missionaries who later arrived in China were scandalized, being of the opinion that the Chinese rites accepted by the Jesuits were idolatrous. Several decades of controversy known as ***The Chinese Rites Controversy"***, raged among the Catholic missionary community until the issue was taken to Rome for adjudication.

From Rome, conflicting decretals and Bulls were issued over several decades. In 1635, ***Pope Innocent X (1644-55)*** declared the rites illicit; in 1656, ***Pope Alexander VII (1655-67)*** sanctioned Ricci's approach and agreed that the rites in question were 'purely civil and political cults'. As to which of the decrees missionaries should follow, the Holy office of Propaganda replied that both were in full force according to the questions and circumstances. The missionary community tried to solve the problem through a series of meetings and finally most of the missionaries from all the Orders—Jesuits, Franciscans, Dominicans and Augustinians agreed

to follow Pope Alexander's decretals of 1656 as it was "based on a very probable opinion". However, there were a few missionaries who were not convinced and who kept the controversy alive until another study of the issues by the Holy Office of Propaganda was ordered by ***Pope Innocent XII (1691-1700)***. The study, which examined all aspects of the controversy, did not conclude until the pontificate of Pope ***Clement XI (1700-21)*** who in 1715 issued a Bull in which it was stated that:
- The Chinese term used to represent God should cease as this was not the same as the true God; and that the tablets bearing such should be removed from all Catholic churches.
- Converts to Catholicism should cease from participating in rites venerating ancestors and Confucius; they were not even to participate as by-standers.
- Catholic converts who were State officials were not to participate in venerating Confucius on the 1st and 15th day of every month.
- Catholic converts were banned from venerating ancestors in family temples.

In reacting to the papal Bull, the ***Emperor K'ang-xi*** considered westerners petty and the papal decree bigoted and nonsensical; he issued a decree of his own expelling all missionaries from his empire in 1721.

The papal legate Ambrose Mezzabarba tried to mitigate the effect of the papal Bull by relaxing some of the rigors of the pontifical interdiction through a pastoral letter called ***"The Mezzabarba Permissions"***. ***Pope Clement XII (1730-40)*** ordered an investigation into the Mezzabarba Permissions which was concluded under the pontificate of ***Pope Benedict XIV (1740-58)***. In 1742, Benedict XIV issued what he thought would be the final Bull on the controversy by affirming emphatically Pope Clement XI's Bull and attached an oath to be taken by all missionaries to China which forbade them from revisiting the controversy again. He condemned and annulled the Mezzabarba Permissions on the grounds that they authorized superstitions.

In 1939, the Vatican revisited the Chinese Rites issue and ***Pope Pius XII (1939-58)*** relaxed the strictures of Pope Clement XI and Benedict XIV stating that:
- Chinese Catholic converts could attend ceremonies in honor of Confucius in Confucius temples or in schools.
- The image of Confucius or tablets on which his name is written were permitted in Catholic schools

- Catholic magistrates and students were permitted to 'passively' attend public ceremonies which have the appearance of superstition.
- It was licit and acceptable to incline the head and show other civil observance before the deceased or their images
- The oath prescribed by Pope Benedict XIV on the Chinese Rites was considered "not fully in accord with recent regulations and superfluous".

India [20, 21]

Catholic missions in India began in earnest with the arrival of *Francis Xavier (1506-1552)* in 1542. He blazed a trail in missionary work by reportedly baptizing thousands in southern India.

After Francis Xavier, many other missionaries followed but made little headway until the arrival of the Italian Jesuit priest, **Roberto de Nobili** *(1577-1656)* in 1605. He carefully observed one of his predecessors, studied the culture and the literature of the Indians and then formulated his strategy for evangelization. He discovered that the caste social system was an obstacle for his predecessors among the elites in India. He found out that because they worked among the pariahs, the Brahmins or higher caste would have nothing to do with them. He discussed his observations and plans with his superiors and obtained their blessings.

Like Matteo Ricci in China, he tried to accommodate the Indian culture and adapt Christianity to it. He then moved to the Brahmin part of town, dressed like them and even had his hair cut the same way. He kept his distance from the other missionaries who worked with the pariahs and in time he had a breakthrough and was able to make converts.

However, the less successful missionaries objected to his methods and made a report to Rome accusing him of promoting heathen customs and idolatry.

The ensuing controversy, known as *"The Malabar Rites Controversy"* was reviewed by the Holy Office of Propaganda in Rome and Pope *Gregory XV (1621-23)* gave a provisional injunction in favor of De Nobili. Therefore, the Catholic converts were allowed to continue such practices as the use of the cords, the sandals and the baths. The separation of the castes was not directly addressed but the Pope urged the Brahmin converts to love and not despise the lower caste brethren. To cater for the pariahs, De Nobili advised the archbishop to consider two tiers of missionaries since the Brahmin priests could not openly minister to pariahs. Therefore, **Pandaram missionaries** emerged, serving as a bridge between the pariahs and other castes. De Nobili continued his work among the Brahmins till his death in 1656.

In 1704, a papal legate, without thorough understanding of the background of the Malabar rites issued a decree to ban it. The issue again came under review by the Holy Office of Propaganda and in 1734 Pope Clement XII issued the revised decree regarding the rites. Some provisions were mitigated while others were retained. The most difficult for the Jesuits was the provision requiring that they openly attend to sick pariahs, an action that could easily torpedo the ministry to the Brahmins.

In 1744, Pope Benedict XIV consented to the formation of a separate band of missionaries to cater to the pariahs. This arrangement lapsed after the suppression of the Jesuit Order in 1773 and the conversion of the higher Hindu castes decreased. The Jesuits returned to India, after their restoration in 1838, with a different approach as missionary educators teaching generations of Brahmins.

Japan [22, 23]

Historians disagree about the presence of Christianity in places like Japan, Burma and the Koreas before the 16th century.

Francis Xavier reportedly reached Japan in 1549 with other Jesuit missionaries and made converts and died trying to reach China. Other Jesuit missionaries followed and by 1579, many princes in west Japan and thousands of their subjects converted to Christianity. Franciscan missionaries also arrived in Japan and the number of Christians grew.

In 1638, the Shogun fearing the increasing influence of Spain and Portugal, banned Christianity, expelled the missionaries and executed natives who refused to renounce their faith. Thereafter, Christianity was effectively suppressed in Japan and those who did not renounce their faith went underground until the proclamation of religious freedom in 1873.

A treaty between France and Japan in 1859 had allowed missionaries into Japan to serve foreigners though proselytizing was still forbidden. It was revealed that several thousands of descendants of Christians had continued to practice Catholicism for over two hundred years underground, sometimes hiding Christian religious symbols behind images of Buddha.

They recognized returning Catholic priests by their celibacy, veneration of the Virgin Mary and allegiance to Rome.

In spite of enshrining freedom of religion in the constitution, re-evangelization has had limited results and Christianity has remained a small minority (c1%) in Japan.

The Philippines [24, 25, 26]

Most historians agreed that Christianity reached the Philippine archipelago when **Magellan (1480-1521)** arrived on the central Island of Cebu in 1521. Legend has it that the son of the chief of the Island was sick and Magellan was able to heal him, therefore the chief allowed about eight hundred of his subjects to be baptized. Unfortunately, Magellan was killed on another Island in the archipelago and many attempts to colonize the nation were unsuccessful until **Miguel Lopez de Legazpi** arrived in Cebu in 1565. He expelled the Moslems who had been in the southern Philippines since the 10th and 11th centuries from Manila.

As Catholic missionaries followed, Catholicism spread quickly among the natives who were previously animists worshiping various deities, spirits and ancestors. The spread was aided by mass conversions and baptisms as well as the administrative policy of relocating and merging small isolated communities into larger bigger communities. The civil authority was often held also by the Catholic priest. The towns' activities were organized around the Church's calendar and the priest learnt the vernacular to conduct his services as very few were educated.

By and large, most philippinos practiced a syncretic form of Catholicism referred to by some as '***Filipinized Catholicism'*** which integrates native customs and traditions.

Initially the priests were trusted because they served as the people's advocates but as time went on they were seen as a part of the problem of colonialism and as a consequence national forms of Christianity emerged.

For about three hundred years, the Spanish held sway in the Philippines until 1898 when the nation was ceded to America and there was an influx of Protestant denominations. These did not make much progress because of their uncompromising stance on syncretic practices and have therefore remained significantly a minority.

Evangelization of the Americas
South and Central America [27, 28, 29, 30, 31, 32, 33, 34, 35]

Catholic missions to the Americas also began during the *Age of Exploration and Discovery* by the Spanish and the Portuguese explorers like *Henry the Navigator (1394-1460)*, *Christopher Columbus (1451-1506)* and *Amerigo Vespucci (1454-1512).*

In 1452 and 1455, **Pope Nicholas V (1447-1455)** issued papal bulls *"Dum Diversas"* and *"Romanus Pontifex"* respectively that gave **King Alfonso V** of Portugal permission to *"invade, capture and subjugate Moslems and pagans or any other group of unbelievers and 'enemies' of Christ wherever they may be, dispossess them of all they have and subject them to perpetual slavery"*. Thus vanquished, all obstacles to making them Christians would have been removed and the conquerors were to build churches and monasteries and have priests and monks sent to such nations.

Pope Nicholas V's two bulls became the justification for the initiation and perpetuation of the Slave trade along the west coast of Africa by the Portuguese prince and explorer, *Henry the Navigator (1394-1460)* who first explored the west coast of Africa and paid for it with revenue from trading in African slaves.

Following the discovery of the New World by Christopher Columbus under the aegis of the Spanish monarchs in 1492, *Pope Alexander VI (1492-1503),* in 1493, also issued a papal bull *"Inter Caetera"* in which Spain was given essentially the same power over all newly discovered inhabited lands west of a particular meridian and lands to the east including Brazil, to Portugal; the two nations that dominated the sea at the time. The arrangement was ratified by the *"Treaty of Tordesillas"* in 1494 and the *"Treaty of Saragossa"* which described the anti-meridian in 1529.

The initial voyages of exploration and discovery under the aegis of the Spanish and Portuguese monarchs were soon followed by *"Voyages of Conquest"* led by conquistadors like *Vasco Nunez de Balboa (1475-1519), Hernando Cortes (1485-1547)* and *Francisco Pizarro (1471-1541).*

In accordance with the goals of the papacy and the monarchs of Spain and Portugal to propagate the Roman Catholic faith, the explorers and conquistadors were usually accompanied by Dominican, Franciscan and later, Jesuit priests. However, most of the time, notwithstanding the presence of priests, the expeditions were often violent as typified by the *"Massacre of Cajamarca"* under the leadership of Francisco Pizarro.

Within decades, the lands of the indigenous peoples of the West Indies, South America, Central America, Mexico and parts of North American continent comprising California, Arizona, Texas, New Mexico and Florida with most of the Philippines formed the huge Spanish empire and were all introduced to the Catholic faith.

However, the coupling of conquests with conversions made the sincerity of the latter questionable. The conquistadors set up a kind of feudal system (*'encomienda'*), ostensibly to teach the indigenes Christianity, but which in actuality enslaved them as they were obliged to pay tribute, usually in form of labor, to the conquistadors in the plantations or mines.

Soon after the colonization of the West Indies and the Americas, the indigenous peoples died in droves, partly from diseases to which they had no immunity such as smallpox introduced into the colonies by the colonists and also as a result of physical abuse and ruthless treatments. This resulted in shortages of workers in the plantations and mines. The steps taken to redress the manpower shortages led to the **"Triangular Trans-Atlantic Slave Trade"** which shipped beads and muskets from Europe to West Africa in exchange for slaves that were then shipped to the West Indies and the Americas and the last leg shipped molasses, tobacco and sugar back to Europe.

The colonists and sellers regarded the natives and slaves as more or less sub-human and treated them as such. The atrocious situation was protested by priests such as the Dominican priest **Bartolome de Las Casas (1484-1566)** and the Jesuit priest **Pedro Claver (1580-1654)** who worked tirelessly and selflessly among the indigenes and the Negro slaves to give spiritual and physical succor. In 1537, Pope Paul III had to issue a bull—*'**Sublimus Dei**'*—stating that Native Indians were rational beings and forbade their enslavement. However, he more or less in the following years issued bulls that to all intent and purposes nullified Sublimus Dei.

However, the economic interests of the settlers often clashed with the missionary goals of the priests, especially the Jesuits who were operating virtually independently being responsible directly only to the Pope. The Jesuits tried to protect the natives from predatory colonists by creating communities called "*reducciones*" (towns and cities built by relocating and merging smaller isolated communities and organized to be self-sustaining) in areas covering parts of Paraguay, Uruguay, Brazil and Argentina today. These communities had better standards of living because the natives shared in the products of their labor and there was no encomienda system in the Jesuit reducciones.

The success of the Jesuit communities displeased the Spanish and Portuguese settlers and eventually the Jesuits were expelled from Brazil in 1759 and from all Spanish Viceroyalties in 1767.

Until the eighteenth century, the clergy and the episcopate were recruited from Europe and appointed by the Spanish Crown; it was felt that the indigenes, the *mestizos* (product of racially mixed marriages) or even American born Europeans were undesirable for the priesthood. However, with time and shortage of clergy, American whites were recruited. Sometimes, the American missions became some sort of *'penal colonies'* for 'unworthy clergymen' from Europe as these were encouraged to go to America to save face and free their superiors from embarrassment.

Conversions and baptisms were usually en mass, instructions poor and instructors sometimes worse than the instructed. Another contributory factor is the method of evangelization. The priests found a parallel between the Indians' religious practices and pagan gods and the Catholic cults of saints and the Virgin Mary. The Aztec eating of divinities was also considered a parallel to the Catholic Communion. Therefore, as in Asia, many syncretic practices were condoned. In fact some priests felt that paganism was an authentic religious experience corrupted by demonic influence. The strategy for evangelization was therefore the shifting of existing beliefs to the Christian paradigm. For these reasons, the Christianity in the empires was superficial and full of syncretism.

By the early nineteenth century, many of the Spanish colonies in America were agitating for independence, and by 1830, most of the colonies in the Americas and the Caribbean with the exception of Cuba and Puerto Rico had gained independence. By the end of the century, virtually all of the Spanish Empire had been dismantled when in 1898, the Philippines, Guam and Puerto Rico were ceded to the United States and Cuba was handed over under a trusteeship.

North America and Canada [36, 37, 38, 39, 40, 41, 42, 43]

The colonization of the south and southwest of the North American continent comprising Florida, Texas, New Mexico, Arizona and California was by Spanish conquistadors and Catholic priests and friars as already discussed.

The eastern part was colonized by several waves of settlers from different European countries and a plurality of Christian sects that resulted from the Reformation and the various wars of religion but the colonies were dominated by the British. Among the various sects were Puritans, Pilgrims, Calvinists, Presbyterians, Mennonites, Lutherans, Catholics and Jews.

The reasons for migration to what came to be the United States and Canada vary; many left Europe to escape religious persecutions from their homelands. This was the case with the Puritans and Catholics during the reign of England's Charles I, Quakers during the reign of Charles II and Huguenots from France after the revocation of the Edict of Nantes. Others migrated for economic reasons, as free men or indentured servants seeking to improve themselves through agricultural or mining endeavors. Some were sent on temporary or permanent exile, as a punishment for various offenses against the Crown. In fact Georgia was reportedly established as a *'penal colony'* for British outlaws and as a buffer between Spanish Florida and the British Carolinas. On the other hand, tens of millions of Africans were brought by force as slaves from Africa to the Americas and the Caribbean Islands.

The earliest viable colony was that of **Jamestown, Virginia** established in **1607** under a proprietary charter by the **Virginia Company of London** hoping to strike it rich in the New World. Later, in **1620**, the **Plymouth colony** was established by the Puritan *'Pilgrim Fathers'* followed in **1628**, by the **Massachusetts Bay colony**, also by Puritan pilgrims. Within decades, thirteen viable British colonies had been established with a sprinkle of smaller ones by the Dutch and the Swedes. France also colonized large tracks of lands in present day Canada and in the United States along the Ohio and Mississippi valleys down to the Gulf of Mexico called the ***colony of Louisiana.***

France lost the control of the territory to the British and the Spanish during 'Seven Year War'. While the British portion became part of the United States following the war of Independence, the Spanish part, returned to France in 1801 and was purchased by the United States in 1803 in the *"Louisiana Purchase".* The British also dispossessed the Dutch and the Swedes of their colonies on the eastern seaboard of North America as well as Spain of Florida and over time dominated as the colonial power in North America.

The thirteen colonies that later evolved into the United States of America were British colonies established under charter, proprietary or provincial colonial type of government. Some, like the Massachusetts colony were established with the intent at doctrinal purity and dissenters such as Anne Hutchinson and Roger Williams were expelled while Mary Dyer, a Quaker and three others were killed. However, other colonies such as Rhode Island and Pennsylvania were known for being tolerant and religious refugees of all persuasions were to be found in these colonies.

The settlers for the most part clashed with the Native Americans ab initio but even in cases where some modicum of peace had been reached, eventually, conflicts arose as the colonies grew and expanded and settlers needed more lands.

A prevalent idea among early settlers about the Native Americans was that they were 'animals in human form' and irrational beings. Others viewed them as 'savages' and 'minions of the devil' who needed to be "civilized to be Christianized". Some colonists therefore had no scruples about plundering, enslaving and killing them. Therefore, as it happened in the Spanish Catholic colonies, Protestant groups colonizing North America also perpetrated atrocities against Native Americans.

One of the earliest serious wars between Native Indians and colonists was the ***"King Philip's War" (1675-1676)*** involving the Wampanoag and Narragansett tribes. The Colonists, under the command Captain Benjamin Church engaged the Natives in a war that started in the Plymouth colony but which later spread to involve practically all of the New England territory. At the end of the war, the colonists lost about a third of their population while the Indians were severely decimated. Those who survived were captured and sold into slavery in the Caribbean and it was estimated that within the one year that the war lasted, the Native Indian population was decimated by about eighty per cent.

Cotton Mather, a Puritan clergyman of Boston Massachusetts hailed the outbreak of smallpox that decimated the region's natives and the ensuing slaughter of the remaining males with the enslavement of the women and children.

Col. John Chivington an ex-Methodist pastor and church elder slaughtered and scalped men, women and children of the ***Cheyenne and Arapaho Indians*** of Sand Creek in what came to be known as ***"The Sand Creek Massacre" (1864-1865)*** despite the fact that they were waving the white flag of surrender. He regarded them as "nits and lice" to be exterminated.

The pacific Islanders did not fare better, following coercive conversions by Protestant missionaries and the introduction of diseases, it was estimated that the population of the Pacific Island of Tahiti was reduced to about six thousands from about two hundred thousands within three decades.

The situation for the Native Indians did not improve even after America's lofty "***Declaration of Independence***" in ***1776*** which declared the equality of all men with divine endowment of inalienable rights.

Thus in 1830, the American Congress passed "***The Indian Removal Act***" which legalized the removal of the ***Cherokee Indians*** from Georgia and it was signed by ***President Andrew Jackson***. The law was contested by the Cherokee nation but after years of legal wrangling, they were removed through a treaty signed with the federal government. Eventually they were rounded up, interned and compelled to move in 1838, marching from Georgia to Oklahoma with thousands dying on the way. The Cherokee immortalized the march by calling it ***"The Trail of Tears"***.

Chapter 19

Three Revolutions and the Impact on Christianity—1760-1850

The Industrial Revolution (c1760-1850) [1, 2, 3]

The industrial revolution which began in Britain with improvements in Agriculture following the invention of mechanized seeders and ploughs became evident in the 1760s with the mechanization of the textile industry. It was characterized by innovations and changes in agriculture, manufacturing, communication, mining and transportation. It spread to Continental Europe, the New World and around the world. It also witnessed the invention of the steam engine used in mining and in other machines, and the development of iron, lead and copper industries.

However, it resulted in socio-economic disruptions as the changes in Agricultural practices rendered many peasant farmers landless and jobless and they migrated to urban centers to seek jobs in factories or to coal mines needed to fuel the steam engines.

The working conditions were poor and child labor was rife before laws were passed to prohibit child labor in Britain in 1833. With the development of mechanization, unemployment became high and social unrest ensued with riots by people who felt displaced by machines and sometimes they resorted to vandalization of the machines. The penalty for such acts was *"transportation"*, that is, exile to the North American colonies for specified number of years or for life.

In 1776 following the American Revolution, transportation to that country stopped and convicts were then shipped to Australia or Tasmania both of which became *'penal colonies'*, although there were also influx of free migrants too. 'Transportation' continued until 1868 when it officially ended. Returning from transportation was a capital offense.

Rural-urban migrations resulted in crowded living conditions with poor sanitation resulting in endemic and epidemic diseases.

The employment of women and children in factories and mines for long hours resulted in the disintegration of the family unit and community. The Church was ill equipped to deal with the emerging situation and the Church of England was more or less moribund while the dissenters seemed exhausted from decades of struggles for toleration. The resulting decrease in the quality and quantity of religious instructions coupled with the social dislocation had a negative impact on the people's spirituality resulting in the fall of moral standards and increases in crimes.

The Wesley brothers and George Whitfield, with no church buildings or elaborate organization or hierarchy, ministered to millions in open fields for decades. They started the *Methodist Movement*, organized the converts into societies for bible study, prayers and personal accountability.

As better labor laws were made, organized labor unions with the power of collective bargaining evolved and better conditions of service and living emerged. In time, the living standards of the people increased and the Industrial revolution spread to other nations around the world.

The American Revolution (1775-1783) [4, 5, 6, 7, 8]

The immediate cause of the American Revolution was the series of legislations promulgated by the British Parliament to regulate the functions of the thirteen American colonies after the Seven-Year War in 1763 when Britain defeated France and took possession of French colonies in North America. Between 1764 and 1765, the legislations included: *the Sugar Act, the Currency Act, the Stamp Act and the Quartering Act.* When the colonists complained, the *Declaratory Act* was also passed in 1766 stating that the British Parliament indeed had the power to legislate for the colonies in everything. The colonists viewed the legislations, most in form of trade levies and taxes as unfair since they had no representation in the British Parliament resulting in the popular saying—*"no taxation without representation"*. In 1767, more regulatory Acts were passed taxing a wide range of items like Tea, paper and glass in the *Townshend Act* and the *Tea Act.* This further enraged the colonists who began to openly attack officials of the British government such as the soldiers leading to deadly clashes such as occurred in 1770 in which civilians were killed in the event dubbed the *"Boston Massacre"*.

In 1772, a British warship enforcing the regulations was burnt by an organized Resistance group called *"The Patriots"*. In 1773, a group of colonists emptied ship loads of tea into the Boston harbor in what came to be known as the *"Boston Tea Party"*. This event unified the British Parliament against the colonists and the *"Boston Port Act"*, which closed the port until the colony of Massachusetts paid reparations to the British East India Company was promulgated. In addition, The Massachusetts Government Act changed the colony's charter such that town meetings were restricted.

In 1774, the **First Continental Congress**, consisting of delegates from all the colonies except Georgia (it was still a penal colony) was convened in Philadelphia with the decision made to petition **King George III *(1738-1820)*** about grievances, to consider the possibility of boycotting British goods and to convene a **Second Continental Congress** in 1775 to train militia to defend the colonies in case the petition and the grievances were not redressed.

Unfortunately, by the time the Second Continental Congress was convened in May 1775, the **American Revolutionary war** had already started; therefore the Congress (comprising delegates from all thirteen colonies including Georgia at last) acted essentially as the de facto national government in executing the war.

Opinions were divided in the colonies regarding the war as some colonists (the loyalists) preferred peace with Britain and loyalty to the King while the majority favored independence. The religious community was also divided, with the Church of England generally loyalist, while the more democratic churches—Baptists, Presbyterian and Congregationalists—were generally in favor of independence. The Quakers were pacifists and neutral and were persecuted as supporters of British rule.

By **1776**, the Congress proposed and declared **Independence on July 4,** after which it drafted and approved the articles of Confederation in 1777 which was ratified by all thirteen colonies finally by 1781. The colonies at various times received help from France, Spain and the Netherlands.

The war lasted till 1783 when the end of hostilities was ratified at the '**Treaty of Paris**'. In the treaty, all the land south of the Great Lakes and east of the Mississippi river were ceded to the United States.

A Constitution adopting a **Republican** form of Government with three branches *(legislative, executive and judiciary)* was drawn with Ten Amendments called the *"Bill of Rights"*. It became operational in 1789 and replaced the Articles of Confederation of 1777.

Various reasons have been adduced for the success of the American War of Revolution; these include the fact that the colonies had no aristocracy and there was religious diversity with no national religion in most of the colonies. In addition, there was widespread ownership of property, relative prosperity and the fear of slavery. The evolving societies in the colonies had become significantly different socially, politically, spiritually and psychologically from their relatives in Europe and so were more open to the idea of self-rule. The aggregate of the colonial experience had, as it were, primed them for what eventually happened. As John Adams put it—***"The Revolution was effected before the war commenced. The Revolution was in the minds and hearts of the people . . . this radical change in the principles, opinions, sentiments and affections of the people was the real Revolution".***

The Revolution resulted in increased suffrage among colonial males and the freedom of religion, speech and the press.

Given the lofty ideals of the Declaration of Independence and the Constitution, some of the Northern States abolished slavery while others committed to gradual abolition and emancipation. Slavery was a sore point in the drafting of the Constitution.

The Southern States were adamant about retaining the practice of enslaving others. In order to solve the issue of representation, the Southerners were willing to count the slaves as humans thus getting more pro-slavery representatives in Congress but not ready to abolish slavery but the Northerners objected.

To break the stalemate, the Northerners demanded that if Southerners would not free the slaves, then, the South would have to count 50,000 slaves per representative while the north would count 30,000 per representative. This was the origin of the infamous perception that the founding fathers regarded slaves as three-fifths of a human being. However, the original intention was actually anti-slavery and was meant to decrease the power of pro-slavery representatives in the Congress!

Thomas Paine (1737-1809) [9, 10, 11]

Thomas Paine was born in England to poor Quaker parents, educated at the local Grammar school and became an excise officer. He was dismissed for absenteeism and agitation for better pay for excise officers.

Thomas Paine was a Deist, a radical and a revolutionary propagandist. He met Benjamin Franklin in London who helped him to emigrate to America.

He arrived in America in late 1774 and became a journalist contributing articles to the Pennsylvania magazine. He entered into the spirit of the revolution that was gathering momentum and wrote a pamphlet titled **"Common Sense"** in early 1776, where he articulated the need for a revolution. The pamphlet was an instant success and spurred public debate throughout the colonies. He followed this with a series titled **"*The Crisis*"** the first of which began with the phrase **"*These are the times that try men's souls . . .*"** The writings were inspirational for the army and the people and for this, Thomas Paine earned a place among the founding fathers of the United States.

He denounced religious pacifism and was an ardent supporter of the right to bear arms against imperialism. His famous quote in this regard was:

> *"The supposed quietude of a good man allures the ruffian; while on the other hand, arms, like the law, discourage and keep the invader and plunderer in awe and preserve order in the world and property. The balance of power is the scale of peace. The same balance would be preserved were all the world destitute of arms, for all would be alike; but since some will not, others dare not lay them aside. Horrid mischief would ensue were one half of the world deprived of the use of them; the weak would become prey to the strong".*

After the war, he returned to England and wrote his book titled **"Rights of Man"** in which he criticized European monarchies, tried to incite the people to a rejection of monarchy and called for the institution of a representative government with social programs to improve the lots of the poor. He was accused of circulating "seditious libel" and was declared an outlaw.

He left England to avoid arrest and became embroiled in the French Revolution; he was given French citizenship and elected into the Convention. When the French Revolution became factionalized, a rival faction arrested and jailed him. While in jail, he wrote **"*The Age of Reason*"** in which he criticized all organized religions—Judaism, Christianity and

Islam—as human inventions designed to terrify and enslave mankind in order to monopolize power and profit. He rejected the Bible and the Koran as revelations from God. He denied faith in any creed or church and declared: *"My own mind is my own church"* and *"my religion is to do good"*. He narrowly, providentially missed the guillotine and was later released in 1794 through the mediation of an American minister.

In 1795 he wrote *"Agrarian Justice"* in which he introduced the concept of a *"Guaranteed Minimum Income"* which many believed influenced America's institution of the *Social Security Administration*. He returned to America in 1802 at the invitation of Thomas Jefferson but arrived to a chilly reception as a result of his book, 'The Age of Reason' which alienated him from many people. He died a lonely man in America in 1809.

The French Revolution and the De-Christianization of France (1789-1799) [12, 13, 14]

The aristocratic system preceding the French revolution favored the Church and the clergy. While the Church, the single largest land owner was exempt from paying taxes to the State, it could levy a tithe on the general population. Therefore, as the concepts of the Enlightenment Age spread, resentment of the power of the Church grew.

In 1789, Louis XVI of France convened the Estates General (that is the First Estate—the Church, the Second Estate—the nobles and the Third Estate—the Commoners represented by the middle class) to find a solution to the National debt incurred largely from the "Seven—Year War" and helping the United States in its Revolutionary war.

To compound the problem, crop failure coupled with high unemployment led to widespread famine and malnutrition in the populace of which the royal court seemed totally unaware. The Queen, *Marie Antoinette*, when told that people had no bread to eat, was famously reported to have quipped—*"let them eat cake"!*

The Estates General made no progress in solving the economic problems, therefore the Third Estate, supported by the First Estate created the National Assembly. The National Assembly enacted legislations for social and economic reforms such as the nationalization of Church lands and the abolition of the Church tithe.

With these steps, the State in essence nationalized the French Church and took over the payment of the French clergy and the care of the poor and the sick. The Church lands were sold to raise revenue, religious orders were dissolved and monastic vows abolished and the monks and nuns were encouraged to return to secular life. The remaining clergy became employees of the State and were required to swear oath of allegiance to the State under the 'Civil Constitution of the clergy'. Some of the clergy and Pope Pius VI rejected the Civil Constitution and the noncompliant priests were exiled or executed as traitors.

In 1793, Louis XVI and Marie Antoinette were guillotined and the *"Reign of Terror"* ensued. A political faction called the *Jacobins* took over government and set up the *"Committee on Public Safety"* led by **Robespierre (1758-1794)**.

Influenced by Enlightenment thinkers like Rousseau, Robespierre's regime was very repressive and he was reputed to have posited that *"The government in a revolution is the despotism of liberty against tyranny"* and that *"Terror is nothing else than swift, severe and indomitable justice; it flows from virtue"*.

With the elimination of the monarchy, the campaign to de-Christianize France, led by atheists *Jacques Herbert* (1757-1794) and *Pierre Chaumette* (1763-1794) who formed the *'Cult of Reason'* sprang up. Private and public worship were outlawed and many churches were closed or converted to temples of the *"Goddess of Reason"*. The churches were ransacked, looted and destroyed while priests were forced to marry, exiled or executed. Robespierre who favored deism proposed the **'Cult of the Supreme Being'** which became an official aspect of the revolution.

The adherents of the Cult of Reason opposed the idea of the Cult of a Supreme Being and considered it a back door return to religion. As dissent was considered counter-revolutionary the protagonists of the Cult of Reason were sent to the guillotine in 1794.

In accordance with the revolution's principle of *Liberty, Equality and Fraternity*, the French convention under Robespierre voted to abolish slavery in 1794.

Eventually, there was a rejection of Robespierre's despotic reign and he was overthrown and also guillotined in 1794. Some historians felt that his despotism was directed against the corrupters of the revolution, the bourgeoisie, who embraced the liberty to trade but ignored the equality and fraternity.

After the death of Robespierre, a bicameral House of Representatives was established with the power to elect a five-member Directory that actually ran the affairs of State; the Directory took over in 1795.

In 1799, following an uprising, ***Napoleon Bonaparte (1769-1821)*** seized power in a coup and later made himself an emperor. He restored order and signed a Concordat with ***Pope Pius VII (1800-1823)*** in 1801 restoring Catholicism as the main but not the State religion of France. The clergy remained State employees and were required to swear allegiance to the State and the Church was to renounce all claims to the land previously confiscated by the State. The Concordat remained in effect until 1905 when it was abrogated with the promulgation of the law on the separation of the Church and State.

Chapter 20

The Great Awakenings and Protestant Missions and Missionaries

The First Great Awakening [1, 2, 3] was that period characterized by a nationwide series of revivals and of increased religious activities that occurred in Britain and its North American colonies from 1730s to 1750s.

In Britain, at the beginning of the eighteenth century, the Rationalists and Deists were in ascendancy in the Church such that belief in miracles was dismissed as superstition. Many of the elites subscribed to the views of freethinkers like (***John Toland 1670-1722)***, an Irish philosopher and theologian who wrote a book titled *"Christianity, not Mysterious"*. Among the working class, there was a fall in church attendance, crimes and moral laxity. It was in this social and cultural milieu that **George Whitefield** and the ***Wesley Brothers*** began the Great Awakening in Britain in the late 1730s.

In the British colonies of North America too, the Enlightenment ideas were pervasive among the elite and religious observance consisted mainly in the teaching of doctrine rather than personal relationship with the Savior by faith.

In America, the Awakening involved preachers from many denominations like the Presbyterians, Congregationalists, Methodists and Baptists. The Great Awakening is considered to have contributed to the development of a concept of democracy different from the Roman republic model to which 'The Enlightenment' philosophies sweeping Europe appeared to support.

The Enlightenment advanced a social order of balance of power between the monarch, the elites and the commoners with due deference to the privileged class. However, the evangelical revivalists preached that, according to Scriptures, all men are equal before God.

They were also advocates for religious freedom and liberty of conscience as inalienable rights of every rational creature. These ideals were believed to have helped in shaping the American Revolution. In addition, the nation wide phenomenon reduced the role and the respect for the clergy as many of the awakening preachers were not ordained ministers. This resulted in the erosion of the authority of the clergy; rendering it open to challenge. Subsequently even the authority of the king was also challenged.

It also led to more efforts to convert the Native Americans and to the establishment of new institutions of higher learning such as Princeton. The awakening preachers included **Jonathan Edwards, George Whitefield, the Wesley brothers and Gilbert Tennent.**

Jonathan Edwards (1703-1758 AD) [4]

Jonathan Edwards was a Puritan preacher, writer and philosophical theologian born into a family of preachers. He succeeded his grandfather as the pastor of one of the largest congregations in Massachusetts. He apparently struggled with the Calvinistic doctrine of 'election' until 1726 when he somehow embraced it and no longer considered it "a horrible doctrine". He was ordained and became an outspoken critic of Arminianism which rejected Calvin's doctrine of election. There was a great revival between 1733 and 1735 with hundreds of people becoming convicted of their sins such that during his sermons they would cry, moan, or convulse. The emotional displays were unfamiliar and evoked criticism from other preachers who accused Edwards of leading his congregation into fanaticism. To compound the problem, the great revival was also accompanied by considerable despair in a lot of people who felt the weight of their sins, were convinced of their damnation but felt no comfort of salvation and therefore committed suicide. After this unsavory turn of events, the revival cooled off until the 1740s when George Whitefield came from England to conduct revival services throughout the colonies. In 1741,

Jonathan Edwards preached his epic sermon, *"The sinner in the hands of an angry God"* which has become the prototype of what is called a *"fire and brimstone"* sermon.

John Edwards fell out with his congregation in 1749 over the qualification to take the 'Lord's Supper' or Communion. He held that only people with proven conversion experience should be entitled while most of the congregation believed, as Edwards' grandfather did, that all who had been baptized could take it and that it was a converting ordinance.

After parting ways with his congregation, he became a missionary to the native Indians while writing many books.

In 1758 he was made the President of the College of New Jersey which later became the Princeton University. He died the same year from the complications of smallpox vaccination.

George Whitefield (1714-1770) [5, 6]

George Whitefield was an itinerant Anglican priest of humble beginnings. He paid for his education at Oxford by being a servant to wealthier students and met the Wesley brothers at the 'Holy Club' at Oxford, forging a life long friendship with them.

He ignited a revival first in England where people had become immoral and later throughout the thirteen British colonies in the 1740s. He held open air services where he preached to thousands of people. He toured all the colonies and cooperated with many other preachers like Jonathan Edwards and the Wesley brothers even though they were not in full agreement on the doctrine of predestination. While he remained a staunch Calvinist with a firm belief in predestination and election, the Wesley brothers believed that God's grace is for all mankind.

In 1749, Whitefield campaigned for the re-legalization of slavery which had been outlawed earlier in the eighteenth century in the colony of Georgia, arguing that slavery was essential for the economic survival of the colony.

He succeeded in 1751 when Georgia re-introduced slavery and he became a slave owner, acquiring slaves to run his plantation and orphanage.

He was a friend of Benjamin Franklin, one of America's founding fathers who used his press to publicize Whitefield's ministry even though he did not agree with him theologically. Whitefield died in the United States in 1770 AD.

John Wesley (1703-1791) [7] & Charles Wesley (1707-1788) [8, 9]

John and Charles Wesley were Anglican priests who co-founded *Methodism* with others like George Whitefield. The sons of a preacher, Charles founded and John later became the leader of a small group at Oxford University that was committed to living strictly in accordance with the discipline of the ***Book of Common Prayer*** observing personal accountability and discipleship. They were given the nickname

"Methodists" and this became the root of the movement that became a separate Methodist denomination.

In 1735, after graduation and ordination, both brothers sailed to North America, to the British colony of Georgia. John hoped to work as a missionary among the settlers while Charles, as Secretary of Indian Affairs to the governor hoped to use his position to evangelize the Native Indians. Both brothers had frustrating experiences and were back in Britain within three years.

In Georgia, they befriended Moravians and observed that they had better assurance of salvation which neither brother had ever experienced. They continued their association with the Moravians and within three days of each other had spiritual experiences of the "New Birth" and for the first time experienced an assurance of salvation by grace through faith.

Realizing that the Church of England was not calling sinners to repentance and that the clergy were corrupt and that many people were dying without the gospel of salvation, the brothers, encouraged by George Whitefield, began to hold open air services. They preached to the high and low and were involved in works of charity. John Wesley, a friend of John Newton and William Wilberforce, was an ardent abolitionist who preached and wrote tracts and pamphlets against slavery and the slave trade. They were also leading voices on other social issues such as prison reforms; all at considerable personal risks. They were opposed and maligned by other preachers, many of whom closed their churches to them.

In 1740, John Wesley preached and published the sermon, "*Free Grace*" which criticized the Calvinist doctrine of "predestination and election". Whitefield, a Calvinist, responded and published his response and the two parted ways splitting Methodism into two streams of Arminianism and Calvinism.

They later reconciled and remained friends with John Wesley preaching at Whitefield's funeral but they remained doctrinally divided, and as John Wesley famously put it, they *"agreed to disagree"*.

John believed and preached '*prevenient grace*' and '*free will*' rather than the Calvinist doctrine of '*Limited grace*' and '*total depravity*'. He considered Calvin's doctrine of predestinated reprobation blasphemous because it "represented God as worse than the devil". He believed in the possibility of "*Christian Perfection*"; the concept that a Christian, empowered by the Holy Spirit can live a holy life free of willful sins.

John Wesley also parted ways with the Moravians when they embraced *"Quietism"-'a state of imperturbable serenity'* with roots in mysticism.

Charles Wesley preached and wrote hundreds of sermons and hymns respectively with an inspirational appeal that has remained unfaded.

He got married in 1749, had eight children with only three surviving.

The brothers preached in England, Wales, Scotland and Ireland, organized converts into societies that met for prayers and Bible study and had many lay preachers to serve them. In 1784, a conference of all the societies they organized was held and the Methodist doctrine on sin and salvation defined.

Both brothers however, sought only to reform the Anglican Church from within and they remained officially Anglicans all their lives. Charles died in 1788 and John in 1791.

Many Holiness Movements and some Pentecostal groups were offshoots of the Methodist Church.

Gilbert Tennent (1703-1764) [10, 11]

Gilbert Tennent was a Presbyterian preacher born in 1703 in Ireland but emigrated with his family (parents and three brothers) to America in 1718. Gilbert's father and all his brothers were also preachers. The Tennent family initiated the first Great Awakening among Presbyterians in Pennsylvania and New Jersey through revivals that generated religious enthusiasm in the middle colonies. Some preachers moved to the south to spread the revival and their efforts were greatly augmented by the itinerant George Whitefield who conducted revival services all over the colonies.

Tennent realized that many professing Christians including the clergy were not actually converted, therefore, he preached about sin, repentance and the importance of spiritual regeneration. While the established clergy preached what they considered "sound theology" with enforcement of church dogmas, Gilbert Tennent preached the need for true conversion of the heart and preached against religion formalism which he considered hollow and meaningless.

The enthusiasm that accompanied the revivals displeased the establishment preachers and congregations who characterized the enthusiasm as overly emotional and disorderly. Gilbert Tennent himself was considered saucy, unpolished, impudent and noisy. He was accused of making salvation more of an escape from hell and less a better way of life.

As his ministry grew, the need for more ministers of similar genre became obvious. The family therefore founded the *"Log College"* where ministers were trained.

Tennent, with some other Yale graduates of the same mind constituted themselves into a presbytery with power to license its own ministers. However, the conservative ministers tried to frustrate this plan by passing a law at the regional synod requiring examination of all non-university graduates before licensing them to preach.

Tennent responded by delivering a fiery sermon titled *"The Danger of an Unconverted Ministry"*, a blistering criticism of the established clergy considered unregenerate and dead by the revivalists. As a result of these controversies, congregations became split into "Old" and "New" Sides and eventually there was a complete schism for several years with the "New Side" advocates forming a separate synod.

In later years, Gilbert used his influence to heal the breach and reconciled the synods.

He also supported and raised funds for the founding of the *College of New Jersey* which later became the *Princeton University*. He died in 1764.

William Wilberforce (1759-1833 AD) [1,2,13]

Although William Wilberforce was not a missionary in the strict or regular sense of the word, he used his position as a member of the British parliament to effect changes that furthered the cause of Protestant missions and missionaries around the world.

William Wilberforce was born in 1759 to a wealthy English family and devoted members of the Church of England. After his Masters degree at the Cambridge University, he entered into politics as a Member of Parliament at the age of twenty-one years in 1780.

In 1785, while on vacation, he read a book by *Philip Doddridge: "The Rise and Progress of Religion in the Soul"* and was convicted and became converted into evangelicalism. As religious enthusiasm was derided in his day, he considered leaving his career in public life to become a preacher or simply live in solitude. He consulted with friends like *John Newton*, a former slave trader turned preacher who advised him to continue his career in politics and that God could use him in that position for His Church and the advancement of His Kingdom.

He resigned from several secular clubs, gave up gambling, theatres and plays which in those days were considered decadent. He also made a decision to cast his vote in parliament only for issues in line with Christian principles. He searched and studied the Scriptures daily to learn principles for his conduct, believing that Christianity should influence a man's thoughts and lifestyle both in private and in the public.

At the time of his conversion, there were only two other evangelicals in parliament, but by the time he died, there were more than one hundred. In 1787, he was instrumental in the formulation of the royal ***"Proclamation for Piety and Virtue and Prevention of Vice, Profaneness and Immorality"*** by ***King George III***. The proclamation encouraged church attendance while drunkenness, lewdness, swearing, cursing and blasphemy were prosecuted. Brothels were closed down, pornographic literatures were destroyed and the publishers prosecuted. William Wilberforce organized grassroots support for the proclamation through *'Proclamation Societies'* among the people to encourage living in the spirit of the Proclamation. This was well received among those already primed by the Great Awakening preachers like Whitfield and the Wesley brothers. He also wrote an exposition on the New Testament comparing *'Real Christianity'* with the *'Prevailing Practices* of *Professing Christians'* of his day, drawing from his own personal life and experience. The book was a success and was translated into many European languages.

William Wilberforce believed in 'small government'; he held that the function of government should be limited to ***defense, justice*** and the maintenance of ***law and order.*** Therefore, he voted against tax increases and government expansion and supported private charities rather than government welfare. Though he was an advocate for improved working conditions for coal miners and campaigned against abuses such as child labor, he was a pragmatist. Therefore, cognizant of the French Revolution across the channel and the tension it generated all over Europe, he voted against workers' rights for Unions in 1799 and for the *'Six Acts'* of 1819 which restricted public meetings and seditious writings. He was accused by his critics of not doing enough for British workers and preaching vital Christianity to savages while tolerating its abuses among the civilized.

William Wilberforce is best remembered for his passion and work to end the ***slave trade and slavery.*** He learnt of the plight of slaves from his friend ***Thomas Clarkson (1760-1846)*** who had researched the subject of slavery for an essay competition at the University of Cambridge. The two, together with many others made the abolition of slavery a life long project. Armed with Clarkson's detailed research, Wilberforce introduced a Bill for the abolition of Slave Trade in 1789; although many members of parliament believed he was right, the vote on the Bill was delayed until 1791 and then it was soundly defeated. The defeat of the Bill was due in part to the change in the political climate created by the French Revolution and in part because the members of parliament feared that the economic consequences would be catastrophic.

Wilberforce did not give up, he and other abolitionists who formed a Christian organization called the *'Clapham Sect'* decided to raise awareness at the grassroots. They printed literature on the slave trade in pamphlets complete with graphic illustrations and widely distributed these at rallies all over the country. Campaigns were held to advocate the boycott of goods grown by slaves such as sugar.

At this time, Wilberforce and his abolitionist group were vilified by other politicians, the merchants, the nobles and even the king and they were called hypocrites and revolutionaries. Eventually, through sheer doggedness, the *Slave Trade Act* which abolished slave trade in the British Empire (but not slavery) passed in **1807** with a landslide. Britain was committed to enforcing the law and the British navy patrolled the Atlantic to intercept any ship carrying slaves.

After the abolition of the slave trade, Wilberforce and friends continued to work for the total emancipation of slaves. He advocated the registration of slaves in the British territories to make it easy to spot infringements of the Slave Trade Act. In 1833, Wilberforce received the news on his death bed that the British government had reached an agreement with slave holders in her territories for the emancipation of slaves. In **1834**, the *Slavery Abolition Act* was passed, emancipating all slaves in the British territories.

He pushed for similar actions in other nations; America abolished the slave trade in 1808 and in 1815, other European nations gave a commitment to end slave trade as soon as possible.

In 1787, Wilberforce, together with other abolitionists founded a settlement for freed slaves in Sierra Leone in West Africa. (Initial missionaries to the West African hinterland were from Sierra Leone).

In 1798, he was instrumental in the launch of the Anglican *Church Missionary Society* which sent missionaries around the world. He supported missionaries like William Carey and others.

In 1804, he cooperated with other denominations—Baptists, Presbyterians, Methodists etc—to form the *Foreign Bible Society*, the first interdenominational society that united Christians committed to the translation of the Bible into other languages around the world.

He also fought hard until in 1813, the parliamentary Act that gave the **British East India Company** a monopoly in British territories in India and forbade missionary activities was reversed. This opened up India to Protestant Christian influence and the subsequent abolition of the caste system, infanticide and suttee (the practice of burning widows with their dead husbands).

He founded the World's first Society for the Prevention of Cruelty to Animals later called the ***Royal Society for the Prevention of Cruelty to Animals***.

A very generous man, he used his personal resources to help the poor and the needy.

He believed that Christianity must permeate every area of a Christian's life and because he lived according to his convictions against all odds, he, together with others of like mind positively influenced and changed the spirit of their age and left indelible footprints on the sand of time for future generations.

William Wilberforce died in 1833 and was buried in Westminster Abbey. The memorial read, inter alia, *"He was among the foremost of those who fixed the character of their times . . . He relied not in vain on God; but in the process was called to endure great verbal abuse and great opposition: He outlived, however, all enmity . . . through the merits of Jesus Christ his only Redeemer and Savior . . ."*

William Carey (1761-1834 AD) [14, 15]

William Carey was born and raised as an Anglican but became involved with the "particular Baptists" and was finally baptized by them.

After his early education, he was apprenticed to a shoe-maker but with the help of educated friends and enormous self effort, Carey learnt Latin, Hebrew, French, Italian and Dutch. He wrote a book on the need to evangelize the heathen in which he:
  i) Established the Scriptural basis for evangelism as Jesus Christ's direct Commands—Mathew 28:18-20.
  ii) Reviewed the previous missionary activities from the early Church to his time,

iii) Compiled the data on world population and religions
iv) Identified the objections to missionary activities based on personal risks and language barrier and
v) Made the call for the formation of missionary societies while proffering suggestions on their sustainability.

Eventually, in 1792, the ***Baptist Missionary Society (BMS)*** was formed.

Carey and Dr. John Thomas were the first foreign missionaries of the society and both sailed to India's Danish colony in West Bengal in 1793 and not British colony because that would have violated the monopoly of the British East India Company.

On arrival, the missionaries tried to find ways to be self sustaining; therefore, Carey took the job of managing a Danish Indigo Plant. He did this for six years while learning the local language and translating the New Testament into Bengali and at the same time formulating the principles of making the missionary community self reliant. His plan included communal living and training of native ministers.

Life was rough for Carey in the early days, he lost a son and his wife suffered a nervous breakdown from which she never recovered until her death in 1807.

The BMS sent more missionaries including school teachers, and a printer all of who settled in Serampore in the Danish colony and were joined by Carey in 1800. Living communally in a big house, they started a school and the printing of the Bible in the Bengali language.

Carey influenced the Danish colonial Governor-General to end infanticide, child prostitution and the Suttee—(the practice of cremating widows with dead husbands).

He founded a college at Serampore in 1820 with the permission of the Danish king and severed association with the BMS when the successors of the founders introduced bureaucratic measures aimed at micromanaging the mission from Britain.

During Carey's lifetime, the mission's printing press translated and published the Bible whole or in part in 44 languages and dialects.

After the death of his first wife in 1807, he remarried in 1808 but she too died in 1821. He married a third time in 1823, his third wife surviving him when he died in 1834.

Carey's maxim was: *"**Expect** great things from God, **attempt** great things for God"*.

William Carey has been dubbed *"the father of Modern Evangelism"*

Adoniram and Ann Judson (1788-1850 AD) [16, 17]

Adoniram Judson was the son of a Congregationalist minister, born in Massachusetts, U.S.A. in 1788. Raised in the Christian faith, he espoused Deism while in college. However, after providentially hearing his Deist friend die, gripped in the terror of death, he sought and found true faith in God again.

He entered the Seminary and committed to becoming a missionary. After graduation, he got married and was commissioned as a missionary to India by the Congregational Church and the ***American Board of Commissioners for Foreign Missions*** in 1812. On the way to India, while studying the theology of Baptism, he became convinced about the '*believers' baptism'* and that it should be done in obedience to the command of Jesus Christ—***Mathew 28:19-20***. Therefore, he was re-baptized together with his wife by an associate of William Carey in Calcutta.

He left Calcutta for Burma due to hostility from the British East India Company. Life in Burma was hard and progress slow, in part because the Burmese king was hostile to evangelism. The Judsons persevered making eighteen converts in ten years.

The progress being made suffered a setback when the first Anglo-Burmese war broke out in 1824 and Adoniram was arrested and jailed for almost two years. After harrowing months in prison, he was released but the exertions of the Burmese mission field took their toll on Ann Judson who died in 1826.

Judson remarried the widow of a fellow missionary, Sarah, in 1834 and they had eight children out of which five survived. Sarah died on the way back to the U.S.A. for health reasons in 1845 at St. Helena. Adoniram continued the journey home and spent time raising awareness about and raising money for mission work.

In 1846, he married his third wife, Emily with whom he had a daughter. In his last years he was troubled with a chronic lung infection for which a voyage was prescribed as treatment; he however died at sea in 1850 and was buried at sea.

Adoniram was a formidable pioneer missionary; he translated the Bible into the Burmese language and planted many churches. He compiled a Burmese-English dictionary but the English-Burmese was completed posthumously.

His need for alternative support following his conviction about 'believers' baptism' led to the nation-wide organization of Baptists in America from which various American Baptist Associations such as the Southern Baptist Convention broke off.

Adoniram was a national figure and he had a 'Liberty Ship', the SS Adoniram Judson named after him during World War II.

David Livingstone (1813-1873 AD) [18, 19]

David Livingstone was a Scottish missionary and explorer born in Blantyre near Glasgow. A medical doctor, he was moved by the speech of **Robert Moffat (1795-1883)** who had been a missionary in Africa. He applied to the **London Missionary Society** (LMS) for sponsorship and he was sent to Kuruman, South Africa in 1841.

He married Mary, the daughter of Robert Moffat in 1845 and after a while, he felt the need to forge further inland and thus began his journeys of exploration which opened up Africa for others. Through several expeditions, (the accounts of which he published), he traversed the Zambezi River from Luanda in the west to the estuary in the Indian Ocean, he crossed the Kalahari Desert and discovered Lakes Nyassa and Victoria as well as other rivers.

In 1856, the LMS withdrew its support because they felt his explorations were conflicting with his missionary work. However, by this time he had become a celebrity and was supported by the government until 1863 after which the Royal Geographical Society picked up the sponsorship of his explorations.

Dr Livingstone was an abolitionist who never failed to call attention to the ravages of the slave trade by the Arabs and the Portuguese in Africa. In an impassioned speech on the slave trade he said: *"I beg to direct your attention to Africa; I know that in a few years I shall be cut off from that country which is now open; do not let it be shut again! I go back to Africa to try to make an open path for commerce and Christianity. Will you carry out the work which I have begun? I leave it with you".*

Unfortunately, the slave traders followed on his heals and profited from his explorations.

Dr. Livingstone died in Africa; his body was returned to England and buried in Westminster Abbey, but his heart was, fittingly, buried in Africa.

Hudson Taylor (1832-1905 AD) [20, 21, 22]

Hudson Taylor was born in 1832 to an English Methodist lay preacher and his wife. Hudson was interested in missions to China and as soon as he was convinced, he made preparations by moving out of the comfort of his parents' home to live in the slum area while learning how to fully depend on God for everything. He went for tutelage under a doctor in order to learn some Medicine; he also spent the time learning Mandarin. Hudson was commissioned by the *"Chinese Evangelization Society"* in 1853 and he was the Society's first missionary to China.

In China, Hudson broke cultural barriers by dressing like the Chinese men complete with a hairstyle with a pigtail. Hudson was a workaholic, not content to remain in the coastal areas; he pressed further inland into the interior of China.

In 1857, he severed relations with the Chinese Evangelization Society and became independent. He formed the '*China Inland Mission*' (CIM). The distinctive features of the CIM include:
- No guaranteed salary
- No appeals for funds
- Dependence on God to supply needs
- Missionaries with the organization expected to dress like the Chinese and\ be ready to work inland.

Taylor's leadership style was exacting and he demanded from others what he demanded from himself and some simply couldn't take it and left to join other missions.

Hudson married Maria Dyer, the daughter of a London Missionary Society (LMS) missionary to Malaysia in 1858. The strains created by his leadership style took its toll also on his family which lost four children before the age of ten years and to cap it all, his wife died at the age of thirty-three in 1870.

He remarried Jennie Faulding, a fellow missionary in 1871.

The CIM was not strictly denominational, it accepted spiritually qualified members from all Protestant groups, nations, gender and marital status. Therefore the organization was able to reach all eighteen provinces of China, founded one hundred and twenty-five schools, established more than three hundred stations and had tens of thousands of converts through the work of more than eight hundred missionaries called and used of God.

Physically and mentally exhausted, Hudson formally retired in 1902 and settled in Switzerland.

His wife Jennie died in 1904 and he returned to China in 1905 visiting the mission stations when he died suddenly and was buried beside his first wife, Maria.

The 1949 take over of China by Communists interrupted the work of CIM but it continued as the *Overseas Missionary Fellowship* (OMF) International.

Hudson has been and continues to be an inspiration for other missionaries and evangelists.

The Second Great Awakening [23, 24, 25]

In the first half of the nineteenth century, another wave of revival swept through the United States and its expanding western frontiers. It was in different forms in different sectors of the country. In the northeast, it took the form of social activism, in parts of New York, growth of new denominations and in the southern states, revival meetings in tents.

The overarching theme however, was personal piety over sterile theological teachings. While the First Great Awakening was dominated by Calvinist preachers that emphasized human depravity, the general theological expression of the Second Awakening was Arminianism which stressed the importance of human responsibility in responding to God's Grace. Methodist and Baptists were active in the south and the frontiers while Presbyterians like **Charles G. Finney (1792-1875),** the evangelist most identified with the Second Awakening was active in New York and the northeast.

The Second Great Awakening resulted in:
- Emphasis on personal piety, temperance, work ethics, frugality etc.
- Evolution of new Christian denominations like the Seventh Day Adventists, the Mormons and the Churches of Christ.
- Interdenominational missionary groups such as the American Bible Society (1816), the American Tract Society (1825) and the American Home Missionary Society (1826).
- Numerical strengthening of Baptists and Methodists relative to the Anglican (Episcopal), Presbyterian and Reformed denominations.

- Emergence of reform groups for the abolition of slavery, suffrage, prisons and care of the handicapped.
- Black congregations and churches from which arose the occasional slave rebellion like the Nat Turner uprising of 1831. (Unfortunately, incidents like this, rather than foster more freedom for slaves led to the curtailment of the freedom of the blacks who were free).

The Second Great awakening made a lasting impact on the religious, political and social fabric of the United States of America.

Charles G. Finney (1792-1875) [26, 27, 28]

Charles Finney was the son of farmers and the youngest of fifteen children. He was an apprentice lawyer when he had a spiritual experience in which he felt himself baptized with the Holy Spirit. He gave up his law career to become an apprentice to a Presbyterian minister, the Reverend George Washington Gale.

Licensed to preach after his tutelage, (his admirers said he refused to pursue a formal theological education while his critics said he was refused admission to a Seminary), he was commissioned as an evangelist in rural New York by the Female Missionary Society. Later he widened his area of evangelism, became very popular with his style of extemporaneous, pithy and sometimes emotional preaching and he popularized the **"anxious bench"** and **"altar calls"**. He believed it was legit to use measures designed to pressurize his listeners to "make a decision" to follow Christ.

His success scandalized the Presbyterian Church that licensed him because, not only was his style considered unorthodox, his theology was also considered uncalvinistic and frankly Pelagian because he believed that true Christian conversion should manifest in better morality based on choices that a professed Christian makes. He was accused of denying the doctrine of Original Sin and believing in "Sinless Perfection". Eventually, he had to resign from the Presbyterian denomination and became affiliated with the Congregationalists.

Finney is also well known for his campaign against Freemasonry; writing a book titled **"The Character, Claims and Practical Workings of Freemasonry"**, he exposed the inner workings of the secret society. He was introduced into Freemasonry by his uncle who assured him that as a member he would always have a friend wherever he went. He joined and attained the Third degree before quitting because he realized 'it was incompatible with real Christianity'. He revealed that the oaths were profane and immoral, that freemasonry was inimical to the government and civil society'. He also revealed that many professing Christians, including the clergy were members.

Finney was regarded as a lone ranger and was criticized for being dismissive of established religion and formal theological education. He was said to be a man of prayer and whatever his faults, his admirers believed he was mightily used of God.

While he is still being vilified by contemporary Reformation orthodoxy theologians, he is highly esteemed by many twentieth century Protestant evangelists and televangelists.

Chapter 21

Theologians and Philosophers of the 19th and 20th Centuries

Friedrich Daniel Ernst Schleiermacher (1768-1834) [1,2]

Freidrich Schleiermacher was a German philosopher and theologian. The son of a Reformed clergyman, he was sent to the Moravian sect school. However, against the counsel of his father, he left the Moravian school and enrolled in a more liberal University of Halle. His main philosophical works were his theories of Hermeneutics (interpretation) and Translation. Schleiermacher's principles of **Hermeneutics** are:

- Hermeneutics is strictly the art of understanding verbal communication (as opposed to explicating or translating.
- Hermeneutics should be universally applied to all disciplines and subjects—Bible, law, literature etc; to oral and written language and to modern and ancient texts whether in foreign or mother tongue.
- The interpretation of sacred texts such as the bible 'may not rely on special principles like divine inspiration' of either the author or the interpreter.
- 'Misunderstanding' (not understanding), occur as a matter of course and interpretation is a more difficult task than generally appreciated because of linguistic and conceptual/intellectual diversity
- Before the interpretation of a text is undertaken, the interpreter must acquire a good knowledge of the text's historical context.
- He also advised having knowledge of the author's psychology in order to resolve linguistic ambiguities and get additional clues to the author's usage.

In his theory of Translation, he highlighted the challenges and difficulties arising from the conceptual gulf that exists between the language of the text and the translator's own language. He believed that the translator's primary goal is the faithful reproduction of meaning and was an advocate of the method of translation that is most faithful to the author's linguistic conceptual world rather than to that of the translator or reader.

On Theology

Schleiermacher is regarded by some as the *"father of modern Protestant Theology"* and his approach to theology is considered philosophical, historical and practical.

While in college, he had a *'crisis of faith'* and wrote his father that he **'did not believe that Jesus died vicariously for his atonement'**. Nonetheless, he completed his theological studies and held preaching positions in many places. His theological ideas were enunciated in many of his works such as that addressed to the elite agnostics and atheists in Berlin—*"On Religion: Speeches to Its Cultured Despisers"* and *"The Christian Faith"*.

He said:
- That religion is neither the outcome of the fear of death nor of the fear of God; neither metaphysics nor morality but that which answers a deep need in man and is essentially intuitive.
- That *"God is optional"* in religion and that God can be included depending on the nature of one's imagination.
- That the Biblical account of creation is *"sacred legend"* rather than literal truth.
- That Christ's redemptive work derives from His being the only one who had the "perfect God-consciousness" and so was able to draw others into perfect God-consciousness.
- He rejected the substitutionary/vicarious atonement of Jesus Christ and like Kant felt that the idea of Christ suffering for the sins of others was 'immoral'.
- That Jesus is not the only mediator or necessarily the last and that the canons be opened to admit new 'revelations'.
- That the desire for personal immortality is indicative of a lack of religion since, according to him, religion assumes a desire to 'lose oneself in the infinite' rather than to preserve one's own future self.

- That, to foster religious harmony, there should be no proselytizing or the belief that salvation exist only for "insiders" and that creeds should not be forced on others.
- That there should be separation of Church and State.

He was said to have backtracked on some of the views later on.

He was described as the ***"Prince of the Vermitters"*** (that is, takers of the middle ground) in philosophy, ethics, religion and theology. Acclaimed as the father of Protestant theology by some, he is considered a heretic by others.

COMMENTS:

Schleiermacher's theology and Christology in large part are unscriptural. For example, his rejection of divine inspiration and illumination in Biblical hermeneutics is diametrically opposed to the teachings of Jesus Christ—John 14:26 and John 16:13. If it is true, as recorded, that he rejected Christ's vicarious atonement and there was never a clear point of reversal of this opinion, it is surprising that he is considered a Christian much less a "father of Protestant theology".

Soren Kierkegaard (1813-1855) [3, 4, 5]

Soren Kierkegaard was a Danish theologian, philosopher, poet and writer.

On Faith and Sin

He believed:
- That faith is not a matter of regurgitating dogma but individual and subjective passion that cannot be mediated by human artifacts.
- That becoming a "true self" comes only through faith
- That there is no mediation between the individual self and God by priest or by any logical system (against Catholicism and Hegelianism respectively).
- That there are paradoxes in the Christian dogma that are offensive to reason and that faith cannot be acquired by reason
- That to believe something higher than reason, it may be necessary to suspend reason.
- That faith is a miracle and a gift from God—an innate eternal truth.

- That the condition of faith is the realization that we are always in sin.
- That faith is not a one time affair and has to be repeatedly renewed.
- That sin cannot evolve from purely human origins and that it was introduced by a "transcendent source". (That Adam probably never thought of eating the fruit until he was forbidding by God).
- That the reaction of temporal human beings to the idea of contact with the infinite transcendent God can be offence or faith.

On the Church
- Kierkegaard was a strong opponent of the national church and believed:
- That State control of churches perverted true Christianity; that in State controlled congregations, people remain spiritually immature and fail to take responsibility for their faith in God.
- That State controlled congregations compromised quality for quantity of membership and were concerned only with the power of the clergy.
- That in State churches, anyone could become a Christian without knowing what it meant to be a Christian.
- That the State church was upholding the values of Christendom (a phenomenon of cultural history) rather than of Christianity which is the vehicle of a passionate and individual inward faith.
- That the clergy were mere political officials and not representatives of God.
- That Christianity had been reduced to a mere "fashionable tradition" embraced by ***"unbelieving believers"***.
- That the single individual had been replaced with the crowd called the congregation
- That struggle had been replaced with mediation; reflections with revolution; works of love with welfare state and that the eternal truth was in danger of being replaced with temporal gossip.

On the Theory of Life
Kierkegaard proposed three stages of life, namely, ***(i) Aesthetic, (2) Ethical and (3) Religious.*** However, he stated that not everyone reaches

all three stages and that some in one stage may retain aspects of other stages too.

The **aesthetic** stage is characterized by hedonism, materialism or intellectual pursuits. The person in the aesthetic stage is a rationalist and relativist who avoids difficult choices and whose approach to life is characterized by self gratification and pleasure. Thinks only of the here and now and has little regard for long term consequences; likely to seek artificial stimuli like narcotics or sexual gratification. After a while, for the aesthetic person, whether hedonist, materialist or intellectual, boredom sets in and then despair.

The **ethical** individual, realizing the despair of the aesthetic stage is compelled to seek greater meaning in life, make choices that build relationships and form enduring ethical systems.

The individual at the **religious** stage experiences faith and suffering and it is only at this level that true 'self understanding' is accomplished.

Rudolf Bultmann (1884-1976) [6, 7]

Rudolf Bultmann was a German Lutheran theologian and New Testament professor. He was an exponent of *"form criticism"* called ***"Demythologization",*** a theological system that strips faith of most, if not all, of history.

He believed that all the historical events recorded in the Bible were like husks which have to be peeled away to get to the real truth. He considered that the historical biblical events were outdated and that the modern man with scientific mind could not take them seriously; therefore he proposed that the Old Testament, the parables, miracles and other stories about Jesus in the New Testament be removed. In Bultmann's theology:
- The bare fact of the crucifixion of Jesus Christ was all that was necessary to faith.
- Sin is nothing more than 'refusal to accept the gift of authentic existence' and has nothing to do with the sin of Adam.
- The significance of the death of Jesus is not the placation of an angry God but that through Him "our authentic life becomes a possibility"
- 'Living in the Spirit does not mean supernatural influence'
- 'God's judgment is not a cosmic event in the future

Bultmann's existential theology dismissed as untenable biblical features like miracles, demonology, eschatology, the significance of the death and resurrection of Jesus Christ and the eternal destinies of heaven and hell. These issues were considered obsolete and frameworks of mythology which believers have to go beyond to reach "the permanent truth". When asked how then Christ crucifixion was still considered relevant to man's salvation, he said it is by the **"Word of Proclamation"** the proof of which he said theologians should not bother to search.

COMMENTS:
It is interesting that Bultmann would 'demythologize' everything in the Bible, including the birth, the life and the most important aspects of Jesus Christ's death and resurrection then suddenly ask that people take a nebulous quantum jump of faith in His crucifixion for salvation. How does the "Word of Proclamation" legitimize the crucifixion while other events had to be demythologized? Bultmann's characterization of core Christian doctrines as myths, and his rejection of Christian doctrines call to question his claim to being a Christian.

Karl Barth (1886-1968) [8, 9]

Karl Barth was born in Switzerland in 1886 to a professor of New Testament and minister. He studied theology under mostly liberal theologians of his day.

Barth was shocked and appalled by the readiness with which his teachers signed on to the plans of the German State during the First World War and the realization that they had turned their backs on the Gospel made him to seek a different theological foundation.

He re-read the Scripture and soon became an ardent opponent of the liberal theology prevalent in his time which was dominated by "scientific study and historical criticism" of texts.

Karl Barth:
- Rejected Schleiermacher's hermeneutics which stressed historical accuracy but discounted authorial revelation.
- Believed that accurate interpretation of the Bible require that the interpreter "stand inside the conviction of the authors"; that failure to do this in the zeal for historical accuracy render the interpretation untruthful to the author's intentions.
- Furthermore, believed that historical criticism of Scriptural texts, although useful for discovering history of the text is the wrong method for finding God as it makes the texts the objects of study and does not allow man to experience God's revelation.

- Believed that human efforts (strivings) to know God through philosophy or religion are doomed to fail and that the only way to succeed is to be positioned to receive God's revelation.
- Held that God is totally unknowable except as He chooses to reveal Himself.
- Barth considered that philosophy, sciences and natural theology only lead to anthropocentricism and idolatry.
- Considered Evangelical theology of his day as religionistic, anthropocentric and humanistic and he agreed with **Feuerbach** (1804-1872) that the Christians of his day had *"created a 'God' in the image of man"* and were guilty of idolatry.

He wrote extensively on Theology, Dogmatics and the Creed. He formed an organization of the *"Confessing Church"* in Germany with pastors of the same mind and wrote a declaration, *the Barmen Declaration*, which condemned the racist and idolatrous policies of the Nazis.

In 1935, he was dismissed from his position in Bonn for refusing to sign allegiance to Hitler. He went to his native Basel where he continued to teach at the University. He retired from the University in 1962 and died in 1968.

Reinhold Niebuhr (1892-1971) [10, 11]

Reinhold Niebuhr was an American theologian and philosopher born in 1892 to immigrant German parents. His father was an ordained minister of the German Evangelical Synod and Reinhold himself studied theology and Divinity and was also an ordained minister.

While ministering in Detroit, he observed the harsh conditions of the automobile workers and this spurred him into social activism. He sought for ways to change the economic and social conditions that produced the problems of the automobile industry workers. He became a critic of capitalism and founded the *"Fellowship of Socialist Christians"* in the 1930s and the *"Union for Democratic Action"* in 1941.

An unabashed liberal theologian, Reinhold:

On Social Justice
- insisted on the necessity of politics in the struggle for *'social justice'*
- Acknowledged the limitations of reason through moral and rational means in solving social injustice.

- Held that religion plays an important role in solving social problems because the 'religious conscience is sensitive as it is judged in the light of 'the absolute.
- Held that the 'spirit of love' cannot prevent social conflict and that the use of the instrument of coercion is inevitable.
- Suggested the application of the *'principles of justice'* (as an approximation of love) to political and socio-economic reality rather than the *'law of love'*.
- Rejected unconditional pacifism because he believed it gives undue preference to tyranny or leads to temptation to remain neutral.

On Morality
- Reinhold differentiated individual morality from group morality; he believed that individuals are capable of making moral adjustments, whereas, the society as a group aggravates individual selfish impulses. Thus compared to individuals, the capacity for morality is lowered in groups.
- He contended that groups are more egoistic, arrogant, hypocritical and ruthless in the pursuit of its goals than the individual and that they lack the capacity for self transcendence.
- He therefore concluded that the religious idealism as espoused by Jesus Christ has a better potential for fulfillment in individuals than in the group.

On Christian Realism
According to Reinhold, Christian realism demands that Christians accept as fact:
- That humans are morally debilitated on account of corruption by sin
- That the promised new life for men and nations in the Gospel has no guarantee of historic success. That the Christian Gospel cannot be transmuted into historical optimism.
- That a Christian realist has to be morally, politically and theologically realistic and should seek to recognize and be attentive to the forces operating in the moral landscape.
- That the 'ultimate' cannot be the normative social ethics and that realism demand a *'step-down'* of ethical ideals to realistic ethical objectives.

- That *'love'* is an *"impossible possibility"*; that the natural man can never attain sacrificial and complete disinterestedness which the ethics of Jesus demand.

On Judaism and Racial Issues

Reinhold, earlier in his career believed in converting Jews to Christianity but as he matured his position evolved to the opposite view. He was a supporter of the Zionist movement and a homeland for the Jews in Palestine.

He abhorred and opposed racial segregation but unlike most liberals, he was reticent about "imposed equality" or integration.

On American History

In a book titled *"The Irony of American History"*, Reinhold stated that there are two types of *"American Idealism", namely—the 'Anti-war, non-interventionists' who are embarrassed by power and—the 'Pro-war Imperialists' who disguise power as virtue.*

The anti-war non-interventionists he said, *"sought to preserve the purity of their souls by denouncing military actions or by demanding that every action taken be unequivocally virtuous; that they exaggerate the sins of their country, excuse the malevolence its enemies and . . . inevitably blame America first"(sounds familiar).*

This, he argued was a sanctimonious way of refusing to face real problems.

The authorship of *"The Serenity Prayer"* has been attributed to Reinhold Niebuhr.

Reinhold Niebuhr has been described as *a "pragmatist and utilitarian who strove for moderation and curtailment of ideals through negotiation of a compromise that accommodate the best of competing propositions"*.

He has also been described as "a situationalist who was tentative and responsive in his ethical formulations; willing to accept the reality of negotiated order and coerced truce". That he envisaged *"a stable society based on the equilibrium between the claims of liberty and equality, freedom and order and need and merit"*.

His demotion of ideals is hailed by some, who consider the idea of *"one Supreme Principle that is valid for all times and in all places"* as the *"Tyranny of Absolutism"*. That he relegated the *"Ultimate to the*

Pen-Ultimate" and that in doing so he rejected the partisanship of both orthodoxy and liberalism.

COMMENT:
An examination of Reinhold's positions in the light of Scriptures reveals that his positions run countercurrent to Biblical standards in most cases. For example, rather than compromise as Niebuhr recommended, the Bible said to avoid doing exactly that—***Romans 12:1-2***

In his reduction of the Ultimate to the pen-ultimate; the question must be asked, whether the Ultimate remains or becomes something else entirely if the post keep shifting in order to compromise.

Dietrich Bonhoeffer (1906-1945) [12, 13, 14, 15]

Dietrich Bonhoeffer was a German Lutheran pastor, theologian and prolific writer born to a University of Berlin professor of Psychiatry and Neurology.

Bonhoeffer was brilliant, getting his doctorate at the age of twenty-one years. He studied in Germany and did a postgraduate course in the United States where he was a student of ***Reinhold Niebuhr*** through whom he came in contact with elements of the *'Liberation Theology'*.

He opposed Hitler and the German national church and was a member of the "Confessional church" becoming the head of the organization's seminary until it was closed down by the Nazis in 1937. In 1940, Bonhoeffer actively joined the anti-Nazi resistance movement until he was arrested in 1943 after being implicated in a plot to assassinate Adolf Hitler. He was subsequently executed in 1945 shortly before the end of World War II.

Bonhoeffer was a prolific writer and the more well known of his writings include:
- The Cost of Discipleship,
- Ethics and
- Letters and Papers from Prison.

In The Cost of Discipleship, Bonhoeffer explored the issue of Grace and Discipleship, the call to discipleship, discipleship and the Cross, individuals and discipleship and the Beatitudes. He differentiated between ***real grace*** and ***cheap grace***.

He said: **Cheap grace**:
- Is presented as grace without price or cost; that the impression is given that the Church has an inexhaustible treasury of it

- 'Is a doctrine, a principle and a system' in which forgiveness is proclaimed as a general truth which he said allowed people to easily cover their sins without discernible contrition or real desire to be set free from sin.
- Is the justification of sin without the justification of the sinner; the Christian follows the world's standard since "grace does everything and to aspire to live differently from the previous sinful life might be presumptuous".
- Is self bestowed; "It is the preaching of forgiveness without repentance; Communion without confession, grace without discipleship, grace without the Cross and therefore grace without Jesus Christ".

On the other hand, real grace:
- Is 'a treasure for which a man will give his all"
- Is "a priceless pearl for which a merchant would sell his all to obtain"
- Is "The rule of Christ for which a man would pluck out his eye if it causes him to stumble".
- Condemns sin and justifies the sinner
- Is costly because it costs God the life of His Son

On discipleship he said:
- ***"Christianity without discipleship is always Christianity without Christ. It remains an abstract idea, a myth which has a place for the Fatherhood of God, but omits Christ as the Living Son; trusts in God but no following of Christ".***
- "The call of discipleship means both life and death . . . it sets the Christian in the middle of the daily arena against sin and the devil".
- "Through the call of God, men become individuals . . . every man is called separately, and must follow alone. But men are frightened of solitude and try to protect themselves from it by merging themselves in the society of their fellow men . . . they are unwilling to stand alone before Jesus . . ."
- ***"Only he who believes is obedient and only he who is obedient believes".***

He concluded that: "the teaching of cheap grace is the ruin of more Christians than any commandment of works".

On Ethics, Bonhoeffer stated that:
- "The foundation of ethics is the reconciliation of the reality of God and the world reality in the reality of Christ". That sharing in the reality of Christ involves being responsible and acting in accordance with the will and reality of God.
- The two guides to discovering God's will in any situation are (i) The needs of one's neighbor and (ii) the Model of Jesus Christ.
- There are no moral certainties and that it is impossible to know what is really good or what is evil because man gained the knowledge of good and evil in rebellion to God.
- That when assaulted by evil, it must be opposed; that failure to oppose evil is to condone it.
- That in resisting evil, ***anything could be done with equal justification***.
- Prior justification of an action is impossible because the knowledge of good and evil is unavailable to man.
- What is worse than doing evil is being evil. That "to lie is wrong, but what is worse than the lie is the liar for the liar contaminates everything he says . . ." Therefore, "it is worse for a liar to tell the truth than for a lover of truth to lie".
- The usual strategies usually employed in attempting to deal with ethical situation, namely—the dictates of reason, conscience, moral dogma, authority, monastic withdrawal and duty—are based on general principles and theories which in the final analysis are destructive to ethics because they interfere with the ability to deal with evil.
- The ethically responsible person is selfless like Jesus Christ and serves the spiritual and material needs of others.
- Using the selfless model of Jesus Christ as guide, the responsible person should not hesitate to act for fear of sin.
- That it is morally reprehensible to avoid conflict because of concern for moral purity.
- It is wrong to refuse to act on behalf of one's neighbor, even violently, for fear of sin or refuse to bear guilt for charity's sake.

- There is no need for advance self-justifying principles since because in "a world come of age", there are no certainties and all must depend on the grace and mercy of God.

COMMENT:
Bonhoeffer's *"responsibility ethics"* is essentially a *"situational ethics"* which is built on rather twisted logic and seems to suggest that *"the end justifies the means"*. On the one hand he said the capacity to know what is evil or good is not available to man, condemned all known approaches and general principles for opposing and resisting evil, and then on the other hand called for a reflexive confrontation of evil. By what means is what is evil to be determined since there is no certainty? If right and wrong cannot be discerned with certainty, is it logical for anyone to fight with reckless abandon, as he proposed, what is perceived as evil?

Bonhoeffer's Other Ethical Positions:
- Life should be free of intentional injury, violation and killing of innocent life. War, which is a complex issue, is exempted.
- Euthanasia is morally wrong; it is arbitrary killing of innocent life
- Suicide is wrong; it shows a lack of faith in God and life's possibilities.
- Abortion is murder
- Perpetual birth control is a violation of man's natural existence.
- Rape, torture and slavery are prohibited.

In his Letters and Papers from Prison, Bonhoeffer said:
- *"... The concept of God as a Supreme Being with absolute power and goodness was spurious and God as a working hypothesis in morals, politics and science should be dropped"*.
- That the world had come of age and religion was no longer necessary. He therefore called for Christianity that is devoid of religion; that a Christian is known not by his beliefs but by his actions.
- He questioned the Virgin birth of Christ, His sinlessness and His deity.
- That "the historicity of the physical resurrection of Jesus Christ was in the 'realm of ambiguity' and one of the mythological elements of Christianity. That such things as miracles and the ascension of Christ were mythological conceptions".

- That Christ is not the only way to God.
- "Faith of the Old Testament is not a religion of salvation" and the book of Genesis was scientifically naïve and full of myths".

Bonhoeffer's place in history is controversial. He has been described as a *"scholar of faith"* by liberal theologians and it's easy to agree with them after reading some of Bonhoeffer's writings such as "The Cost of Discipleship". He has also been called a *"practical atheist"*, a "*religious humanist"* and a ***blasphemer.*** Again, it is hard to disagree when one reads his Letters and Papers from Prison and his other writings such as Ethics. He was a twentieth century martyr to some and a blasphemer to others. The harsher critics have even compared his writings to a *"garbage can, a dangerous place to seek for nourishment even though it is possible to occasionally find something useful in it".*

He is believed to have been a great influence on the developers of the Liberation Theology.

COMMENT

It is hard to believe that Bonhoeffer who wrote so succinctly about discipleship and grace wrote the papers and letters from prison. If he did, was he in his right mind? Was he writing under duress? Or, did he recant his faith in prison?

It is simply impossible to reconcile the man who wrote the excellent exposition on God's grace and Christ's Cross with the man who practically renounced God in the Letters from Prison. It is either he had changed profoundly through his prison experiences (whatever those were) or he was not the author and they were only attributed to him.

Chapter 22

Global Trends in Christianity in the 19th and 20th Centuries

Latin America and the Liberation Theology [1,2,3,4]

In the nineteenth century, the Latin American nations gained independence from Spain and Portugal. However, this did not result in the improvement of the lives of the majority of the people who were impoverished because the wealth of the nations was concentrated in the hands of only a few. The poverty of the people was blamed on the social and political structures and perceived exploitation by developed countries.

Because the Catholic Church was intimately involved in the conquest and colonization of Latin America, the Catholic hierarchy was considered by some to be complicit with the oppressors of people.

Some Latin American clergy in the 20th century felt that the traditional Catholic theology was inadequate to address the situation of the people. The dogmas were described as hollow and irrelevant to real life.

Therefore, in the 1960s, Latin American theologians, influenced by the Enlightenment liberal theologians from Europe like Bultmann and Bonhoeffer and others from North America began developing the **"Liberation Theology"**.

The leading exponents of the Liberation Theology were the Peruvian Dominican priest and theologian **Gustavo Gutierrez (1928—)**, Uruguay Jesuit priest and theologian, **Luis Segundo (1925-1996),** Brazilian Franciscan priest, theologian and philosopher, **Leonardo Boff (1938—)** and Salvadorian Jesuit priest and theologian **Jon Sobrino (1938—)**. The development of the theology was boosted by the Vatican II Council held from 1962 to 1965 which overhauled many Catholic Church practices. For instance, it was decided at the Council that mass could be said in the vernacular and social inequality among others was condemned. In 1968, at the conference of Latin American Bishops, Gutierrez gave the outline of a Liberation Theology.

The Premise:
The Liberation Theology was based on the premise that:
- All theologies are biased and reflect the economic and social classes of the developers
- Theology is not a systematic collection of timeless and acultural truths.

The Structure:
- The liberation theology is built on the concept of "**Praxis**" that is "doing". According to Gutierrez, theology is not just doctrines to be learned, it is to be done.
- The pre-understanding of preferential option for the poor.
- The concept of Liberation as enunciated in Isaiah 61:1

According to Gutierrez, the starting point for liberation theology is 'praxis' which consists of *"revolutionary struggle"* for the poor; out of the actions will emerge "theological perceptions". Therefore instead of Orthodoxy (right doctrine), Orthopraxis (right doing) is emphasized.

Ideology/methodology

The ideology and methodology of Liberation theology is unabashedly Marxism.

In fact in its documents, it is stated that "Marxist categories" were used for social and economic analysis.

Basic Principles:

Sin

In liberation theology, sin is not defined in terms of individual falling short of God's glory; rather sin is social, economic and collective. Hence capitalist countries that allegedly exploit the underdeveloped countries are oppressors, guilty of institutionalized violence and therefore in a state of sin.

The oppressed also sin by not offering resistance to oppression, if necessary by violent means. Killing in the course of resisting oppression is not considered sinful, whereas, if the perceived oppressor kills, it is sinful.

Salvation

Salvation in liberation theology is not about individual repentance from sin, faith in Jesus Christ and hope of eternal life; rather it is "bringing about the kingdom of God" which is an egalitarian social order. Salvation is collective and is achieved through social change.

Jesus Christ

Liberation theology is not very clear about Jesus Christ. His significance is in the incarnation where he is presented as God's total identification with the suffering of the poor. Most Liberation theologians do not believe in Christ's vicarious sacrifice, rather, He was crucified because He offended the religious and political leaders. In fact, Leonardo Boff said the followers fabricated the salvific significance associated with His death.

The Church

The Church is defined more by its mission than by its nature; it is expected to protest and challenge injustice at all times and not be concerned about saving individual souls. Small groups called *'Ecclesia Based Communities'* which meets for bible study, prayer and the discussion of social concerns were formed at the grassroots. These groups were used for the effective dissemination of the concept of liberation. In the liberation theology, there is no clear demarcation between the church and the world, according to Gutierrez, *"a theology of the church in the world should be complemented by a theology of the world in the church"*.

The Catholic hierarchy through papal encyclicals—*Pope Paul VI (1963-1978) and John Paul II (1978-2005)* approved the idea of socio-economic upliftment of the poor and criticized capitalist systems for its obsession with profit at the expense of human beings and counseled development through consensus rather than struggle. However, the Vatican appeared to have allowed even armed resistance in case of prolonged tyranny saying: *"We know that revolutionary uprising—(save where there is manifest long-standing tyranny which would do great damage to fundamental personal rights and dangerous harm to the common good of the country)—produces new injustices, throws more elements out of balance and brings new disasters"*.

As liberation theology spread, the Vatican issued cautionary statements in 1984 and 1986 through the Sacred Congregation of Doctrine and Faith. While the Catholic Church acknowledged the legitimate concern for the poor, it rejected the use of Marxist principles because it is believed that this will eventually lead to the use of Marxist methods and the embrace of Marxist goals. In a preliminary report on Liberation theology, then

Cardinal Joseph Ratzinger said: *"An analysis of the phenomenon of liberation theology reveals that it constitutes a fundamental threat to the faith of the Church"*. He however conceded that liberation theology as a phenomenon is indicative of "a lack of conversion in the Church and a lack of radical faith". He believed that only with such a conversion can the Church adequately address the question of liberation theology.

Liberation theology led to socio-political tensions in many countries in Latin America. In El Salvador and Nicaragua it led to the formation of resistance armies and civil wars.

A few Catholic priests identified so much with the radical resistance to political authorities that they joined the revolutionaries and took up arms. Perhaps the most prominent was **Father Camilo Torres** (1929-1966) who joined the Colombian liberation movement and paid the ultimate price in 1966.

However, with the collapse of Marxist regimes of the former USSR and Eastern Europe and violent revolutions and counter-revolutions in Central America without discernible results in socio-economic and political justice or spiritual dividends, confidence in socialism waned and calls have been made for a review of Liberation Theology. The proponents of Liberation Theology have therefore shifted their emphasis more to spirituality than Marxist social analysis.

Another theory on which liberation theology was built that has been found to be fallacious was the "dependency theory" which stated that the developed capitalist countries maintain their development at the expense of the poor countries. Sociologists have cited the success of Asian nations like Japan, Hong Kong, Singapore, South Korea and Taiwan on the one hand and the absence of any real successful socialist state to debunk the dependency theory of the Liberation theologians.

The Liberation Theology, though it has its roots in Latin America and the Catholic Church, has become both international and interdenominational with variants in North America, Asia and Africa. This has led to the **Black Liberation Theology** and **Feminist Liberation Theology** with race and gender playing central roles.

COMMENTS:

If Liberation Theology is accepted as a true theological system, it is hard to label it a Christian theology for the following reasons:

i) The foundation of any genuine Christian theology is centered on Jesus Christ; His birth, life, teachings, death and resurrection. The significance of His death in relation to sinners and sin and the importance of His resurrection for time and eternity. The biblical revelations on these issues are for the Christians, timeless truths that transcend epochs, cultures, race, political systems and gender. Any theological system that is fuzzy about the biblical revelations of Jesus Christ is something other than Christianity, so also is any system that views Christian theology as a system in a state of flux rather than a system of timeless truths.

ii) The idea of an evolving theology based on the so called 'Orthopraxis' turns things upside down. While 'doctrine without doing' is untenable, praxis without sound doctrine (based on balanced and correct scriptural interpretation) is downright dangerous. It is important to first discern the will of God through sound doctrine and learn His ways before doing anything. Therefore Orthodoxy should precede Orthopraxis.

iii) The redefinition of sin as collective and social rather than individual and particular also contradicts the biblical concept of sin and undermines the need for personal repentance and faith in the process of redemption. There is nowhere the Bible talked about collective sin or collective salvation—John 3:16; Ezekiel 18:4, 20.

iv) Preaching salvation in terms of ushering in an utopian "kingdom of God" here on earth is also unbiblical; Jesus clearly taught that His Kingdom is not of this world.

v) The liberation theologians' biblical exegesis and hermeneutics through the "lenses" of the poor, thereby reducing biblical revelations to mainly socio-economic and political issues of poverty is ludicrous. In the matter of justice, God's instruction is that no partiality be shown to the poor or the rich; each of them stands equal before the law and justice must be dispensed in righteousness without fear or favor—Leviticus 19:15. A poor man who steals still has to pay the price—Proverbs 6:30-31. Jesus Christ taught that those who have should voluntarily take care of those that do not have; he never taught that anything should be taken from the rich and given to the poor by those in authority.

vi) In fact when a man wanted Jesus to "redistribute" his brother's wealth to his advantage, Jesus rebuked him and warned him to beware of covetousness—Luke 12:13-15.

Essentially, it seems the advocates of Liberation Theology would like to achieve societal redemption through politics and ideology disguised as theology.

The following comment of ***Cardinal Joseph Ratzinger (now Pope Benedict XVI)*** about Liberation Theology encapsulates the pretensions and the fallacies of the Liberation theologies; He said:

"Whenever politics tries to be redemptive, it is promising too much. Where it wishes to do the work of God, it becomes, not divine but demonic".

Trends in Africa [5, 6, 7]

By the turn of the 20th century, Africa had been carved up between the European nations, mainly France, Britain, Germany, Italy and Portugal with the exception of Ethiopia and Liberia.

Contrary to the vision of David Livingstone of commerce and Christianity for the African continent, what the people got from the colonists was colonialism and imperialism so rapacious and so brutal as to sometimes border on genocide.

Such was the case in the Congo Free State of the Belgian ***King Leopold II*** where his officials imposed a reign of terror killing and maiming the natives if they failed to produce allotted quota of rubber and ivory. Millions, young and old, male and female who escaped execution had their hands amputated and maimed for life and between 1885 and 1908 the population was reduced to less than a half.

The atrocities in the Congo Free State produced international outcry and inspired **Joseph Conrad *(1857-1924)*** to write the book titled ***"Hearts of Darkness"***. The people of Belgium were scandalized and they dispossessed the King of the colony converting it to a State colony, the Belgian Congo.

In the neighboring French Congo, the situation was much the same as the people were conscripted into forced labor to build railways causing the death of many and the decimation of the population by half.

In Southwest Africa under the Germans, the ***Hereros*** and the ***Namaqua*** peoples revolted after being reduced to penury when rinderpest that was probably introduced by the colonists destroyed the cattle on which their livelihood depended. The Germans' response was swift and brutal; those who escaped were forced into the arid Namibian desert where thousands perished. By the time the outcry from Europe caused the recall of the German commander, ***Lothar von Trotha (1848-1920),*** there were only twenty per cent of Hereros and fifty per cent of Namaqua people remaining in the realm. For his genocidal campaign, von Trotha got a medal of honor for devotion to the fatherland from the German Emperor, William II.

To assuage the feelings of Europeans and win public support, the colonial lobby resorted to propaganda of the worst kind, employing **social Darwinism** and perverting science **(scientism).** Native Africans were captured and exhibited in *"human zoos"* in European capitals and the United States and some were presented as the "missing link" between Apes and Man. The false appeal to perverted science obscured the racist and eugenic agenda of the colonial lobby and dulled the sense of outrage of the unsuspecting populace who went in droves to see human beings caged like animals usually nude or semi nude. Thus, sanitized by pseudo-science, the Scramble for Africa and colonialism became acceptable and was even considered philanthropic by some people.

The poet ***Rudyard Kipling (1865-1936),*** who was called the *"prophet of British imperialism"* belong to this group hence his poem *"The White Man's Burden"* in which he considered the colonized people devilish nitwits—*half-devil* and *half-child.*

Thankfully, there were voices of dissent and other poets replied Kipling with sensible poems of their own, ***H.T. Johnson*** with *"The Black Man's Burden*** and ***George McNeill*** with *"The Poor Man's Burden"*.

However, following the punitive invasion of the Benin Kingdom by Britain in 1897 and the discovery of the Benin Bronze sculptures, the racist pseudo scientists and anthropologists had to re-think their stereotypes about indigenous cultures. The kingdom's work of art were looted and sold to Museums in Europe.

The plunder and exploitation of Africa went on for decades and colonialism on the whole was in most cases slavery in another form. The case for civilization is debatable as many of the people groups had cultures much older and arguably more sophisticated in many respects than that of their colonizers.

African Initiated (Independent, Instituted, Indigenous) Churches—(AICs) [5, 6, 7, 8, 9, 10]

As the name implies, these are churches started by indigenous peoples in Africa and not by expatriate missionaries. The reasons for the evolution of AICs include: political, Scriptural and cultural.

Political

As colonialism took root in Africa, the relationship between some expatriate missionaries on the one hand and the local chiefs with the people on the other changed. Many missionaries were too cozy with colonists and colonial merchants with whom they worked to subvert the interests, hopes and aspirations of the natives. In addition, some missionaries were treating the natives as second class citizens by segregating white churches as happened in South Africa. There was also the pervasive practice of preventing the natives from leadership positions in the church. This was what led to the separation of the '**African Church**' from the **Anglican Communion** in Yorubaland in 1901. In doctrine and liturgy, it remains essentially Anglican but the hierarchy from inception was totally indigenous.

Scriptural/Doctrinal Viewpoints

Another bone of contention between expatriate missionaries and the indigenes was what has been described as ***"the Africans' natural spiritual views of reality as a cosmic spiritual battleground between good and evil"***.

Africans generally believe in demons, the fact that diseases can have spiritual causes and the fact that deliverance and cures can also be obtained through spiritual means. The western missionaries on the other hand, considered the belief in demons and witches as pagan and mere superstitions and trusted in hospitals for treating and curing diseases rather than exorcism and faith healing.

Although the African Christians' viewpoint was in close agreement with the biblical view, the western missionaries considered their own position as more "scientific and rational". Most expatriate Mission churches therefore had the triumvirate mission of preaching, teaching and 'healing' supported by building churches, schools and hospitals. Consequently, it has been alleged that the expatriate missionaries had been more interested in the African converts being more 'western than biblical'.

Culture

Some African cultural practices such as circumcision were retained by many converts but prohibited by the missionaries. This was the case in South Africa where even male circumcision was grounds for expulsion from the church although this was also a practice approved of in the Bible as pointed out by the natives.

The culture of polygamy, which was rife in Africa, also caused conflicts with the expatriate missionaries many of whom refused to give

Communion to polygamists. This was particularly serious as many of the paramount rulers of necessity were culturally expected to have many wives. The church's position on the issue meant that the local leaders were essentially excluded from communion, a serious issue in churches where communion is sacramental.

In due time, many converts became disillusioned and frustrated with the brand of Christianity being practiced by the western missionaries and fractures appeared within the Protestant Mission churches, with breakaway groups forming the **AICs.** These range from churches that mirrored the Mission churches to those that were practically African Traditional Religion in the garb of Christianity.

However, although the AICs 'share the basic cultural assumptions with traditional African culture about good and evil, most reject the practices of Traditional religions as evil'. These churches exist all over Africa but more numerous in Nigeria, Kenya and South Africa.

In Nigeria, many of the AICs were off-shoots of Anglican and Methodist churches which started as prayer groups. The first was the **Christ Apostolic Church** which started as a prayer group in 1918 during an influenza epidemic. The group believed in miracles, renounced the use of medicine whether native or western and rejected infant baptism. Eventually, they were forced to separate from the Anglican Communion due to irreconcilable doctrinal differences. Other groups like the **Cherubim and Seraphim** and the **Aladura** groups also separated between 1925 and 1930. Since these earlier AICs, there have been hundreds of others in Nigeria among which are **The Redeemed Christian Church of God, the Deeper Life Ministries, Mountain of Fire** and the **Winners' Chapel.**

In the Belgian Congo in 1921, Kimbangu, a Baptist catechist started a movement based on biblical teachings, miraculous healings and holy living. Although he was imprisoned by Belgian authorities for most of his life and died in prison, his movement survived and adherents of Kimbanguism run into millions today in the Democratic Republic of Congo.

COMMENT:
Many of these AICs are no longer 'African' in the real sense of the word as they have become international in outreach and are found in all continents of the world. While the idea of African initiated churches used to raise the spectre of syncretism, the areas of acculturation in beliefs and practice in most cases are totally scriptural and the Gospel and sound Christian doctrines are not compromised.

The lively worship style with music, drumming and dancing are in the realm of contextualization and not syncretism; and the belief in angels, demons and miracles are all scriptural. For the African, religion is not head knowledge of hair splitting philosophical theology but something that is relevant to every aspect of life. Therefore, rather than an intellectual approach to Christianity, Africans tend to be Pentecostal, believing in the power of God, Jesus Christ and the Holy Spirit to defeat evil. While African Christians believe in the after-life, they expect their faith to work for them also in the here and now.

While the Church everywhere must be on guard to avoid syncretism, acculturation in Christianity is not new. The early Church replaced many heathen worship days with Saints' Days and the celebrations of Christmas and Easter have burrowed a lot from non Christian festivals.

As of today, Christianity is growing faster in Africa than Europe and America where in fact it seems to be on the decline.

The Call for Africanized Christianity [11, 12, 13]

Christianity in Africa was affected by colonialism; therefore, with the struggles for Independence also came the call to **"Africanized Christianity"**. After Independence, there was a clamor for indigenization at every level, including the Church and Mission hierarchy. In addition, many sought to find ways of accommodating the African culture or even some aspects of the African religion within Christianity.

Foremost in this quest were the late Patriarch of the Nigerian Methodist Church, ***Bolaji Idowu (1913-1993),*** the late Ghanaian Presbyterian theologian, ***Kwame Bediako (1945-2008)*** and the Kenyan Anglican priest and theologian, ***John Mbiti (1931—)***. All averred that, before the advent of the western missionaries, Africans had a complete system of religion that touched every part of their lives. John Mbiti summed it up succinctly that—***"Missionaries did not bring God to Africa; rather it is God who brought the missionaries here"***. Kwame Bediako suggested that God revealed Himself to the African ancestors the same way He did to the Biblical patriarchs. Bediako felt that the Biblical teaching about angels and demons replaced the belief in non-human spirit divinities of African religions and suggested that, since ancestor veneration/worship is rife in African religions, there should be a ***"theology of ancestors"*** to explain the role of Jesus Christ who would then become the "Supreme Ancestor" and the ancestors become part of the "communion of saints".

These theologians advocated the development of an ***"African Theology"*** in the context of African culture and religions.

The idea of an African theology contextualized in African culture and religions was opposed by **Byang Kato (1936-1975)** of the Evangelical Churches of West Africa (ECWA). Kato warned of an incipient syncretism in the development of an 'African theology' and insisted that the Bible be held as the sole revelation for salvation and authority on legitimate Christian theology. He held that the proper understanding of the Gospel entail an exclusive approach to other religions. He rejected Mbiti's charge that the Church in Africa is without a distinct theology because it did not seriously engage with African culture. He believed that the issues of African traditions and beliefs like polygamy, family life, communal life and the afterlife can be adequately addressed by adhering to the tenet of ***Sola Scriptura.***

He argued that, fundamentally, the philosophies of African religions and culture are at variance with the Gospel and that to truly embrace Christianity requires a radical break from such philosophies. He posited that Christianity is not 'western theology' and that the Gospel is ***'acultural'***. He warned that attempts to 'domesticate' the Gospel will vitiate its integrity and that scriptural truths should not be sacrificed on the altar of ***'regional theology'***.

Although Kato, like the advocates of an African theology condemned the injustice of colonialism, apartheid in South Africa and racism in America at the time, he rejected the politicization of theology in dealing with political oppression and social injustice that is inherent in the **Black Liberation Theology** which he opined confused the fruit of salvation with the substance.

For his views, Kato was severely vilified by proponents of the African Christian theology across the Continent and accused of repudiating the African culture for the western, colonial culture.

In spite of the obvious syncretism in the so called African Christian theology, the mention of syncretism is still a taboo in the circle of advocates. At a recent lecture by John Mbiti on: **"The Dialogue between African Religion and Christianity"**, questions were raised about **"how to go beyond scholarly syncretism in religious studies"** and about **"the place of sin in African Traditional Religion and African theology** because Africans tend to have more of a concept of 'evil' rather than of sin".

Professor Mbiti's response, rendered verbatim here was very revealing. On the question of syncretism, he said: ***"I'm not happy about the use of the term syncretism. It is a one-sided term used by certain Christians*** *who think their version of Christianity is more faithful. If someone says they are a Christian, I'm satisfied with that. I'm not concerned whether it is syncretism, or Anglicanism, or African Independentaism . . . I'm just happy that Jesus is being proclaimed. I'm not going to take part in discussions about syncretism".*

On the question of sin in African Theology, he said: *"I don't like sin. In doing translation work, that word is very difficult to put into an African language. In translating into Kikamba, I almost had to put a related word in brackets. There are a few other words which are difficult to translate into an African language.*

COMMENT:

The professor's answers raised more questions than they tried to elucidate. For example, how can the Christian Gospel of Salvation, through Jesus Christ, be fully preached without the knowledge of what Sin is? How accurate can the theology of a Holy God be without an understanding of sinful humanity?

How does refusing to discuss legitimate concerns about syncretism advance the dialogue on the development an "African Christian Theology"? Did not Jesus Himself warn about putting new wine in old wine skin?—Mathew 9:16-17.

When Kwame Bediako suggested affirming the Africans' desire to connect with their dead ancestors in the Christian doctrine of the "Communion of Saints", obviously, a theological line was crossed.

The call by the advocates of an African Christian theology for the incorporation of such aspects of African religion as ancestor worship or veneration into Christianity or looking for Christian 'revelation' in African Traditional Religions has crossed the line into the realm of syncretism.

It would seem that what the developers of the 'African Christian Theology" are doing is trying to put the new wine of Christianity in the old skin of African Traditional Religion; it cannot work.

Byang Kato's warning about domesticating the Christian theology and the fact that the Gospel is acultural should be taken seriously by anyone concerned about real Christianity.

Trends in Europe [14, 15, 16, 17, 18]

The trend in Europe in the 19th and 20th centuries was influenced by the Age of Enlightenment, industrialization, scientific theories especially Darwinism and the development of liberal theology and it was generally a move away from religious observance to secularization of the society.

However, there were also revivals in many Protestant nations, for example in England where groups like the Holiness Movement and Higher Life Movement were formed in Keswick, Oxford and Brighton and in Scotland the Faith Mission. The period also witnessed Protestant missionary activities from Europe to other areas of the globe.

In the Protestant communities, the division between Arminianism and Calvinism continued to deepen and other groups like the Unitarians and Universalists emerged.

Protestant theology also witnessed the development of the so called Higher Biblical Criticism and Liberal theologies that embrace Deism and reject miracles.

The Catholic world and by extension much of Europe received a flurry of new dogmas out of **Vatican 1 Council (1869-1870)**. Some of the new dogmas included: **Papal Infallibility** and **Papal Supremacy** in certain situations and Marian **Immaculate Conception**.

The issue of papal infallibility caused a minor schism with the breakaway of the **See of Utrecht** from communion with Rome and entering into communion with the Anglicans. The schismatic group is also often referred to as the *"Old Catholic Church"*.

Because of the traditional alliance between the Church and the State, the Church is often treated with distrust in revolutions.

The upheaval of the French Revolution which began in the 18th century continued well into the 19th century and was mostly anti-clerical and anti-religion. The Church was also a target during the Spanish civil war (1936-1939). The Bolshevik Revolution of early 20th century in Russia was also anti-clerical and anti-religion and it eventually became a kind of State sponsored atheism which involved Eastern Europe as the region came under the sphere of influence of the Soviet Union.

The two World Wars and their aftermath also contributed to the de—Christianizing and secularizing trends in Europe.

The Trend in North America (United States and Canada) [19]

The arrival of Christianity in the United States of America was multi-denominational. Catholicism arrived with the Spanish conquistadors in the regions of Florida, Texas and California. Anglicanism, similar in liturgy to Catholicism, was brought by the early colonists who recognized the King of England as the head of the Church. Eastern Orthodoxy arrived in Alaska in the 18th century from Russia and the Congregationalists arrived at the Massachusetts Bay in 1620 establishing an independent theocratic congregation in Calvinistic tradition. The Puritans, also a breakaway group from the Anglican Communion landed in Plymouth, Massachusetts in 1649 and established a community based on the teachings of John Calvin and the New Testament and they founded Harvard, the first American College.

These were followed by Methodists from Great Britain who settled in the mid-Atlantic colonies of New Jersey, New York, Maryland, Pennsylvania and Virginia. The Lutherans from Germany, Norway, Sweden, Denmark and Finland settled on the East coast and the Midwest.

Presbyterians also came from the Swiss Reformation and also from England, Scotland and Ireland. Quakerism, founded by George Fox, an English preacher, was brought to America by William Penn, the founder of Pennsylvania.

Initially these were discrete national congregations, often with services being held in the native language until they became Americanized and similar communions became consolidated into synods or conferences and conventions.

From this mixed grill beginning, Christianity has evolved greatly along many tracks in America.

Evangelicalism [20, 21]

Evangelicalism is defined as: *'a Protestant Movement which emphasizes personal conversion and commitment to sharing the gospel'*. It has its roots in the reformation but became a recognized movement in the early 18th century following the Great Awakenings. Apart from personal conversion and sharing the gospel, adherents also subscribe to ***Biblical inerrancy, Biblical authority, the substitutionary death and resurrection of Jesus Christ***. These tenets have been summed up as: ***'Conversionism, activism, Biblicism and Crucicentricism'***.

Before, during and after the American civil war, evangelicals, who had become the leading Christian sects as a result of the Awakenings, impacted the United States socially and politically through the various reforms such as the ***abolitionist*** and the ***temperance*** movements. However, after the war, with increasing urbanization, industrialization and increase in non Protestant immigrants, the influence of the evangelicals began to wane. The greatest challenge to Evangelicalism however was the rise of Liberal Theology in the late 19th century.

Liberal Theology and Liberal Christianity [22, 23]

Liberal Theology has its roots in the Age of Enlightenment and the subsequent enthronement of Reason. Although Liberal theology is not based on any unifying creed or dogma, certain characteristics are commonly found among adherents.

In Liberal Theology:
- The teachings of Jesus Christ, devoid of what is considered the pagan and cultic traditions such as the belief in miracles or the supernatural, as standards for civilization is the lynch-pin of Liberal Theology.
- The Bible is regarded as an "anthology of human beliefs and feelings about God at the time of writing and written within a historical and cultural context rather than factual statements or truth propositions".
- The inerrancy of the Bible is denied and the authorship of most texts is rejected.
- *The Virgin birth, substitutionary death and the bodily resurrection of Jesus Christ are denied and belief in the reality of the events generally regarded as unnecessary.*
- Prophets are regarded as speaking only for their generations and the truthfulness of futuristic prophesies is denied.
- The reality of hell is denied.

Liberal theology infiltrated the mainline Protestant churches in the late 19th and early 20th century and resulted in the development of the *Social Gospel Movements* which was an attempt to apply Christian ethics in solving social problems. The advocates of Social Gospel were predominantly post-millennialists who believed in making the earth socially suitable for Christ's return. Therefore, reforms were proposed to address racial inequalities, labor issues, crimes, slums and poor schools.

In the Catholic Church, the influence of Liberal Christianity led to the development of the *Liberation Theology* and its various forms such as the *Black Liberation Theology.*

The introduction of Liberal theology into the mainline Protestant churches created crises within many resulting in the *Fundamentalist Movements* to counter the influence of liberalism.

Many critics of Liberal Christianity wonder if it can be designated "Christian" at all.

J. Gresham Machen said: *"It may appear that what the liberal theologians has retained after abandoning to the enemy one Christian doctrine after another is not Christianity at all but a religion which is so different from Christianity as to belong in a distinct category".*

Fundamentalism [24, 25, 26, 27, 28]

Fundamentalism began as an organized movement within Protestant Churches especially Baptists and Presbyterians in reaction to the influence of liberal theology on the mainline Protestant churches in the late 19th and early 20th century.

Fundamentalists spiritedly defended what they considered the *"Fundamentals of the Christian faith"* namely: **the virgin birth, Biblical inerrancy, sola Scriptura, substitutionary atonement, bodily resurrection and the second coming of Christ**.

The basics of Fundamentalism were first developed at the Presbyterian Princeton Theological Seminary and were espoused by other Protestant churches. Many also subscribe to *"Dispensationalism"*, a theological concept of progressive revelation from the Old Testament through to the New Testament and the End-Times popularized by *John Nelson Darby* of the *Plymouth Brethren Movement—(An Anglo-Irish movement which started in Dublin in 1827 and spread to the British Isles by people who were tired of religious sectarianism and who sought to promote a non-denominational, non-hierarchical and non-dogmatic/creedal fellowship among Christians. They were believers in Dispensationalism, priesthood of all believers, ceasationism, eternal security of true Christians and pre-tribulation, pre-millennial eschatology).*

With the financial support provided by the '*Stewart Brothers*' in 1909, and using the *Scofield's Reference Bible* which was heavy on Dispensationalism, the essence of fundamentalism was compiled by dozens of theologians and scholars in twelve booklets called *"The Fundamentals"* between 1910 and 1915. Three million copies of the booklets were reportedly freely distributed.

In the 1920s they also opposed the teaching of Darwinism in schools believing that it has an erosive effect on the moral fabric of the society by justifying hegemony and the crushing of the weak by the strong through its concept of the "survival of the fittest".

The opposition of Fundamentalists to Darwin's theory of evolution was epitomized by the *"Scopes Trial"* of 1925 in which a teacher was prosecuted for teaching evolution at a school in Tennessee. The media, which nationally sensationalized the trial, portrayed the Fundamentalists as conservative, narrow-minded, separatist and obscurantist, in short, hicks and jerks. On the other hand, the Liberal Christians were considered scientific, educated and tolerant.

Although Fundamentalists won the case from the standpoint of the law, the fundamentalist label suffered and became pejorative.

In the 1960s, Fundamentalists developed the *"Creation Science"* and pushed to have it taught as a counter-point to the theory of evolution but the move was opposed by the *"Scientific Community"* and its teaching declared unconstitutional by the United States Supreme Court in 1987.

Fundamentalists became more political in the latter half of the 20th century following the United States Supreme Court rulings prohibiting prayers and bible reading in public schools in 1962 and 1963 respectively.

The political groups include *"The Moral Majority"* started by **Jerry Falwell,** the *"Christian Voice"* by **Robert Grant** and *"The Christian Coalition"* and the *"Family Research Council"* by **James Dobson**. They all constitute a bloc for political influence.

Neo-Evangelicalism [29, 30, 31, 32]

Neo-evangelicalism started towards the middle of the 20th century as a breakaway group from Fundamentalism as a result of controversies between Protestant fundamentalists and Protestant liberals on doctrinal issues of: the historicity of the Bible, biblical inerrancy, the deity of Christ, His virgin birth, His bodily resurrection, the Second Advent, and creationism versus evolution.

Dr. Harold Ockenga (1905-1985), born in Chicago to Methodist parents, was one of the leading figures at the inception of the movement; others are scholars like **Drs. Donald Barnhouse, Edward Carnell, Carl Henry and Evangelist Dr. Billy Graham**.

Neo-evangelicals sought to reform what they considered the anti-intellectual tendencies of Fundamentalism and therefore rejected separatism and embraced social, cultural and political involvement.

Doctrinally, the position of neo-evangelicals has been described as: **Dialogue, Intellectualism, Non-judgmentalism and Appeasement.**

Therefore, they are considered to be characterized by:

I. Lower view of the Scripture—that is they espouse the so called *'Higher Biblical Criticism'* and tolerate questionable views of Scripture.
II. Acceptance as reliable, the "learned opinions" of "experts" in Biblical interpretation for the determination of reliable revelation.
III. Open, inclusive spirit towards liberalism and in the name of ecumenical peace, de-emphasize real doctrinal differences. They also try to Christianize pagan ideas.
IV. Belief in the authority of science and willingness to make Scriptural truths subservient to it.
V. Ecumenism in evangelism and cooperation with every shade of doctrine including questionable ones.
VI. Espousal of Social gospel and attempt to water down Biblical truths in order to make it acceptable to the world rather than make the gospel applicable to the world.
VII. Compromise and the preaching of "positive messages" and platitudes with the excuse that the important mission was to win souls and not criticize others. Therefore, God's love is preached while his justice, judgment and holiness are suppressed or ignored so as to make the gospel more attractive and non-threatening.
VIII. Growing appeasement through the acceptance of the ways of the world and methods such as music, theater, fiction, sports, etc.
IX. "Christian Activism" and emphasis on social justice; also encourage political involvement with a view to Christianizing the society through cultural influence rather real spiritual transformation.
X. Reliance on psychology and psychotherapy and promoting these rather than a Biblical perspective of life.
XI. A critical and intolerant attitude towards fundamentalists whom they regard as hypocritical, anti-intellectual, obscurantist and unloving.

Neo-evangelicalism has been described as:
"A movement born of compromise, nurtured on the pride of intellect, growing on the appeasement of evil, and doomed by the judgment of the Word of God".—William Ashbrook.

* * *

"A movement with a new mood (toleration of false teachers, ridicule of fundamentalists), with a new method (the end justifies the means), a new theology (questioning the Canon of the Bible, its inerrant authority and the nature of its content), and a new ethics (repudiation of personal separation for interaction with culture)—following a downward path of toleration of error, accommodation of error, cooperation with error, contamination by error and capitulation to error"—Charles Woodbridge

* * *

A movement that*: ". . . lacks moral courage in the face of the great conflict with apostasy. It lacks doctrinal clarity in important areas of theology. It makes unwarranted concessions to the enemies of the Cross of Christ".—Ernest Pickering*

* * *

"Neo-evangelicalism is a religious philosophy. It attempts to minister to man through his felt needs. It seeks to commend man for his achievements and re-align his energies for good. It emphasizes unity at the expense of truth and reduces the Biblical requirements of purity and separation unto God until they are obscure. Man and his present circumstances rather than God and His eternal precepts are the core of its concern".—Francis Stiles.

The Holiness Movement [33, 34, 35, 36, 37]

The Holiness Movement was an offshoot of Methodism based on John Wesley's doctrine of *"Christian Perfection"* (a belief in the possibility of the attainment of a high degree of virtue and entire sanctification with the help of divine 'sanctifying grace'). By Christian Perfection, Wesley is understood as not saying freedom from temptations or the possibility of involuntary transgressions, therefore, the Christian is still required to continue to pray for forgiveness and holiness. He also did not teach *"salvation by perfection"* but *"perfection as a result of salvation"*. Therefore, *"perfection"*, to Wesley was not *'the inability to sin'* but rather *'choosing not to sin'* as a consequence of a changed life, freedom from pride, impure intentions and willful disobedience against God. He also did not consider it as a permanent state—2Corinthians 10:12.

The Holiness Movement was a response to the decline of Wesleyan holiness in the Methodist Church as 'unconverted people', some say **Freemasons**, crept into leadership positions in the church. The Holiness Movement therefore endeavored to promote a Christianity that is personal, life changing, committed to a consecrated lifestyle and revivalist.

The key beliefs include:
- Regeneration by grace through faith and the assurance of salvation by the witness of the Holy Spirit being the first work of grace.
- The second work of grace, which is "entire sanctification", enables the believer to live a holy life free of willful sin. The second work of grace is dependent of the first without which it is impossible.

Holiness Movement members reject antinomianism and hold that God's moral laws are still pertinent for successive generations.

In the Holiness tradition, the Church is a spiritual communion of the saved and sanctified.

The movement was launched in 1867 at the National Holiness Camp Meeting Association. Prominent among the founders was **Phoebe Palmer (1807-1874)** whose house fellowship was the earliest nucleus for the movement. While the earlier frontier revival camp meetings focused on the conversion experience, the Holiness Movement moved beyond conversion to providing avenues for nurturing the converts' faith through religious education towards spiritual renewal and sanctification.

The Movement was opposed by the leadership of the Methodist Church and this led to the schism of the Holiness churches but it spread to other denominations like the Quakers and the Salvation Army.

Notable persons who were involved were D.L. Moody, Oswald Chambers and Hannah Whithall Smith.

There were many objections and controversies surrounding the Movement. On the creedal front were those who contest the issues of:
- Instantaneous versus progressive maturity in personal holiness
- Eradication versus retention of the sinful nature

- And the validity of the second grace for sanctification separate from the grace that effected salvation.

According to **Keith Drury**, a pastor of one of the Holiness churches, the Holiness churches have for the most part abandoned the Holiness Movement. Lamenting the trend in Holiness churches, Drury identified the reasons the Movement is to all intent and purposes dead. He said:
- The members craved to be 'normal' so as to 'fit in' and be accepted and respectable.
- They dropped the 'holiness tag and label and got assimilated into evangelicalism
- They gave up the preaching of holiness consistently and with urgency and substituted optional holiness for entire sanctification.
- The leaders became elitist by ditching regular lay people committed to holiness in favor of the uncommitted educated people.
- The leaders got swept into the "Church Growth Movement" which considers holiness as of secondary importance and as a result 'have accommodated too much to the world in order to win the world'.
- That **"people oozed"** into the church without ever being **saved**, that '**accepting Christ**' replaced **repentance**, **sinners** were branded **seekers**, **absolutes** traded for **options** and **theology** for **therapy**. As a result of the *"non-conversion"* conversion models, *transformational conversion* is replaced with *assimilation evangelism*.

Therefore, there is no difference between the world and Christians in vices and crimes.

Pentecostalism [38, 39, 40, 41, 42]

Pentecostalism began in the United States at the beginning of the 20th century. It has its roots in disparate small groups in the Holiness and Higher-life Movements who had been preaching and teaching on the gifts of the Holy Spirit and divine healing.

The fore-runners were people like preacher, theologian and founder of the Christian and Missionary Alliance, A.B. Simpson who experienced divine healing for a chronic illness; the founder of the Christian Catholic Apostolic Church, John Alexander Dowie, Evangelist Mariah Woodworth Etter and others.

Pentecostalism became a popular movement through the ministry of **Charles Parham** who in 1901 was teaching (even before he had the experience) the gift of speaking in tongues as the sign of the baptism of the Holy Spirit at his non-denominational Bethel Bible School in Topeka, Kansas. One of the students, Agnes Ozman, after being prayed for by the others, spoke in tongues. The effect at the school was electrifying and the event soon became widely advertised as many more had the experience.

In 1905, Parham extended the ministry to Houston, Texas and admitted into his school an African-American student minister—**William Seymour**—who was willing to learn about the new spiritual experience despite the indignity of having to sit in the hallway, apart from the white students, and listen through the window as dictated by the segregation law.

In 1906, William Seymour was invited to a Holiness church in Los Angeles that was in need of a preacher. In his first sermon, he mentioned speaking in tongues as a sign of the baptism of the Holy Spirit and had the door of the church locked against him. He continued to meet with a small group in the home of a member who was receptive to his message and soon the group had to move to a ramshackle warehouse in Azusa Street.

In Azusa Street, the congregation exploded as people heard about the nature of the worship services there which were characterized by speaking in tongues, supernatural healings, and significant lifestyle changes in the members. The church attracted real seekers across denominational lines as well as critics from far and wide.

The secular media and the theologians disparaged the church members of what was considered outrageous emotional displays. Some Christians accused them of being hyper-emotional and focusing more on the Holy Spirit than on Jesus Christ. The members were called epithets like *"Holy Rollers", "Holy Jumpers"* and *"Tangled Tonguers"*.

Nonetheless, the movement spread quickly in the United States as visiting pastors carried the experience back to their congregations. While many considered the multiracial non-denominational congregation a clear evidence of the workings of the Holy Spirit and a true revival, many 'orthodox' Christians were appalled.

Surprisingly, this included **Charles Parham,** William Seymour's erstwhile teacher in Houston, allegedly a Klu Klux Klan (KKK) sympathizer who criticized the free racial mixing and the ecstatic nature of the worship services at Azusa Street. Eventually the two fell out, parted ways, and Pentecostalism went into schism virtually at birth.

Parham's group went on to form essentially *"The Assemblies of God Church"* while the Azusa Street revival gave rise to *"The Apostolic Faith Mission";* others include the United Pentecostal Church and Pentecostal Church of God.

From the Azusa Street Revival also evolved ethnic Pentecostal movements like the "Italian Pentecostal Mission" and the "Spanish Apostolic Faith Mission". Pentecostalism was ignited around the world by missionaries from the church, reaching about fifty nations within two years. Today, the Pentecostal movement is the fastest growing brand of Christianity and is second only to the Roman Catholic Church with a membership of about half a billion worldwide.

The newer movements include the **Word of Faith**, the **Positive Confession** and **Laughter Revival**. These are dubbed by critics as the *"Health and Wealth"*, *"Prosperity"* or the *"Name it Claim it"* gospel represented by people like **Kenneth Hagin, Kenneth Copeland** and **Charles Capps etc**.

The Pentecostal movements have been dogged by racism, divisiveness, and allegations of fraud, occultic mysticism and sexual scandals.

Pentecostalism has sipped into mainline denominations including the Roman Catholic Church as the **Charismatic Movement.**

The four core beliefs of Pentecostals (the four-square) are:
- Salvation by Jesus Christ according to *John 3:16*
- Baptism with the Holy Spirit according to *Acts 2:4*, separate from the salvation experience.
- Bodily healing by Jesus Christ according to *James 5:15*
- The return of Jesus to take the redeemed according to *1Thessalonians 4:16-17.*

Pentecostals are generally Arminian theologically, believing in salvation by grace through faith and literal heaven and hell for those who accept God's gift of salvation and those who reject it respectively.

Like all evangelicals, Pentecostals subscribe to the divine inspiration and inerrancy of Scriptures but unlike them reject *cessationalism* in regards to the 'Gifts of the Holy Spirit'. Therefore they believe that the gifts of the Holy Spirit like speaking in other/unknown tongues, prophecy, interpretation of tongues, healings etc are as relevant today as they were during the apostolic era. Most Pentecostals hold that the baptism of the Holy Spirit follows after salvation and not an experience necessary for salvation except the **"Oneness Pentecostals"** who believe that it is an integral part of the process of salvation.

Pentecostals, except the Oneness branch, also observe the ordinances of Believer's baptism and the Lord's Supper but do not believe they have any sacerdotal significance.

Pentecostals have a tradition of ordaining women and having them in other positions of authority in the church unlike most mainline denominations.

Charismatic Renewal Movement [43, 44, 45, 46]

The Charismatic Renewal Movement is a trans-denominational movement which started in the 1960s. It involves the adoption of the beliefs and practices similar to those of Pentecostals in regard to the baptism of the Holy Spirit within the mainline Protestant, the Roman Catholic and the Orthodox Churches.

This development could have been midwifed, at least in part, by the non-denominational *Full Gospel Business Men's Fellowship International* launched by **Demos Shakarian**, a millionaire business man in 1951. The purpose of the movement was the spreading of the Pentecostal message of tongues and healing across sectarian lines through business luncheons and breakfasts.

Doctrinally, Charismatics believe:
- The necessity of a personal encounter with Jesus Christ as a prelude to the Spirit baptism.
- That the Spirit baptism empowers for victorious Christian living
- That worship and prayer are enhanced by the baptism of the Holy Spirit.
- That the gifts of the Spirit are meant for today
- That the Bible is the source of divine revelation and that those baptized by the Spirit have a deeper revelation of biblical truths.
- That evangelism is more effective with the baptism of the Holy Spirit.

The main difference between Pentecostals and Charismatics is that many of the latter do not regard speaking in tongues as the necessary sign of the baptism in the Holy Spirit.

There was also what was called the third wave of Pentecostalism which started in the 1980s epitomized by the "*Vineyard Churches*" started by **John Wimber** (1934-1997).

In addition to beliefs like other Charismatics, Vineyard adherents also believe:
- That signs and wonders are essential for effective evangelism especially among the "primitive" people and therefore expounded the idea of ***"Power Evangelism"*** and ***"Dominion theology"***.
- In spiritual warfare and the possibility of demon possession or oppression of Christians
- That an illness can be caused by the state of the mind, Satan and demons and therefore practice "psychic healing" and exorcism.
- That Christians should be able to do what Jesus Christ did while on earth.

Dispensationalists who also subscribe to cessationalism generally condemn all forms of Pentecostalism and feel:
- That the concept of the baptism of the Holy Spirit as an experience separate from conversion is scripturally and theologically erroneous because: (i) "the bible says there is only one baptism, (ii) Pentecost was an historical event not intended for continuation, (iii) the signs and wonders performed by Jesus and the Apostles was meant to validate their offices and not meant to continue beyond the transitional period.
- That "Pentecostals and Charismatics are trading the birthright of the Holy Scripture for a bowl of pottage named experience".
- That lasting faith does not require signs and wonders to validate God's truth and that it is the flesh that desire signs.
- That the sign gifts of the Holy Spirit like speaking in tongues, prophesy, healings and miracles were temporary and had ceased therefore it is heretical of Pentecostals and Charismatics to claim that they are meant for today.
- That the miracles claimed by Pentecostals and Charismatics are usually exaggerated, that real physical ailments were hardly ever cured and sometimes claims are frankly fraudulent.
- Charismatics foster and encourage worldliness in speech, dress, music, sport etc to entertain members and attract the lost rather than promote holiness.

Specific Charismatics like John Wimber were accused of:
- Reliance on psychological "methods" and experimentation.
- Being influenced by Morton Kelsey, a non Christian who compared Jesus to a witchdoctor and Agnes Sanford, a psychic healer.

- Downgrading the divinity of Jesus Christ to justify his failure to perform real signs and wonders
- Claiming to hear messages from God, and
- Of seeing demons behind every physical and emotional illness.

Perhaps the most acerbic criticism of Pentecostalism and Charismaticism was by ***John MacArthur***, a Reformed Church pastor who likened both movements to the deadly disease, the Acquired Immune Deficiency Syndrome—"AIDS". He alleged that both destroyed the Church's immune system and make her susceptible to 'theological diseases" being unable to ward off doctrinal errors.

COMMENT:

The doctrine of the Baptism of the Holy Spirit (BHS) is a major controversy in contemporary Church. All sides of the issue feel very passionate about their positions and what is intended to unite Christians has been made one of the biggest divisive issues of our day.

Considering all sides and angles of the controversy, the Holy Spirit has become like the *"Elephant in the room"* among blind people who are feeling different parts of it and insisting that the part they hold is the whole or some not even getting near the elephant and insisting it was not in the room at all. All sides of the argument quote the Bible to support their positions but it is obvious that in many cases, texts are interpreted to suit previously held positions through speculations and generalizations; and sometimes, Creeds are appealed to in support of positions rather than scripture.

What are the facts, as presented in the Bible regarding the Holy Spirit?

To answer this question, the questions that have given rise to the main quibbles will be considered and scriptural answers sought which will hopefully clear some of the fogs in the controversy.

1) **Is the Baptism of the Holy Spirit merely an historical event or is it relevant for today?**

The most ardent opponents of the BHS believe that it was a unique historic event that fulfilled the prophecy of the prophet Joel mentioned by Peter in *Acts 2:16-21* on the day of Pentecost to explain what happened that day. To them, Pentecost signified the birth of the Church and therefore can never be repeated.

A careful look at some of the Scripture advanced to support this position and others do not support the idea of BHS as simply a historic event marking the birth of the Church.

First, Joel's prophecy, according to Peter spoke of the "Last days" and not just a single day—*Acts 2:17*. It is generally believed that the "Last days" refer to the 'End Times', before the second coming of Jesus Christ; and since He has not retuned, the contemporary Church fits within the frame of the fulfillment of the prophecy and therefore the promised outpouring of the Spirit is relevant for today.

2) **If it is relevant for today, is it a separate post conversion event or obtained at conversion or with water baptism?**

While there is general agreement on the need for the Holy Spirit, there is controversy about how and when a believer receives Him. i) Some are of the opinion that since conversion itself requires the work of the Holy Spirit, anyone who believes already has the Holy Spirit and does not need another experience. ii) Some believe that the Holy Spirit enters the believer at the time of water baptism because the Spirit descended on Jesus Christ at His baptism—*Mathew 3:13-17*. iii) Some hold that BHS is a separate and distinct event subsequent to conversion.

While all acknowledge the work of the Holy Spirit in conversion, careful examination of the evidence from scriptures suggest that the baptism of the Spirit is a separate, post conversion event.

- Jesus Christ said that to "enter the kingdom of God", it is necessary to be born of <u>water</u> and of the <u>Spirit</u>. If water baptism automatically confers the Spirit, Jesus would not have emphasized the need for the two baptisms—*John 3:5.*
- Jesus told the disciples before His ascension that though they had received water baptism, they would receive the baptism of the Holy Sprit—*Acts 1:4-5.*
- John the Baptist who offered water baptism to converts stressed the importance of the baptism of the Holy Spirit which he said would occur through Jesus Christ—*Mathew 3:11*
- The Samaritan believers had water baptism in the Name of Jesus and yet did not receive the baptism of the Holy Spirit until Peter and John prayed for them and laid hands on them—*Acts 8:14-17.*

It has been suggested by some that the Samaritans did not receive the Holy Spirit baptism at conversion or water baptism because Philip was not an Apostle and therefore did not possess the "sign of an Apostle". However, In Acts 9, Ananias, a disciple, who was not an Apostle was sent to Paul (then Saul) to restore his sight and fill him with the Holy Spirit—*Acts 9:(17)1-18.*

Others have tried to explain why the Samaritan converts did not receive the Holy Spirit when they believed and were baptized by suggesting that somehow this was to let the Samaritans know that the Apostles, though Jews, were the authoritative leaders. The Samaritans knew that Jesus was a Jew and that Philip who evangelized them was also a Jew, yet they listened and were converted including even a magician.

The idea that God withheld the Holy Spirit from the Samaritans to affirm the Apostles and make a historical point is highly speculative and preposterous.

In *Acts 19:1-7*, the account of another set of disciples (believers) who had had John's baptism and had never even heard of the baptism of the Holy Spirit was given. Opponents of a separate baptism of the Spirit said they were not believers in Jesus, but then Paul called them disciples. What this encounter shows is that during the apostolic era, it is expected that converts be baptized in the Holy Spirit as a separate event or Paul's question would not have arisen or Peter and John raise the issue with the Samaritan converts.

- In *Acts 10*, Cornelius, a devout gentile centurion who feared God was instructed by an angel to send for Peter to help him straighten out his theology. Peter who had also had a vision was instructed to oblige the centurion and while he was speaking to his household, they were baptized with the Holy Spirit. There was no laying-on of hands and they had not been baptized with water. This showed that no importance could be attached to laying-on of hands, though it is sometimes associated and that it is not associated with water baptism either.

3) **Is 'speaking in tongues' the <u>sine qua non</u> sign of the Baptism of the Holy Spirit?**

In *Acts 2, 10 and 19*, it was recorded that those baptized with the Holy Spirit spoke in tongues. In addition, they prophesied; In Acts *2:4*, is written: "they began to speak with other tongues as the Spirit gave them utterance" and *Acts 2:11* says "... we do hear them speak in our tongues <u>the wonderful works of God</u>".

Acts 10:43-46 recounted that "... the Holy Spirit fell on them which heard the Word ... for they heard them speak with tongues and magnify God".

In *Acts 19:6,* it is written: "And when Paul laid hands on them, the Holy Spirit came upon them and they spoke with tongues and prophesied".

In the Old Testament, one of the commonest sign of the Holy Spirit coming on people and Prophets is that they prophesied. In *Numbers 11*, Moses was instructed to choose seventy elders among the people to share the burden of leadership and God promised that He would put His Spirit on them. On that occasion, two of the elders who were in the camp and not even at the Tabernacle also received the Spirit and prophesied in the camp—*Numbers 11:24-26*. Joshua felt that it was inappropriate for the two to prophesy in the camp and asked that they be stopped but

Moses declined and said he wished all the people were prophets filled with God's Spirit—*Numbers 11:27-29*. Joel echoed Moses and prophesied that God would do just that—"pour out His Spirit on all flesh . . ." in the "Last Days"—*Joel 2:28.*

King Saul prophesied when the Spirit of God came upon him—*1Samuel 10:10-11; 1Samuel 19:22-24*.

Moreover, in *1Corinthians 12*, Paul expounded on the gifts of the Spirit and made it clear that speaking in Tongues was one of them but that not everyone had the gift.

Therefore, contrary to the position of Pentecostals, Speaking in Tongues is not the sine qua non sign for the Baptism of the Holy Spirit.

However, it would appear that something has to signify the Baptism of the Holy Spirit—either prophesying or speaking in Tongues—to mark the moment of baptism, but may not necessarily continuing as a gift.

In the book of Numbers, it was recorded that the elders prophesied when the Spirit came on them but they never prophesied again—*Numbers 11:25*. Also, King Saul prophesied only on occasions when the Spirit came upon him but was never a prophet in the real sense of the word.

4) **What are the "Gifts / Manifestations of the Holy Spirit?**

Three texts—*Romans 12:4-8; 1Corinthians 12:7-11, 28 and Ephesians 4:11*—dealt with the gifts of the Spirit which include: Word of Wisdom, Word of Knowledge, faith, gifts of Healings, working of Miracles, Prophecy, Discerning of Spirits, different kinds of Tongues, Interpretation of tongues, Apostles, Prophets, evangelists, pastors, teachers, Helps and Administrations.

5) **What are the purposes of the Gifts of the Holy Spirit?**

The purposes of the gifts of the Spirit are given in *Ephesians 4:12-14* as:
- The equipping of the saints (believers)
- The work of ministry
- The edification of the Body of Christ (the Church)
- The unification of faith
- The attainment of the knowledge of the Son of God (Jesus Christ)
- The maturity of believers in Christ
- The grounding of believers in sound doctrine

6) **Are some gifts of the Holy Spirit meant to be temporary and therefore not relevant for today?**

Because for centuries, the manifestations of the Holy Spirit were suppressed in the Church, many have advanced the idea that some of the gifts were temporary and meant only for the transition period of the apostolic era. Critics of Pentecostalism have also maintained that what happened at Pentecost to the

Apostles was a historic event and that gifts such as speaking in tongues, healings, miracles, prophets and apostles ceased with the death of the apostles and the completion of the canons of the Bible.

The *ceasationist* position is held by many mainline Fundamentalist denominations but most rigidly by the Reformed Calvinist tradition. Their position is predicated on:

- The fact that Pentecostal and Charismatic tongues are usually 'unintelligible' languages but rather what they consider "gibberish" not recognizable by linguists. In addition, that in *1Corinthians 13:8-12* Paul affirmed that prophecy, and tongues will cease.
- Difficulty in authenticating the healings and miracles claims of modern day Pentecostals and Charismatics.
- The fact that the baptism of the Holy Spirit did not feature prominently in the teachings of the Church for several centuries.

The issue of the baptism of the Holy Spirit as a historic event has been dealt with in part. It was claimed that tongues by Pentecostals and Charismatics are unbiblical because they are unintelligible and that when Paul spoke about "the tongue of angels"—*1Corinthians 13:1*, he was speaking subjunctively.
However:

- Paul did say that those speaking in tongues are "speaking mysteries to God and not men"; that they are "praying in the Spirit and edifying themselves" but not the church especially if speaking in public without interpretation—*1Corinthians 14:2, 4, 14.* This suggests that people could speak in tongues that are quite unintelligible to the hearers but quite meaningful and acceptable to God. Therefore recognition by linguists is immaterial.
- Paul actually affirmed speaking in tongues; he resolved to pray and sing in the Spirit and he thanked God that he spoke in tongues *more than* all in the Corinthian Church—*1Corinthians 14:15, 18.* He never said that he always interpreted when he spoke and sang in the Spirit, he did to worship God, period. In fact he warned the Corinthians not to forbid anyone from speaking in tongues—*1Corinthians 14:39.*
- As regards prophecy, the passage cited to buttress the claim of ceasation cannot refer to the completion of the canons as suggested but the time we shall see Jesus. It was important that Paul put everything in perspective for the Corinthians who seemed to be getting too caught up in the gifts of the Holy Spirit with some probably feeling they had the more important gifts etc. In *1Corinthians 12* where he emphasized the Church as a body

with every part as important to the whole, he gave the background to the conclusion in *1Corinthians 13:8-12.* In essence he was saying that no one with any particular gift knows it all and that full understanding will come only when we see our Lord and Savior. Then faith will become sight, all prophecies fulfilled, no need for tongues and partial knowledge will give way to full comprehension.

As to the fact that the baptism of the Holy Spirit and the gifts were not taught by the early Fathers or the Church for centuries; if this were to be the criterion for authenticity then many denominations today, including the most critical of Pentecostals would be considered unbiblical, null and void. This is because, until the sixteenth century, the idea of *sola fide* and *sola gracia* in regard to salvation were not taught either. Apart from this, the records of sects like the Montanists who in fact believed in the baptism of the Holy Spirit were wiped out by those who considered them heretics.

Finally, on healings and miracles which opponents of Pentecostalism said were only meant to validate Jesus and the Apostles during the transition period; does it seem reasonable, from utilitarian standpoint, that God would consider it necessary to validate Jesus Christ and the Apostles who lived with Him but consider it unnecessary for those of us who would come to learn of Him but not see Him physically?

What does the Bible say about signs and wonders and evangelism?

- Jesus, at the beginning of His ministry declared that the Spirit of the Lord was upon Him and that "*He was anointed to preach the gospel and <u>sent</u> to heal, proclaim liberty to captives, give sight to the blind and free the oppressed*—*Luke 4:18. In John 17:18 and John 20:21,* Jesus Christ told the assembled disciples (not just the apostles, in fact Thomas, an apostle was absent—*John 20:19-29*) that he was sending them just as the Father had sent Him.
- In several instances in the Bible, people believed because they saw the miracles—*John 2:11; John 11:45; John 12:10-11.*
- In *John 5:36-37; 10:25-26, 37—38 and 14:11*, Jesus called on the people and the disciples to believe Him based on the miracles He had performed and in fact said that those who disbelieved Him in spite of the fact that they had seen His works of miracle were guilty of sin on that account—*John 15:24.*
- In *Mark 16:17-18*, Jesus promised that signs will follow those who believe, that in His Name they will cast out demons, speak new tongues, heal the sick, etc.

- Jesus also said that "*anyone who believes in Him* will do what He did and *even greater works* because he was going to the Father"—*John 14:12*.
Could the problem be unbelief rather than ceasation of the gifts?
- Paul declared that his "preaching was not with enticing words of man's wisdom but in demonstration of the Spirit and of power—*1Corinthians 2:4.* Again in *1Thessalonians 1:5* he said: " . . . our gospel did not come to you in word only, but in power and in the Holy Spirit.
- The gospel was not meant to be preached without empowerment by the Holy Spirit. Jesus instructed the disciples to wait until they were empowered by the Spirit before attempting to be His witnesses—*Luke 24:49; Acts 1: 4-5, 8.*
- Jesus promised that the Father will send the Holy Spirit who will abide with believers and help, teach, remind, testify about Jesus, guide the believer, empower him and glorify Jesus—*John 14:16-17, 26; John 15:26; John 16:13.*
- Peter said the promise of the Holy Spirit is for all who repent, are baptized and who obey—*Acts 2:38-39; Acts 5:32*

To say that Christ would promise the Holy Spirit to all believers and yet empower only some at some point and not others when all are expected to be His witnesses defies rationality. If God gave the apostles and the early Church both the Word and the Power, why would He give subsequent believers only the Word and expect them to be as effective as the earlier Christians? The promise is: *"You shall receive power after the Holy Spirit has come upon you and you shall be my witnesses . . ."—Acts 1:8.*

It is clear that it is impossible to witness effectively without the empowerment by the Holy Spirit because Jesus Christ instructed the disciples to wait until filled with the Spirit before making any attempt to witness and they did.

The man born blind that Jesus healed demonstrated the power of experience, badgered by unbelieving scribes and Pharisees as to how he was healed and who healed him and whether or not his healer was a sinner or saint, the man stood firm on what he had experienced and said: *"Whether He is a sinner or not I do not know. One thing I know; though I was blind, now I see".*

No wind of doctrine could take away from him what he experienced.

The Church Growth (a.k.a Seeker Sensitive / Seeker Friendly) Movement [47, 48, 49, 50, 51, 52, 53, 54]

The Seeker Sensitive Church Growth Movement is considered by many as the modern mutant of the late 19th century Christian Liberalism spear-headed by ***Harry Fosdick (1878-1969)*** after passage through ***Norman Vincent Peale's (1898-1993)*** 'Positive Thinking' and ***Robert Schuler's (1926-**)*** 'Possibility Thinking'. Also cited in the founding of the Church Growth Movement is ***Donald McGavran (1897-1990),*** a missionary and son of missionaries to India who wrote the books—"The Bridges of God" and "How Churches Grow" in which he highlighted the social and economic barriers to evangelism in the Indian society. In 1965, he set up a School of World Missions at the Fuller Theological Seminary which later became an institution on Church Growth.

The Seeker-Friendly Church Growth Movement is a trans-denominational Movement. The pioneers and models are ***The Willow Creek Community Church*** founded in 1975 by ***Bill Hybels*** in Chicago and the ***Saddleback Valley Community Church***, Lake Forest, California, founded by ***Rick Warren*** in 1980.

- **The philosophy** of the Seeker Sensitive Church Growth Movement is that the numbers is an indicator of a healthy church; therefore all barriers that could prevent people from attending church must be removed. To this end, the church has to be made familiar, comfortable and acceptable to prospective attendees.
- **The goal** is the desire to reach the greatest number possible 'for Christ' by making Christianity contagious through innovative, culturally relevant means.
- **The strategies** to achieve this include:
- Market surveys of the neighborhood to find out demographics and the needs of the people
  - Church architecture that is neutral and not overly religious and without symbols; designed to have fixtures like Day-care or Adult-care centers, Fitness centers, Sports arenas, eateries etc.
  - Worship style that is non-threatening; that is short, pithy, anecdotal sermons, usually on self-help topics regarding jobs, family and interpersonal relationships in informal settings. The goal is to address the ***"felt needs"*** of the target population.
  - Positive, upbeat and motivational messages always and avoidance of words considered "offensive" to "seekers" such as sin, sinner, lost, unsaved, hell, suffering, Cross, etc and substitution of "seekers" or "unchurched" for sinners. No preaching on doctrines or theology on Sundays.

- Use of contemporary music like pop, rock, and rap instead of traditional hymns to satisfy an entertainment oriented culture. In addition using drama, movies and mimes.
- The dress code must be casual, no suits, ties, dress etc.
- Mid-week services for believers, mostly along same lines and small group meetings where doctrinal issues were supposedly handled.
- Support groups for addictions—Alcohol, narcotics, pornography, sex etc and for divorced, separated, family and friends of homosexuals, depression, eating disorders etc.
- Profession based ministries—doctors, lawyers, hairdressers etc

In the Seeker-Sensitive Movement, *"the church is not regarded as a 'religious meeting place' but a 'service agency' that exists to meet the needs of the audience"*. Therefore, as in the world's market place, the audience (consumer) is the most important, not the message; and the method takes precedence over theology.

It is believed that if the "unchurched" is brought to church and encouraged to stay, in time, they will come to trust Christ, therefore anonymity is promoted and no direct demands are made on the seekers.

Judging by the numbers, the Seeker-Friendly Movement was a huge success, not only had the models, the Willow Creek and Saddleback churches blossomed into mega-churches; they have helped spurn other mega-churches within and outside of the United States.

The Willow Creek Church formed an Association of affiliated churches in 1992 comprising over eleven thousand churches across about ninety denominations in forty-five countries. Through this Association and its annual leadership conferences, Willow Creek church has propagated its ideas around the world.

The Saddleback Valley Community church of Rick Warren has also propagated the Seeker-Sensitive ideas globally through his books, "The Purpose Driven Church" and "The Purpose Driven Life" and seminars for thousands of pastors annually. The two, by their numerical success have influenced mainline and other churches in America and around the world.

However, there have been many critics who have accused the advocates of the Seeker-Friendly methodology of:
- Minimizing and suppressing scriptural truth by characterizing them as "offensive".

- Being overly concerned about people's physical and emotional "felt needs" while neglecting their spiritual needs.
- Using corporate marketing strategies to produce a politically and culturally correct church.
- Providing solutions to worldly problems rather than salvation from sin
- Endangering the Gospel message with the method.
- Neutralizing the power of the Gospel Truth by trying to make it more palatable to the natural man.
- Conforming the church to the world to reach the world.
- "'Burger King'—(have it your way) Christianity".

After three decades of the Seeker-Friendly model, in spite of its ostensible success, it would seem that the critics were right.

Greg Hawkins, the executive pastor of the Willow Creek church conducted a survey of one thousand two hundred affiliated churches and two hundred and eighty thousand congregants in a project dubbed 'REVEAL'. The result of the survey confounded the leadership of the church and the whole idea of the Seeker-Friendly Movement. It was revealed that:

- The methods were not producing spiritually mature Christians
- Those who were already Christians or become Christians were not been ministered to in ways that help them grow.
- "Church activity is not a blueprint for spiritual growth"
- Some are dissatisfied with the church's role in their spiritual growth
- Many were stalled in their spiritual growth and some were leaving.
- Love for God and others is defined by relationship with Jesus Christ.

The study also revealed that the people, among other things, wanted to:
- Understand the Bible in greater depth
- Develop a closer personal relationship with Christ
- Be challenged to grow in faith

After agonizing over the results of the study, the church leadership decided to overhaul their practices and make major changes in their methods. They admitted that they had been mistaken!

They replaced the midweek service with Scripture reading, Bible teaching and prayers and dropped the policy of anonymity. They also developed a Survey tool to help congregants to assess and track their spiritual progress called **MAP**—which is supposed to help the congregant to **M**easure his or her spiritual reality, help them to take **A**ction on top priorities and track **P**rogress. The information was disseminated to members of the Willow Creek Association churches in seminars, CDs and through other media.

Many believe that the Emerging/Emergent Church Movement is a natural product of the Seeker-Sensitive Church Growth Movement and it would appear that some Seeker-Sensitive churches are evolving along the Emergent line. It is reported that Willow Creek Community church is partnering with mystics and teaching Catholic, Quaker and Eastern mystic methods of *lectio divina, quietism and mantras* respectively at its women fellowship.

COMMENT:

Although it is very important to take seriously Jesus Christ's charge to evangelize, usually called the 'Great Commission', it is also important to approach it according to the principle that He (Jesus Christ) laid down.

The Seeker-Sensitive Movement's approach can only be characterized as "zeal without knowledge".

First, the Bible tells us that *"All Scripture is inspired by God and useful for doctrine, for reproof, for correction and for instruction in righteousness"*—**2Timothy 3:16.** It is therefore sacrilegious to deem some Biblical words which accurately describe the state of the unregenerate man and the Cross and all that pertains to it, by which it pleased the Almighty to bring redemption to a lost world as "offensive".

Second, the 'Emergers' demonstrated a lack of understanding of the "Church" and her relationship with the world. The Church is not something you do, the Church is the congregation of believers—the "Body of Christ", and there are clear guidelines as to how to be a part of that body. For Emergers to think that attracting people to meet in a building by worldly means is growing the Church is a tragic misunderstanding. Tragic because it has eternal consequences as the hordes of people who thought they were Christians by the Seeker-Sensitive Movement methods actually aren't according to the Scripture and were being deceived.

Thirdly, the idea of making the Church culture compliant to "grow the Church" also flies in the face of Scripture which clearly taught separation from the world. Jesus stated several times that Christians are not of the world and the Church is actually those "called out" of the world. To develop a system that blurs the line between the church and the world, or bring the world into the church, goes against Christ's instructions. It is true that Christ socialized with people considered sinners but he never condoned or excused sin; He never put gloss over sin, he preached repentance and urged all to sin no more. The way of the master is simple—"And I if I be lifted up . . . will draw all men unto me"—**John 12:32.**

The danger with the SSM is that changing the method while at the same time neglecting or suppressing core doctrinal truths and values eventually led to significant change of the message.

It was really not surprising but sad, that after three decades, the Willow Creek Community church found out they had been wrong. It is hard to ignore or reject the manufacturer's instructions and expect the machine to function optimally or the product to be perfect.

The Emerging (Emergent) Church Movement [55, 56, 57, 58, 59, 60, 61]

The Emerging Church Movement (ECM) is a trans-denominational movement that began in the late 20th century and early 21st century by those who were disgruntled about the organized/institutional churches.

The ECM is difficult to define because there are a spectrum of beliefs and practices among adherents. A humorous sketch of the movement is giving thus:

Emergents or Emergers:

Description	Meaning
- Confess their faith like Mainliners	- Publicly declare what they don't really believe.
- Drink like Southern Baptists	- They are teetotalers when judicious
- Talk like Catholics	- Curse and use naughty words
- Evangelize and theologize like Reformers	- Rarely evangelize yet theologize all the time
- Worship like Charismatics	- That is emotionally with whole bodies
- Vote like Episcopalians	- They are left of the political spectrum
- Deny the Truth	- They are students of ***Derrida***, the apostle of Deconstruction

The philosophy of the Emerging Church Movement (ECM) is *"Deconstruction"—(that is dismantling and re-construction)*—of Christian worship, evangelism and the nature of Christian community and to radically redefine and re-invent Christianity.

The goal of the ECM is the transformation of the secular society through the imitation of Jesus Christ based on the Emerging church's 'trinity' of Worship, Mission and Communion. It seeks to remove divisions by blending, through the abolition of hierarchy and the fusion of theology and experience, faith and feeling, reason and prayer, worship and social concerns and the Clergy with the laity.

The ECM is characterized by:

a) **Generous Orthodoxy**—The ECM believes in the egalitarianism of differing theological opinions and is therefore radically inclusive. It is open to diverse perspectives within Christianity as well as sharing narratives in interfaith dialogues including ancient mysticism. It holds that every theology will 'remain a conversation about the Truth and that no systematic theology can be final'. It rejects the idea of absolute Truth and therefore rejects doctrines and dogmas based on propositional statements of truth. In the ECM, the quest for truth is an unending journey. The ECM also subscribes to orthopraxis and believes that ***"the way you live is more important than what you believe"***. As the story and narratives replace doctrine and dogma, in the Emerging church, "the story of the Good Samaritan carries more weight and is regarded as more important than the Ten Commandments"! Missional living, which is, living the 'faith' by being involved in the community is promoted.

b) **Post-Liberal Hermeneutics**—ECM accepts multiplicity of approaches as well as plurality of scriptural interpretations. It favors the use of Bible translations that have been made contemporary culture compliant but which sometimes contain subtle and not so subtle changes that radically alter the original meaning. It holds that the world is changing radically and that the Church must also change drastically, ***not just her methods but to "a new kind of Christianity"***. The ECM therefore, rather than converting the world, essentially brought the world into the Church.

c) **Lower View of the Bible**—In the ECM, the Bible is neither authoritative nor a foundation for faith; it is also not considered a principal source of guidance on morality. This view of Scriptures also translated into disbelief, condescension and hostility towards core Christian doctrines of soteriology and ecclesiology. For instance, a leader of the ECM, **Steve Chalke** said of Christ's death on the Cross: *"How then have we come to believe that at the Cross, this God of love suddenly decides to vent his anger and wrath on His own son? The fact is that the Cross isn't a form of cosmic child abuse—a vengeful father punishing His son for an offense he has not committed. Understandably, both people inside and outside of the Church have found this twisted version of events morally dubious and a huge barrier to faith"*.

Another frontline ECM advocate, **Dallas Willard** said: *"The divine conspiracy"—"atonement centered understanding of the gospel create vampire Christians who want Jesus for His blood and little else"*.

d) **Experiential Worship and Spirituality**—The ECM describes itself as creative, experiential and sensory, blending elements of worship from a wide variety of traditions, namely Catholic, Anglican, Orthodox, mystics etc. There is a variety of worship styles, ranging from 'Charismatic funky to liturgical, mystical and ritualistic'. The goal is to offer worshippers a sensory experience through the senses of touch, smell, hearing, taste and sight through the use of icons, relics, prayer beads, incense, candles, music and communion.

e) **'Non-Conversion' Evangelism**—The ECM believes that Christianity is just a voice among many; therefore it believes in applying 'humility and respect' in making "truth claims". It seeks to "deliver the gospel in a non-aggressive, 'more loving' and 'affirming' manner rather than what is considered the 'overly redemptive and condemnatory' ways of Fundamentalists and Evangelicals". It recommends 'Christian charity' instead of 'condemnation' and promotes non-critical 'interfaith conversations' instead of dogma driven evangelism and apologetics which are considered confrontational. Members of the ECM reject the evangelical dividing line between Christians and non-Christians and avoid the use of words like—unsaved, lost, hell, the cross, the world as darkness etc. **Rev. Bruce Epperly**, a leader in the Emerging Church said: *"As we share our faith, we do not seek* *to convert one another, but grow together by sharing a common spiritual adventure".* Another leading figure in ECM circles, **Brian McLaren** said: *"I don't believe making disciples must equal making adherents to the Christian religion. It may be advisable in many, if not all circumstances to help people become followers of Jesus and remain within their Buddhist, Hindu or Jewish contexts . . . rather than resolving the paradox via pronouncements about the eternal destiny of people more convinced by or loyal to other religions than ours, we simply move on . . . to help Buddhists, Hindus, Moslems and everyone else experience life to the full in the way of Jesus (while learning it better myself), I would gladly become one of them, to join them, to enter into their world without judgment but with saving (?) love as mine has been entered by the Lord".*

f) **Syncretism**—Because the ECM affirms other religions, many also practice inter-spirituality and see nothing wrong in dabbling in the rituals of Eastern mysticism such as Zen Buddhism, Yoga, Transcendental Meditation (TM), labyrinth, lectio divina etc. Rev. Bruce Epperly again said: *"Persons of faith are called to be global pioneers. Although you may be rooted in a particular religious tradition, you may also find spiritual nurture through the insights and practices of the historical religious traditions, native spiritualities or the new spiritual movements of our time, (Ancient-future). You may for example attend church on Sunday morning, share fully in the ritual of the Holy Communion but, throughout the week, you may practice Zen Buddhist meditation or Transcendental Meditation, receive reiki or acupuncture treatment or attend a Native American sweat lodge".*

g) **Universalism**—Many in the ECM believe that God saves everyone and the idea that some may not be saved is considered painful to even contemplate. **Rob Bell**, an ECM bigwig wrote in his book "Love Wins": *"Salvation is realizing you are already saved. We are all forgiven. We are all loved, equally and fully by God who has made peace with everyone. That work is done. Now we are invited to believe that story and live it".* Furthermore he said: *"God has already forgiven us whether we ask for it or not, whether we repent or not, whether we are born again or not, God* *isn't waiting for us to get it together, to clean up, shape up, get up—God has already done it".*

h) **Political and Social Activism**—The goal of the ECM is an Utopian secular society where everyone sort of gets along without rocking any boat. Adherents of ECM, because of their lack of belief in absolute truth propositions or moral standards, they have no definite stand on social and moral issues such as homosexuality, drinking, pornography, profanities etc. However, they are very involved in social justice and environmental issues about 'saving the planet'.

The Emerging Church concept is spreading among the younger generation and infiltrating into churches and colleges.

COMMENT:
The Emerging Church Movement, strictly speaking is not a Christian Movement. This is so because:
- Jesus Christ says: *"I am the Way, the Truth and the Life. No one comes to the father except through me"—John 14:6.* This is a statement of absolute certainty that leaves no room for other considerations and has to be believed or rejected. The Emergers say *"that Truth is larger than any religious tradition, that all theology will remain a conversation about the Truth . . ."* The apostle Paul characterized people like this as: *"Ever learning but never able to come to the knowledge of truth . . ."—2Timothy 3:7.* To reject Jesus as the Truth is to reject Him.
- The Christian faith is built on Jesus Christ who Emergers don't really believe in but are studying in conjunction with a plethora of other deities.
- The Bible, a compilation of God's laws and prophets that Jesus Christ affirmed and said He came to fulfill is to the Emergers just another book; with stories and narratives they love to tell but not instructions they are willing to obey.
- The Christian doctrine of salvation is based on the atonement of Jesus Christ for the sins of the world on the Cross; the Bible says that "without the shedding of blood, there could be no remission for Sin". The Emergers found the idea of the Cross, sacrifice and blood repugnant judging by the statements of some front-liners of the movement. The Emergers' concept of soteriology contradicts Jesus Christ who said attaining eternal life depends on believing in Him, His sacrificial death, repenting and being

"born again"—**John 3:3-7; 16-18**. Therefore, the Emergers reject Jesus Christ's prescription for salvation.

Jesus Christ commanded Christians to make disciples of all nations—**Mathew 28:19-20,** but Emergers opposed the injunction, think it is offensive to talk of converting anyone and instead choose to affirm all religions and in fact believe in the equality of all opinions!

The Bible warned believers not to be unequally yoked with unbelievers and not to partake of the table of demons but Emergers see nothing wrong in sitting and eating at the shrine of Buddha and other gods—**(2Corinthians 6:14, 17; 1Corinthians 10:20-21)**. While true Christians through the ages oversee the burning of pagan fetishes and idols, Emergers promote the use of questionable objects and methods in worship and meditation.

Jesus said "By their fruits, you will know them"—**Mathew 7:20**. While the Seeker-Sensitive Movement neglected core Christian doctrines, the ECM rejected them; while the SSM suppress Biblical truths so as not to offend, the ECM discounted them and is willing to embrace contrary opinions from other faiths.

Finally, while the SSM convinced itself it was only changing the method without changing the message, the ECM, true to its deconstructive philosophy has radically changed both the method and the message. It is very clear that what the Emerging church is evolving into is anything but Christianity. The ECM is not "a new kind of Christianity"; it is a Frankenstein monster of anything goes kind of faith which is totally un-Christian and Christians should not be deceived—**1Timothy 4:1-2; 2Timothy 3:1-8; 2Peter 2:1-3.**

Trends in Asia [62]

Asia is the largest, most populous and diverse continent on earth being home to more than half of the world's population. It is broadly divided into six geographical regions, namely—West (the Middle East), South, South East, Central, East and North.

West Asia (the Middle East) [63, 64, 65, 66, 67, 68]

In spite of the fact that West Asia, (the Middle East) is the cradle of Christianity and home to various forms of ancient Christian traditions and rites such as the Assyrian, Chaldean, Armenian, Syrian and Maronite rites; today, Christians remain a minority in all the countries in this region. The population of Christians in the region range from virtually nil as in the Gulf States (where there are virtually no indigenous Christians) to about

38 percent as in Lebanon. In most others States, the Christian population is under 5 percent and declining.

Although some of the countries have constitutions that protect the rights of Christians such as Iran, Jordan and Iraq, the reality is different and they are subjected to discrimination in employment and politics leading to social and economic deprivation which makes them second class citizens to the Moslem majority. In many of the countries, the populations of Christians are dwindling due to emigration in order to escape persecution or seek better standards of living and also lower birth rates compared to the Moslem compatriots.

In a few countries in the region, the persecution of Christians has taken a violent turn with bombings of churches packed with worshippers as have occurred in Iraq and Egypt and even religious civil war as in Lebanon. The Christians in the region have lamented the apathy and indifference of the West to the plight of Christians in the Middle East.

South and South East Asia [69, 70, 71, 72, 73, 74, 75, 76, 77, 78, 79, 80, 81, 82, 83]

The countries in this region differ in their composition and treatment of Christians. Christianity is a minority in the vast majority of the countries in this region and there is a wide variation in the Christian population among the countries. In Afghanistan Christianity is non-existent officially though a few thousands Christians are said to exist underground. The only Church in the country is a Roman Catholic chapel within the premises of the Italian Embassy which construction was allowed in appreciation of Italy's support of Afghanistan's independence in 1919. A Protestant Church built and dedicated in 1970 in Kabul was destroyed in 1973. The construction of the Church was negotiated by President Eisenhower to reciprocate the construction of a mega mosque and Islamic cultural center in Washington D.C in 1959.

In Pakistan, Indonesia and Malaysia Christian populations range between 1 to 10 percent and is the same in Sri Lanka, Myanmar, and Thailand. While Islam predominates in Pakistan, Indonesia and Malaysia, Buddhism predominates in Sri Lanka, Myanmar and Thailand and both Christians and Moslems are a minority. In India, Hinduism is the major religion while in Vietnam, a syncretic combination of Buddhism, Confucianism and Taoism is practiced. Christians in Indonesia and Malaysia are fairly tolerated while they face serious persecutions from Moslems in countries like Pakistan where the Governor of Punjab State, **Salman Taseer (1944-2011)** and a federal minister, **_Shabazz Bhatti (1968-2011)_** were killed for supporting the abrogation of the Blasphemy Law which is very discriminatory to Christians. Christians are also persecuted in countries like Vietnam, India and Myanmar but tolerated in Thailand.

Trends in Central and East Asia [84, 85, 86, 87, 88, 89, 90, 91, 92]

The region commonly referred to as Central Asia include the '-Stan' States of Kazakhstan, Uzbekistan, Turkmenistan, Kyrgyzstan and Tajikistan, parts of China and Mongolia while East Asia comprise parts of China, North and South Koreas and Japan.

In most of the 'Stan' States of Central Asia, Christianity is a minority and Islam predominates in most. The country with the most Christian population was Kazakhstan which had 46 percent identified as Christian following independence from communist rule in 1990. However, the population of Christians has declined sharply to 26 percent in 2009 while Islam has risen to 70 percent. In virtually all the countries, religious freedom is enshrined in the Constitution but in practice, it is virtually non existent. In some proselytizing is prohibited and in all, religious activities are closely regulated and monitored.

In Mongolia, Christianity was introduced in the 7th century AD by Nestorian Christians. It was tolerated and it flourished under the rule of the 'Khans' of the Mongolian Empire. However Christianity virtually disappeared with the dissolution of the Mongol Empire and re-evangelization was truncated by the Soviet Communist rule. Christian groups returned after Mongolia's Independence from the Soviet Union in 1990 and Christians now account for 4 percent of the population comprising 90 percent Protestants, 9 percent Mormons and 1 percent Roman Catholic and Russian Orthodox. The majority of Mongolians, 80 percent, are Buddhists while 5 percent are Moslems.

North Korea [93]

The People of North Korea were predominantly Buddhists and Confucians before the Communist assumed power and took control of everything including religious activities.

After the Communists came to power, they initially tried to exterminate all forms of religion from the land and replace them with "cult of personality" and the concept of "self reliance" called "Juche" in Korean language. However, under State controlled freedom of religion, the State now builds Seminaries, churches of different denominations all under the Korean Christian Federation. Buddhist temples are also renovated and the State controls the training of the clergy.

It is reported that there are underground churches the size of which is difficult to ascertain.

South Korea [94, 95, 96, 97]

In South Korea, almost half of the population, 46.5 percent express no religious preference, 29.2 percent Christians (18.3% Protestant and 10.9% Catholic) and others 22.8 percent. The rest include minority religions like Confucianism, Hinduism, Islam, Shamanism and a host of new religious movements.

Koreans are generally eclectic in their approach to religion which probably explains why almost half could not state a religious preference; rather, ideas from various religions are absorbed into the culture. Whatever the religious leaning in South Korea, there is a pervasive belief in spirits and their influence on the living. Therefore, ancestor veneration is viewed as mere social and cultural practice rather than religious and shamans are consulted by those not primarily adherents of Shamanism.

South Korea has witnessed a surge in Christianity since after World War II and has the highest number of Christians in Asia after the Philippines. In contrast to most countries in Asia where Christianity is either static or in decline, Christianity in South Korea is robustly expanding and has been doubling in every decade for the last three decades of the 20th century.

South Korea is home to one of the world's largest single congregations, the Yoido Full Gospel Church with a membership of about 750,000 people.

China [98, 99]

In the 19th century, there had been a sort of "scramble for China". Foreign powers of Britain, Germany, France, Russia and Japan had all carved out spheres of influence in China and signed treaties which favored the foreigners but disadvantaged the Chinese. To compound the problem, the expatriates were often exempted from local Chinese laws. This resulted in discontent among the Chinese and the formation of anti-imperialist groups.

The "Boxer Rebellion" against western imperialism of 1900 also instigated anti-Christian sentiments and so many indigenous Christians and missionaries were killed. As the rebellion spread, all western foreigners were besieged in the "Legation Quarters" in Beijing and an eight nation alliance comprising Austria, France, Germany, Italy, Japan, Russia, United Kingdom and the United States of America attacked China to free them.

It is alleged by eyewitness westerners that the liberators committed atrocities against innocent Chinese people by looting, raping and killing. So horrific was the violence against the weak and helpless Chinese that it is reported that many committed suicide after being raped or to avoid being raped. To make matters worse, some missionaries like ***William Scott Ament*** allegedly guided American troops through Chinese villages on orgies of looting ostensibly to compensate Christians whose properties had been destroyed by the Boxers. An eyewitness journalist, ***George Lynch*** wrote: ***"There are things I must not write and that may not be printed in England, which would seem to show that this Western civilization of ours is merely a veneer over savagery".***

After the Alliance's victory, the peace treaty included reparations to be paid by China and privileges for foreigners in the country.

By 1922, the special privileges for foreigners sparked discontent and nationalistic fervor among the people with the formation of Nationalist Movements. These Nationalist movements translated into anti-imperialist and by extension, anti-Christian movements as many missionaries were seen as imperialist agents by their conduct and association with trading companies such as the East India Trading Company.

With the emergence of the Communist Movement formed by those inspired by ***Karl Marx (1818-1883)***, China entered a period of political instability with the various groups engaged in struggle for supremacy. However, the common enemy as perceived by the groups, is the foreigners whom they wanted expelled.

In 1949, the Communist Party of China declared the Republic of China and took over power and control of virtually everything. Religion became regulated such that religious bodies have to register with membership open only to those eighteen years of age and above and the missionaries left the country. Three main groups of Christians emerged, namely:
- The Three Self Patriotic Movement which was formed by Y.T. Wu in 1951 and is Self-supporting, Self-governing and Self-propagating. It was formed in order to reassure the government that the church would be free of foreign influence and patriotic.

- The Patriotic Catholic Association which is largely independent of the Pope and is regarded as being schismatic.
- The Underground (House) churches comprising both Protestants and Catholics which are not officially registered.

It is believed that Christianity is growing in China, against all odds.

Japan [100, 101, 102]

Christianity has had a checkered fortune in Japan since it was introduced in the 16th century by the Jesuits and later the Franciscans and Dominican Catholic priests. Christianity was banned by the mid 17th century and the ban remained till mid 19th century after which missionary activities once again resumed.

Anticipating the possibility of war based on the global political situation, Japan enacted the "Religious Bodies Law" which recognized Shintoism, Buddhism and Christianity as the official religions in Japan in 1940. The law curtailed the activities of foreign missionaries, barring them from financially supporting the native church workers or giving any assistance to the Japanese churches with strings attached. However, foreign missionaries' salaries could still be paid by their home mission boards. In addition, the law stipulated that Christians must participate in the "Shrine Shinto" ceremonies and all the denominations were under pressure to comply.

Forty-two Protestant denominations merged to form the United Japanese Christian Church excluding the Episcopal and the Seventh Day Adventist. Also excluded from the union were the Roman Catholic Church and the Russian Orthodox Church. The churches complied after government's written assurance that the observance of the Shrine Shinto was purely a patriotic and irreligious ceremony like the civic ceremony at the tomb of an Unknown Soldier.

Nonetheless, many missions withdrew their missionaries and the Japanese Church became indigenized. After Japan's defeat in World War II, the nation was forced to democratize, abolish State Shinto and institute freedom of religion. Nevertheless, in spite of the contribution of Christianity to the educational and economic growth of Japan, it remains a minuscule religion among the Japanese at less than one percent of the population.

Trends in North Asia (Russia) [103, 104, 105]

Russia adopted the Byzantine rites brand of Christianity in the tenth century AD by the evangelization of Kievan Rus. It remained in the Byzantine orthodoxy until the fall of Constantinople in 1453 when the Metropolitanate of Moscow became a Patriarchate and Moscow saw itself as the "***Third Rome***".

After the ***Bolshevik Revolution of 1917***, the separation of Church and State was declared but the ideological policy of the Communist regime in power was the elimination of religion. The Russian Orthodox Church, the biggest religious bloke was targeted for persecution and many bishops, priests and believers were sent to mental hospitals, exiled to labor camps, imprisoned, tortured or killed. Many churches and monasteries were also either destroyed or converted to secular use. Anti-religion propaganda, which the Church could not respond to, harassment of believers and ridicule of religion were sanctioned by the government throughout the Soviet Union. Many Christians and people of other faiths were subjected to psychological punishment or subjected to mind control experimentation.

However, sometimes attempt were made to use the Church for political ends. Hence, in 1922, the State backed the schismatic Renovated Church and prevented the election of a new Moscow Patriarch on the death of the incumbent in 1925.

In 1927, the deputy of the Patriarch-elect capitulated and cooperated with the Soviet government, accepted the authority of the government over the Church and condemned political dissent. Notwithstanding this cooperation, the onslaught of the government against the Church was reported to have reduced the number of Orthodox churches in the Russian Republic from almost thirty thousand to just about five hundred between 1927 and 1940.

When Germany attacked the Soviet Union in 1941, ***Joseph Stalin (1879-1953)*** revived the Church to rally ethnic support for the war. He opened Seminaries and churches that have been closed for decades. This continued until 1959 when another wave of persecution of the Russian Orthodox Church began under ***Nikita Khrushchev (1894-1971)*** and continued under ***Leonid Brezhnev (1906-1982)***.

The Church—State relationship did not improve until Gorbachev's reforms through perestroika and Glasnost. In 1990, with the disintegration of the former Soviet Union, churches were returned and monasteries re-opened.

The Russian Orthodox Church has been operating more or less as a State religion and over 73 percent identified with it though less than 5 percent is fully integrated into church life. There are also Protestant denominations like Baptists, Lutherans, Methodists, Seventh Day Adventist as well as others like the Jehovah's Witness and Mormons. These, together with Roman Catholics constitute only about 1.5 percent of the population. Other officially recognized religions are Islam (about 6 percent, Judaism and Buddhism (less than I percent). The rest of the people are either atheists or agnostics.

Chapter 23

The Christian and Christianity Today

Global Overview [1,2,3,4]

Christianity is ostensibly the predominant religion in the Americas, Europe, East, Central and South Africa, Russia, the Philippines and Oceania. The countries with the largest Christian populations are found in the Americas. The United States of America has the largest Christian population in the world followed by Brazil and Mexico respectively.

There are about thirty-nine thousand denominations but the largest denomination is the Roman Catholic Church which, with over a billion members, account for about half of all the Christians in the world.

The results of various surveys reveal that Christians make up about one third of the world's population and this proportion has remained essentially unchanged over the last century. However, there have been significant regional changes; for instance, at the beginning of the 20th century, 80 percent of all world Christians were in Europe but by 2010, European Christians accounted for fewer than 30 percent.

Region	Population	Christian Population	%Christian	%Total Christians
Africa	1,012,956,000	482,240,000	47.6%	22.43%
Americas	935,120,000	804,140,000	85.99%	37.41%
Asia	4,119,629,000	278,273,000	6.75%	12.94%
Europe	727,083,000	550,911,000	75.77%	25.63%
Middle East	365,305,000	17,354,000	4.75%	0.80%
Oceania	35,103,000	25,754,000	73.36%	1.19%

Christianity by Regions of the World*

* Data from Wikipedia, the free Encyclopedia—http://en.wikipedia.org/wiki/ChristianitybyCountry

A Christian is defined by the World Christian Encyclopedia as:
"One, who believes in, professes or confesses Jesus Christ as Lord and Savior or is assumed to believe in Jesus Christ" [3]
Or:
"Followers of Jesus Christ as Lord of all kinds, all traditions and confessions, and all degrees of commitment"
Evangelical Christians are a subset of the general definition of Christians. They have a higher level of commitment to the person of Jesus Christ, to His Great Commission (through organized evangelism), and to the Gospel by their lifestyle while looking forward to His Second Advent [3].

Using data from various sources, the **Joshua Project** compared the percentages of Evangelical Christians to that of all Christians in some regions of the world.

Analyzing data from various sources but mainly from Greater Europe Mission, the Joshua Project considered issues like commitment measured by regular church attendance, being part of some religion and importance of God in the individual's life. Also considered were: belief in a personal God, in Spirit or life force and belief in one true religion, many true religions and no true religion. The regions surveyed were West Africa, South-east Asia, Western Europe, Eastern Europe, Latin America, North America Oceania or Pacific.

They found that commitment and other indicators such as church attendance and doctrinal beliefs reveal that Christianity in many countries and regions regarded as Christian is at best historical and mostly superficial. Although the Americas, Europe and Oceania scored highly for the percentage of the population considered Christian, commitment, measured in terms of the percentage of evangelicals and church attendance was considerably low for the regions.

More surprising was the finding that, although Christianity is a monotheistic religion, only about one in five persons in North America and Western Europe belief there is only one true God. In fact more than three times as many people in North America belief in 'many true religions' as believe in only one true religion (71% vs 20%)

Based of the results of the various surveys, the Joshua Project made the following observations and conclusions about Europe:
- Though ostensibly highly evangelized through its Catholic and Protestant heritage, Europe has many unevangelized people

groups and the lowest percentage of evangelical Christians in the world except the Pacific region.
- Europe has the lowest percentage of church attendance among the world regions.
- More than half of Europe's population do not consider God as important in their lives
- Europe has the highest percentage of agnostics and many of the most resistant people to Christianity.

United Kingdom [5,6,]

A more detailed look at the situation in the UK, one of the more populous European countries further elucidates the dire state of Christianity in the region.

A research result on 'Churchgoing in the UK" published in 2007 by ***Tearfund*** *in the United Kingdom provided a broader analysis of the state of Christianity in the country. Although 53 percent of adults identified themselves as Christians, only 10 percent regularly attended church weekly, increasing to 15 percent when monthly attendees are included and to 26 percent when the occasional attendees (Christmas, Easter, weddings, baptisms and funerals) are included. Six percent are affiliated with other religions while 39 percent are not affiliated with a church or any other religion.

The research also found that women are more interested in church than men by a 2:1 margin. Also regular church-goers are more likely to be older; 82% of those above 75 years and 75% of those between 65 and 74 years while only 33% of those aged 16-34 years are regular church attendees. In fact, for adults below the age of 45 years, the non-religious predominate. About 60 percent of the adult population, comprising older de-churched and younger unchurched people makes up the secular majority who are closed to attending church in the future. Hence, the older people, though more regular churchgoers are 'de-churched'; while the younger ones are 'unchurched'.

As a result, thousands of churches have closed or face closure, demolition or conversion to mosques, places of worship for other religions, homes, offices and restaurants. For instance, it is said that in 1961, there were 55,000 churches in Britain and only 7 mosques. In 2005, the number of churches were down to 47,600 (a difference of 7,400) while the number of mosques were up to 1689. It is feared that if the trend continues, some denominations may become extinct. The Methodist churches are closing at a rate of almost 100 per year; numbering 14,000 in 1932, there were only about 6,000 in 2005.

This scenario is replicated in much of Europe and Christianity is therefore in serious decline.

- **Data and statistics culled from Tearfund. Church—going in the UK (30-04-07)—by permission Copyright © Tearfund UK 2007 www.tearfund.org**

Oceania
Australia [8, 9]

In Australia, the largest country in Oceania, the 2006 census put Christians at about 64 percent of the population down from 96.1 percent in 1901. *The National Church Life Survey*, (the nationwide census of Australian church attendance); put the weekly church attendance at 7.5 percent.

While Christianity declined by about 32 percentage points in a century, other religions as well as atheists and agnostics made gains. Between 1986 and 2006, Christianity declined from 73 percent to 63.9 percent, Buddhism rose fourfold from 0.5 to 2.1 percent, Islam doubled from 0.7 to 1.7 percent, Hinduism from 0.1 to 0.7 percent and 'No Religion' from 12.7 to 18.7 percent. Judaism remained unchanged at 0.4 per cent of the population.

United States of America [10, 11, 12, 13]

In the United States, the most populous country in the Americas and the country with the largest Christian population in the world, surveys by the *American Religion Identification Survey (ARIS)* revealed that Christianity has declined from 86.2 percent in 1990 to 76 per cent in 2008.

The decline was reflected in all the major denominations; thus Catholics fell from 26.2 percent in 1990 to 25.1 percent, Baptists from 19.4 to 15.8 percent, and the Mainline Protestants (Methodists, Lutherans, Presbyterian, Episcopalian and United Church of Christ) from 18.7 to 12.9 percent. During the same period, the percentage of Agnostics and Atheists almost doubled from 8.2 to 15 percent.

The declining numbers is not the only problem plaguing the Church in the United States; there are serious signs of declining commitment and other problems too.

The ***Gallup International Poll*** and other surveys have reported weekly church attendance of adult Americans at about 40 percent; though there is variation between the States ranging from 24 to 58 percent. However, these figures are considered as exaggerated and have been challenged. It is believed that the actual national average weekly church attendance is about 21 percent.

The ***Barna Group*** has conducted many surveys that have shed light on a wide range of issues about Christianity in the United States of America.

In 2006, the Group conducted a study on the commitment of those who identified themselves as Christians and found that only 18 percent of churchgoers believed in spiritual development within the community of faith such as a church. Even among the evangelicals and 'Born Again' Christians, only about 33 percent affirm the concept of spiritual growth within the local church.

In another study, the Barna Group examined the prevalence of biblical worldview (***defined as believe in absolute moral truth, accuracy of the Bible on the principles it teaches, salvation not by good works, sinlessness of Jesus while on earth, all-knowing and all powerful God who is still in control of the universe and the reality of Satan rather than as a symbol***) among the general population and various subgroups among Christians. The result was as follows:

Subgroup	% with Biblical Worldview
Adult Americans	9%
Born Again Christians	19%
Catholics	2%
Democrats	4%
Liberals	0.5%
18-23 year olds	0.5%

Biblical Worldview among Subgroups of Adults in the United States of America*

* Data culled from Barna Survey (March 6, 2009)—Changes in Worldview among Christians over the past thirteen years. By Permission, Copyright, Barna Group www.barna.org

Other surveys by the Barna Group and other groups also revealed the following: [14,15,16,17, 18, 19, 20*, 21, 22, 23, 24].

- The majority of Christians do not understand the concept of holiness, do not believe God expect them to be holy and therefore do not desire to be holy.
- Even among regular church attendees, only 15 percent ranked relationship with God as a priority in their lives though the majority claims to be deeply spiritual.
- About 75 percent of teenagers were found to have dabbled into occultism involving psychic or witchcraft activity such as games involving sorcery or witchcraft, reading of books on Wicca, use of Ouija board, palmistry, horoscope or fortune telling. On the contrary, only about 33 percent of teenagers had had any teaching on the supernatural in their churches.
- The age group 16 to 29 years is more skeptical and critical of Christianity and is generally more resistant to evangelization.
- Most American Christians do not believe that the Holy Spirit and Satan are real entities; rather they are considered as merely symbols of good and evil respectively.
- Most Americans lack interest in spiritual principles. Socio-economic pressures and distractions hamper spiritual practices such as meditation, contemplation, solitude etc.
- Faith in the lives of Americans is compartmentalized and seldom influences other areas of life or play a part in crucial decisions.
- American Christians are becoming theologically illiterate
- The rate of divorce among Born-Again and non Born Again Christians is statistically the same.
- Many adult Americans subscribe to '*universalism*' and '*pluralism*'. Fifty-nine percent believe Moslems and Christians worship the same God, 43 percent agreed with the idea that the Bible, the Book of Mormon and the Koran teach the same spiritual truths and 40 percent believe everybody will be saved no matter what because God loves all His creation.
- Even among the 'Born Again' Christians, 40 percent believe that Christians and Moslems worship the same God and 25 percent embrace the idea that it does not matter what religion is practiced, everyone gets saved because they all teach the same lessons.

From these and other findings, the Barna Group made some important observations and drew some important conclusions:
- Most Americans see themselves as a people of faith but they do not have accurate views in regard to spirituality.
- American Christians are not as devoted to their faith as they like to believe. They feel positively about faith but it is rarely the focal point of their lives or a critical factor in their decision making.
- Few Americans bother to evaluate their spiritual journey or develop benchmarks or indicators for their spiritual health. Therefore, they have a distorted view of the prominence and purity of faith in their lives.
- Measured against biblical standards, most American Christians are lukewarm, make little effort towards spiritual growth, lack clear spiritual goals and have many distractions.
- The American Christians' approach to faith is superficial and they consider surviving the present much more important than eternal security or spiritual possibilities.
- The American Church has been cowered by the postmodern insistence on tolerance. This coupled with theological illiteracy and ignorance of spiritual principles has resulted in the lack of discernment regarding choices on crucial social issues by the church for fear of being labeled judgmental. Therefore the church has become tolerant of a host of morally and spiritually dubious behaviors and philosophies.
- "Religious organizations have become materialistic, competing for dollars, bodies and talents rather than promoting and upholding core values like service, obedience, accountability, responsibility, humility" etc.
- Christians have abdicated their traditional roles as moral and spiritual leaders and have taken their value cues from the political and business sectors, therefore the bar of character and vision have been lowered.
- Many indicators and statistics point to the demise of the family, schools, churches, the media and government, all of which are America's fundamental institutions. The nation is therefore in a precarious position with its energy shifting from a willingness to work hard to achieve desired outcomes to an attitude of entitlement.

- *The influence of Christianity on the contemporary culture and individuals is regrettably largely invisible.*

* Data from multiple Barna Group Survey Reports (2006-2011). Barna Group, www.barna.org

As in Europe, churches in the United States of America have been experiencing declining membership and churches are closing at a greater rate than new ones are being founded. In the 1990s, the annual rate of church closure across the United States was about 3200, this has increased to about 3,700 churches in the year 2000. The Catholic Church is closing down parishes across the country while merging others to make them viable. The decline is not only in the Catholic Church but across all denominations.

It is reported that only 15 percent of churches are growing and only 2.2 percent by actual conversion. In addition, there is a shortage of priests in the Catholic Church and pastors are leaving the ministry in other denominations as a result of contentions with the congregation, spiritual burnout syndrome or moral turpitude.

Some church leaders are aware and are concerned about these trends. They have sought to find the reasons with a view to seeking solutions. Among the reasons identified are:
- Increasing secularization of the western culture
- A sense of cultural disconnect among the young people who feel that church is irrelevant to their lives. They crave authenticity, repudiate empty religiosity and desire something practical and applicable to their daily lives.
- Lack of spiritual zeal among the church people and what they called a "spectator mentality" which made them believe that evangelism is the duty of the paid pastor alone.
- Friction between pastors and evangelists. Evangelists think that pastors feel threatened by them and therefore are usually reticent about collaborating with them or sharing church resources.
- Many churches and denominations have poorly defined missions
- Credibility crisis in the Church due to sexual molestation, fraud and other scandals involving priests, pastors and other prominent church leaders.

- Heretical theology and the preaching of a gospel that promises salvation without repentance and faith without the fear of God.

West Africa

Although West Africa has a relatively lower percentage of Christians (48.4%) compared to Europe, the Americas and Oceania, the region scored higher on indices such as belonging to a religion (99%), believe in a personal God (64%) and believe in only one true religion (62%). The region, more than any other, also scored highly on regular church attendance (82%) and on the importance of God in the lives of the people (97%).

Nigeria [25]

Nigeria, the most populous nation in Africa—(Every 1 in 4 African, and every 1 in 5 black persons in the world is a Nigerian)—has the highest score for church attendance in the world at 89%.

Nigeria is emblematic of the state of Christianity in Africa.

Gideon Para-Mallam, a Nigerian and the Lausanne Deputy Director for Anglophone Africa observed that in spite of mega-churches with single congregations exceeding fifty thousand weekly attendees, the impact on the general society is largely indiscernible. He decried the dichotomy between what Christians profess and what is practiced and their failure to be Christ's Ambassadors in their various walks of life.

He also identified doctrinal distortions, the peddling of the "Gospel for Gain" which he dubbed "Cash for Christ", the preaching of a "Cross-less Christianity" and the "Gospel of Greed" as other malaise in the Nigerian church.

It is obvious that Christianity is in decline in many regions where it was once strongly rooted around the world. It is said that the European region is one of the most resistant to evangelism and in April of 2010, the Newsweek magazine published an edition titled "The Decline and Fall of Christianity in America".

Of all the regions surveyed, only the West African region showed consistent growth. This has made some to conclude that the centre for Christian growth in the coming decades would be in Africa.

However, the rosy picture has been tarnished by the observation that Church growth in Africa is characterized by an emphasis on numerical rather than spiritual growth and that ministry success is measured by quantity rather than quality. The world renowned missiologist, **John Stott** commenting on Church growth in Africa reportedly said*: "Numerical growth of Christianity in Africa is an inch deep and a mile wide".*

Sadly, although many churches across Africa South of the Sahara experienced explosive numerical growth, they have very weak doctrinal and discipleship foundations. Unless these inherent weaknesses are corrected, Christianity in the region will experience the same fate as in other places where it once held sway but is now in decline.

Chapter 24

Evolutionary Trends from the Early Church to the 21st Century

It is obvious that the Church today is significantly different from the Church of the 'Acts of the Apostles'. Jesus and all the Apostles warned the disciples to watch out for false teachers and false doctrines. John stated that "the spirit of the antichrist" was already operative in the world even as he wrote his epistle.

Many historians believed that before the 'conversion' of the Emperor Constantine, the Church had been plagued by compromise, accommodation, corruption and acculturation into the Roman culture, the process that was accelerated the said conversion of the emperor.

The following are some of the discernible processes in the evolution of the Church through the ages to the present time:

(I) Philosophization of the Gospel [1, 2, 3, 4, 5, 6, 7]

During the apostolic period, the Church was vibrant and was led and controlled by the Holy Spirit. The Apostles preached by the power of the Holy Spirit and their message was accompanied by signs and wonders. The believers, as true disciples, experienced God.

By the end of the first century, several sinister trends were creeping into the Church which prompted the Apostles to warn believers to be vigilant. One such trend was the tendency towards explaining the Gospel by philosophy.

After the first century AD when the first generation of Christians had passed away from the scene, many of the leading Christians from the Second century onward were philosophers. These philosophers considered **Platonism**, the prevalent philosophical thinking at the time, the *"best available instrument for understanding and defending the teachings of the Scripture and Church traditions."* Many therefore used philosophy as a tool to spread orthodox Christianity.

This was diametrically opposed to how Jesus instructed that the gospel be preached. Jesus expressly charged His followers to first be endued with the Power of the Holy Spirit, then to go preach, teach and be His witnesses—*Luke 24:46-49; Acts 1:4-5, 8.*

Paul warned the Colossians not to be *"deceived through philosophy and the tradition of men"*—*Colossians 2:8*; and constantly testified that his preaching was not with wise and persuasive words of human wisdom, but with the demonstration of the Power of the Holy Spirit. This he held to be crucial to the end that the faith of his converts might not rest on human wisdom but on the power of God—*1Corinthians 2:4-5.*

He made it clear that understanding the gospel require the work of the Holy Spirit who alone can reveal spiritual truth and grant understanding of what God has freely given to Believers. He asserted that a man without the Holy Spirit could neither accept nor understand the gospel—*1Corinthians 2:13-14.*

In fact he said*: "to preach the gospel with words of human wisdom would <u>empty the Cross of Christ of its power</u>"—1Corinthians 1:17 (NIV).*

Paul repeatedly warned his protégé, Timothy, a Greek youth to avoid the lure of philosophical arguments which he said led to ungodliness and had derailed the faith of some even during his time—*1Timothy 6:20-21; 2Timothy 2:16.*

Tertulian of Carthage, one of the very few early 'Church Fathers' who rejected philosophy as a credible vehicle for Christianity believed that Philosophy perverted Christian doctrines and bred heresies. He opined that philosophers lacked understanding of God's revelation and were devoid of real faith. Therefore, they changed Christian doctrines by creating **confusions, uncertainties and complexities** out of simple issues. He also noted that philosophers never seem to agree on anything.

Greek philosophy has been described as "confusing and sometimes presenting ambiguities or outright contradictory concepts". It has also been characterized as *"an amalgam of rival world views based on premises that differ from biblical revelation and often fail to establish means of resolving disputes"*[13].

Cicero (106-43 B.C) in his treatise on The Nature of God said*:*

"So various and so contradictory are the opinions of the most learned men on this matter as to persuade one of the truth of the saying that 'philosophy is a child of ignorance'".

Yet, it was this same human wisdom that many of the acclaimed *'Church Fathers'* such as **Justin Martyr, Origen, Clement of Alexandria and Augustine of Hippo** espoused as the vehicle for spreading the Gospel in the first five centuries AD and what they used in the development of what became the accepted Christian Creed and Dogma.

Dependence on philosophical speculations in doctrinal matters continued into the medieval period in form of *Scholasticism*. Many of the Church Scholastics, rather than returning to Biblical revelations, instead dumped *Plato* only to embrace another philosopher, *Aristotle*. Unfortunately, the result was the same—confusion, uncertainties and complexities that fail to spiritually impact man in any positive way.

Al Ghazali (1058-1111), a medieval philosopher of Iranian extraction summed up the attempt of philosophers to explain God by reason as **"incoherent"** and not based on anything that was demonstrable.

The incoherence of the philosophers was seen in the writings of early fathers such as **Origen of Alexandria** and even **Augustine of Hippo** whose exegesis were sometimes plagued with contradictions and patently unscriptural concepts. The same incoherence and contradictions characterized the writings of the *"Schoolmen"* of the Middle Ages such as **Anselm** and **Abelard**.

As philosophic speculations about the nature of God, Jesus Christ and the Holy Spirit flourished, several schools of thought sprang up and logic replaced faith. Genuine pursuit of the true knowledge of God by revelation and true experience of His power gave way to mere intellectual speculations upon which formalized doctrines were then built.

As philosophy replaced the Holy Spirit, the State sponsored Greek Orthodox and Roman Catholic Churches began to evolve into entities that differed considerably from the New Testament model and the Gospel was gradually emptied of its power.

As Tertullian of Carthage observed, many others have also noted the corruption of the Christian doctrines by pagan philosophies.

Friedrich Nietzsche (1844-1900) dubbed Christianity as *"Platonism for the people"*.

And the historian, *Edward Gibbons* observed that: *"If paganism was conquered by Christianity, it is equally true that Christianity was corrupted by paganism . . ."*

II) **Sacerdotal Ecclesiology** [8, 9, 10]

At the core of what came to be known as the Roman Catholic faith and what the whole structure is built on are the doctrines of:
- *The Apostolic succession and*
- *The Power of the Keys*

These doctrines are based on the conversation of Jesus Christ with the disciples in *Mathew 16:13-20.* Jesus had asked the disciples who the people thought He was and they replied that some thought He was Elijah, others John the Baptist etc. He then asked them: *But what about you? Who do you say I am?* Simon Peter answered: *"You are the Christ, the Son of the living God"—Mathew 16:15-16*

Jesus replied: *"Blessed are you, Simon son of Jonah, for this was not revealed to you by man, but by my Father in heaven. <u>And I tell you that you are Peter, and on this Rock I will build my Church and the gates of Hades will not overcome it.</u> I will give you the keys of the kingdom of heaven; whatever you bind on earth will be bound in heaven, and whatever you loose on earth will be loosed in heaven"—Mathew 16:17-19*

The Apostolic succession doctrine is based on *Mathew 16:18* (underlined above) and purports that Jesus Christ promised to build His Church on the person of the Apostle Peter. In addition, Peter was given the *"power of the keys"* to bind and loose in Mathew 16:19; the same power was given to the other Apostles in *Mathew 18:18.*

From the doctrines of the *Apostolic succession* and *the Power of the keys* grew the Roman Catholic doctrine of what constitutes a church which can be summarized thus:

1) The Church, based on *Mathew 16:18,* is built on the person of Peter the Apostle.
2) Peter and the Apostles were given the 'power of the keys' to loose and bind which was passed to their successors, the popes and the bishops.
3) Jesus breathed the Holy Spirit on the Apostles and sent them as the Father sent Him—*John 20:21*; therefore, only the Pope and the bishops, who are the successors of the Apostles have the Holy Spirit which they can then impart to others by laying on of hands and by delegation, for instance on the priests and the deacons. They were also given the power to remit sins.

4) The *'saving mission'* that God entrusted to Jesus Christ was committed to the Apostles and their successors who alone "received His Spirit to act in His Name and His Person".
5) Only the Pope (the successor of Peter) and the bishops (successors of the other Apostles) who constitute ***the Magisterium*** are entrusted with authentic interpretation of the word of God.
6) The popes and the bishops are repositories of vital information passed on by tradition that were not written in the Scriptures, therefore, this ***"deposit of tradition"*** is a treasure of *'equal weight' as the Scripture*—this doctrine is usually supported by ***2Timothy 2:2***.
7) Therefore, it is believed that: ***The validity and authority of the Christian ministry are derived from the Apostles and true churches are those that can be traced back (unbroken), to the Apostles.***

COMMENT

It is essential to examine the veracity of each of these doctrinal points in the light of the Scriptures.

1) How sound is this *'Peter/ clergy-centric'* doctrine of ecclesiology?

Did Jesus in ***Mathew 16:18*** actually promised to build on the person of the Apostle Simon Peter?

To test the veracity of this doctrine, the following questions should be considered:

i) In the context of Mathew ***16:13-19;*** which is more important for 'Time and Eternity',—the Holy Spirit inspired revelation of Jesus Christ as the Messiah and the Son of God confessed by Peter or the person of Simon Peter?
ii) Which is central to the Gospel and the Church; the revelation of Jesus as the Son of God and Messiah and its implication for the eternal destiny of humanity or the person of Peter?
iii) On which is Jesus likely to build His Church; the Eternal Truth of His Divinity or on the person of Peter, a mere human being.
iv) Is traceability to the Apostles the litmus test of the true church?

In the context of **Mathew 16:13-19** and not just an isolated verse 18; it is obvious that the revelation of Jesus as ***'the Christ and Son of God'*** confessed by Peter was the crucial point Jesus wanted the disciples to grasp when he initiated the conversation in verse 13 and concluded in verse 20.

❖ ***Peter's confession*** as revealed by the Father and not ***Peter the person*** is the central point in the salvation of mankind and the Gospel—**John 3:16.**

It is therefore clear that **the Rock** referred to by Jesus Christ in **Mathew 16:18** on which He promised to build His Church was the ***revelation*** in Peter's ***confession*** and not his ***person***. The allusion to Peter's alias "I say to you that you are Peter . . ." must have been a pun or a metaphor.

That this is the case is shown by what happened shortly afterwards when Jesus shared His impending passion with the disciples and Peter remonstrated with Him displaying a total lack of understanding of what he had just confessed. Jesus Christ rebuked him sharply, realizing that he was being influenced by Satan *(Mathew 16:21-23).* The Scriptures say (and it cannot be broken*), "not to put trust in princes nor the son of man . . ."—Psalm 146:3; and in fact says "Cursed is he who trusts in man and make flesh his strength . . ."—Jeremiah 17:5.*

No one is called to be saved and no one can be saved by believing in Peter.

It is therefore preposterous, all things considered, to assert that the Church is built on Simon Peter.

The assignment that Jesus Christ gave to Peter was for him to preach and teach what he had confessed and make disciples of all nations and to tend and feed His sheep—**Mathew 28:19-20; John 21:15-17**.

In the New Testament, the Church is the body of Christ and He is the Head—**Colossians 1:18.** *The body is composed of baptized believers; that is, those who have confessed their sins, repented and professed their faith in Jesus Christ as Lord and Savior—John 3:16; Acts 2:37-39; Romans 10:9-13; Acts 16:29-31.*

It is the communion of those who worship God in Spirit and in truth—John 4:21-24.

The idea of the true Church as a group that traces its genealogy or pedigree to the apostles is alien to Scriptures.

2) On the issue of **'the power of the keys'**, it is important to know what the keys are:
   i) Are the keys literal keys to the gate of heaven?
   ii) Are the keys for absolving or withholding forgiveness?
   iii) Were the keys given to Peter and the Apostles alone for binding and loosing?
   iv) Were the keys passed on to only direct successors of the Apostles and no one else?

To discern what the keys Jesus referred to mean, we need to examine other texts in the Scriptures.

In Mathew 18:18, Jesus, while speaking to the disciples, not just Peter or the Apostles, repeated the promise of giving to them *'the power to bind and loose'* that he had made while apparently addressing only Peter in Mathew 16:19, without the express mention of the keys. Since this promise was linked to the keys in Mathew 16:19, it can be surmised that it meant that they too would get the keys.

In **Mathew 23:13,** Jesus said: *"Woe unto you Scribes and Pharisees, hypocrites, for you shut off the kingdom of heaven from men; you do not enter in yourselves, nor do you allow those who are entering to go in."* (Remember, what Jesus promised to give Peter was the keys of the kingdom of heaven)

It would appear that the Scribes and the Pharisees also had the keys to the kingdom of heaven (otherwise they would not have been able to shut the door), but they used the keys to shut people out rather than let them in.

In **Luke 11:52,** the meaning of *the keys* was revealed when Jesus said: *"Woe to you lawyers, for you have taken away <u>the key of Knowledge,</u> you did not enter in yourselves, and those who were entering in you hindered."*

It is clear that **the key** that the Scribes, Pharisees and lawyers use against or take away from people is *the knowledge of the truth about God, Jesus Christ and the kingdom of heaven.*

In John 8:32, He said: *"And you shall know the TRUTH and the TRUTH shall set you free."* Again, Jesus said: *"I am the Way, the Truth and the Life, no man comes unto the Father but by me"—John 14:6.*

When Jesus therefore promised to give the keys, He was speaking figuratively about the knowledge of the Truth about Himself and about God and how such knowledge can set men free and lead to eternal life.

Another interpretation for the "keys" is that it gave Peter and the Apostles the power to absolve people of sins or withhold forgiveness from them. This again was used to support the doctrine that the clergy is essential for salvation since anyone whose sins are not absolved cannot go to heaven.

However, Jesus' teaching on forgiveness is that Christians should as a matter of practice, forgive those who offend them and also seek forgiveness from all they offend—*Mathew 5:23-24; Mathew 6:14; Mathew 18:15-35; Mark 11:25-26.*

Jesus taught that Christians should practice reciprocal forgiveness so that the Father can also forgive them. It is clear that the keys, if they are for absolution of sins are not limited to the Apostles and their successors.

The key that will be used to bind and loose is ***the knowledge of the Truth which is essential for salvation and holy living*** and not ***a literal or mystical key*** given to Peter or the Apostles alone to literally open the gates of heaven.

3) On the issue of the Holy Spirit:

a) Were the Apostles and their successors the only repository of the Holy Spirit?
b) Is the 'saving mission' committed only to the Apostles and their direct successors?

The idea of the Holy Spirit being the exclusive preserve of the Apostles and by succession the Pope and the bishops are unscriptural. Many Scripture passages corroborate the fact that the Holy Spirit is promised to *everyone* who *believes* and *obeys*—*John 7:38-39; John 14:17, 26; John 15:26; John 16:13-14; Acts 1:4-8; Acts 5:32.*

As Peter addressed the curious people on the day of Pentecost, he reminded them of the promise of God to pour out His Spirit on **"all flesh"**, not just a few or select group who 'succeed' the Apostles. He called on them to repent, get baptized and receive the Holy Spirit because *the promise was not only for them but also for their Children and for 'all' who are called of God—Acts 2:37-39.*

In *Acts 5:32*, Peter testified that *God gives the Holy Spirit to all who obey Him.*

Although the Holy Spirit can be imparted by the laying on of hands, this is not a requirement. No one laid hands on the disciples on the day of Pentecost or for that matter, surprisingly, the household of Cornelius before they were baptized with the Holy Spirit—**Acts 10:44-48**.

In the Old Testament, at the consecration of the **seventy elders** selected to help Moses, **sixty-eight** were around the Tabernacle and prophesied but so also did *Eldad* and *Medad* who were not even in the vicinity but in their tents, to the consternation of Joshua, Moses' helper—**Numbers 11:16-30.**

4) On the question of the "saving mission", the Roman Catholic Church teaches that this was committed to the Apostles and their successors who alone are authorized to act in the Name of Jesus".

This position; again is not supported by Scriptures. Jesus Himself, during his lifetime, commissioned others, apart from the Apostles to be missionaries in their communities. Apart from the Apostles, Jesus also sent out seventy other disciples in pairs with the same assignment he gave to the twelve, to preach, teach and heal—*Luke 10:1-20.*

Many Samaritans became believers on the witness of the woman at the well—*John 4:39 (1-42)*

In Mark *5:18-20 (1-20);* Jesus told a man he healed of demon possession and who wanted to follow him, to go home and be a witness to God's grace. The man effectively proclaimed Jesus in Decapolis and all marveled. Also, in Mark **9:38-39 and Luke 9:49-50**; John reported to Jesus Christ that they had forbidden a man who was casting out demons in the Name of Jesus because he did not follow them. Jesus asked them not to stop him; that the man was obviously on their side. Again, following the persecution that arose after the martyrdom of Stephen; the scattered disciples all went about preaching, the Gospel and not only the Apostles—*Acts 9:1-8.*

In *1Corinthians 12:1-31,* Paul made it clear that as members of Christ's body, each person has a role to play under the direction of the Holy Spirit and that every role is important. It is incumbent on every disciple to make disciples; Stephen and Philip were elected to serve food as deacons, but God used both mightily in evangelism—*Acts 6:8; Acts 8:4-8.*

5) Another dogma tied to the doctrines of Apostolic Succession and the power of the keys is that of the **"Magisterium of the Church"**.

This dogma states that only the Magisterium, (that is the Pope and all the bishops in communion with him) can give "authentic" interpretation of the Word of God, whether in the written form of in the form of tradition. The faithful are expected to *"receive with docility"* the teachings and directives that their priests give them in different forms.

This unquestioning reception of the teachings of the Magisterium is also unscriptural. Jesus promised to give the Holy Spirit to all obedient believers to help, teach and guide—*John 14:16-17, 26; John 16:13.*

The Holy Spirit, not the Church or the Magisterium is the believer's Teacher, Guide, Helper and the Revealer of all truth.

Jesus also told the multitude and the disciples that only Christ is their teacher and only God is their father—*Mathew 23:8-10.*

Paul commended the Berean Christians for their respectful sense of doubt of new teachings when they diligently searched the Scripture to corroborate what they were being taught—*Acts 17:10-12.*

6) The Magisterium is also credited with the possession of unwritten "treasure of deposit" of oral tradition considered of equal weight in authority with the Scriptures.

Moses said: *"the secret things belong unto the Lord our God, but those things which are revealed belong unto us and to our children for ever, that we may do all the words of this law"*—Deuteronomy 29:29 (KJV).

Paul also declared: *"You know that I have kept back nothing that was profitable unto you, and have taught you publicly and from house to house"*—Acts 20:20 (KJV).

Again he said: *"Therefore I declare to you today that I am innocent of the blood of all men. For I have not hesitated to proclaim to you the whole counsel of God"*—**Acts 20:26-27 (NIV).**

All through the Scriptures, prophets and priests kept nothing from God's people. The idea that some special people have some secret knowledge is unbiblical and smacks of Gnosticism; God's messengers are expected to declare the whole counsel of God.

III) Sacerdotal Soteriology—The Ritualization and Formalization of Worship [10, 11, 12]

The clergy-centered Roman Catholic Church doctrine led to the believe that there can be no salvation outside of the Roman Catholic Church since the clergy is seen as "*the essential link between the laity and Christ*".

St. Augustine of Hippo said: *"one cannot have salvation except in the (Catholic) Church. Outside of the Catholic Church, one can have everything except salvation." ". . . One can have faith in the Name of the Father and of the Son and of the Holy Spirit; and preach, but never can one find salvation . . ."*

St. Cyprian of Carthage said: *"No one can have God as Father who does not have the (Catholic) Church as mother."*

In Roman Catholic soteriology, **the sacraments, (of which seven are described, namely—baptism, Confirmation or Chrismation, Eucharist, Penance, Extreme Unction or Anointing of the sick, Holy Orders and Matrimony) are necessary for salvation**.

The celebration of the Eucharist and other sacraments are believed to provide *"an encounter between Christ and the church and dispense divine life"*.

Consequent on the doctrine of Apostolic Succession, only the clergy can administer the sacraments (except baptism which can be administered by anyone and marriage which couples can administer on each other in the presence of witnesses).

It is believed that the *"priesthood of ordained ministers"* (as opposed to the *baptismal priesthood*, which includes the laity) is the *sacramental bond or link in the encounter between Christ and the Church*.

Therefore, *according to the Roman Catholic Church dogma, the clergy is essential for salvation because the laity can encounter Christ only through the clergy*!

It is believed that Christ is present in:
- The church's liturgical celebrations
- The Eucharistic species
- The person of the minister
- In the Word which the Magisterium alone can interpret
- The church's singing and prayer.

"The celebration and administration of the sacraments are according to 'specified formulae' codified into liturgical rites which the clergy follow. For the laity to worship, participation in these liturgical rituals is essential".

With the ritualization of worship also came the formalization; for example, in the Roman Catholic doctrine of transubstantiation, when the priest celebrates the Eucharist, Christ has a real presence, not only through the priest, but in what the priest offers—the Eucharist. Jesus is believed to be offering Himself for sins again in the Eucharistic mass as a "victim". The liturgical rites and celebration of sacraments are according to specified codes and formulas. The rituals are complete with elaborate liturgical codes, formulae, ceremonies and vestments which are the exclusive preserve of the clergy, the episcopate or the papacy but have no basis in the Scriptures.

In addition, by the power of the keys, the clergy is believed to hold the power to bind and loose, interpreted to mean the power to remit or retain sins. Therefore, it is believed that the eternal destiny of the laity for heaven or hell is in their power too.

COMMENT

Contrary to the Catholic Church doctrine of sacerdotal soteriology, believers do not need the mediation of a priest to encounter Jesus Christ.

- ❖ Jesus Christ Himself promised to abide with and live in every obedient believer; in ***John 14:23***; he said: *"... If anyone loves me, he will keep my commandment; and My Father will love him and We will come to him and make Our home with him."*

1Corinthians 3:16-17 say: *"Do you not know that you are the temple of God and that the Spirit of God dwells in you? If anyone defiles the temple of God, God will destroy him. For the temple of God is holy, which temple you are."*

- ❖ Although corporate worship is promoted in the Scriptures, Jesus said true worshipers are those who worship Him in Spirit and in truth—*(John*

4:24)—never did He say believers need to encounter Him through the Apostles or their successors in order to worship acceptably.

- The idea of Jesus Christ as a 'sacrificial victim' is unscriptural. Jesus was not a victim, He laid down His life voluntarily—***John 10:17-18; John 15:13***.
- Furthermore, the Bible teaches that: *"Jesus was offered as sacrifice for the sins of the world once for all"*—*(Hebrews 10:1-14)*; therefore, the idea of the repetition of the sacrifice is unscriptural
- (though the Roman Catholic Dogma denies repeating, but merely celebrating).
- Every obedient believer has Christ living in him and through the Blood of Jesus Christ has **direct access** to the Father. Unlike in the Old Testament Covenant, there is no longer a partitioning veil separating the laity from the Holy of Holies; there is no longer a sacred place where only the High Priest can enter. The Scriptures say that: *with His own Body and Blood, Jesus Christ provided a direct access to the throne of Grace for every believer—Hebrews 4:14-16, Hebrews 10:19-23.*

This is the Good News; the Gospel in a nutshell!

- While there are valid mysteries, whatever mystery it has pleased God to reveal are for the benefit of all true believers and not a select few—***Psalm 25:14; Mathew 13:10-11; John 14:16-17, 26; John 16:13-14.*** The idea of mysteries to which only a select few are privy smacks of Gnosticism. This mystification of worship only empowers the ecclesiastics through which undue control of the laity is achieved as the doctrines had anathemas attached for any dissident.
- Christian leaders, as Disciples of Christ, are expected to make more disciples, teaching others all that Jesus Christ has commanded—***Mathew 28:19-20***; and not fail to declare the whole counsel of God.
- The function of the minister of God in the New Covenant is to preach and teach the Good News—*(Mathew 28:19-20)*; not the performance of rituals and this priestly function is given to all believers—*1Peter 2:9*.
- The Communion that believers share in the Eucharist is possible because they are all sealed in the New Covenant which is in the Blood of Jesus Christ. They have access to the Communion table because they are already saved not because they are seeking salvation. The Eucharistic meal nourishes believers spiritually because they qualify to eat it, otherwise it would be a snare if they eat it unworthily—*1Corinthians 11:23-32*.

IV) The Paganization of Worship and the Perversion of Piety [13, 14, 15, 16, 17]

The imperial favor enjoyed by Christianity following the 'conversion' of the Emperor Constantine led to the rapid growth of the Church. However, this was not due to actual conversions but rather the embrace of Christianity from expediency. There were moral and spiritual decline of those who called themselves Christians and this set the stage for the insidious paganization of Christian worship and piety.

The rigorous catechumenate which subsisted during the period of persecution was relaxed in time of peace and syncretism became rife.

During the time of the Cappadocian fathers and Chrysostom, syncretism was dealt with simply by offering *"Christian alternatives"* to the laity's pagan practices. Making the sign of the cross replaced occultic marks and infant baptism replaced the use of amulets for the protection of children. The *"cult of martyrs and saints"* which replaced the hordes of Roman pagan gods and heroes also developed.

Relics and icons became regular fixtures in the inauguration of churches and monasteries which also stocked and traded in them. Shrines were also built in other places for the relics of martyrs and saints. Pilgrimages to the churches, monasteries and shrines for the veneration of the relics and icons were encouraged as signs of piety. The teaching was that the icons were mediums that provided access to and communion with the saints, the angels or the holy being for the holder and afforded the pilgrims or icon holders participation in the saints' or martyrs' sanctity. The veneration of relics in the Middle Ages reportedly came to rival the sacraments in the daily life of the medieval Church. This is a perversion of piety because according to Scriptures, true piety consists of doing what the word of God says and being a true witness of Jesus in charitable living. In addition, the only mediator between God and man is Jesus Christ—*1 Timothy 2:5;* and the intercessors are Christ and the Holy Spirit—*Hebrews 7:24-25; Romans 8:26-27.*

As already discussed, there is absolutely no need for any dead or living intermediate intercessor between believers and Jesus Christ or the Holy Spirit since both live in the true and obedient child of God.

The only difference between icon veneration and pagan idol worship appears to be only semantics.

Another way in which piety was perverted was monasticism. Those appalled by the worldliness and corruption around them withdrew from society; others withdrew thinking they could tame or overcome the demons in them. However, judging by the reputation (or lack thereof) of most monks and nuns through the ages until now, it is clear that this approach to piety has never worked.

What the Bible taught was not physical separation but genuine spiritual transformation that can resist the devil and the lure of the world—***John 17:14-23.***

The process of paganization is not limited to the early church. As conversion by conquest continued during the Middle Ages, the practice of compromise and accommodation of pagan practices continued through merely inventing Christian alternatives to pagan festivals in many cultures. For example, The Roman winter festival of **Saturnalia** and the Nordic and Germanic pagan winter festival of **Yule** were converted to **Christmas**; the celebration of Christ's birth (though the exact date of Christ's birth is unknown). Aspects of those celebrations such as decorations, exchange of gifts, singing, dancing etc have been retained in Christmas celebrations. For centuries, the drunkenness, licentiousness and acts of depravity that characterized the pagan celebrations continued in spite of the new label. As a result, some Puritans in the 17th century banned the celebration of Christmas. Today, the mythical character, Santa Claus and commercialization dominate Christmas celebrations in many countries.

In the same way Halloween, the Celtic pagan celebration in honor of the 'lord of darkness', **Sawhain,** and the day on which the souls of the dead as well as other spirits, good and evil were believed to roam about became incorporated into Christianity. The Roman Catholic Church invented the "All Saints' Day to counter and down play the pagan celebrations. Most of the other Christian groups today have approached the festival much like the Catholic Church by creating alternatives and re-labeling the festival but still celebrating it with all the pagan trappings of decorations, costumes, candies even horror themed projects etc. Some new labels for churches with no saint days are 'Harvest festival' and 'Reformation Day'.

(V) The Romanization of the Ecclesiastical Structure [18, 19]

Many historians believe that the hierarchical structure of the Catholic Church developed as a process of Roman acculturation, with Christians adapting the Roman model of government to Church organization. The administrative units were grouped into provinces called Diocese which were headed by bishops. Under the bishops were parishes headed by priests who report to the bishop. The bishops of large cities were later called Metropolitans and have authority over the bishops in their provinces. The bishops of regions were later called Patriarchs; there were five Patriarchates namely—Rome, Antioch, Jerusalem, Alexandria and Constantinople. Initially, though these Patriarchs communicate on matters of mutual interest, there was no subordination of one to the other though most considered the Patriarch of Rome as *"primus inter pares"* due to the recognition given to Rome as the capital of the Empire and the centre of Christendom.

Later, the doctrine of Apostolic Succession and the Power of the Keys with the belief that Jesus said He would build the Church on Peter led to the development of the doctrine that regarded the bishop of Rome, as the head of the universal Church.

With the fall of Rome and the western half of the empire, the Bishop of Rome rose to prominence and filled the void left by the emperor and came to be known as the Pope. The supremacy of the bishop of Rome as the head of Christendom, though accepted in the west has never really been accepted in the east, and it remained a bone of contention until the final east-west schism of 1054 AD.

While the early churches had deacons, elders, overseers or bishops administering them, the idea of an 'emperor' more or less over a Christian kingdom was unknown in Scriptures and in fact discouraged by Jesus Christ who resisted the effort by the people to crown him king—***John 6:14-15*** and said over and over again that His Kingdom is not of this world—***John 18:36***.

Therefore the hierarchical Roman Catholic Church system that developed is not supported in the Scriptures much less the doctrines used to prop them up such as those of the Magisterium and Papal infallibility.

The extent to which the Roman culture influenced Roman Catholicism is expressed succinctly by historian **J.J. Blunt** thus:

> *"In the transition from pagan to papal Rome, much of the old material was worked up. The heathen temples became Christian churches, the altars of the gods became Christian altars, the curtains, incense, tapers, votive tablets remained the same; the aquaminarium was still the vessel for holy water; St. Peter stood at the gate instead of Lardea; St. Sebastian in the bedroom instead of the Phrygian Penates; St. Nicholas was the sign of the vessel instead of Castor*

> *and Pollux; the Mater Deum became the Madonna . . . the festival of the Mater Deum, the festival of the Madonna or Lady Day; the Hostra, or victim was now the 'Host'; the Lugentes Campi or dismal regions, purgatory; the offering to the Manes wore masses to the dead . . . . Indeed, so much of the Roman had been grafted upon the Roman Catholic system during the Dark Ages (as they are called) that the confusion of ideas and of terms resulting from it forms quite a feature in the writings of the Italian authors who lived at the revival of letters. Images holy and unholy are by them crowded together without the slightest regard for decency . . . ."*

VI) The Secularization and Militarization of the Clergy and the Monastics [18, 21, 22, 23, 24]

The secularization of the ecclesiastics of the Roman Catholic Church began when it was made the only acceptable form of Christianity by Emperor Constantine. The emperor placed all cadres of the clergy on salary and ensured that the Bishop pays them as scheduled.

Later, when Emperor Theodosius made Christianity the only lawful religion of the realm, ascetic monks called ***circumcellions*** were used as vigilantes by Bishops in North Africa and other parts of the empire to ensure conformity to the tenets of the faith by all. They roamed the land ransacking homes looking for idols to destroy.

After the fall of Rome and the fragmentation of the western empire, the Pope and the bishops of the region filled in the administrative void created by the elimination of the civil administration. The Popes were careful to align with the strongest warlords. Beginning with Clovis to the Carolingian dynasty when in 800 AD, Charlemagne was declared the Holy Roman Emperor and others till the final divorce of the Church and State in the 19th century.

This marriage of Church and State increased the State's intrusion in Church affairs and vice versa. The Emperors appointed bishops who were usually also princes who held both temporal and spiritual powers and many of whom had their own armies.

The Church was very much a part of the European feudal system. In Britain, the Lord Chancellor was almost always a bishop until Henry VIII deposed Cardinal Woolsey and broke away from the Catholic Church and even today, the bishops of the Church of England are members of the House of Lords as the "Lords Spiritual".

In France, bishops and abbots, usually from noble families, constituted the First Estate of the realm before the French Revolution in 1789. In every other European nation, bishops also held high political offices.

Many of the princes also endowed monastic orders with lands to build monasteries, but when needed, such monasteries provided the princes/bishops with fighting men.

The militarization eventually involved the whole echelon of the Clergy such that some Cardinals and Popes were known to have led their armies into battle. The increased involvement of the State in spiritual matters led to the '*Investiture Controversy*'.

The Crusades, launched essentially to free the Holy land from Moslems also culminated in the formation of military orders within the Church, namely, the Knights Templar, the Knights Hospitaller and the Teutonic knights. All served as crusading knights during the Middle Ages and the last mentioned was used principally to force Eastern European tribes to convert to Christianity.

The secularization of the clergy probably reached its apogee by the twelfth and thirteenth century when the papacy groaning under the yoke of the imperial powers, began the effort to break off the imperial hold on the ecclesiastic structure. The process began in the eleventh century with Pope **Nicholas II (1058-1061)**, was advanced greatly by **Gregory VII (1073-1085)** but sealed and delivered by **Pope Innocent III (1198-1216)** who made virtually every European nation a vassal of the papacy. With the deft use of ecclesiastical power of excommunication and interdict combined with not so subtle diplomacy, he, more than any other pope brought the European monarchs under papal authority.

He believed in the spurious **"Donation of Constantine"** document which purported that the Emperor Constantine had ceded the temporal power of the old Western Roman Empire to the Pope and his successors. As such, the Pope, possessing both spiritual and temporal powers, was sovereign over all the kings and the emperor in Europe.

(VII) **The Relaxation of the Penitential Discipline and Commercialization of Penance** [24, 25, 26, 27, 28]

During the Apostolic Age, believers had zero tolerance for sin. As much as Jesus associated with sinners, His message was consistently the need for sinners to repent. In fact, He stated that the purpose of His coming was to *"call sinners to repentance"—Mathew 9:13, Mark 2:17; Luke 5:31-32(NKJV)*. Jesus taught the disciples to have Zero tolerance for sin saying: ***"If your hand or your foot causes you to sin, cut it off and throw it away. It is better for you to enter life maimed or crippled than to have two hands or two feet and be thrown into eternal fire. And if your eye causes you to sin, gouge it out and throw it away. It is better for you to enter life with one eye than to have two eyes and be thrown into the fire of hell—Mathew 18:8-9 (NIV).***

When Ananias and Sapphira his wife thought that they could deceive the Holy Spirit, they received instant justice—*Acts 5:1-11.*

When Simon the sorcerer offered Peter and John money for the baptism of the Holy Spirit, he was sharply rebuked by Peter who advised him to repent and make his heart right with God.—*Acts 8:14-24.*

When Elymas the sorcerer openly opposed the ministry of Saul and Barnabas to the official Sergius Paulus; he was struck with instantaneous blindness—*Acts 13:6-12.*

In all of their epistles, the Apostles encouraged believers to live righteous and holy lives and to have Zero tolerance for sin—*1Corinthians 5&6; Ephesians 4:20-5:11; Colossians 3:1-17; 1Thessalonians 4:1-8.*

They recommended that repeat or unrepentant offenders of serious sins be excommunicated—*1Corinthians 5:11; 2Thessalonians 3:6, 14; Titus 3:10-11.* They warned that sin, like yeast through dough, would spread through the church if not appropriately dealt with.

However, with time, the penitential discipline of the Church was gradually relaxed.

1) The first recorded relaxation was by the Bishop of Rome (Pope) ***Callistus I (217-222)*** who began the readmission into communion those with capital or mortal sins and precipitated the **'Hippolytus Schism'.**

During the Decian and the Diocletan persecutions of the Church, huge numbers 'lapsed', that is, they denied the faith in one form or the other. Many expressed the wish to return into fellowship and the Church considered the issue at the ***Council of Ancyra in 314 AD***. At the Council, various types of penance were prescribed depending on the level of culpability. The less rigorous approach was adopted also because of the emerging doctrine of the Church as the vehicle of salvation. The thinking was that since the bishops had the power to bind and loose, if absolution was withheld for anyone, it meant that person had no hope on earth or in heaven.

2) In 440 AD, *Pope Leo I (440-461 AD)* abrogated public penance which was previously the norm, except for capital sins of idolatry, murder and uncleanness and decreed that private confession to a priest was sufficient. He explained that many people were not presenting themselves for confession because of fear and shame of public penance or of exposure to enemies. This was contrary to the position of many early Church fathers like Cyprian, Augustine and Gregory of Nyssa.

3) *Pope Gregory I (590-604 AD)* called for*: "treating sinners in power with the art of tenderness lest instead of being reformed, they should be hardened"*! He counseled against making frontal attacks or direct mention of known sins and advocated public penance for only public and notorious transgressions.

COMMENT

Pope Gregory 1's counsel is contrary to many biblical injunctions in both the Old and the New Testament—*Leviticus 19:17; 1Timothy 5:20-21.* The Bible clearly warned against showing partiality in the course of justice. Moreover, the prophets did not handle sinners in high places with kids gloves—Nathan confronted David—*2Samuel 12:1-14*; Elijah confronted Ahab—*1Kings 17:1; 1Kings 21:17-24*; and John the Baptist confronted Herod—*Mark 6:17-19*.

In spite of Pope Gregory I's effort to improve the penitential discipline by relaxation, his method did not seem to work; although private confessions occurred, many among the clergy and the people refused to do public penance. The situation was complicated by the fact that there was no way to compel public penance for privately confessed sins. Following an Augustinian principle, the Church had determined that it would be improper to threaten or actually excommunicate such persons as the bishop cannot be both the witness and the judge.

Gregory's relaxation did not help the morals of his time as judged by the record of a contemporary who wrote *"both the priests and the people ran riot in wickedness".*

4) In 680 AD, *Theodorus (602-690 AD),* the Archbishop of Canterbury systematized the private penance instituted by Pope Leo I and wrote the *Private Penitential* for both the priest and the people.

The method changed the old Penitential order. In the old order, the sinner was bound to the prescribed austerities and absolved after the fulfillment of same then restored to previous privileges. However, in the new order, the sinner is first loosed, and then bound because the priest ***absolved*** and ***restored*** following confession if the sinner **promised** to follow the prescribed ***austerity***; as already noted, many didn't.

Private confession therefore became the norm "whatever the nature of the sin, the circumstance or the inducement", contrary to previously established tradition.

5) Another change that crept into the penitential discipline was the number of times it could be repeated by an individual. Prior to the time of St. Augustine, an individual was allowed one *'Solemn Penance'*. In the new penitential discipline, penance became *'toties quoties'*; that is, as needed and as many times as required without limitation.

6) Redemption of the public canonical penance by pecuniary and other commutations known as ***Indulgence*** gradually became the norm in the Middle Ages.

The foundation for this was laid in the canons of the Council of Ancyra which gave bishops the discretionary power to shorten or lengthen a penitent's prescribed penance based on the penitent's behavior and compliance. Another factor in the development was the practice of the early martyrs who gave the *'libellus pacis'* to Christians who lapsed and who sought readmission into the Church. From this developed the idea of vicarious satisfaction which the Church supported with the words of the Apostle Paul in Colossians 1:24.

By the seventh century, penitential redemption was mentioned and methodized in ***Theodorus' Penitential***. He was denounced by some as the innovator of the practice but others defended him as a mere regulator; that the practice was so ingrained he only tried to regulate it, as there was no hope it could be totally removed. There were documented cases of such redemption of canonical penance by commutation of austerities that predated Theodorus by more than a century.

In commutations, gifts were made to God, His saints and the Church; the rich could build and endow churches while the less affluent could render military service against infidels in crusades.

The process became prominent during the crusades when indulgences were declared for those taking part. In time, the almsgiving branch of penance overshadowed the other areas and in time people thought this and other commutations could be given in lieu of other forms of penance like fasting, prayers etc.

Indulgence is defined as: *"An extra-sacramental remission of temporal punishment due, in God's justice to <u>sin that has been forgiven(?)</u>, which remission is granted by the Church in the exercise of the 'power of the keys' through the application of the superabundant merits of Christ and the saints . . ."*

Indulgence is said to be from the "merits" of Jesus Christ and the saints which together constitute the "Treasure" of the Church from which the pope and the episcopate can dispense based on 'the power of the keys'. To gain indulgence, the faithful must be free from mortal sins; for plenary indulgence, confession and communion are required while for partial indulgence, a disposition of contrition is all that is required.

Indulgences can be local or universal, temporary or perpetual, Plenary or partial and for the living or the dead. A universal indulgence is accessible to any faithful anywhere and a plenary indulgence remits the entire temporal punishment that would have been served in purgatory.

The pope can grant every kind of indulgence while the cardinals, archbishops and bishops can grant indulgences as allowed by the pope.

According to the doctrine of indulgence:
- Sin attracts two kinds of punishment: eternal and temporal.
- Guilt is associated with sin and it incurs punishment (it is unjust to punish the guiltless)
- The sacrament of baptism removes (remits) the guilt of sin and therefore the penalties (since guilt was the reason for punishment, once that is removed, there is no longer any grounds for penalties)
- **For mortal sins (committed after baptism),** *"penance removes the guilt and the eternal punishment but the temporal punishment is still required by Divine justice"*
- The temporal punishment can be served in life or after death in purgatory.
- An indulgence offers the penitent sinner the means of paying off the debt during his lifetime on earth.
- It releases the penitent from his indebtedness to the Church, (from his obligation of performing canonical penance), and

from temporal punishment. Rather than the penitent having to do penance—fasting, prayers, alms etc, to get personal 'merits' to pay for sins, the merits of Christ and the saints are offered to him—(at a price)—such as a specified sum of money, pilgrimage or participation in a crusade.

It is stated that Indulgence is not:
- Permission to commit sin.
- A pardon for future sin.
- An exemption from any law or duty
- The forgiveness of the guilt of sin (it presupposes that sin has already been forgiven). **
- Not the purchase of a pardon that secures the buyer salvation and does not (?) release the soul from purgatory (!)**

COMMENT

The reasoning behind the doctrine of indulgence is confusing and raises a lot of questions.

The questions are:
- ❖ First, why should one sin, after it has been repented of, attract two kinds of punishment—an eternal and a temporal?
- ❖ Why would penance remit the guilt and the eternal punishment but somehow leave intact the temporal punishment?
- ❖ If indulgence is being given for "sin that has already been forgiven"; what guilt is left to which the temporal punishment is attached?
- ❖ If there is no more guilt, because the sin has been forgiven, on what basis is there a 'temporal punishment? Since, according to the sacrament of penance, the removal of guilt removes the penalties?
- ❖ Although it is stated that only God knows what precise amount of penalty that remains in severity and duration, specific numbers of days of indulgence are given.
- ❖ If indulgence presupposes the effects of confession, contrition and sacramental satisfaction, why is it still maintained that indulgence does not release from guilt and punishment?
- ❖ If indulgence is not the purchase of a pardon that secures the buyer a release from purgatory, why does the doctrine say it is a means of 'paying off' during the penitent's lifetime, the debt that could keep him in purgatory?

The whole idea of the 'Indulgence' is kind of nebulous and those who formulated it did not seem to know exactly what it is and what it actually does.

It is therefore not surprising that the doctrine faced opposition from within the Church. John Wycliffe, the English theologian and scholar of the fourteenth century said: *"It is foolish to believe in the indulgence granted by the pope and the bishops".*

This was one of the 'errors' for which Wycliffe was condemned at the Council of Constance.

Martin Luther, a monk in the sixteenth century said: *"Indulgences are pious frauds of the faithful"*

The gradual relaxation of the penitential discipline and later introduction of pecuniary redemption in the form of indulgences corrupted the Church hierarchy and the laity with the result that both 'wallowed in wickedness' until the revolt of the Reformation and subsequent schisms of various forms of Protestantism from the Roman Catholic Church.

(VIII) The Reformation and the Fragmentation of the Church [29]

As already seen, corruption had become systemic in the Church long before Martin Luther. Groups like the Albigensians, Waldensians, Wycliffites and the Hussites that tried to break away from the Roman Catholic Church or introduce reforms were persecuted and crushed by the powers of the papacy and the states.

In the early sixteenth century, the excesses and corruption of the Roman Catholic Church hierarchy led to the Schism of the Lutheran church from the Catholic Church led by Martin Luther. Soon after, other groups like the Calvinists, the Anabaptists and the Anglicans emerged and the principle of *"Cuius regio, eius religio"* was adopted in much of Europe and the various forms of Christianity became associated with the various nation States.

Initially dissidents were exiled but later accommodated with various degrees of deprivation of civil liberties. During this period, Catholicism predominated in Italy, France, Spain and Portugal; Britain Anglicanism, Germany Lutheranism and other European countries, mixed Catholicism and Protestantism. The Christian faith was exported around the world in this fragmented form which has only multiplied in the last three centuries.

(IX) Liberalization and Tribalization of Christianity [30]

From the Renaissance humanists philosophers and Reformation theologians evolved the Enlightenment Age and modern day liberal theologies. These liberal theologians are found in every denomination and have undermined traditional faith and doctrine. Many have denied the core doctrines of Christianity such as the virgin birth, the divinity of Christ, the need and significance of the crucifixion and the resurrection. The idea of a system of timeless acultural theological truths is being jettisoned for racial, social or even gender based theologies.

Rather than teaching that man order his life in accordance with the dictates of a sovereign all-wise and all-knowing God, theologies are being developed that tries to create a god that will fit every man's situation, whatever that may be. Sin and salvation are redefined to suit social and political ideologies and the Scriptures are remade so as not to offend the sensibilities of the 'sophisticated' modern man or conflict with his science.

Modern writers and commentators claim to have better knowledge and insight into biblical accounts than the eyewitness recorders several millennia before; and the amazing thing is, many believe them and trust their phony exegesis and hermeneutics.

Even among those who claim to believe the traditional timeless truths, there is a wide gulf between the conduct and the confession.

X) The Secularization of the Gospel and the Perversion of Compassion [31, 32, 33, 34, 35]

Secularism, which is defined as the principle of the separation of government, its institution and officials from religious institutions and dignitaries has its roots in the Enlightenment Age. From the concept arose the idea of the 'Separation of Church and State' which initially meant the reversal of what obtained in the era of '*Cuius regio, Eius religio*' in Europe when State religion meant exile for dissenters. It was meant to afford citizens freedom of religion with non-imposition of any particular religion on them by the State as was enshrined in the American Constitution. Over time, the meaning of the separation of Church and state has been expanded from toleration of all shades of religion to the exclusion of and resistance to all religious influence on the executive, legislative and judicial arms of government. Unfortunately, in an attempt supposedly to protect minorities, the secularization process has progressively morphed into a situation in which the majority is often marginalized and even criminalized. The initial idea of freedom of religion in which government does not interfere in what people believe and how they believe is rapidly changing. Governments, individually and sometimes collectively through the United Nations (UN), under the pretext of protecting the rights of minorities are beginning to infringe on the beliefs of the people through legislations. Laws are being enacted that force people to conform to positions that are contrary to their religious beliefs in areas of scientific research, sex education, sexuality, abortion and birth control etc.

The lofty ideal of secularism was equality for all citizens, the reality is a lie and more and more, the secular agenda is being driven by atheists and agnostics many of whom are rabidly intolerant of the people of faith. It is a fact that, within the secularist movements are those whose core agenda is anti religion and whose goal is to transform the society by diminishing religious influence on institutions and denigrating religious values. Hence, there have been concerted efforts of effect institutional paradigm shift from religious to secular such as happened in Harvard and many others; at the individual level, there is increasingly a shift in mentality from the "ultimate to the proximate" and at societal level, a shift from church charities to welfare states.

The Church has also been infected with the secularization bug. The process also began during the Enlightenment Age and progressed through the liberal theology of Social Gospel Movements to the Hippie Jesus Movements, the Church Growth Movements and present day Emerging Church Movements.

In the last half of the 20th century, the "***Beat Generation***" or "***Beatniks***" emerged between the late forties and the early sixties. The movement consisted of artists with non-conformist, anti-capitalism, anti-materialism and anti-militarism ideology. Self described as "down beat and out but believing in the beatitudes, beatific and beautiful in an ugly but graceful way".

Led by notable figures like Allen Ginsberg and Jack Kerouac, the movement lived by a code of rebellion and mutiny against constituted authority and they sought freedom from what they considered sexual repression. In their quest for self awareness and what is considered expansion of consciousness, they embraced the use of drugs like cannabis, LSD, mescaline, amphetamines and heroin. They also dabbled in Eastern religions like Buddhism.

In the mid-sixties, another movement, essentially the progeny of the Beatniks, consisting of young 15-25 year old Americans emerged called the *"Hippies"*. They were also a counter-cultural movement that embraced sexual liberation, free love and sex and the use of psychedelic drugs. ***Their creed was "free love, peace and freedom", the philosophy was: "do your own thing whenever and wherever you want to"; while the anthem was the Beatles' "All you need is love".***

The Hippie culture spread around the world through music and other entertainment media.

They lived in communes usually (but not always) governed by democratic principles in which things were shared in common.

The Hippies embraced the Beatniks' idea of 'Sexual Revolution' which calls for loosening all societal restrictions on issues of sex. They live by the code "If it feels good, do it" and "free love" which means: "feel free to love whomever, wherever, whenever and however they pleased" in an atmosphere of "open relationships" of love without jealousy. They experimented in public and group orgies and gave free rein to all sorts of fantasies hitherto considered taboos.

The ideology of free love led to sexual permissiveness and promiscuity with heterosexual, bisexual and homosexual practices. The movement was characterized by violence at its gatherings and communes. Eventually, the more exuberant public displays waned suddenly with the emergence of the deadly sexually transmitted disease HIV/AIDS in the 1980s.

The Hippie culture infiltrated every fiber of the American society and transformed it in many ways. As pacifists, they protested the Vietnam War until the draft was cancelled and the war was ended. They influenced the manner of dressing, the music, and especially sexual norms and mores. Abortion was legalized, homosexuality and trans-sexuality were decriminalized, pornography in print and on the screen became free speech and the society became permissive in sexual matters.

Although many of the hippies renounced Christianity and embraced paganism, Wicca or Eastern religions like Buddhism and Taoism for spirituality, some formed what became known as the **"Jesus Movement"** which theologically is evangelical, and believes in miracles, faith healing, the Bible and the Holy Spirit. While some lived in communes others did not.

The Jesus Movement is considered by some as the Hippie element within Protestant churches and by others as the Christian element within the Hippie counter-culture. No matter how it is perceived, it is an incontrovertible fact that it has left its mark on Christianity in the United States of America; and the effect is being exported around the world.

The Jesus Movement climaxed at the Expo 1972 in Dallas Texas where the Jesus Movement and youths from the mainline denominations were brought together by *"Campus Crusade for Christ"*.

As time went on, those in the group or associated with them got into leadership positions within the churches and the hippie legacy in worship and music styles permeated the churches. With time the theology is also changing from pure evangelical to the seeker-friendly and emergent type of theology. Even within the mainstream mainline churches, balanced Gospel of salvation by grace based on faith in Jesus Christ and true repentance from sin has been replaced by the Hippie theology, shaped by the Hippie ideology of 'rights without responsibility and liberty without accountability'. Therefore, the message of salvation is presented as *"unconditional love"* and *"once saved always saved"* because Jesus is love.

People are invited to come to Christ as they are, but in the name of love are never told of Christ's power to transform them and that real change is required if salvation is genuine.

The lawless, irresponsible Hippie concept of love was introduced into the church with attendant perversion of love and compassion; so also cultural and political correctness; therefore all manner of immorality fester unchecked as Satan is transformed into an angel of light—2Corinthians 11:14-15.

The Great Question

". . . But, when the Son of Man comes, will He find faith on the earth?"—Luke 18:8.

Christianity has been battered through the ages such that, two millennia later, the product presented to the modern man differs from the Christianity found in the Acts of the Apostles. Over the ages, as philosophy replaced revelation, logic supplanted faith; the Gospel has been emptied of its power. Without demonstrable power and impact on the daily lives of people, Christianity has become little more than empty rituals for most and self hypnosis for others. Rather than making efforts to find out where and how the faith got derailed, generation after generation have only tried to rationalize, misinterpret and misrepresent the Word of God to the point where what is called Christianity today is nothing more than ***"Systematic or Systematized Unbelief"***. Christians profess words that make them feel good but in reality dishonor God and are nothing but unconscious and sometimes blatant blasphemies.

Today, ***Christians today preach and teach:***

- Confession without Contrition
- Salvation without Sanctification
- Redemption without Repentance
- Reconciliation without Regeneration
- Discipleship without Discipline
- Liberty without Responsibility
- Religion and Rituals without Righteousness
- Charity without Character
- ***And Expect:***
- God's comforts while ignoring His Commandments
- God's Blessings while disbelieving His promises
- Prosperity while lacking Integrity
- Miracles without Morality

In spite of this dismal picture, God has never failed to have true witnesses in every generation. For He has said:
"*. . . **I will build My Church, and the gates of hell shall not prevail against it**"—Matthew 16:18*

References

Introduction
1) Richard N. Ostling (Associated Press, May 19, 2001). "Researcher tabulates World's believers". About.com: http://www.adherents.com/misc/WCE.html

Chapter 1
1) Send the Light Trust (1969): Gems from Tozer, Extracts from the writings of a 20th Century Prophet.

Chapter 2
1) Send the Light Trust (1969): Gems from Tozer, Extracts from the writings of a 20th Century Prophet.
2) Salvation—Wikipedia, the free encyclopedia. http://en.wikipedia.org/wiki/salvation
3) Christian salvation—Religion Facts. http://www.religionfacts.com/Christianity/beliefs/salvation
4) Maas, A. (1912). Salvation. In The Catholic Encyclopedia. New York: Robert Appleton Company. Retrieved September 27, 2011 from New Advent: http://www.newadvent.org/cathen/13407a.htm

Chapter 5
1) Clement of Rome. ANFO1. The Apostolic Fathers with Justin Martyr and Iranaeus/ Christian Classic Ethereal Library. http://www.ccel.org/ccel/schaff/anf01.ii.ii.xlix.html
2) Ignatius of Antioch. ANF01. The Apostolic Fathers with Justin Martyr and Iranaeus/ Christian Classic Ethereal Library. http://www.ccel.org/schaff/anf01.html
3) Polycarp. ANF01.The Apostolic Fathers with Justin Martyr and Iranaeus/ Christian Classic Ethereal Library. http://www.ccel.org/ccel/schaff/anf01.html

4) Justin Martyr. ANF01.The Apostolic Fathers with Justin Martyr and Iranaeus/Christian Classic Ethereal Library. http://www.ccel.org/ccel/schaff/anf01.html
5) Justin Martyr. Synopsis. http://www.earlychurch.org.uk/justin.php
6) Iranaeus. ANF01. The Apostolic Fathers with Justin Martyr and Iranaeus/Christian Classic Ethereal Library. http://www.ccel.org/ccel/schaff/anf01.html
7) Iranaeus of Lyons. Synopsis. http://www.earlychurch.org.uk/iranaeus.php
8) ANF02. Fathers of the Second Century: Hermas, Tatian, Athenagoras, Theophilus and Clement of Alexandria (Entre)/Christian Classic Ethereal Library. http://www.ccel.org/ccel/schaff/anf02.toc.html
9) Ante-Nicene Fathers, Vol. II. http://www.tertullian.org/fathers2/ANF-02/anf02-60.html
10) Tertullian of Carthage: Synopsis. http://www.earlychurch.org.uk/Tertullian.php
11) A treatise on the soul. ANF03. Latin Christianity: Its Founder, Tertullian/ Christian Classic Ethereal Library. http://www.tertullian.org/ccel/schaff/anf03.html
12) Ante-Nicene Fathers, Vol. III. http://www.tertullian.org/fathers2/ANF03/toc.html
13) Edward Moore (updated May 2, 2005). Origen of Alexandria [Internet Encyclopedia of Philosophy]. http://www.iep.utm.edu/origen-of-alexandria/
14) Prat, F. (1911). "Origen and Origenism". In The Catholic Encyclopedia. New York: Robert Appleton Company. Retrieved October 7, 2010 from New Advent: http://www.newadvent.org/cathen/11306b.htm
15) "Origen of Alexandria" (c185-c254). Synopsis. http://www.earlychurch.org.uk.php
16) James Keifer. Cyprian of Carthage, Bishop and Martyr: http://satucket.com/lectionary/cyprian.htm
17) Edelhard L. Hummel. Cyprian of Carthage—Synopsis. http://www.earlychurch.org.uk/cyprian.php
18) ANF05. Fathers of the Third Century: Hippolytus, Cyprian, Caius, Novatian, Appendix. http://www.ccel.org/ccel/schaff/anf05.iv.v.html

19) Chapman J. (1908). St. Cyprian of Carthage. In The Catholic Encyclopedia. New York: Robert Appleton Company. Retrieved October 12, 2010 from New Advent: http://www.newadvent.org/cathen/04583b.htm
20) Chapman J. (1909). Firmilian. In The Catholic Encyclopedia. New York: Robert Appleton Company. Retrieved October 12, 2010 from New Advent: http://www.newadvent.org/cathen/06080b.htm
21) Lapsi (Christianity)—Wikipedia, the free encyclopedia. http://en.wikipedia.org/wiki/lapsi_(Christian)#
22) Nathaniel Marshall, D.D. "The Penitential Discipline of the Primitive Church for the first four hundred years after Christ together with its Declension from the Fifth Century, downwards to its present state: Impartially presented. New Edition: Oxford, John Parker: MDCCCXLIV

Chapter 6

1) Emperor Constantine (c274-337). http://www.earlychurch.org.uk/constantine.php
2) Paul Halsal. Medieval Sourcebook: Eusebius: Conversion of Constantine. http://www.fordham.edu/halsal/source/conv-const.html
3) Hans A. Pohlsanser. Roman Emperors—DIR Constantine I. http://www.roman-emperors.org/conniei.htm
4) Rev. M.B. Cowell. Priscillianus and Priscillianism, Priscillian. Dictionary of Christian Biography and Literature to the end of the Sixth Century A.D., with an Account of the Principal Sects and Heresies. http://www.ccel.org/ccel/wace/biodict.html?term=priscillianus%20and%20priscillianism,%20priscillian
5) Healy, P. (1911). Priscillianism. In The Catholic Encyclopedia. New York: Robert Appleton Company. Retrieved October 20, 2010 from New Advent. http://www.newadvent.org/cathen/12429b.htm
6) Fortescue A. (1912). Theodosius. In The Catholic Encyclopedia. New York: Robert Appleton Company. Retrieved December 25, 2009 from New Advent: http://www.newadvent.org/cathen/14577d.htm
7) David Woods. Roman Emperors—DIR Theodosius I. http://www.roman-emperors.org/theoI.htm

8) Hunter-Blair, O. (1910). St. Gregory of Nazianzus. In The Catholic Encyclopedia. New York: Robert Appleton Company. Retrieved December 25, 2009 from New Advent: http://www.newadvent.org/cathen/07010.htm
9) McSorley, J. (1907). St. Basil the Great. In The Catholic Encyclopedia. New York: Robert Appleton Company. Retrieved December 30, 2009 from New Advent. http://www.newadvent.org/cathen/023330b.htm
10) Catholic Information Network. "St. Basil the Great (329-379)—Bishop and Doctor of the Church. http://www.cin.org/saint/basilgre.html
11) Leclercq, H. (1910). St. Gregory of Nyssa. In The Catholic Encyclopedia. New York: Robert Appleton Company. Retrieved December 25. 2009 from New Advent: http://www.newadvent.org/cathen/07016a.htm
12) Vasiliki Limberis. "The cult of Martyrs and the Cappadocian Fathers". In Byzantine Christianity—Derek Krueger Ed.—Vol. 3, ch. 2: http://www.augsburgfortress.org/copyrights/contents.asp
13) NPNF2—06. Jerome: The Principal Works of St. Jerome/ Christian Classic Ethereal Library. http://www.ccel.org/ccel/schaff/npnf206.html
14) NPNF1—09. St. Chrysostom: On the priesthood, Ascetics, Treatises, Select Homilies and Letters, Homilies on Statutes/ Christian Classic Ethereal Library. http://www.ccel.org/ccel/schaff/npnf109.html
15) Portalie, E. (1907). Life of St. Augustine of Hippo. In The Catholic Encyclopedia. New York: Robert Appleton Company. Retrieved December 25, 2009 from New Advent: http://www.newadvent.org/cathen/02084a.htm
16) Augustine of Hippo (354-430 AD). http://www.earlychurch.org.uk/augustine.php
17) Church Fathers: On Nature and Grace (St. Augustine). http://www.newadvent.org/fathers/1503.htm
18) Church Fathers: On Merit and the Forgiveness of Sins, and Baptism of Infants. (Augustine). http://www.newadvent.org/fathers/1501.htm
19) Church Fathers: On Grace and Free Will (St. Augustine). http://www.newadvent.org/fathers/1510.htm

20) Church Fathers: On the Predestination of the Saints (Augustine). http://www.newadvent.org/fathers/1512.htm

Chapter 7
1) Fall of Rome—why did Rome fall?: http://ancienthistory.about.com/cs/rome/allarticles/a/falloffrome.htm
2) Alaric and the Fall of Rome: http://ancienthistoriy.about.com/alaricthevisigoth
3) Decline of the Roman Empire—Wikipedia, the free Encyclopedia. http://en.wikipedia.org/wiki/Decline_of_the_Roman_Empire
4) Huddleston, G. (1911). Monasticism. In The Catholic Encyclopedia. New York: Robert Appleton Company. Retrieved October 6, 2009 from New Advent: http://www.newadvent.org/cathen/10459a.htm
5) Butler, E.C. (1907). St. Anthony. In The Catholic Encyclopedia. New York: Robert Appleton Company. Retrieved October 30, 2010 from New Advent: http://www.newadvent.org/cathen/01553d.htm
6) St Anthony the Great. Photo Album. http://www.qozhaya.com/St.Anthony.html
7) Bacchus, F.J. (1911). St. Pachomius. In The Catholic Encyclopedia. New York: Robert Appleton Company. Retrieved October 31, 2010 from New Advent: http://www.newadvent.org/cathen/11381a.htm
8) Christian Monasticism and its Evil History: http://www.Muhammed.net/other-scriptures-mainmenu-43/73-otherideologies/710-monasticism-and-its-evilhistory.htm
9) Kurth, G. (1908). Clovis. In The Catholic Encyclopedia. New York: Robert Appleton Company. Retrieved October 27, 2010 from New Advent: http://www.newadvent.org/cathen/04070a.htm
10) Simeon Stylites—Wikipedia, the free Encyclopedia. http://en.wikipedia.org/wiki/Simeon_Stylites
11) Christian Monasticism and its Evil History: http://www.Muhammed.net/other-scriptures-mainmenu-43/73-otherideologies/710-monasticism-and-its-evilhistory.htm

12) Kurth, G. (1908). Clovis. In The Catholic Encyclopedia. New York: Robert Appleton Company. Retrieved October 27, 2010 from New Advent:
13) Paul Halsall. (1996). Medieval Sourcebook: Gregory of Tours: On Clovis. http://www.fordham.edu/halsall/source/gregtours1.html
14) Kurth, G. (1908). Charles Martel. In The Catholic Encyclopedia. New York: Robert Appleton Company. Retrieved December 25, 2009 from New Advent: http://www.newadvent.org/cathen/03629a.htm
15) Kampers, F. (1911). Pepin the Short. In The Catholic Encyclopedia. New York: Robert Appleton Company. Retrieved December 25, 2009 from New Advent: http://www.newadvent.org/cathen/11662b.htm
16) Shahan, T. & MacPherson, E. Charlemagne. In The Catholic Encyclopedia. New York: Robert Appleton Company. Retrieved December 24, 2009 from New Advent: http://www.newadvent.org/cathen/03610c.htm
17) Durant, Will. "King Charlemagne", History of Civilization Vol. III, The Age of Faith. Electronic Version in the Knighthood, Tournaments and Chivalry Resource Library. Brian R. Price (Ed.). http://www.chronique.com/Library/Medhistory/Charlemagne.htm
18) Charlemagne/King of the Franks/Emperor of the Holy Roman Empire: http://www.lucidcafe.com/library/96apr/charlemagne.html
19) Gascoigne Bamber. 'History of the Holy Roman Empire". History World. From 2001, Ongoing. http://www.historyworld.net/wrldhis/PlainTextHistories.asp?
20) Kelly, L. (1909). Council of Frankfort. In The Catholic Encyclopedia. New York: Robert Appleton Company. Retrieved December 9, 2009 from New Advent: http://www.newadvent.org/cathen/06236b.htm
21) Leclercq, H. (1911). The Second Council of Niceae. In The Catholic Encyclopedia. New York: Robert Appleton Company. Retrieved December 9, 2009 from New Advent: http://www.newadvent.org/cathen/11045a.htm
22) Louis the Pious: Biography from Answers.com. http://www.answers.com/topic/louis-the-pious

23) Charles III. (2010). In Encyclopedia Britannica. Retrieved November 04, 2010 from Encyclopedia Britannica online: http://www.britannica.com/EBchecked/topic/106899/charlesIII
24) Mann, H. (1912). Pope Stephen VI (VII). In The Catholic Encyclopedia. New York: Robert Appleton Company. Retrieved December 9, 2009 from New Advent: http://www.newadvent.org/cathen/14289d.htm
25) Kirsch, J.P. (1909). Pope Formosus. In The Catholic Encyclopedia. New York: Robert Appleton Company. Retrieved December 9, 2009 from New Advent: http://www.newadvent.org/cathen/061396b.htm
26) Mann, H. (1910). Pope John IX. In The Catholic Encyclopedia. New York: Robert Appleton Company. Retrieved December9, 2009 from New Advent: http://www,newadvent.org/cathen/08425a.htm
27) Kirsch, J.P. (1910). Pope John XII. In The Catholic Encyclopedia. New York: Robert Appleton Company. Retrieved December 9, 2009 from New Advent: http://www.newadvent.org/cathen/108426b.htm
28) Otto I. (Soylent Communications): http://www.nndb.com/people/921/000092645/
29) Mann, H. (1910). Pope Leo VIII. In The Catholic Encyclopedia. New York: Robert Appleton Company. Retrieved December 9, 2009 from New Advent: http://www.newadvent.org/cathen/09160b.htm
30) Kampers, F. (1911). Otto II. In The Catholic Encyclopedia. New York: Robert Appleton Company. Retrieved December 9, 2009 from New Advent: http://www.newadvent.org/cathen/11355a.htm
31) Kampers, F. (1911). Otto III. In The Catholic Encyclopedia. New York: Robert Appleton Company. Retrieved December 9, 2009 from New Advent: http://www.newadvent.org/cathen/11356a.htm
32) Charles Manley Roberts. A treatise on the history of confession . . . —Charles Manley Roberts—Google Books. http://books.google.com/book?id
33) Newton Reader. Present position of Catholics—lecture 3. http://www.newmareader.org/work/england/lecture3.html

34) Leigh Ann Craig. Wandering Women and Holy Matrons—Google Books. http://books.google.com/books?id
35) Paul Halsall. Internet History Source Books. http://www.fordham.edu/halsall/basis/boniface-letters.asp
36) William Palmer. A compendious Ecclesiastical History. http://www.archives.org/stream/acompendiousecc02palmgoog#page
37) Brian R. Price. Charlemagne's Biography. http://www.chronique.com/library/MedHistory/Charlemagne.htm
38) Lillian Goldman Law Library. The Avalon Project: Capitulary of Charlemagne issued in the Year 802. http://avalon.law.yale.edu/medieval/capitula.asp
39) The Church of Christ in the Middle Ages: an historical sketch compiled from . . . Jesus Christ, Author of Essays on the Church—Google Books. http://books.google?id
40) Finch G. A sketch of the Romish Controversy—Google Books. http://books.google.com/books?id

Chapter 8

1) Fall of Rome—why did Rome fall?: http://ancienthistory.about.com/cs/rome/allarticles/a/fallofrome.htm
2) Alaric and the Fall of Rome: http://ancienthistoriy.about.com/alaricthevisigoth
3) Decline of the Roman Empire—Wikipedia, the free Encyclopedia. http://en.wikipedia.org/wiki/Decline_of_the_Roman_Empire
4) Huddleston, G. (1911). Monasticism. In The Catholic Encyclopedia. New York: Robert Appleton Company. Retrieved October 6, 2009 from New Advent: http://www.newadvent.org/cathen/10459a.htm
5) Butler, E.C. (1907). St. Anthony. In The Catholic Encyclopedia. New York: Robert Appleton Company. Retrieved October 30, 2010 from New Advent: http://www.newadvent.org/cathen/01553d.htm
6) St Anthony the Great. Photo Album. http://www.qozhaya.com/St.Anthony.html
7) Bacchus, F.J. (1911). St. Pachomius. In The Catholic Encyclopedia. New York: Robert Appleton Company. Retrieved October 31, 2010 from New Advent: http://www.newadvent.org/cathen/11381a.htm
8) Christian Monasticism and its Evil History: http://www.Muhammed.net/other-scriptures-mainmenu-43/73-otherideologies/710-monasticism-and-its-evilhistory.htm

9) Kurth, G. (1908). Clovis. In The Catholic Encyclopedia. New York: Robert Appleton Company. Retrieved October 27, 2010 from New Advent: http://www.newadvent.org/cathen/04070a.htm
10) Simeon Stylites—Wikipedia, the free Encyclopedia. http://en.wikipedia.org/wiki/Simeon_Stylites
11) Christian Monasticism and its Evil History: http://www.Muhammed.net/other-scriptures-mainmenu-43/73-otherideologies/710-monasticism-and-its-evilhistory.htm
12) Kurth, G. (1908). Clovis. In The Catholic Encyclopedia. New York: Robert Appleton Company. Retrieved October 27, 2010 from New Advent:
13) Paul Halsall. (1996). Medieval Sourcebook: Gregory of Tours: On Clovis. http://www.fordham.edu/halsall/source/gregtours1.html
14) Kurth, G. (1908). Charles Martel. In The Catholic Encyclopedia. New York: Robert Appleton Company. Retrieved December 25, 2009 from New Advent: http://www.newadvent.org/cathen/03629a.htm
15) Kampers, F. (1911). Pepin the Short. In The Catholic Encyclopedia. New York: Robert Appleton Company. Retrieved December 25, 2009 from New Advent: http://www.newadvent.org/cathen/11662b.htm
16) Shahan, T. & MacPherson, E. Charlemagne. In The Catholic Encyclopedia. New York: Robert Appleton Company. Retrieved December 24, 2009 from New Advent: http://www.newadvent.org/cathen/03610c.htm
17) Durant, Will. "King Charlemagne", History of Civilization Vol. III, The Age of Faith. Electronic Version in the Knighthood, Tournaments and Chivalry Resource Library. Brian R. Price (Ed.). http://www.chronique.com/Library/Medhistory/Charlemagne.htm
18) Charlemagne/King of the Franks/Emperor of the Holy Roman Empire: http://www.lucidcafe.com/library/96apr/charlemagne.html
19) Gascoigne Bamber. 'History of the Holy Roman Empire". History World. From 2001, Ongoing. http://www.historyworld.net/wrldhis/PlainTextHistories.asp?
20) Kelly, L. (1909). Council of Frankfort. In The Catholic Encyclopedia. New York: Robert Appleton Company. Retrieved

December 9,2009 from New Advent: http://www.newadvent.org/cathen/06236b.htm

21) Leclercq, H. (1911). The Second Council of Niceae. In The Catholic Encyclopedia. New York: Robert Appleton Company. Retrieved December 9, 2009 from New Advent: http://www.newadvent.org/cathen/11045a.htm

22) Louis the Pious: Biography from Answers.com. http://www.answers.com/topic/louis-the-pious

23) Charles III. (2010). In Encyclopedia Britannica. Retrieved November 04, 2010 from Encyclopedia Britannica online: http://www.britannica.com/EBchecked/topic/106899/charlesIII

24) Mann, H. (1912). Pope Stephen VI (VII). In The Catholic Encyclopedia. New York: Robert Appleton Company. Retrieved December 9, 2009 from New Advent: http://www.newadvent.org/cathen/14289d.htm

25) Kirsch, J.P. (1909). Pope Formosus. In The Catholic Encyclopedia. New York: Robert Appleton Company. Retrieved December 9, 2009 from New Advent: http://www.newadvent.org/cathen/061396b.htm

26) Mann, H. (1910). Pope John IX. In The Catholic Encyclopedia. New York: Robert Appleton Company. Retrieved December9, 2009 from New Advent: http://www,newadvent.org/cathen/08425a.htm

27) Kirsch, J.P. (1910). Pope John XII. In The Catholic Encyclopedia. New York: Robert Appleton Company. Retrieved December 9, 2009 from New Advent: http://www.newadvent.org/cathen/108426b.htm

28) Otto I. (Soylent Communications): http://www.nndb.com/people/921/000092645/

29) Mann, H. (1910). Pope Leo VIII. In The Catholic Encyclopedia. New York: Robert Appleton Company. Retrieved December 9, 2009 from New Advent: http://www.newadvent.org/cathen/09160b.htm

30) Kampers, F. (1911). Otto II. In The Catholic Encyclopedia. New York: Robert Appleton Company. Retrieved December 9, 2009 from New Advent: http://www.newadvent.org/cathen/11355a.htm

31) Kampers, F. (1911). Otto III. In The Catholic Encyclopedia. New York: Robert Appleton Company. Retrieved December 9, 2009 from New Advent: http://www.newadvent.org/cathen/11356a.htm

Chapter 9
1) Gerland, E. (1908). The Byzantine Empire. In The Catholic Encyclopedia. New York: Robert Appleton Company. Retrieved March 2, 2010 from New Advent: http://www.newadvent.org/cathen/03096a.htm
2) Richard Hooker. The Byzantine Empire. http://www.wsu.edu:8080/~dee/MA/BYZ.HTM
3) James Allan Evans (1998). Roman Emperors—DIR Justinian (527-565). http://www.romans-emperors.org/justinian.htm
4) Scott Moore, R. (1997). Roman Emperors—DIR Heraclius (610-641). http://www.romans-emperors.org/hereclis.htm
5) Bronwen Neil (2000). Roman Emperors—DIR Leo III (717-741). http://www.roman-emperors.org/leoiii.htm
6) Shaun Tougher (2004). Roman Emperors—DIR Constantine V Copronymus (741-775). http://www.roman-emperors.org/constanv.htm
7) Byzantine Iconoclasm. http://www.mlahanas.de/Greek/medieval/LX/Iconoclasm.html
8) Paul Halsall (1996). Medieval Source Book: Iconoclastic Council, 754. http://www.fordham.edu/halsall/source/icono-cncl754.html
9) Lynda Garland. Constantine VI (780-797) and Irene (797-802). Roman Emperors—DIR Irene (wife of Leo IV). http://www.roman-emperors.org/irene.htm
10) John of Damascus: Icons. http://www.balamand.edu.ib/theology/Jicons.HTM
11) Leo V the Armenian—Wikipedia, the free Encyclopedia. http://en.wikipedia.org/wiki/leo_v_the_Armenian
12) Michael II. Wikipedia, the free Encyclopedia. http://en.wikipedia.org/wiki/Michael_II
13) Theophilus, Emperor—Wikipedia, the free Encyclopedia. http://en.wikipedia.org/wiki/theophilus_(emperor)
14) Michael III—Wikipedia, the free Encyclopedia. http://en.wikipedia.org/wiki/Michael_III
15) Nick Trakeikes. What was the Iconoclastic Controversy About : http://www.theandros.com/iconoclast.html
16) Iconoclastic Controversy. http://encyclopedia.jrank.org/articles/pages/3376/iconoclasticcontroversy.html

17) The Council of Elvira. http://community2.webtv.net/tales_of_the_western_world/RLELVIRA
18) Fortescue, A. (1911). Photius of Constantinople. In The Catholic Encyclopedia. New York: Robert Appleton Company. Retrieved December 16, 2009 from New Advent: http://www.newadvent.org/cathen/12043b.htm
19) Photius the Great: http://orthowiki.org/photius_the_Great
20) Patriarch Ignatius of Constantinople—Wikipedia, the free Encyclopedia. http://en.wikipedia.org/wiki/Patriarch_Ignatius_I_of_Constantinople
21) Basil II—Wikipedia, the free Encyclopedia. http://en.wikipedia.org/wiki/Basil_II
22) Fortescue, A. (1912). The Eastern Schism. In The Catholic Encyclopedia. New York: Robert Appleton Company. Retrieved December 8, 2009 from New Advent: http://www.newadvent.org/cathen/13535a.htm
23) Fortescue, A. (1911). Michael Caerularius. In The Catholic Encyclopedia. New York: Robert Appleton Company. Retrieved December 8, 2009 from New Advent: http://www.newadvent.org/cathen/10273a.htm
24) On Michael Caerularius. <<Eirenikon: http://wordpress.com/2009/11/09/On-Michael-Caerularius/
25) Mann, H. (1910). Pope St. Leo IX. In The Catholic Encyclopedia. New York: Robert Appleton Company. Retrieved December 2009 from New Advent: http://www.newadvent.org/cathen/09160c.htm
26) Drogo of Hauteville—Wikipedia, the free encyclopedia. http://en.wikipedia.org/wiki/Drogo_of_Hauteville
27) Constantine IX Monomachus—Wikipedia, the free encyclopedia. http://en.wikipedia.org/wiki/Constantine_IX_Monomachus
28) Battle of Manzikert—Wikipedia, the free encyclopedia. http://en.wikipedia.org/wiki/Battle_of_Manzikert

Chapter 10
1) Kampers, F. (1910). St. Henry II. In The Catholic Encyclopedia. New York: Robert Appleton Company. Retrieved November 22, 2010 from New Advent: http://www.newadvent.org/cathen/07227a.htm

2) Henry II, Holy Roman Emperor—Wikipedia, the free Encyclopedia. http://en.wikipedia.org/wiki/Henry_II_Holy_Roman_Emperor
3) Mann, H. (1907). Pope Benedict VIII. In The Catholic Encyclopedia. New York: Robert Appleton Company. Retrieved November 20, 2010 from New Advent: http://www.newadvent.org/cathen/02428e.htm
4) Conrad II, Ruler of the Holy Roman Empire—Infoplease.com: http://www.infoplease.com/ce6/people/A0813269.htm
5) Conrad II, Holy Roman Emperor: http://encyclopedia2.thefreedictionary.com/conrad+II,+Holy+Roman+Emperor
6) Henry III, Holy Roman Emperor—New World Encyclopedia. http://www.newworldencyclopedia.org/entry/Henry_III,_Holy_Roman_Emperor
7) Mann, H. (1907). Pope Benedict IX. In The Catholic Encyclopedia. New York: Robert Appleton Company. Retrieved November 24, 2010 from New Advent: http://www.newadvent.org/cathen/02429a.htm
8) Pope Benedict IX. (Soylent Communications). http://www.nndb.com/people/236/000094951
9) Mann, H (1910). Pope St. Leo IX. In The Catholic Encyclopedia. New York: Robert Appleton Company. Retrieved December 9, 2009 from New Advent:
http://www.newadvent.org/cathen/09160c.htm
10) Weber, N. (1911). Pope Nicholas II. In The Catholic Encyclopedia. New York: Robert Appleton Company. Retrieved December 9, 2009 from New Advent: http://www.newadvent.com/cathen/11055a.htm
11) Pope Nicholas II. (Soylent Communications). http://www.nndb.com/people/517/000103208
12) Laughlin, J. (1907). Pope Alexander II. In The Catholic Encyclopedia. New York: Robert Appleton Company. Retrieved December 9, 2009 from New Advent: http://www.newadvent.org/cathen/01286.htm
13) Oestereich, T. (1909). Pope St. Gregory VII. In The Catholic Encyclopedia. New York: Robert Appleton Company. Retrieved December 10, 2009 from New Advent: http://www.newadvent.org/cathen/06791.htm

14) Kampers, F. (1910). Henry IV. In The Catholic Encyclopedia. New York: Robert Appleton Company. Retrieved December 11, 2009 from New Advent: http://www.newadvent.org/cathen/07230a.htm
15) Loffler, K. (1910). Conflict of Investitures. In The Catholic Encyclopedia. New York: Robert Appleton Company. Retrieved December 11, 2009 from New Advent: http://www.newadvent.org/cathen/08084c.htm
16) Butler, R.U. (1912). Pope Bl. Urban II. In The Catholic Encyclopedia. New York: Robert Appleton Company. Retrieved December 11, 2009 from New Advent: http://www.newadvent.org/cathen/15210a.htm
17) Laughlin, T. (1911). Pope Paschal II. In The Catholic Encyclopedia. New York: Robert Appleton Company. Retrieved December 11, 2009 from New Advent: http://www.newadvent.org/cathen/11514b.htm
18) Kampers, F. (1910). Henry V. In The Catholic Encyclopedia. New York: Robert Appleton Company. Retrieved December 11, 2009 from New Advent: http://www.newadvent.org/cathen/07232a.htm
19) MacCaffrey, J. (1908). Pope Callistus II. In The Catholic Encyclopedia. New York: Robert Appleton Company. Retrieved December 11, 2009 from New Advent: http://www.newadvent.org/cathen/03185a.htm
20) Kent, W. (1907). St. Anselm. In The Catholic Encyclopedia. New York: Robert Appleton Company. Retrieved March 26, 2010 from New Advent: http://www.newadvent.org/cathen/01546a.htm
21) Ben Bayliss. Henry1 of England: http://www.suite101.com/context/henry-i-of-england-a238469
22) Crusades—Wikipedia, the free Encyclopedia. http://en.wikipedia.org/w/index.php?title=crusades&printable=yes
23) Pope Urban II. http://www.crusades-encyclopedia.com/urbanII.html
24) Brehier, L. (1908). Crusades. In The Catholic Encyclopedia. New York: Robert Appleton Company. Retrieved February 6, 2010 from New Advent: http://www.newadvent.org/cathen/04543c.htm
25) Al-Hakim-bi-Amr-Allah—Wikipedia, the free Encyclopedia. http://en.wikipedia.org/wiki/Al_Hakim_bi_Amr_Allah
26) Ali-az-Zahir—Wikipedia, the free Encyclopedia. http://en.wikipedia.org/wiki/Ali_az_Zahir

27) Paul Halsall. (1997). Medieval Source Book: Urban II: Speech at the Council of Clermont, 1095, five versions of the speech. http://www.fordham.edu/halsall/source/urban2-5vers.html
28) Ott, M. (1910). Pope Innocent III. In The Catholic Encyclopedia. New York: Robert Appleton Company. Retrieved February 6, 2010 from New Advent: http://www.newadvent.org/cathen/08013a.htm
29) Pope Innocent III. (Soylent Communications). http://www.nndb.com/people/536/000093260
30) Andrew Holt. (June 2005). Pope Innocent III. http://www.crusades-encyclopedia.com/innocentIII.html
31) Paul Halsall. (December 1997). Medieval Source Book: The Fourth Crusade, 1204: collected sources: http://www.fordham.edu/halsall/source/4cde.html#sack
32) Robert of Clari. The Sack of Constantinople by the Crusaders: http://www.shsu.edu/~his_ncp/1204.html
33) The Fifth Crusade—Wikipedia, the free encyclopedia. http://en.wikipedia.org/wiki/The_fifth_Crusade
34) The Sixth Crusade: http://www.medievality.com/sixth-crusade.html
35) Rickard J. (24March 2001). Sixth Crusade, 1228-1229; http://www.historyofwar.org/articles/wars_crusades6th.html
36) Rickard, J. (24 March 2001), Seventh Crusade, 1248-1254. http;//www.historyofwar.org/articles/wars_Crusades7th.htm
37) The Eighth Crusade—Wikipedia, the free encyclopedia. http://en.wikipedia.org/wiki/The_Eighth_Crusade
38) Effects of the Crusades: http://www.middle-ages.org.uk/effect-of-crusades-.htm
39) Christina Pomoni. (World History Net Blog>>Blog Archive>). The lasting effects of the crusades. http://www.worldhistorynet.com/blog/?p=25
40) Oestereich, T. (1907). Pope Boniface VIII. In The Catholic Encyclopedia. New York: Robert Appleton Company. Retrieved February 10, 2010 from New Advent: http://www.newadvent.org/cathen/02662a.htm
41) Paul Halsall. (Jan. 1996). Medieval Source Book: Boniface VIII, Unam Sanctam, 1302. http://www.fordham.edu/halsall/source/b8-unam.htm

42) Pope Boniface VIII: Biography from Answers.com: http://www.answers.com/topic/pope-boniface-VIII
43) Lynn H. Nelson. The Avignon Papacy (1305-1378). ORB: The Online Reference Book for Medieval Studies. http://www.the-orb.net/textbook/nelson/avignon,html
44) Avignon Papacy—Wikipedia, the free Encyclopedia. http://en.wikipedia.org/wiki/Avignon_Papacy
45) The Avignon Papacy: http://www.christianchronicler.com/history1/avignon_papacy.html
46) Salembier, L. (1912). Western Schism. In The Catholic Encyclopedia. New York: Robert Appleton Company. Retrieved April 13, 2010 from New Advent: http://www.newadvent.org/cathen/13539a.htm
47) Lynn H. Nelson. The Great Schism. ORB: The Online Reference Book for Medieval Studies: http://www.the.orb.net/textbook/nelson/great_schism.html
48) Conciliarism—Wikipedia, the free Encyclopedia. http://en.wikipedia.org/wiki/conciliarism

Chapter 11

1) Toke, L. (1911). St. Peter Damian. In The Catholic Encyclopedia. New York: Robert Appleton Company. Retrieved March 24, 2010 from New Advent: http://www.newadvent.org/cathen/11764a.htm
2) Holopainen, Toivo J. "Peter Damian", The Stanford Encyclopedia of Philosophy (winter 2008 Edition), Edward N. Zalta (ed.). http://plato.stanford.edu/archives/win2008/entries/peter-damian/
3) Pierre J. Payer (Translator). "Book of Gomorrah: an eleventh century treatise against clerical homosexual practices . . . By Saint Peter Damian. Wilfrid Laurier University Press (1982). http://books.google.com/books?id=hr4AAAAMAAJ&dq=Peter+damian&Source=gbs_navlinks
4) Randle Engel. St Peter Damian's Book of Gomorrah: A Moral Blueprint for Our Times—Part1. http://www.ourladyswarriors.org/articles/damian1.htm
5) Proslogium; Monologium; an Appendix in Behalf of the Fool by Gaunilon; and Cur Deus Homo/Christian Classics Ethereal Library. http://www.ccel.org/ccel/anselm/basic_works.toc.html

6) Anselm of Canterbury—Wikipedia, the free Encyclopedia. http://en.wikipedia.org/wiki/Anselm_of_Canterbury
7) William, Thomas. "Saint Anselm": The Stanford Encyclopedia of Philosophy (Fall 2008 Edition), Edward N. Zalta (ed.). http://plato.stanford.edu/archives/fall2008/entries/anselm/>
8) Greg Sadler. (October 20, 2006): Anselm [Internet Encyclopedia of Philosophy]. http://www.iep.utm.edu/anselm/
9) King, Peter. "Peter Abelard". The Stanford Encyclopedia of Philosophy. (Spring 2010 Edition), Edward N. Zalta (Ed.). http://plato.stanford.edu/archives/spring2010/entries/abelard/>
10) Abelard of Le Pallet on Theology: "Logic has made me hated among men"—Abelard. http://www.abelard.org/abelard/abelard2.htm#superstition-magic
11) Pierre (Peter) Abelard, introduction and short biography. http://www.abelard.org/abelard/abel-hi.htm
12) The Logic of ethics—Abelard, with commentary on Abelard's ethical teaching. http://www.abelard.org/ethics.htm
13) Peter Abelard (1079-1142)—ReligionFact. http://www.religionfacts.com/Christianity/people/abelard.htm
14) Vacandard, E. (1907). Arnold of Brescia. In The Catholic Encyclopedia. New York: Robert Appleton Company. Retrieved March 24, 2010 from New Advent: http://www.newadvent.org/cathen/01747b.htm
15) Arnold of Brescia—New World Encyclopedia—http://www.newworldencyclopedia.org/entry/Arnold_of_Brescia
16) Ghellinck, J. (1911). Peter Lombard. In The Catholic Encyclopedia. New York: Robert Appleton Company. Retrieved March 24, 2010 from New Advent: http://www.newadvent.org/cathen/11768d.htm
17) Lombard, Peter [Internet Encyclopedia of Philosophy]. http://www.iep.utm.edu/lombard/
18) Master Peter Lombard: First Book of Sentences. http://www.franciscan-archive.org/lombardus/1-sent.html
19) Master Peter Lombard: Second Book of Sentences. http://www.franciscan-archive.org/lombadus/II-sent.html
20) Kennedy, D. (1907). St. Albertus Magnus. In The Catholic Encyclopedia. New York: Robert Appleton Company. Retrieved March 27, 2010 from New Advent: http://www.newadvent.org/cathen/01264a.htm

21) Fuhrer, Markus. "Albert the Great". The Stanford Encyclopedia of Philosophy. (Winter 2010 Edition). Edward N. Zalta (Ed.). http://plato.stanford.edu/archives/win2010/entries/albert-great/
22) Albertus Magnus: Biography from Answers.com. http://www.answers.com/topic/albertus-magnus
23) Kennedy, D. (1912). St. Thomas Aquinas. In The Catholic Encyclopedia. New York: Robert Appleton Company. Retrieved June 5, 2009 from New Advent: http://www.newadvent.org/cathen/14663b.htm
24) Aquinas, Thomas [Internet Encyclopedia of Philosophy]. http://www.iep.utm.edu/aquinas/
25) Thomas Aquinas—Wikipedia, the free Encyclopedia. http://en.wikipedia.org/wiki/Thomas_Aquinas
26) Minges, P. (1909). Bl. John Scotus. In The Catholic Encyclopedia. New York: Robert Appleton Company. Retrieved April 5, 2010 from New Advent: http://www.newadvent.org/cathen/05194a.htm
27) Williams, Thomas. "John Duns Scotus". The Stanford Encyclopedia of Philosophy (Spring 2010 Edition), Edward N. Zalta (Ed.). http://plato.stanford.edu/archives/spr2010/entries/duns-scotus/>
28) Duns Scotus—Wikipedia, the free Encyclopedia. http://en.wikipedia.org/wiki/Duns_Scotus
29) Sharon Kaye (January 2007). Ockham, William of [Internet Encyclopedia of Philosophy]. http://www.iep.utm.edu/Ockham/
30) Spade, Paul Vincent. "William of Ockham". The Stanford Encyclopedia of Philosophy (Fall 2008 Edition), Edward N. Zalta (Ed.). http://plato.stanford.edu/archives/fall2008/entries/ockham/
31) William of Ockham—Wikipedia, the free Encyclopedia. http://en.wikipedia.org/wiki/William_of_Ockham
32) John Wycliffe. http://www.greatsite.com/timeline-english-bible-history/john-wycliffe.html
33) John Wycliffe: Life, Works, Teachings and Resources—Religionfacts. http://www.religionfacts.com/Christian/people/Wycliffe.htm
34) J. Loserth. "Biography of John Wycliffe": http://www.tlogical.net/biowycliffe.htm

35) Paul Halsall. (1998). Medieval Source Book: Condemnation of Wycliffe, 1382. http://www.fordham.edu/halsall/source/1382wycliffe.html
36) Twelve Conclusions of the Lollards—Wikisource—http://wikisource.org/wiki/Twelve_Conclusions_of_the_Lollards
37) Lollardy—Wikipedia, the free encyclopedia. http://en.wikipedia.org/wiki/Lollardy
38) David S. Schaff. (1915). John Huss—His Life, Teachings and Death after five hundred years. New York: Charles Scribner's Sons. Retrieved April 18, 2010. http://books.google.com/books
39) John Hus. http://www.greatsite.com/timeline-english-bible-history/john-hus.html
40) James E. Keifer. John Huss, Priest and Martyr: http://Justus.anglican.org/resources/bio/7.html
41) David S. Schaff. (1915). De Ecclesia: The Church, by Jan Hus. New York: Charles Scribner's Sons. Retrieved April 18, 2010. http://books.google.com/books
42) Wilhelm, J. (1910). Hussites. In The Catholic Encyclopedia. New York: Robert Appleton Company. Retrieved June 5, 2009 from New Advent: http://www.newadvent.org/cathen/07585a.htm
43) Louis B. Weeks. "Hussites", Microsoft Encarta Online Encyclopedia, 2009. http://encarta.msn.com/text_761577157_O/Hussites.html
44) Hussites. http://www.fact-index.com/h/hu/hussite.html

Chapter 12

1) Sauvage, G. (1907). Berengarius of Tours. In The Catholic Encyclopedia. New York: Robert Appleton Company. Retrieved March 31, 2010 from New Advent: http://www.newadvent.org/cathen/02487a.htm
2) Berengarius [Berengar] . . . Online Information article about BERENGARIUS [BERENGAR]. http://encyclopedia.jrank.org/BEC_BERENGARIUS_BERENGAR_d_i088.html
3) Cathars and Cathar Beliefs in the Languedoc. http://www.cathar.info/
4) Weber, N. (1908). Cathari. In The Catholic Encyclopedia. New York: Robert Appleton Company. Retrieved March 21, 2010 from New Advent: http://www.newadvent.org/cathen/03435a.htm

5) Albigensian Crusade (1209-1255). http://xenophongroup.com/montjoie/albigens.htm
6) Weber, N. (1912). Waldenses. In The Catholic Encyclopedia. New York: Robert Appleton Company. Retrieved March 31, 2010 from New Advent: http://www.newadvent.org/cathen/15527b.htm
7) Stuart Murray Williams. The Waldensians / The Anabaptists Network. http://www.anabaptistnetwork.com/waldensians
8) Waldensians (Chapter 19). http://www.prca.org/books/portraits/walden.htm
9) Al Van Heldon (2003). "The Galileo Project"/Christian/The Inquisition. http://galileo.rice.edu/chr/Inquisition.html
10) Blotzer, J. (1901). Inquisition. In The Catholic Encyclopedia. New York: Robert Appleton Company. Retrieved April 21, 2010 from New Advent: http://www.newadvent.org/cathen/08026a.htm
11) The Inquisition—http://www.thenazareneway.com/inquisition.htm
12) The Cathars: The Medieval Inquisition—Inquisitors in the Languedoc. http://www.cathar.info/1209_inquisition.htm
13) Spanish Inquisition—Wikipedia, the free encyclopedia. http://en.wikipedia.org/wiki/Spanish_Inquisition#organization
14) Caroll Anne W. "The Inquisition". In Christ the King; Lord of History. Rockford. Illinois: Tan Books and Publishers Inc. 1994. http://www.catholiceducation.org/articles/history/world/uh0009.html
15) The Inquisition—http://www.exposingchristianity.com/Inquisition.html
16) Vacandard E. The Inquisition. http://www.freefictionbooks.org/books/i/11316-the-inquisition-by-e-vacandard
17) John Chrysostom—OrthodoxWiki. http://orthodoxwiki.org/John_Chrysostom
18) Popes vs. Christ—2. http://sorrypope.com/popesvschrist-2.html

Chapter 13
1) Steven Kreis (2008). "Renaissance Humanism". http://www.historyguide.org/intellect/humanism.html
2) Renaissance—Wikipedia, the free encyclopedia. http://en.wikipedia.org/wiki/Renaissance
3) Loffler, K. (1910). Humanism. In The Catholic Encyclopedia. New York: Robert Appleton Company. Retrieved May 5, 2010

from New Advent: http://www.newadvent.org/cathen/07538b.htm
4) Gardner, E. (1908). Dante Alighieri. In The Catholic Encyclopedia. New York: Robert Appleton Company. Retrieved May 5, 2010 from New Advent: http://www.newadvent.org/cathen/04628a.htm
5) Dante Alighieri—Wikipedia, the free encyclopedia. http://en.wikipedia.org/wiki/Dante_Alighieri
6) Rex Pay (2004). Petrarch. http://www.humanistictexts.org/petrarch.htm
7) Ford, J. (1911). Francesco Petrarch. In The Catholic Encyclopedia. New York: Robert Appleton Company. Retrieved May 5, 2010 from New Advent: http://www.newadvent,org/cathen/11778a.htm
8) Nauta, Lodi. "Lorenzo Valla": The Stanford Encyclopedia of Philosophy. (Summer 2009 Edition), Edward N. Zalta (Ed.). http://plato.stanford.edu/sum2009/entries/lorenzo-Valla
9) Lorenzo Valla—Wikipedia, the free encyclopedia. http://en.wikipedia.org/wiki/Lorenzo_Valla
10) Steven Kreis (2004). "Desiderius Erasmus", 1466-1536": http://www.historyguide.org/intellect/erasmus.html
11) Erasmus. http://www.greatsite.com/timeline-english-bible-history/erasmus.html
12) John Wilson's 1688 Translation: Desiderius Erasmus—"In Praise of Folly"/ Christian Classic Ethereal Library. http://www.ccel.org/ccel/erasmus/folly
13) Jokinen, Anniina. "The Life of Sir Thomas More". Luminarium. 13 June 2009. Retrieved December 18, 2010. http://www.luminarium.org/renlit/morebio.htm
14) Utopia by Thomas More—http://oregonstate.edu/instruct/ph/302/texts/more/utopia-contents,html
15) Charles Manley Roberts. A treatise on the history of confession . . . —Charles Manley Roberts—Google Books. http://books.google.com/book?id
16) Newton Reader. Present position of Catholics—lecture 3. http://www.newmareader.org/work/england/lecture3.html
17) Leigh Ann Craig. Wandering Women and Holy Matrons—Google Books. http://books.google.com/books?id

18) Paul Halsall. Internet History Source Books. http://www.fordham.edu/halsall/basis/boniface-letters.asp
19) William Palmer. A compendious Ecclesiastical History. http://www.archives.org/stream/acompendiousecc02palmgoog#page
20) Brian R. Price. Charlemagne's Biography. http://www.chronique.com/library/MedHistory/Charlemagne.htm
21) Lillian Goldman Law Library. The Avalon Project: Capitulary of Charlemagne issued in the Year 802. http://avalon.law.yale.edu/medieval/capitula.asp
22) The Church of Christ in the Middle Ages: an historical sketch compiled from . . . Jesus Christ, Author of Essays on the Church —Google Books. http://books.google?id
23) Finch G. A sketch of the Romish Controversy—Google Books.

Chapter 14

1) Steven Kreis (2008). "Renaissance Humanism". http://www.historyguide.org/intellect/humanism.html
2) Renaissance—Wikipedia, the free encyclopedia. http://en.wikipedia.org/wiki/Renaissance
3) Loffler, K. (1910). Humanism. In The Catholic Encyclopedia. New York: Robert Appleton Company. Retrieved May 5, 2010 from New Advent: http://www.newadvent.org/cathen/07538b.htm
4) Gardner, E. (1908). Dante Alighieri. In The Catholic Encyclopedia. New York: Robert Appleton Company. Retrieved May 5, 2010 from New Advent: http://www.newadvent.org/cathen/04628a.htm
5) Dante Alighieri—Wikipedia, the free encyclopedia. http://en.wikipedia.org/wiki/Dante_Alighieri
6) Rex Pay (2004). Petrarch. http://www.humanistictexts.org/petrarch.htm
7) Ford, J. (1911). Francesco Petrarch. In The Catholic Encyclopedia. New York: Robert Appleton Company. Retrieved May 5, 2010 from New Advent: http://www.newadvent,org/cathen/11778a.htm
8) Nauta, Lodi. "Lorenzo Valla": The Stanford Encyclopedia of Philosophy. (Summer 2009 Edition), Edward N. Zalta (Ed.). http://plato.stanford.edu/sum2009/entries/lorenzo-Valla
9) Lorenzo Valla—Wikipedia, the free encyclopedia. http://en.wikipedia.org/wiki/Lorenzo_Valla

10) Steven Kreis (2004). "Desiderius Erasmus", 1466-1536": http://www.historyguide.org/intellect/erasmus.html
11) Erasmus. http://www.greatsite.com/timeline-english-bible-history/erasmus.html
12) John Wilson's 1688 Translation: Desiderius Erasmus—"In Praise of Folly"/ Christian Classic Ethereal Library. http://www.ccel.org/ccel/erasmus/folly
13) Jokinen, Anniina. "The Life of Sir Thomas More". Luminarium. 13 June 2009. Retrieved December 18, 2010. http://www.luminarium.org/renlit/morebio.htm
14) Utopia by Thomas More—http://oregonstate.edu/instruct/ph/302/texts/more-utopia-contents.html

Chapter 15

1) Jacque Lefevre d'Etaples—Wikipedia, the free encyclopedia. http://en.wikipedia.org/wiki/Jacque_Lefevre_d'Etaples
2) Great Marketing (1997-2008) Martin Luther. http://www.greatsite.com/timeline-english-bible-history/martin-luther.html
3) David M. Whitford (2005). Luther, Martin [Internet Encyclopedia of Philosophy]. http://www.iep.utm.edu/luther/
4) Jacobs C.M. "An Open Letter to the Christian Nobility: "The Three Walls of the Romanists by Martin Luther" (1520). In Project Wittenberg; Rev. Robert E. Smith (Ed.). http://www.iclnet.org/pub/resources/text/wittenberg/luther/web/nb/ty-03.html
5) Jacobs C.M. "An Open Letter to the Christian Nobility: Proposals for Reform II, by Martin Luther" (1520). In Project Wittenberg; Rev. E. Smith (Ed.). http://www.iclnet.org/pub/resources/text/wittenberg/luther/web/nblty-06.html
6) Jacobs C.M. "An Open Letter to the Christian Nobility: Proposals for Reform I, by Martin Luther" (1520). In Project Wittenberg; Rev. Robert E. Smith (Ed.). http://www.iclnet.org/pub/resources/text/wittenberg/luther/web/nblty-05.html
7) Jacobs C.M. "An Open Letter to the Christian Nobility: Proposals for Reform III, by Martin Luther" (1520). In Project Wittenberg; Rev. Robert E. Smith (Ed.). http://www.iclnet.org/pub/resources/text/wittenberg/luther/web/nblty-07.htm
8) Grignon, R.S. "Concerning Christian Liberty: Letter of Martin Luther to Pope Leo X" (1520). In Project Wittenberg; Rev.

Robert E. Smith (Ed.). http://www.iclnet.org/pub/resources/text/wittenberg/luther/web/cclib-1.html

9) Jacobs C.M. "An Open Letter to the Christian Nobility: Abuses to be discussed in the Council, by Martin Luther" (1520). In Project Wittenberg; Rev. Robert E. Smith, (Ed.). http://www.iclnet.org/pub/resources/text/wittenberg/luther/web/nblty-04.html

10) Bente, F; Dau, W.H.T. "The Large Catechism: Of Baptism by Martin Luther". In Project Wittenberg; Rev. Robert E. Smith (Ed.). http://www.iclnet.org/pub/resources/text/wittenberg/luther/catechism/web/cat-13.html

11) Bente, F; Dau, W.H.T. "The Large Catechism: Of Infant Baptism by Martin Luther". In Project Wittenberg; Rev. E. Smith (Ed.). http://www.iclnet.org/pub/resources/text/wittenberg/luther/catechism/web/cat-13a.html

12) Bente, F; Dau, W.H.T. "The Large Catechism: Of the Sacrament of the Altar by Martin Luther. In Project Wittenberg; Rev. Robert E. Smith (Ed.). http://www.iclnet.org/pub/resources/text/wittenberg/luther/catechism/web/cat-14.html

13) Bente, F; Dau, W.H.T. "The Large Catechism: Conclusion by Martin Luther. In Project Wittenberg; Rev. Robert E. Smith (Ed.). http://www.iclnet.org/pub/resources/text/wittenberg/luther/catechism/web/car-15.html

14) Bente, F; Dau, W.H.T. "The Large Catechism: Of the Creed by Martin Luther". In Project Wittenberg; Rev. Robert E. Smith (Ed.). http://www.iclnet.org/pub/resources/text/wittenberg/luther/catechism/web/cat-10.html

15) Shane Rosenthal. "The Law and the Gospel: Martin Luther and Others—A Reformation Sampler. http://homepage.mac.com/shanerosenthal/reformationink/lawgospel.htm

16) Adolph Spaeth, Reed L.D, Jacobs H.E. "A Treatise on Good Works by Martin Luther (1520). In Wittenberg Project, Rev. Robert E. Smith (Ed.). http://www.iclnet.org/pub/resources/text/wittenberg/luther/work-02a.txt

17) Grignon R.S. "Concerning Christian Liberty, by Martin Luther—Part 2"—(1520). In Project Wittenberg; Rev. Robert E. Smith (Ed.). http://www.iclnet.org/pub/resources/text/wittenberg/luther/web/cclib-2.html

18) Grignon R.S. "Concerning Christian Liberty by Martin Luther—Part 3" (1520). In Project Wittenberg; Rev. Robert E. Smith (Ed.). http://www.iclnet.org/pub/resources/text/wittenberg/luther/web/cclib-3.html
19) Erika Bullman Flores. "Let Your Sin Be Strong: A Letter from Luther to Melanchton" (1521). In Project Wittenberg; Rev. Robert E. Smith (Ed.). http://www.iclnet.org/pub/resources/text/wittenberg/luther/letsinbe.txt
20) Martin H. Bertram (1971). "Of Jews and their lies by Martin Luther—(1543)"/ Fortress Press & Augsburg Fortress. http://www.humanitas-international.org/showcase/chronography/document/luther-jews.htm
21) Richard Hooker (1966). Ulrich Zwingli. http://wsu.edu/~dee/REFORM/ZWINGLI.HTM
22) Ulrich Zwingli: Reformer of Zurich. http://www.prca.org/books/portraits/zwingli.thm
23) Victor Shepherd. Heinrich Bullinger. http://www.victorshepherd.on.ca/other%writings/heinrich_bullinger.htm
24) Heinrich Bullinger—Wikipedia, the free encyclopedia. http://en.wikipedia.org/wiki/Heinrich_Bullinger
25) William Tyndale. http://www.greatsite.com/timeline-english-bible-history/william-tyndale.html
26) The William Tyndale Homepage: William Tyndale and the History of the English Bible: http://www.williamtyndale.com/0welcomewilliamtyndale.htm
27) Barry, W. (1908). Calvinism. In The Catholic Encyclopedia. New York: Robert Appleton Company. Retrieved September 30, 2009 from New Advent: http://www.newadvent.org/cathen/03198a.htm
28) Marian Hillar. Sebastian Castellio. http://www.socinian.org/castellio.html
29) Chris Trueman (2000-2010). John Calvin. http://www.historylearningsite.co.uk/John_Calvin.htm
30) Kent R. Rieske. "Calvinism False Doctrines, Depravity, Election, Atonement, Irresistible Grace. http://www.biblelife.org/calvinism.htm
31) Richard Hooker. (1996).Reformation: John Calvin. http://www.wsu.edu/~dee/REFORM/CALVIN.HTM
32) Arminianism—Wikipedia, the free encyclopedia. http://en.wikipedia.org/wiki/Arminianism

33) Victor Shepherd. Jacobus Arminius. http://www.victorshepherd.on.ca/others%20writings/jacobus_arminius.htm
34) Jacobus Arminius and Arminianism. http://www.ondoctrine.com/10armini.htm
35) Ronald J. Gordon. (2001) Anabaptism in 16th Century Europe. http://www.cob.net.org/anabaptism.htm
36) "Schleitheim Confession (Anabaptist, 1527)": Global Anabaptist, Mennonite Encyclopedia Online. Retrieved December 29, 2010. http://www.gameo.org/encyclopedia/contents/S345.html
37) Hall of Church History: The Anabaptists. http://www.spurgeon.org/~phil/anabapt.htm

Chapter 16
1) Augsburg Confession—Wikipedia, the free encyclopedia. http://en.wikipedia.org/wiki/Augsburg_Confession
2) Schmalkaldic War—Wikipedia, the free encyclopedia. http://en.wikipedia.org/wiki/Shmalkaldic_War
3) Augsburg Interim—Wikipedia, the free encyclopedia. http://en.wikipedia.org/wiki/Augsburg_interim
4) Leipzig Interim—Wikipedia, the free encyclopedia. http://en.wikipedia.org/wiki/Leipzig_Interim
5) Peace of Augsburg—Wikipedia, the free encyclopedia. http://en.wikipedia.org/wiki/Peace_of_Augsburg
6) Frank E. Smitha. The Thirty Year War. http://www.smitha.com/h3/h25-wars.com
7) The Thirty-Year War, 1618-1648. http://www.caveonline.com/APEH/thirtyyearswar.html
8) English Reformation—Wikipedia, the free encyclopedia. http://en.wikipedia.org/wiki/English_Reformation
9) Richard Hooker. (1996). Reformation: Protestant England. http://www.wsu.edu/~dee/REFORM/ENGLAND.HTM
10) 1517-1564: The Reformation. http://justus.anglican.org/resources/timeline/06reformation.html
11) Steven Kreis (2002). Lecture 7: "The English Civil War". http://www.historyguide.org/earlymod/lecture7c.html
12) The Great Controversy—Chapter 12: "The French Reformation". http://www.prepareforeternity.com/gc/gc12.htm

13) The French Wars of Religion—Wikipedia, the free encyclopedia. http://en.wikipedia.org/wiki/French_Wars_of_Religion
14) Chris Trueman. (2000-2010). French Wars of Religion. http://www.historylearningsite.co.uk/FWR.htm
15) Richard Hooker (1996). Reformation: Religious Wars. http://www.wsu.edu/~dee/REFORM/WARS.HTM

Chapter 17
1) Kirsch, J.P. (1912). Council of Trent. In The Catholic Encyclopedia. New York: Robert Appleton Company. Retrieved May 26, 2010 from New Advent: http://www.newadvent.org/cathen/15030c.htm
2) The Council of Trent. CT Table. http://history.hanover.edu/texts/trent.html
3) Richard Hooker (1996). Reformation: The Counter-Reformation. http://www.wsu.edu/~dee/REFORM/COUNTER/HTM
4) Gascoigne Bamber. "History of the Jesuits". (From 2001 ongoing). http://www.historyworld.net/wrldhis/PlainTextHistories.asp?historyid=ab30
5) Theodore Greisinger (1903). "The Jesuits: A Complete History of their open and secret proceedings from the foundation of the Order to the present time". http://books.google.com
6) CARRIE: Full Text Electronic Library—chapter 19: "The Counter-Reformation". http://vlib.iue.it/carrie/texts/carrie_books/gilbert/19.html
7) Centre for Reformed Theology and Apologetics, chapter 4: "Moral Code of the Jesuits". In The History of Protestantism by Rev. J.A. Wylie. http://www.reformed,org/master/index.html?mainframe=misc/the_jesuits.html
8) Ian Paisley (1999). EIPS—The Jesuits. http://www.ianpaisley.org/article.asp?ArtKey=gavazzi

Chapter 18
1) Paul Brians (2000). The Enlightenment. http://www.wsu.edu/~brians/hum_303/enlightenment.html
2) Brendan Connoly. The Natural Religion. http://www.thenaturalreligion.org/

3) "Towards a Natural Religion"—St. Petersburg Times. http://www.tampabay.com/news/perspective/toward-a-natural-religion/1056081
4) Thomas Hobbes: A short Biography. http://www.njgeib,com/thoughts/nature/hobbes-bio.html
5) Garrath Williams (2005). Hobbes, Thomas: Moral and Political Philosophy [Internet Encyclopedia of Philosophy]. http://ww.iep.utm.edu/hobmoral/
6) Lloyd, Sharon A, Sreedhar, Susanne. "Hobbes' Moral and Political Philosophy". The Stanford Encyclopedia of Philosophy (Spring 2009 Edition). Edward N. Zalta (Ed.). http://plato.stanford.edu/archives/spr2009/entries/hobbes-morals/
7) Nadler, Steven. "Baruch Spinoza". The Stanford Encyclopedia of Philosophy. (Winter 2009 Edition), Edward N. Zalta (Ed.). http://plato.stanford.edu/archives/win2009/entries/spinoza/
8) Kelley L. Ross (1999). Baruch Spinoza. http://www.friesian.com/spinoza.htm
9) William Uzgalis (2007). John Locke. The Stanford Encyclopedia of Philosophy. (Summer 2010 Edition), Edward N. Zalta, (Ed.). http://plato.stanford.edu/entries/locke/
10) Anonymous (2001). Locke, John. [Internet Encyclopedia of Philosophy]. http://www.iep.utm.edu/locke/
11) William Popple. "John Locke: A Letter concerning Toleration—(1689)". http://www.constitution.org/jl/tolerati.htm
12) Russell, Paul. (2005). "Hume on Religion". The Stanford Encyclopedia of Philosophy. (Winter 2008 Edition), Edward N. Zalta (Ed.). http://plato.stanford.edu/archives/win2008/entries/hume-religion/
13) James Feiser (2004). "Hume, David: Life and Writings [Internet Encyclopedia of Philosophy]. http://www.iep.utm.edu/humelife
14) James J. Delaney (2005). Rousseau, Jean-Jacques. [Internet Encyclopedia of Philosophy]. http://www.iep.utm.edu/rousseau/
15) Robin Chew (1995-2010). Jean-Jacques Rousseau/philosophy. http://www.lucidcafe.com/library/96jun/rousseau.html
16) Thomas Robert Malthus—Wikipedia, the free encyclopedia. http://en.wikipedia.org/wiki/Thomas_Robert_Malthus
17) Malthusian Catastrophes—Wikipedia, the free encyclopedia. http://en.wikipedia.org/wiki/Malthusian_Catastrophes

Chapter 19
1) The Story of Africa/BBC World Service. http://www.bbc.co.uk/worldservice/africa/features/storyofafrica/8chapter1.shtml
2) History of Christianity in Africa. http://www.allaboutreligion.org/history-of-christianity-in-africa-faq.htm
3) Sub-Saharan African Christianity: The Church among the Kongo. http://www.bethel.edu/~letnie/AfricanChristianity/SSAKongo.html
4) Crowther, Samuel Ajayi (1807-1891), Anglican, Nigeria. http://www.dacb.org/stories/nigeria/legacy_Crowther.html
5) The Story of Africa/BBC World Service. http://www.bbc.co.uk/worldservice/africa/features/storyofafrica/8chapter3.shtml
6) The Story of Africa/BBC World Service. http://www.bbc.co.uk/worldservice/africa/features/storyofafrica/8chapter4.shtml
7) Gascoigne Bamber. "History of Africa". History World from 2001, ongoing. http://www.historyworld.net/wrldhis/PlainTextHistories.asp
8) Scramble for Africa—Wikipedia, the free encyclopedia. http://en.wikipedia.org/wiki/Scramble_for_Africa
9) Berlin Conference of 1884-1885 to Divide Africa. http://wysinger.homestead.com/berlinconference.html
10) Mary Slessor, Scottish Missionary, Nigeria: Africa Missionary Biographies. http://www.wholesomewords.org/missions/bioslessor2.html
11) The Story of Africa/BBC World Service. http://www.bbc.co.uk/worldservice/africa/features/storyofafrica/8chapter5.shtml
12) Pentecostal Missions in Africa (1840-1960). http://www.bethel.edu/~letnie/SSAcolonialprotestant.html
13) Sub-Saharan Christianity—A History of the Christian Church in Sub-Saharan Africa. http://www.bethel.edu/~letnie/AfricanChristianity/subsaharahomepage.html
14) The Story of Africa/BBC World Service. http://www.bbc.co.uk/worldservice/africa/features/storyofafrica/8chapter7.shtml
15) T.V. Philip. East of the Euphrates: Early Christianity in Asia. http://www.religiononline.org/shobook.asp?tittle=1553
16) Christianity in Asia—Wikipedia, the free encyclopedia. http://en.wikipedia.org/wiki/Christianity_in_Asia

17) Brucker, J. (1912). Matteo Ricci. In The Catholic Encyclopedia. New York: Robert Appleton Company. Retrieved January 7, 2011 from New Advent: http://www.newadvent.org/cathen/13034a.htm
18) "Chinese Rites Controversy"—New World Encyclopedia. http://www.newworldencyclopedia.org/entry/chinese_Rite_Controversy
19) Chinese Rites Controversy—Wikipedia, the free encyclopedia. http://en.wikipedia.org/wiki/Chinese_Rites_Controversy
20) Brucker, J. (1910). Malabar Rites. In The Catholic Encyclopedia. New York: Robert Appleton Company. Retrieved January 7, 2011 from New Advent: http://www.newadvent.org/cathen/09558b.htm
21) Malabar Rites—Wikipedia, the free encyclopedia. http://en.wikipedia.org/wiki/Malabar_Rites
22) Christianity in Japan—New World Encyclopedia. http://www.newworldencyclopedia.org/entry/Christianity_in_Japan
23) Balette, J, Ligneul, F (1910). Japan. In The Catholic Encyclopedia. New York: Robert Appleton Company. Retrieved December 7, 2010 from New Advent: http://www.newadvent.org/cathen/08297a.htm
24) Susan Russell. Christianity in the Philippines. http://www.seasite.niu.edu/crossroads/russell/Christianity.htm
25) Jack Miller (2008). Religion in the Philippines/Asia Society. http://asiasociety.org/countries-history/religion-philosophies/religion-philippines?page=%2CO
26) Miguel Lopez de Legazpi. Encyclopedia Britannica. Retrieved December 8, 2010. http://www.brittanica.com/EBchecked/topic/334927/Miguel-lopez-de-Legazpi
27) Gascoigne Bamber. "History of the Spanish Empire". History World from 2001 ongoing. http://www.historyworld.net/wrlhis/PlainTextHistories.asp
28) Pope Nicholas V—Wikipedia, the free encyclopedia. http://en.wikipedia.org/wiki/Pope_Nicholas_V_and_slavery
29) Popes for Slavery—Romanus Pontifex by Pope Nicholas V. http://www.romancatholicism.org/popes-slavery.htm
30) "The Bull Inter Caetera". http://www.nativeweb.org/pages/legaliindig-inter-caetera.html
31) Treaty of Tordesillas. http://.u-s-history.com/pages/h/028.html
32) The Atlantic Slave Trade—Wikipedia, the free encyclopedia. http://en.wikipedia.org/wiki/Atlantic_Slave_Trade

33) Paraguay—The Sword of the Word. http://countrystudies.us/paraguay/s.htm
34) James E. Keifer. "Bartolome De Las Casas, Missionary, Priest, Defender of the Oppressed". http://justus.anglican.org/resources/bio/203.html
35) Jesuit Saints and Blesseds: "St. Peter Claver". http://www.sjweb.info/jesuits/saintshow.cfm?
36) Cambridge Theological Seminary: Christian Colonization, "Doctrine of Discovery and Papal Bulls. http://www.ministers-best-friends.com/colonisation-Doctrine-of-Discovery.html
37) History of Christianity: Christian Colonization, genocide and extermination in the Americas. http://freetruth.50webs.org/A4a.htm
38) European colonization of the Americas—Wikipedia, the free encyclopedia. http://en.wikipedia.org/wiki/European_colonisation_of_the_Americas
39) Plymouth Colony—Wikipedia, the free encyclopedia. http://en.wikipedia.org/wiki/Plymouth_Colony
40) Massachusetts Bay Colony—Wikipedia, the free encyclopedia. http://en.wikipedia.org/wiki/Massachusetts_Bay_Colony
41) Christianity: Christianity in North America—Encyclopedia of Religion/Encyclopedia.com—http://www.encyclopedia.com/article-IG2-3424500547/Christianity-Christianity-north-america.html
42) Richard White: "Trail of Tears". http://www.powersource.com/cocinc/history/trail.htm
43) History of Christianity: Colonization and genocide in the Pacific, Missions and Colonialism. http://freetruth.50webs.org/A4e.htm

Chapter 20
1) Industrial Revolution—Wikipedia, the free encyclopedia. http://en.wikipedia.org/wiki/Industrial_Revolution
2) Richard Hooker. "The Industrial Revolution of the Enlightenment Century". http://www.wsu.edu/~dee/ENLIGHT/INDUSTRY.HTM
3) David Luke. "The Church in the Age of Revolution: Society, Church and Technological Change" (16 December, 2007, Gilnahirk Baptist Church website). http://www.gilnahirkbaptist.org.uk/resources/frontiers/1/2/luke-church-revolution.php

4) American Revolution—Wikipedia, the free encyclopedia. http://en.wikipedia.org/wiki/American_Revolution
5) The Gilder Lehrman Institute—Modules on American History. http:////www.gilderlehrman.org/teaches/modules.php?module_id=24
6) Declaration of Independence—Transcript. http://www.archives.gov/exhibits/charters/declaration_transcript.html
7) Transcript of the Constitution of the United States—Official. http://www.archives.gov/exhibits/charters/constitution_transcript.html
8) Bill of Rights. http://www.archives.gov/exhibits/charters/bill_of_rights.html
9) Steven Kreis (2006). "Thomas Paine, 1737-1809". http://www.historyguide.org/intellect/paine.html
10) Thomas Paine—Wikipedia, the free encyclopedia. http://en.wikipedia.org/wiki/Thomas_Paine
11) What the Founding Fathers said: http://www.sunlink.org/wa2joc/guns.html
12) French Revolution—Wikipedia, the free encyclopedia. http://en.wikipedia.org/wiki/French_Revolution
13) Frank E. Smith (2009-2011). "French Revolution". http://www.fsmitha.com/h3/h33.htm
14) Reign of Terror—Wikipedia, the free encyclopedia. http://en.wikipedia.org/wiki/Reign_of_Terror

Chapter 21
1) The Great Awakening [UShistory.org]. http://www.ushistory.org/us/7b.asp
2) The Great Awakening. http://www.wfu.edu/~matchet/perspective/four.htm
3) Lex Loizoides (2009). A Great Awakening in Great Britain <<Church History Blog>> http://lexlois.wordpress.com/2009/06/15/a.greatawakening-in-great-britain/
4) Jonathan Edwards (theologian)—Wikipedia, the free encyclopedia. http://en.wikipedia.org/wiki/Jonathan_Edward_theologian
5) Rimas, J. Orentas (Baltimore UBF). "George Whitefield: Lightening Rod of the Great Awakening. http://washingtonubf.org/Resources/Leaders/Georgewhitefield.html

6) George Whitefield—Wikipedia, the free encyclopedia. http://en.wikipedia.org/wiki/George_Whitefield
7) John Wesley—Wikipedia, the free encyclopedia. http://en.wikipedia.org/wiki/John_Wesley
8) Charles Wesley—Wikipedia, the free encyclopedia. http://en.wikipedia.org/wiki/Charles_Wesley
9) Douglas Graham. "John and Charles Wesley". http://www.seekinggod.org.uk/main/preacher/method1.htm
10) Gilbert Tennent—Conservapedia. http://www.conservapedia. http://www.conservapedia.com/Gilbert_Tennent
11) Gilbert Tennent—Wikipedia, the free encyclopedia. http://en.wikipedia.org/wiki/Gilbert_Tennent
12) William Wilberforce—Wikipedia, the free encyclopedia. http://en.wikipedia.org/wiki/William_Wilberforce
13) Peter Hammond. "William Wilberforce—Setting the Captives Free". http://www.frontline.org.za/articles/settingcaptives_free.htm
14) William Carey (Missionary)—Wikipedia, the free encyclopedia. http://en.wikipedia.org/wiki/William_Carey_(Missionary)
15) William Carey—Father of Modern Protestant Missions/Christian History. http://www.christianitytoday.com/ch/131Christians/missionaries/carey.html?start=2
16) Eugene Myers Harrison. "Adoniram Judson Biography". http://www.reformedreader.org/rbb/judson/ajbio.htm
17) Adoniram Judson—Wikipedia, the free encyclopedia. http://en.wikipedia.org/wiki/Adoniram_Judson
18) David Livingstone—Wikipedia, the free encyclopedia. http://en.wikipedia.org/wiki/David_Livingstone
19) David Livingstone (1813-1873), Missionary and Explorer Believers. http://www.believersweb.org/view.cfm?ID=74
20) Hudson Taylor—"Faith Missionary to China". http://www.Christianitytoday.com/ch/131Christians/missionaries/htaylor.html?start=1
21) J. Hudson Taylor—Missionary Biographies—Worldwide Missions. http://www.wholesomewords.org/missions/biotaylor.html
22) Hudson Taylor—Wikipedia, the free encyclopedia. http://en.wikipedia.org/wiki/Hudson_Taylor

23) The Second Great Awakening. http://www.u-s-history.com/pages/h1091.html
24) Second Great Awakening—http://www.america.gov/st/educ-english/2008/April/200804071135/eaifs0.3545038.htm
25) Second Great Awakening—Wikipedia, the free encyclopedia. http://en.wikipedia.org/wiki/Second_Great_Awakening
26) William P. Farley. "Charles Finney: The Controversial Evangelist. http://enrichmentjournal.ag.org/200601/200601_118_Finney.cf
27) Charles Grandison Finney—Wikipedia, the free encyclopedia. http://en.wikipedia.org/wiki/Charles_Grandison_Finney
28) The Character, Claims and Practical Workings of Freemasonry (1869) By Rev. C.G. Finney. http://www.gospeltruth.net/1869freemasonry/indexfreemasonry.htm

Chapter 22

1) Foster Michael. "Friedrich Daniel Ernst Schleiermacher": The Stanford Encyclopedia of Philosophy (Fall 2008 Edition), Edward N. Zalta, (Ed.). http://plato.stanford.edu/archives/fall2008/entries/schleiermacher/
2) Friedrich Schleiermacher—Wikipedia, the free encyclopedia. http://en.wikipedia.org/wiki/Friedrich_Schleiermacher
3) William McDonald. "Kierkegaard, Soren". [Internet Encyclopedia of Philosophy]. http://www.iep.utm.edu/kierkega/
4) McDonald, William. "Soren Kierkegaard". The Stanford Encyclopedia of Philosophy (summer 2009 Edition), Edward N. Zalta (Ed.). http://plato.stanford.edu/archives/sum2009/entries/kierkegaard/
5) Soren Kierkegaard—Wikipedia, the free encyclopedia. http://en.wikipedia.org/wiki/5%C3%B8ren_Kierkegaard
6) David L. Edwards. "Rudolf Bultmann: Scholar of Faith". http://www.religion-online.org/showarticle.asp?title=1827
7) Wesley J. Wildman (1994-2008). "Rudolf Bultmann". Bolton Collaborative Encyclopedia of Western Theology. http://people.bu.edu/wwildman/weirdwildweb/courses/mwt/dictionary/mwt_themes_760_bultmann.htm
8) Karl Barth—Wikipedia, the free encyclopedia. http://en.wikipedia.org/wiki/Karl_Barth

9) Wesley J. Wildman (1994-2008). "Karl Barth". Boston Collaborative Encyclopedia of Western Theology. http://people.bu.edu/wwildman/Weirdwildweb/courses/mwt/dictionary/mwt_themes_750_barth.htm
10) Reinhold Niebuhr—Wikipedia, the free encyclopedia. http://en.wikipedia.org/wiki/Reinhold_Niebuhr
11) Wesley J. Wildman (1994-2008). "Reinhold Niebuhr": Boston Collaborative Encyclopedia of Western Theology. http://people.bu.edu/wwildman/WierdWildweb/courses/mwt/dictionary/mwt_theme_770_niebuhrreinhold.htm
12) Douglas Huff. "Bonhoeffer, Dietrich". [Internet Encyclopedia of Philosophy]. http://www.iep.utm.edu/bonhoeff/
13) John Beardsley. "Dietrich Bonhoeffer—General Teaching/Activities". http://www.rapidnet.com/~jbeard/bdm/exposes/bonhoeffer/general.htm
14) Todd Kappelman. "Dietrich Bonhoeffer". http://www.leaderu.com/orgs/probe/docs/bonhoeffer.html
15) Dietrich Bonhoeffer—Wikipedia, the free encyclopedia. http://en.wikipedia.org/wiki/Dietrich_Bonhoeffer

Chapter 23

1) Ron Rhodes. "Liberation Theology" (By Ron Rhodes). http://home.earthlink.net/~ronrhodes/Liberation.html
2) Marian Hillar. "Liberation Theology". http://www.socinian.org/Liberty.html
3) Philip Berryman. "Liberation Theology: Essential Facts about the Revolutionary Movement in Latin America and Beyond". Temple University Press, Philadelphia 19122. http://books.google.com/books
4) Liberation Theology. http://mb-soft.com/believe/txn/liberati.htm (Retrieved August 12, 2010).
5) Scramble for Africa—New World Encyclopedia. http://www.newworldencyclopedia.org/entry.Scrmble_for_Africa (Retrieved February 01, 2011
6) Berlin Conference of 1884-1885 to Divide Africa. http://wysinger.homestead.com/berlinconference.html

7) Gascoigne Bamber. "History of Africa", History World from 2001 Ongoing. http://www.historyworld.net/wrldhis/PlainTextHistotries.asp?historyid=ab24
8) Aladura—Wikipedia, the free encyclopedia. http://en.wikipedia.org/wiki/Aladura
9) African Initiated Church—Wikipedia, the free encyclopedia. http://en.wikipedia.org/wiki/African_Initiated_Church
10) World Council of Churches: "The African Church". http://www.oikoumene.org/gr/member-churches/religion/africa/nigeria/the-african-church.html
11) Reverend Alan Morris. "A Review: Christianity in Africa" by Kwame Bediako. http://www.staidanlindisfarne.org/vsItemDisplay.dsp
12) John Mbiti: "The Dialogue between African Religion and Christianity (lecture notes). http://benbyerly.wordpress.com/2010/05/24/john-mbiti-the-dialogue-between-african-religion-and-Christianity
13) Byang Kato (1936-1975). Evangelical Church West Africa, Nigeria. http://www.dacb.org/stones/nigeria/kato-legacy.html
14) Christianity in Europe, 1910-2010. http://www.atlasofglobalchristianity.org/images/samplepages_4.pdf
15) B.A. Robinson: "New Age Spirituality". http://www.religiontolerance.org/newage.htm
16) New Age—Wikipedia, the free encyclopedia. http://en.wikipedia.org/wiki/New_Age
17) Religion in European Union—Wikipedia, the free encyclopedia. http://en.wikipedia.org/wiki/Religion_in_the_European_Union
18) "PC Nonsense: European Union removes Christian Holidays from calendar but maintains Muslim Holidays. http://cubachi.com/2011/01/161/pcnonsense-european-union-removes-christian-holiday-from-calendar-but-maintain-muslim-holidays
19) History of Religion in America. http://www.u-shistory.com/pages/h3787.htm
20) Evangelicalism—Wikipedia, the free encyclopedia. http://en.wikipedia.org/wiki/Evangelicalism
21) "Defining Evangelicalism": <<Institute for the Study of American Evangelicals>> http://isae.wheaton.edu/defining-evangelicalism/

22) Liberal Christianity—Wikipedia, the free encyclopedia. http://en.wikipedia.org/wiki/Liberal_Christianity
23) What is Liberal Christianity? http://www.gotquestions.org/Liberal-Christianity-theology.html
24) Fundamentalist Christianity—Wikipedia, the free encyclopedia. http://en.wikipedia.org/wiki/Fundamentalist_Christianity
25) Terry Mathews. "Fundamentalism". http://www.wfu.edu/~mathewtl/index.html
26) Plymouth Brethren—Wikipedia, the free encyclopedia. http://en.wikipedia.org/wiki/Plymouth_Brethren
27) "Dispensationalism'—Wikipedia, the free encyclopedia. http://en.wikipedia.org/wiki/Dispensationalism
28) Dr. Ken Blue. "Dispensationalism". http://www.biblebelievers.com/BlueDisp.html
29) Neo-Evangelicalism—Wikipedia, the free encyclopedia. http://en.wikipedia.org/wiki/Neo-evangelicalism
30) Harold Ockenga—Wikipedia, the free encyclopedia. http://en.wikipedia.org/wiki/Harold_Ockenga
31) John Beardsley. "Neo-Evangelicalism—Characteristics and Positions'. http://www.rapidnet.com/~jbeard/bdm/psychology/neoe.htm
32) John Beardsley. "Christian Activism"? http://www.rapidnet.com/~jbeard/bdm/psychology/amr/cact2.htm
33) Holiness Movement—Wikipedia, the free encyclopedia. http://en.wikipedia.org/wiki/Holiness_Movement
34) Gary Gilley. "The Holiness Movement". http://www.svchapel.org/resources/articles/19-charismatics/29-the-holiness-movement
35) Holiness Movement—Conservapedia. http://www.conservapedia.com/Holiness_Movement
36) Keith Drury. "The Holiness Movement: Dead or Alive?" http://www.crivoice.org/hmovement.html
37) Ttt. "Holiness Movement, American". http://www.Mathew548.com/d-American.html
38) Pentecostalism—Wikipedia, the free encyclopedia. http://en.wikipedia.org/wiki/Pentecostalism
39) The Azuza Street Revival—Wikipedia, the free encyclopedia. http://en.wikipedia.org/wiki/Azuza_Street_Revival

40) Kevin Sack. "The Pentecostal Church in America". http://partners.nytimes.com/library/race/060400sack-church-side.html
41) Robert Longman Jr. (1997-2010). "The Azuza Street Timeline". http://www.spirithome.com/histpen1.html
42) David W. Cloud. "The Strange History of Pentecostalism part 2 of 3". http://www.deceptioninthechurch.com/strnge2.htm
43) Charismatic Movement—Wikipedia, the free encyclopedia. http://en.wikipedia.org/wiki/Charismatic_Movement
44) David C. Forsyth. "History of the Charismatic Movement". http://www.Christianfallacies.com/articles/forsyth/historyofcharismaticmovement.html
45) Albert James Dager—"John Wimber and the Vineyard"—http://www.rapidnet.com/~jbeard/bdm/explores/wimber/john.htm
46) Fundamental Evangelistic Association: "Charismatic Movement is Dangerous". http://cnview.com/on_line_resources/charismatis_movement_is_dangerous.htm
47) Church Growth—Wikipedia, the free encyclopedia. http://en.wikipedia.org/wiki/Church_Growth
48) Ken Silva. "John MacArthur: Seeker Friendly Movement is the new Liberalism". [Apprising Ministries]—http://apprising.org/2009/05/07/john-macarthur-seeker-friendly-movement-is-the-new-libralism
49) McMahon T.A. "The Seeker Friendly Way of Doing Church/the Berean call.org. http://www.thebereancall.org/node/2587
50) VW: Rick Warren's "Purpose Driven (Seeker-Friendly) Church Growth Strategy. http://www.a-voice.org/discern/Saddle.htm
51) John H. Armstrong. "Problems of Seeker-Sensitive Worship/Brethren Revival Fellowship. http://www.brfwitness.org/?p=635
52) Willow Creek Association/REVEAL—What is it? http://www.reveal.revealnow.com
53) Matt Branaugh. "Willow Creek's Huge Shift"—Influential Mega church Moves away from Seeker-Sensitive Services. http://www.Christianitytoday.com/ct/2008/june/5.13.html
54) Mary Fairchild (March 2003). "Protestant No More: Willow Creek Infiltrated by a mystic Quaker Movement called Renovare. http://www.cephas-library.com/renovare-willow-creek.html

55) Emerging Church—Wikipedia, the free encyclopedia. http://en.wikipedia.org/wiki/Emerging_Church
56) Scot McKnight. "Five Streams of the Emerging Church". http://www.Christianitytoday.com/ct/2007/february/11.35.html
57) Roger Oakland. "The Emerging Church: Revival or Return to Darkness?" http://www.understandingthetimes.org/commentary/c29.shtml
58) The Emerging/Emergent Church and their use of "diaprax". http://www.deceptioninthechurch.com/emergingdiaprax.html
59) Roger Oakland. "How to know when the Emerging Church shows signs of emerging in your church". http://www.understandingthetimes.org/commentary/c54.shtml
60) David Kowalski. "Appropriate Response to the Emerging Church Movement/Apologetic Index. http://www.apologeticindex.org/290-emerging-church
61) Emerging Church—Distinctive Teaching and Goals /Apologetic Index. http://www.apologeticindex.org/291-emerging-church-teachings
62) Asia Map, Map of Asia. http://www.mapsofworld.com/asia/
63) Christianity in the Middle East—Wikipedia, the free encyclopedia. http://en.wikipedia.org/wiki/Christianity_in_the_Middle_East
64) BBC News/Middle East/Guide: Christians in the Middle East. http://news.bbc.co.uk/2/hi/middle_east/4499668.stm
65) Pierre Tristam. Christians of the Middle East: Country by Country Facts and Figures on Christians of the Middle East. http://middleesat.about.com/od/middleeast101/a/Christians-Middleeast.htm
66) Jonathan Addman, Agota Kuperman. "The Christian Exodus from the Middle East". http://www.jewishvirtuallibrary.org/jsource/arabs/Christianme.html
67) Eden Naby, Jamsheed K. Choksy. "The End of Christianity in the Middle East? / Foreign Policy. http://www.foreignpolicy.com/articles/2010/11/02/the_end_of_Christianity_in_the_middle_east
68) George Weigel. "Christian in the Middle East / First Things. http://www.firstthings.com/onthesquare/2011/04/Christians-in-the-middle-east

69) Christianity in Afghanistan—Wikipedia, the free encyclopedia. http://en.wikipedia.org/wiki/Christianity_in_Afghanistan
70) Christianity in Pakistan—Wikipedia, the free encyclopedia. http://en.wikipedia.org/wiki/Christianity_in_Pakistan
71) Christianity in India—Wikipedia, the free encyclopedia. http://en.wikipedia.org/wiki/Christianity_in_India
72) Somini Sengupta. "Hinduism vs. Christianity in India: The New York Times. http://www.nytimes.com/2008/10/13/world/asia/13iht-orrssa.1.16901648.html
73) Christianity in Indonesia—Wikipedia, the free encyclopedia. http://en.wikipedia.org/wiki/Christianity_in_Indonesia
74) Report: "Christianity Growing in Indonesia"—World—CBN News—Christian News 24-7—CBN.com. http://www.cbn.com/cbnnews/world/2010/April/Report-Christianity-Growing-in-Indonesia
75) Religion in Malaysia—Wikipedia, the free encyclopedia. http://en.wikipedia.org/wiki/Religion_in_Malaysia
76) Christianity in Malaysia—Wikipedia, the free encyclopedia. http://en.wikipedia.org/wiki/Christianity_in_Malaysia
77) Religion in Vietnam—Wikipedia, the free encyclopedia. http://en.wikipedia.org/wiki/Religion_in_Vietnam
78) Christianity in Thailand—Wikipedia, the free encyclopedia. http://en.wikipedia.org/wiki/Christianity_in_Thailand
79) Religion in Burma—Wikipedia—the free encyclopedia. http://en.wikipedia.org/wiki/Religion_in_Burma
80) Susan Russell. Christianity in the Philippines. http://www.seasite.niu.edu/crossroads/russell/Christianity.htm
81) Christianity in the Philippines—Wikipedia, the free encyclopedia. http://en.wikipedia.org/wiki/Christianity_in_the_Philippines
82) East Timor—Wikipedia, the free encyclopedia. http://en.wikipedia.org/wiki/East_Timor
83) Religion in Sri Lanka—Wikipedia, the free encyclopedia. http://en.wikipedia.org/wiki/Religion_in_Sri_Lanka
84) Religion in Kazakhstan—Religion. http://atheism.com/library/FAQS/Islam//countries/bl_kazakstanIndex.htm
85) Religion in Kazakhstan—Wikipedia, the free encyclopedia. http://en.wikipedia.org/wiki/Religion_in_Kazakhstan

86) The Beliefs of Kazakhstan People. http://www.hope4astara.com/Beliefs/default.htm
87) Christianity in Uzbekistan—Wikipedia, the free encyclopedia. http://en.wikipedia.org/wiki/Christianity_in_Uzbekistan
88) Freedom of Religion in Uzbekistan—Wikipedia, the free encyclopedia. http://en.wikipedia.org/wiki/Freedom_of_Religion_Uzbekistan
89) Christianity in Turkmenistan—Wikipedia, the free encyclopedia. http://en.wikipedia.org/wiki/Christian_in_Turkmenistan
90) Religion in Kyrgyzstan—Wikipedia, the free encyclopedia. http://en.wikipedia.org/wiki/Religion_in_Kyrgyzstan
91) Religion in Tajikistan—Wikipedia, the free encyclopedia. http://en.wikipedia.org/wiki/Religion_in_Tajikistan
92) Christianity in Mongolia—Wikipedia, the free encyclopedia. http://en.wikipedia.org/wiki/Christianity_in_Mongolia
93) Religion in North Korea—Wikipedia, the free encyclopedia. http://en.wikipedia.org/wiki/Religion_in_North_Korea
94) Religion in South Korea—Wikipedia, the free encyclopedia. http://en.wikipedia.org/wiki/Religion_in_South_Korea
95) Religion in South Korea: Religious Beliefs in South Korea: Religious Beliefs in South Korea. http://www.asiarooms.com/en/travel-guide/south-korea/culture-of-south-korea/religion-in-south-korea.html
96) Andrew E. Kim. "A History of Christianity in Korea: From Its Troubled Beginning to Its Contemporary Success". http://www.tparent.org/library/religion/cta/korean-Christianity.htm
97) Christophe Landau. Will South Korea become Christian? http://news.bbc.co.uk/2/hi/8322072
98) Boxer Rebellion—Wikipedia, the free encyclopedia. http://en.wikipedia.org/wiki/Boxer_Rebellion
99) Christianity in China—Wikipedia, the free encyclopedia. http://en.wikipedia.org/wiki/Christianity_in_China
100) Religion: Christianity in Japan—TIME. http://www.time.com/time/magazine/article/0,9171,795198,00.html
101) Christianity in Japan/OMF. http://www.omf/japan/about_japan/Christianity_in_japan
102) Christianity in Japan—New World Encyclopedia. http://www.newworldencyclopedia.org/entry/Christianity_in_Japan

103) Russian Orthodox Church—Wikipedia, the free encyclopedia. http://en.wikipedia.org/wiki/Russia_Orthodox_Church
104) Christianity in Russia—Wikipedia, the free encyclopedia. http://en.wikipedia.org/wiki/Christianity_in_Russia
105) Demographics of Russia—Wikipedia, the free encyclopedia. http://en.wikipedia.org/wiki/Demographics_of_Russia

Chapter 24

1) Todd Johnson. Lausanne World Pulse—World Christian Trends, Update 2007. http://www.lausanneworldpulse.com/766/08-2007?pg=all
2) Christianity by Country—Wikipedia, the free encyclopedia. http://en.wikipedia.org/wiki/Christianity_by_Countries
3) European Christian Demographics. http://www.joshuaproject.net/assets/UnreachedEurope.pdf
4) Church Attendance—Wikipedia, the free encyclopedia. http://en.wikipedia.org/wiki/Church_Attendance
5) Juanita Ashworth, (Research Matters); Ian Farthing, (Tearfund)—"Church—Going in the U.K". http://news.bbc.co.uk/2/shared/bsp/hi/pdfs/30_04_07_tearfundchurch.pdf
6) BBC NEWS/UK/ "One in 10 attends church weekly". http://news.bbc.co.uk/2/hi/Uk_news/6520463.stm
7) Jessica Ravitz (CNN). "Catholic faithful face church closures—CNN. http://articles.cnn.com/2009-03-25/living/cleveland.catholic.parish.closures_1_church-closures-parishes-official-catholic-directory?_s=pm:LIVING
8) Religion in Australia—Wikipedia, the free encyclopedia. http://en.wikipedia.org/wikiReligion_in_Australia
9) Christianity in Australia—Wikipedia, the free encyclopedia. http://en.wikipedia.org/wiki/Christianity_in_Australia
10) Barry A. Kosmin, Ariela Keysar. American Religious Identification Survey (ARIS) 2008. http://b27.cc.trincoll.edu/webblogs/AmericanReligiousSurvey-ARIS/reports/ARIS_Reports_2008.pdf
11) Religion in the United States—Wikipedia, the free encyclopedia. http://en.wikipedia.org/wiki/Religion_in_the_United-States#church_attendance
12) The Barna Group (April 16, 2006). "Americans Have Commitment Issues, New Survey Shows". http://www.barna.org/faith-

spirituality/267-american-have-commitment-issues-new-survey-shows

13) The Barna Group (March 6, 2009). Barna Survey Examines Changes in Worldview among Christians Over the past 13 years. http://www.barne.org/transformation-articles/252-barna-survey-examine-changes-in-worldview-among-Christians

14) The Barna Group (February 20, 2006): "The Concept of Holiness Baffles Most Americans". http://www.barna.org/barna.org/barna-update/articles/5-barna-update/162-the-concept-of-holiness-baffles-most-Americans

15) The Barna Group (December 20, 2006). "Barna lists the 12 most Significant Religious Findings". http://www.barna.org/faith-spirituality/141-barna-lists-the-12-most-significant-religious-findings

16) The Barna Group (December 13, 2010). "Six Mega-themes Emerge from Barna Group Research in 2010". http://www.barna.org/culture-article/462-six-megathemes-emerge-from-2010

17) The Barna Group ( ). "Most American Christians do not believe that Satan or the Holy Spirit Exist. http://www.barna.org/barna-update/article/12-faithspirituality/260-most-american-Christian-do-not-believe-that-satan-or-the-holy-spirit-exist

18) The Barna Group (March 31, 2008). "New Marriage and Divorce Statistics Released. http://www.barna.org/family-kids-article/42-new-marriage-and-divorce-statistics-released

19) The Barna Group (April 18, 2011): "What Americans Believe About Universalism and Pluralism". http://www.barna.org/faith-spirituality/484-what-americans-believe-about-universalism-and-pluralism

20) The Barna Group (April 24, 2009): "America's seven tribes hold the key to National Restoration". http://www.barna.org/culture-articles/262/america's-seven-tribes-hold-the-key-to-national-restoration

21) Church Attendance Statistics—Countries compared worldwide—Nationmaster. http://www.nationmaster.com/graph/rel-chu-att-religion-church-attendance

22) "In America, 3500 to 4500 churches close their doors each year; if we lose our small churches, we lose America". http://www.keepgodinamerica.com/statistics.asp

23) "Churches Closing and Pastors Leaving">djchuang.com. http://djchuang.com/2010/churches-closing-and-pastors-leaving/?utm_source=feedburner&utm_medium=feed&utm
24) J. Lee Grady (Charisma online). Open Heaven.com—"Leading Evangelists blame Record Church Closing on Spectator Mentality". http://www.openheaven.com/forums/forum_posts.asp?TID=19271
25) Gideon Para-Mallam. Lausanne Reports (March 2008). Theological Trends in Africa: Implications for Missions and Evangelism. http://www.lausanneworldpulse.com/lausannereports/03_2008

Chapter 25
1) Tertullian of Carthage: Synopsis. http://www.earlychurch.org.uk/Tertullian.php
2) Plato, Platonism and Neo-Platonism (Synopsis). http://www.earlychurch.org.uk/plato.php
3) Turner, W. (1911). Plato and Platonism. In The Catholic Encyclopedia. New York: Robert Appleton Company. Retrieved June 28, 2009 from New Advent: http://www.newadvent.org/cathen/12159a.htm
4) Christian Classic Ethereal Library: "Platonism and Christianity". http://www.ccel.org/s/schaff/encyc/encyc09/htm/ii.cxxxiii.htm
5) Phil Norfleet (2007-2011). Platonism, Paganism and Early Christianity. http://Platonism347.tripod.com/
6) Cicero: Philosophy, Metaphysics of Cicero's 'Nature of Gods'. Quotes, Pictures, Biography Cicero. http://www.spaceandmotion.com/philosophy-cicero-philosopher.htm
7) The Incoherence of the Philosophers—Wikipedia, the free encyclopedia. http://en.wikipedia.org/wiki/The_Incoherence_of_the_Philosophers
8) John Salza (2001-2007). "Scripture Catholic—Apostolic Authority and Succession". http://www.scripturecatholic.com/apostolic_succession.html
9) Apostolic Succession—Wikipedia, the free encyclopedia. http://en.wikipedia.org/wiki/Apostolic_Succession
10) Joyce, G. (1910). Power of the Keys. In The Catholic Encyclopedia. New York: Robert Appleton Company. Retrieved May 24, 2011 from New Advent: http://www.newadvent.org/cathen/08631b.htm

11) Jim Crawley (1997). Catechism of the Catholic Church, Part Two: The Celebration of the Christian Mystery, section one—The Sacramental Economy. http://www.Christusrex.org/www1/CDHN/liturgy2.html
12) Jim Crawley (1997). Catechism of the Catholic Church—Part Two: The Celebration of the Christian Mystery. Article 2—The Paschal Mystery in the Church's Sacraments. http://www.christusrex.org/www1/CDHN/paschal.html
13) John Beardsley. Roman Catholicism: The Paganization of Christianity—Constantine and the Catholic Church State. http://www.rapidnet.com/~jbeard/bdm/cults/catholicism/ch-state.htm
14) Vasiliki Limberis. "The cult of Martyrs and the Cappadocian Fathers". In Byzantine Christianity—Derek Krueger Ed.—Vol. 3, ch. 2: http://www.augsburgfortress.org/copyrights/contents.asp
15) Christianity and Paganism—Wikipedia, the free encyclopedia. http://en.wikipedia.org/wiki/Christianity_and_Paganism
16) Lawrence Kelemen. Origin of Christmas/The Real Story of Christmas/How it began. http://www.simpletoremember.com/vitals/Christmas_TheRealStory.htm
17) Halloween—Wikipedia, the free encyclopedia. http://en.wikipedia.org/wiki/Halloween
18) Kenneth Scot LaTourette: Christianity through the Ages: ch.4; The Initial Five Centuries of Christianity. http://www.religion-online.org/showchapter.asp?title=532&C=575
19) J.J. Blunt (1794-1855). Sketches of the Reformation in England. http://www.archives.org/stream/sketchesreformatio1blungoog#page/n98/mode/2up
20) Life of Clergy in the Middle-Ages. http://www.medievaltimes.info/medieval-life-and-society/life-of-clergy-in-the-middle-ages.htm
21) Pope Innocent III. (Soylent Communications). http://www.nndb.com/people/536/000093260
22) Bishop—Wikipedia, the free encyclopedia. http://en.wikipedia.org/wiki/Bishop#Bishop_and_civil_government
23) Parliament of the United Kingdom—Wikipedia, the free encyclopedia. http://en.wikipedia.org/wiki/Parliament_of_the_United_Kingdom
24) Hippolytus of Rome—Wikipedia, the free encyclopedia. http://en.wikipedia.org/wiki/Hippolytus_of_Rome

25) Nathaniel Marshall, D.D. "The Penitential Discipline of the Primitive Church for the first four hundred years after Christ together with its Declension from the Fifth Century, downwards to its present state: Impartially presented. New Edition: Oxford, John Parker: MDCCCXLIV. http://www.archive.org/stream/penitential00marsuoft
26) Hanna, E. (1911). The Sacrament of Penance. In The Catholic Encyclopedia. New York: Robert Appleton Company. Retrieved May 31, 2011 from New Advent: http://www.newadvent.org/cathen/11618c.htm
27) Bernadeare Carr. "Myths about Indulgences". http://www.catholic.com/library/Myths_About_Indulgences.asp
28) Richard Hooker. Glossary of Indulgences. http://www.wsu.edu/~dee/GLOSSARY/INDULGE.HTM
29) Protestant Reformation—Wikipedia, the free encyclopedia. http://en.wikipedia.org/wiki/Protestant_Reformation
30) Liberal Christianity—Wikipedia, the free encyclopedia. http://en.wikipedia.org/wiki/Liberal_Christianity
31) Secularism—Wikipedia, the free encyclopedia. http://en.wikipedia.org/wiki/Secularism
32) Secularization—Wikipedia, the free encyclopedia. http://en.wikipedia.org/wiki/Secularization
33) Beatnik—Wikipedia, the free encyclopedia. http://en.wikipedia.org/wiki/Beatnik
34) Hippie—Wikipedia, the free encyclopedia. http://en.wikipedia.org/wiki/Hippie
35) Jesus Movement—Wikipedia, the free encyclopedia. http://en.wikipedia.org/wiki/Jesus_Movement

Epilogue
1) Philip Schaff. A select Library of the Nicene and . . .—Saint Augustine (Bishop of Hippo), Saint John Chrysostom, Philip Schaff—Google Books. http://books.google.com/books?id
2) Charles Manley Roberts. A treatise on the history of confession . . .—Charles Manley Roberts—Google Books. http://books.google.com/book?id
3) Newton Reader. Present position of Catholics—lecture 3. http://www.newmareader.org/work/england/lecture3.html

4) Leigh Ann Craig. Wandering Women and Holy Matrons—Google Books. http://books.google.com/books?id
5) Paul Halsall. Internet History Source Books. http://www.fordham.edu/halsall/basis/boniface-letters.asp
6) William Palmer. A compendious Ecclesiastical History. http://www.archives.org/stream/acompendiousecc02palmgoog#page
7) Brian R. Price. Charlemagne's Biography. http://www.chronique.com/library/MedHistory/Charlemagne.htm
8) Lillian Goldman Law Library. The Avalon Project: Capitulary of Charlemagne issued in the Year 802. http://avalon.law.yale.edu/medieval/capitula.asp
9) The Church of Christ in the Middle Ages: an historical sketch compiled from . . . Jesus Christ, Author of Essays on the Church—Google Books. http://books.google?id
10) Finch G. A sketch of the Romish Controversy—Google Books. http://books.google.com/books?id
11) Paul Halsall (January 1999). Internet History Source Book Project (Medieval Sourcebook: Bruno of Segni: A pamphlet on Simoniacs, Late eleventh century. http://www.fordham.edu/halsall/source/1brunosegni-simony.asp
12) J.J. Blunt (1794-1855). Sketch of the Reformation in England. http://www.archives.org/stream/sketchreformatio1blungoog#page
13) Herbert Lockyer. All the Doctrines of the Bible—Herbert Lockyer—Google Books. Http://books.google.com/books?id
14) History of Christianity: Christian colonization, genocide and extermination in the America. http://freetruth.50webs.org/A4a.htm
15) J.A. Siena. The Legend of Hatuey, from the History of Cuba. http://www.historyofcuba.com/history/oriente/hatuey.htm
16) The complete Works of Swami Vivekananda/vol.8/Notes of class talks and lectures/Christianity in India. (2008, May 8). In Wikisource, The Free Library. Retrieved 07.42, December 27, 2011, from//en.wikisource.org/w/index.php?title=The_complete_works_of_swami_vivekananda/volume_8/Notes_of_class_talks_and_lectures/Christianity_in_India&oldid=648240
17) The complete works of Swami Vivekananda/volume 8/ Notes of class talks and lectures/Hindus and Christians (2008, May 8). In Wikisource, The Free Library. Retrieved 07.51, December 27, 2011, from //en.wikisource.org/w/

index.php?title=The_complete_works_of_swami_vivekananda/volume_8/notes_of_class_talks_and_lectures/Hindus_And_Christians&oldid=648243

18) Boxer Rebellion—Wikipedia, the free encyclopedia. http://en.wikipedia.org/wiki/Boxer_Rebellion

19) Meacham. The End of Christian America—Daily Beast. http://www.thedailybeast.com/newsweek/2009/the-end-of-christianity-in-America.html

CPSIA information can be obtained at www.ICGtesting.com
Printed in the USA
BVOW020412220312

285669BV00002B/41/P